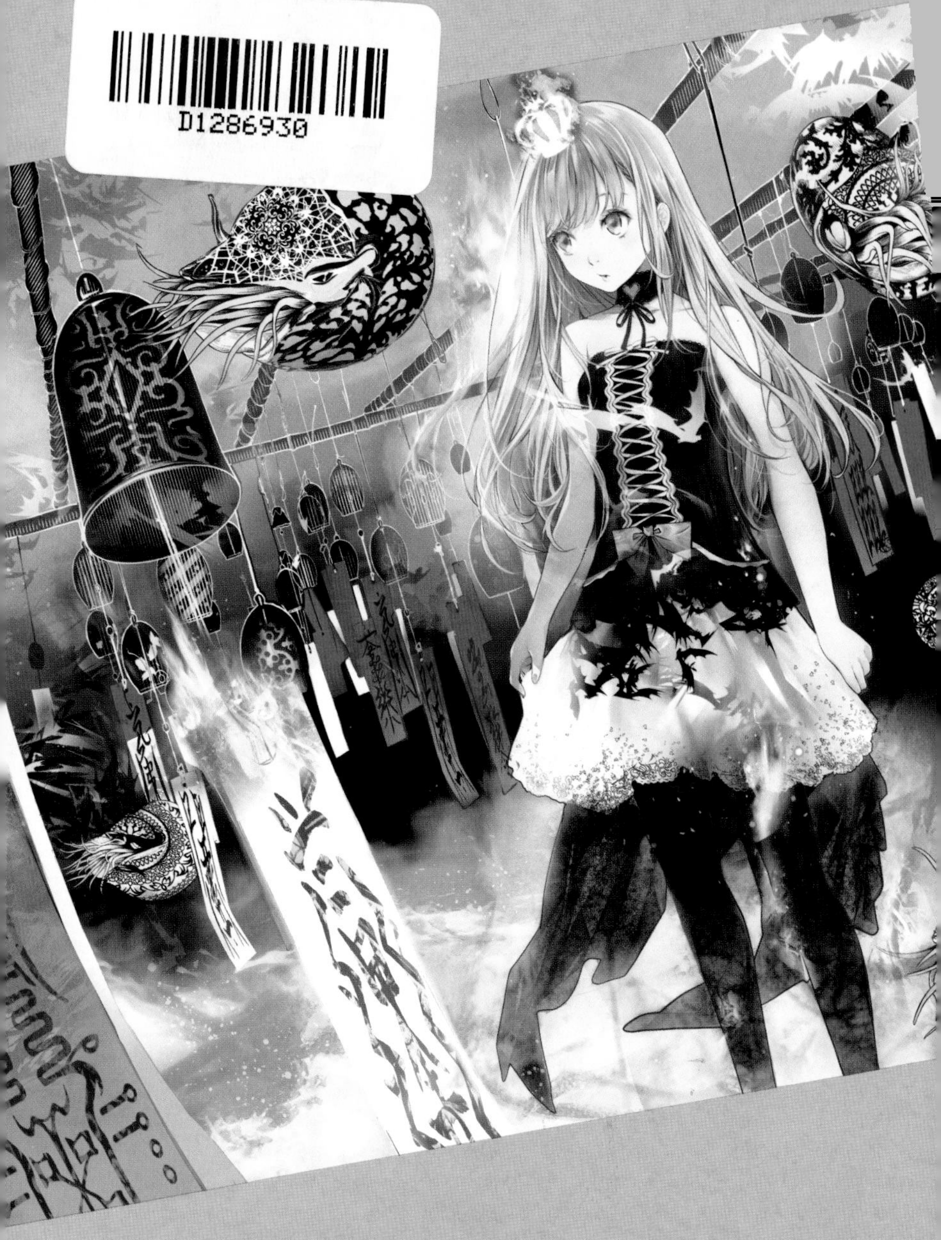

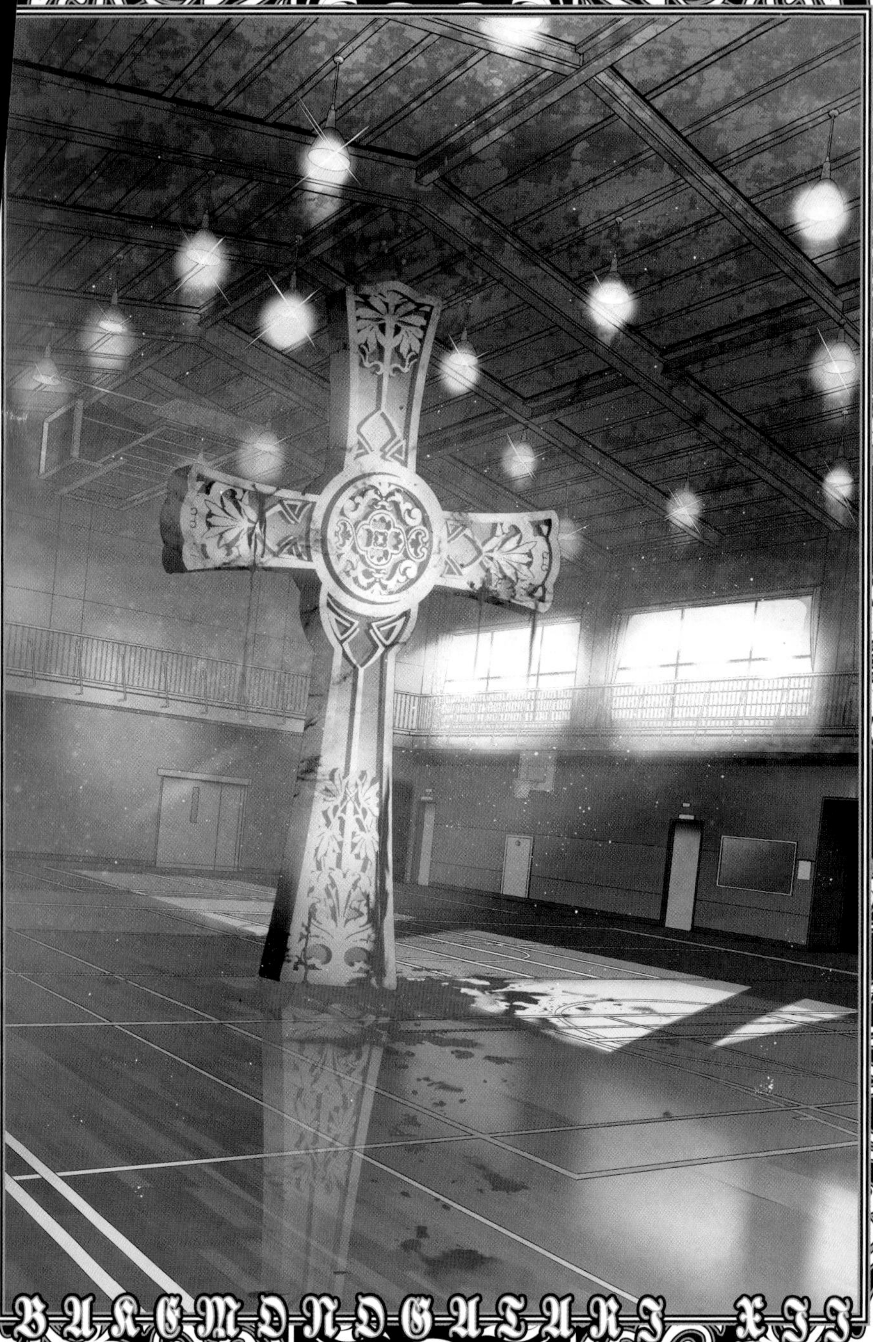

BAKEMONOGATARI XII

BAKEMONOGATARI

OH!GREAT

ORIGINAL STORY:
NISIOISIN

ORIGINAL CHARACTER
DESIGN: VOFAN

12

MAIN CHARACTERS

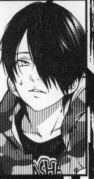

Koyomi Araragi

A boy who became Kiss-Shot's thrall after saving her. To regain his humanity, he must now fight three vampire hunters.

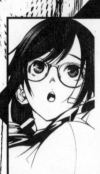

Tsubasa Hanekawa

Koyomi's friend who goes to the same school as him, and an honor student that few honors could sufficiently describe. She goes out of her way to save Koyomi, even putting herself at risk in the process.

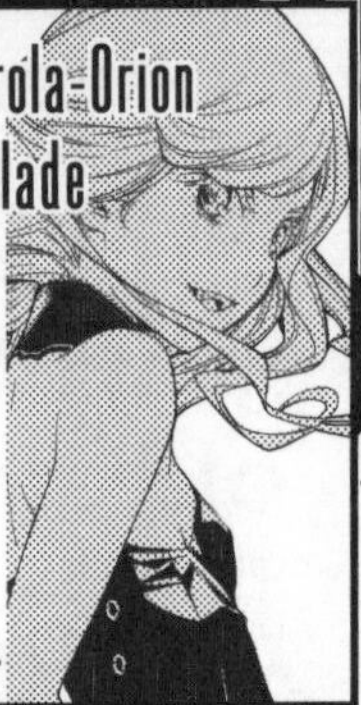

Kiss-Shot Acerola-Orion Heart-Under-Blade

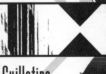

A vampire powerful enough to be called the "king of aberrations" who Koyomi saved from near-certain death. She has regained a tiny bit of her powers.

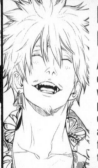

Mèmè Oshino

A self-described expert on aberrations who suddenly appeared before Koyomi one day. He now acts as a go-between for Koyomi and the hunters.

Guillotine Cutter

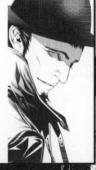

A vampire hunter who, despite being human, took both of Kiss-Shot's legs from her. A user of strange tools and techniques.

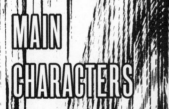

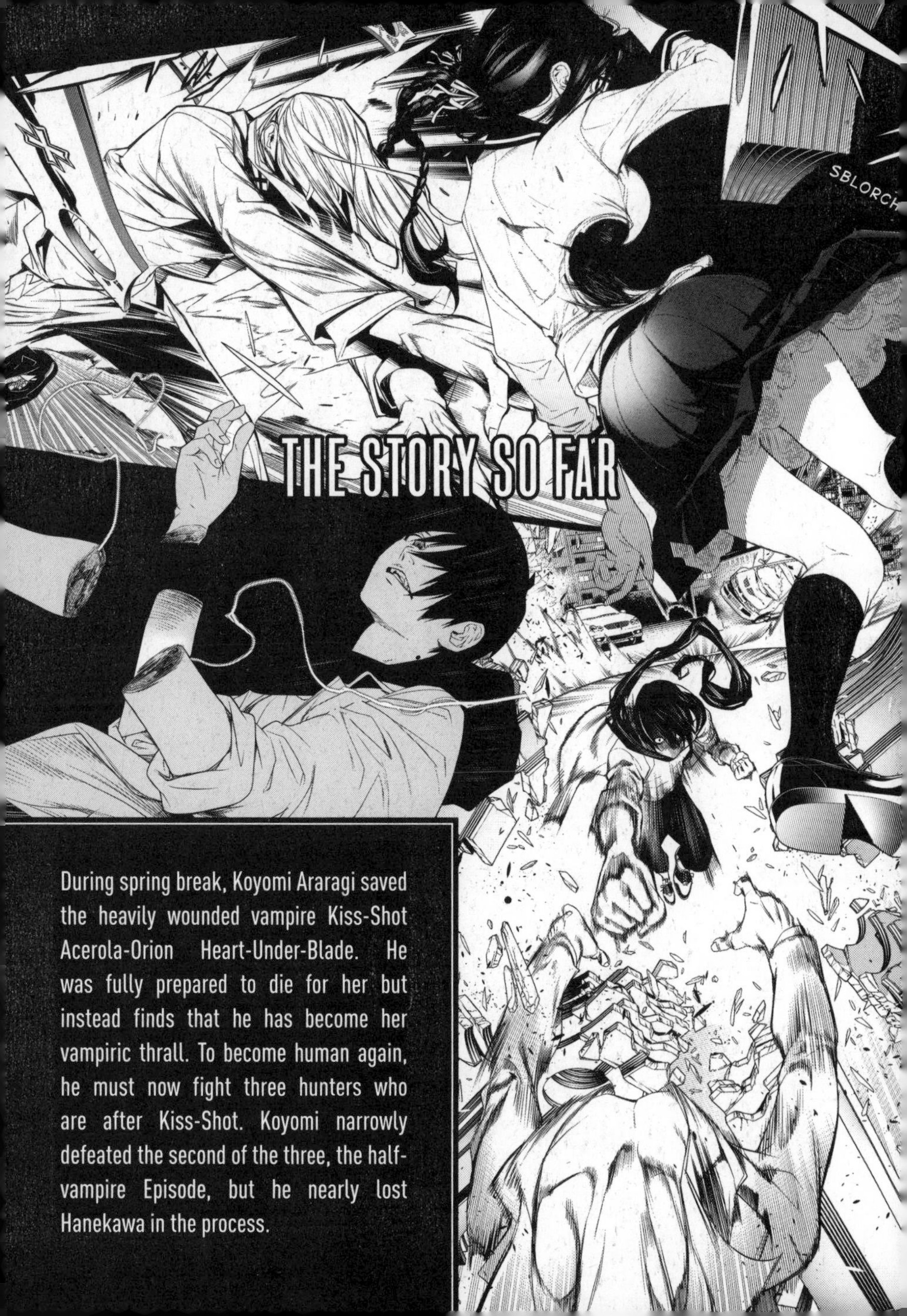
SBLORCH

THE STORY SO FAR

During spring break, Koyomi Araragi saved the heavily wounded vampire Kiss-Shot Acerola-Orion Heart-Under-Blade. He was fully prepared to die for her but instead finds that he has become her vampiric thrall. To become human again, he must now fight three hunters who are after Kiss-Shot. Koyomi narrowly defeated the second of the three, the half-vampire Episode, but he nearly lost Hanekawa in the process.

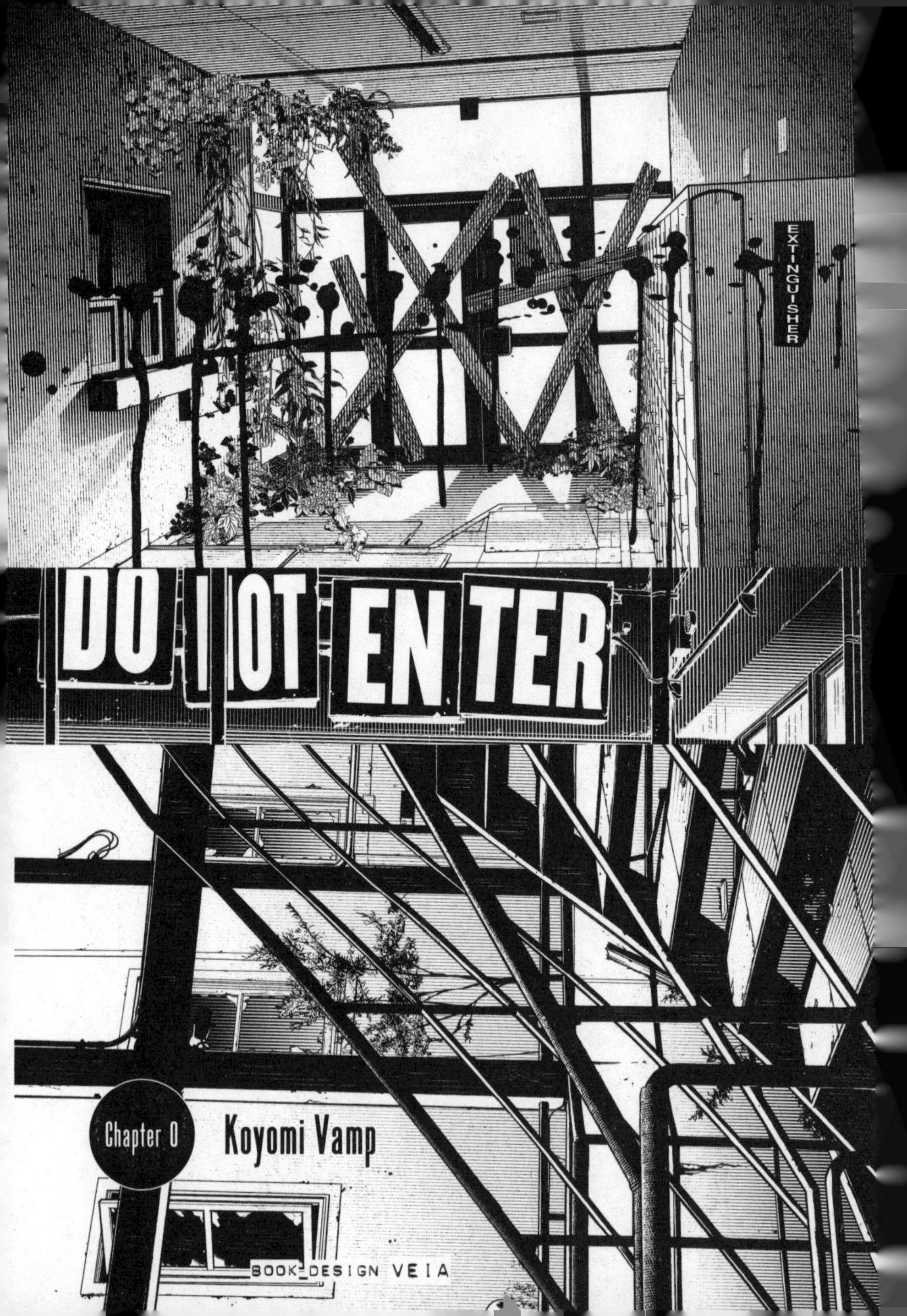
EXTINGUISHER
DO I OT EN TER
Chapter 0
Koyomi Vamp
BOOK_DESIGN VEIA

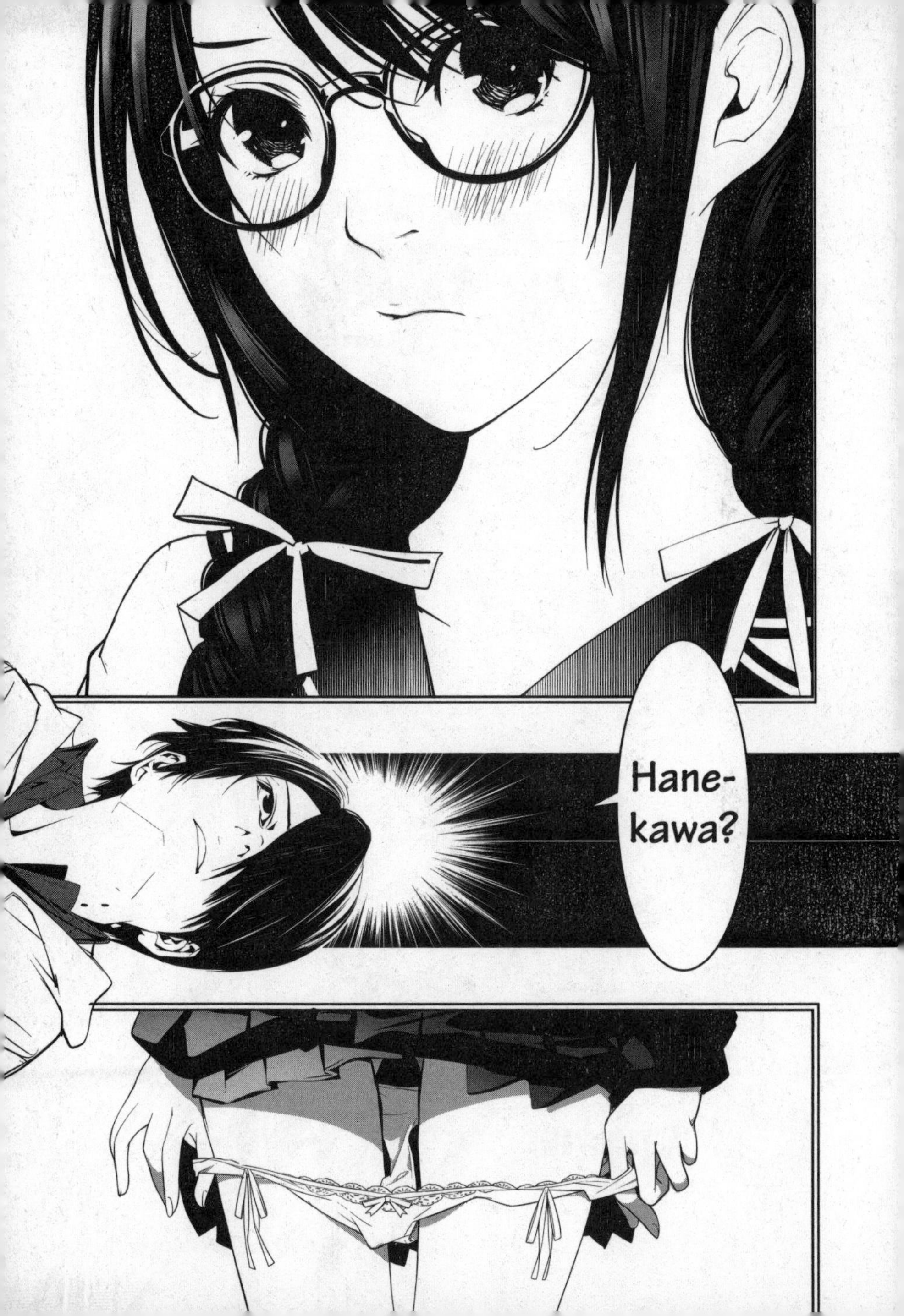
Hane-
kawa?

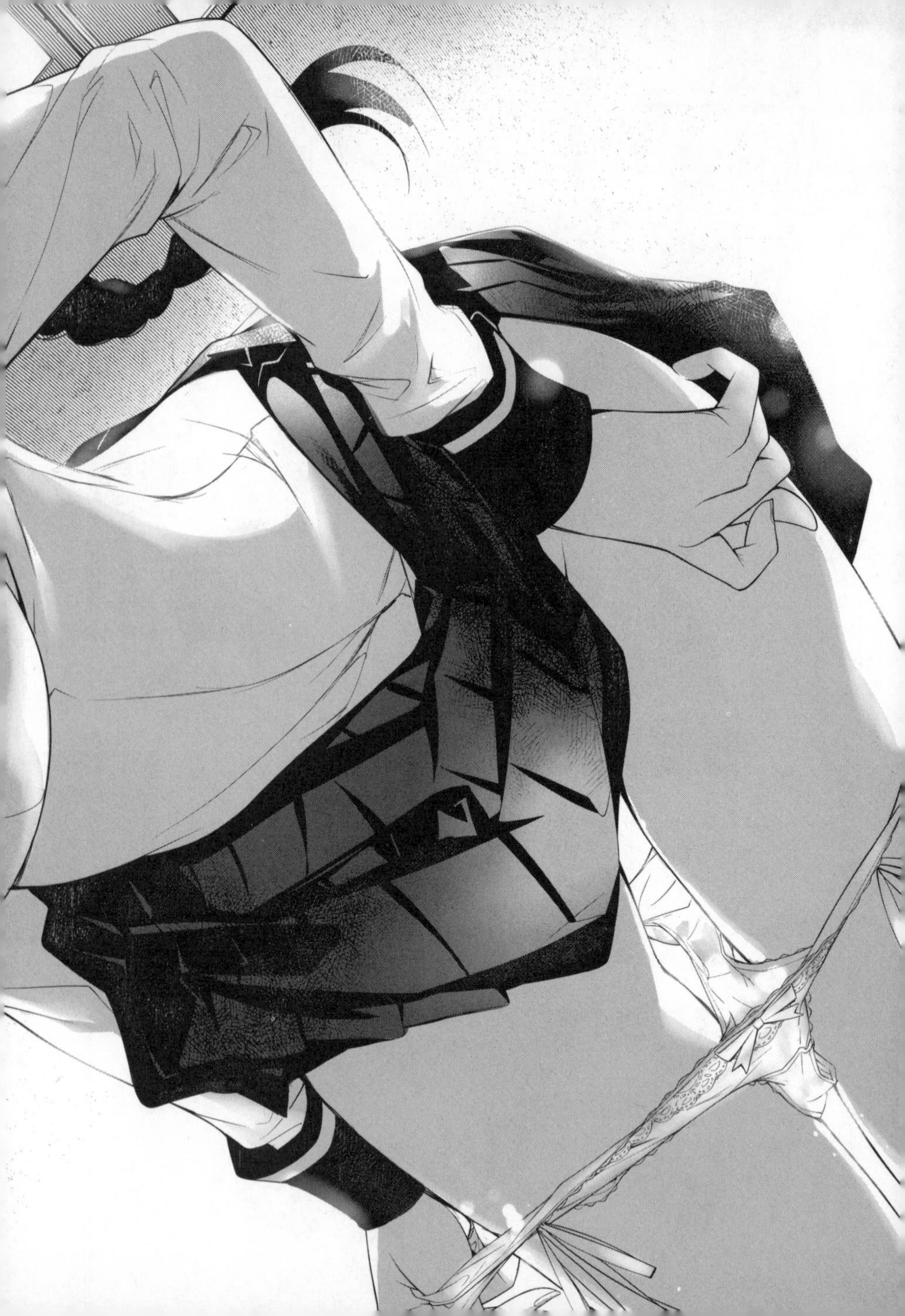

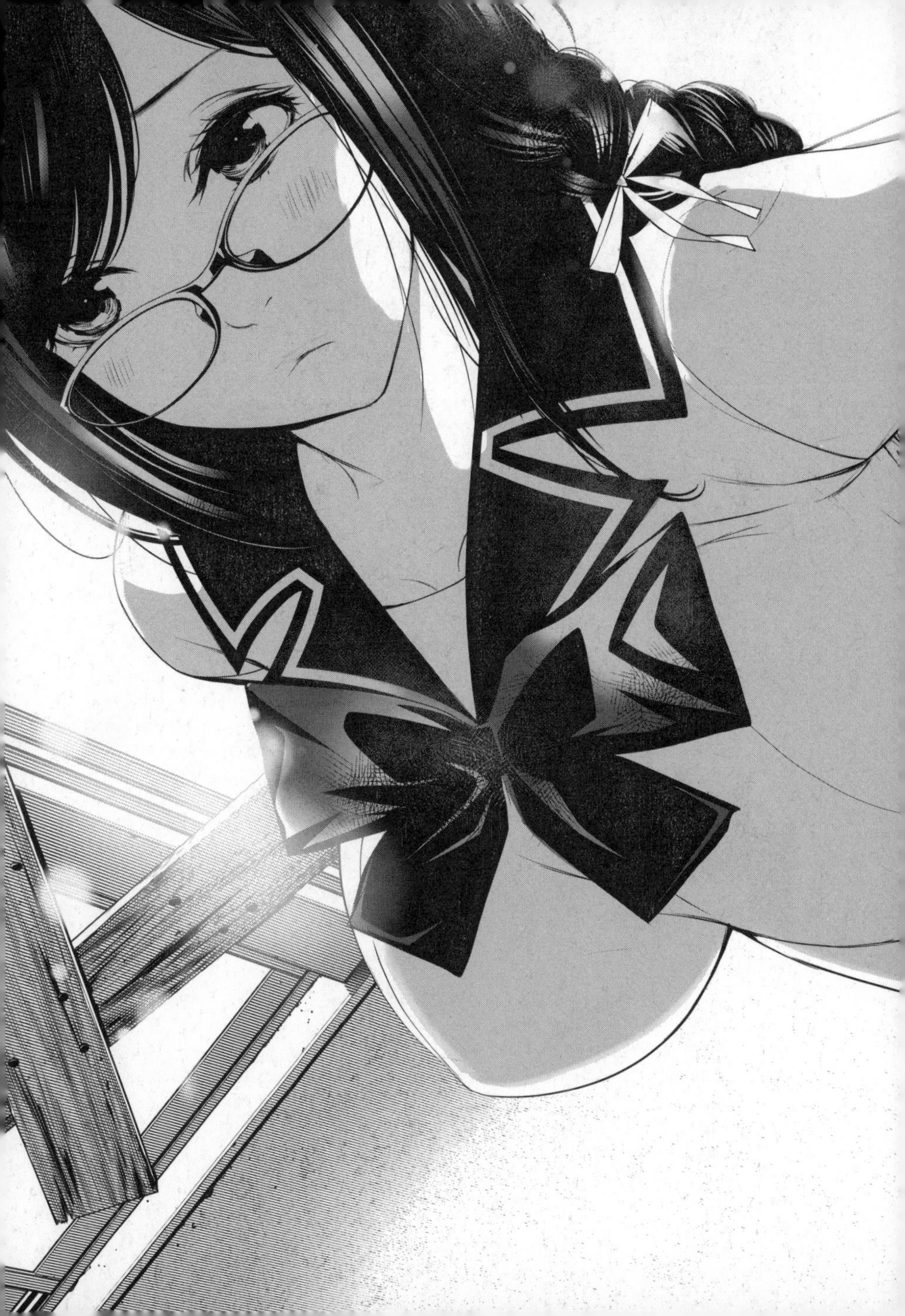

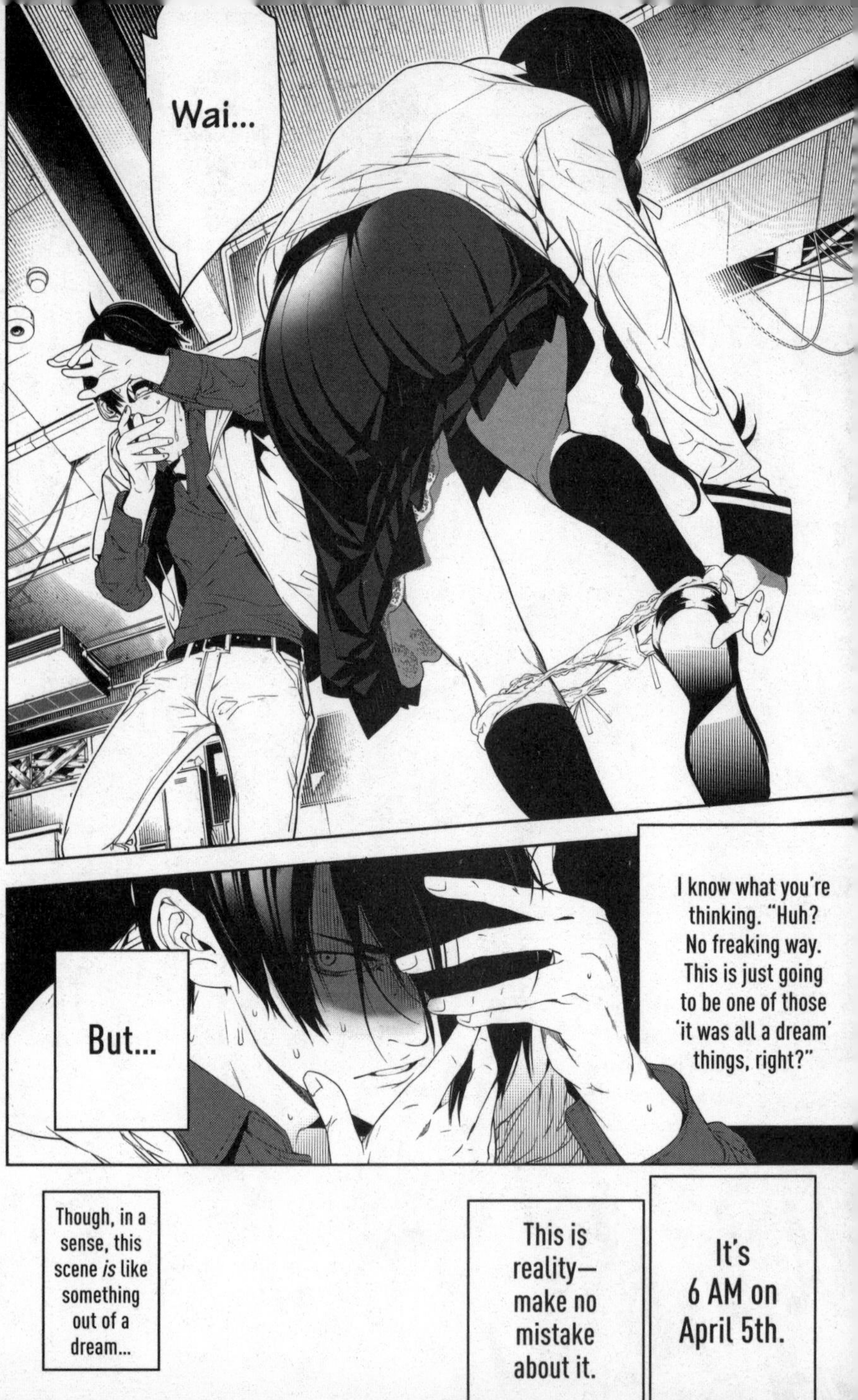
Wai...
I know what you're thinking. "Huh? No freaking way. This is just going to be one of those 'it was all a dream' things, right?"
But...
It's 6 AM on April 5th.
This is reality—make no mistake about it.
Though, in a sense, this scene *is* like something out of a dream...

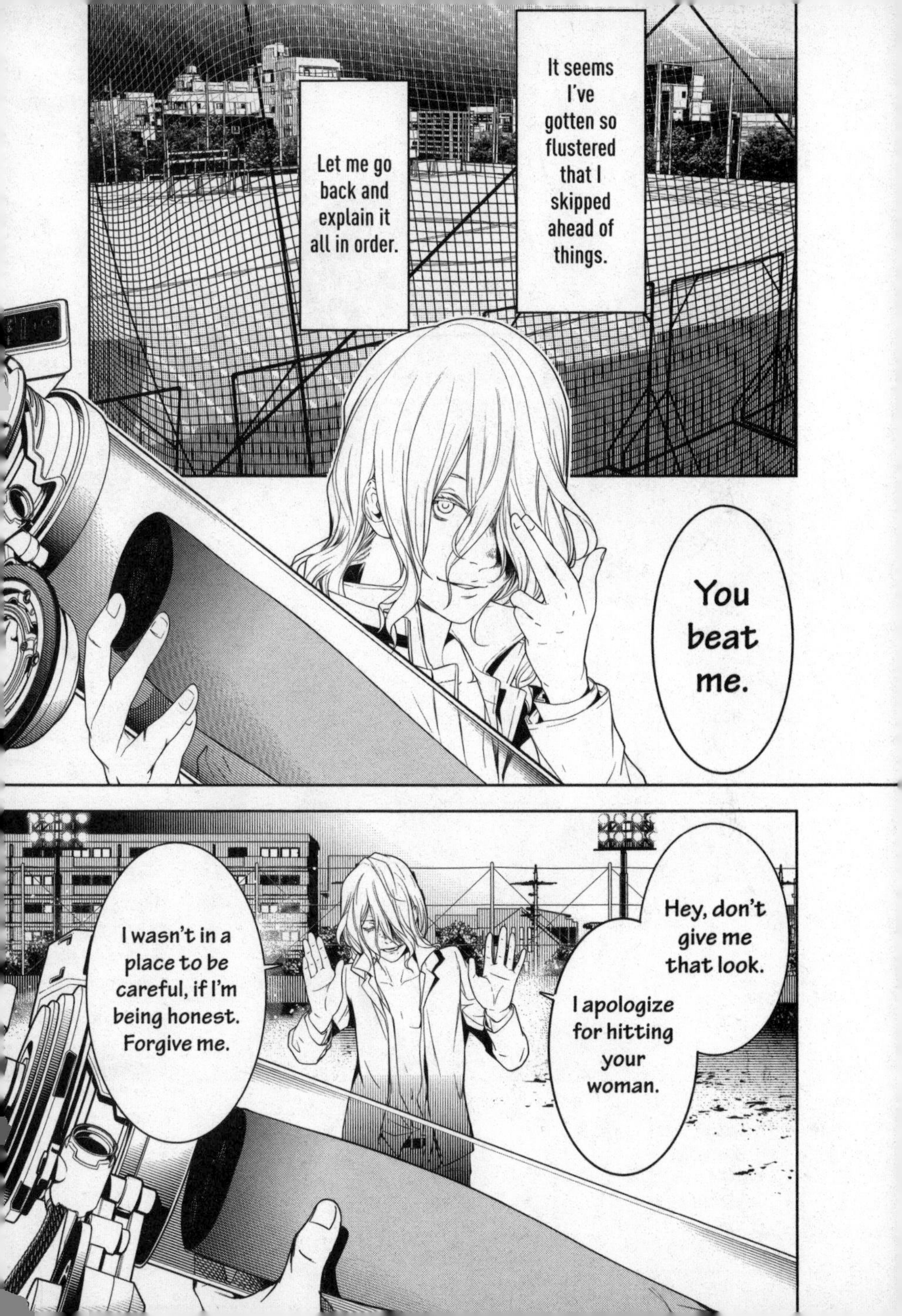
It seems I've gotten so flustered that I skipped ahead of things.
Let me go back and explain it all in order.
You beat me.
Hey, don't give me that look.
I apologize for hitting your woman.
I wasn't in a place to be careful, if I'm being honest. Forgive me.

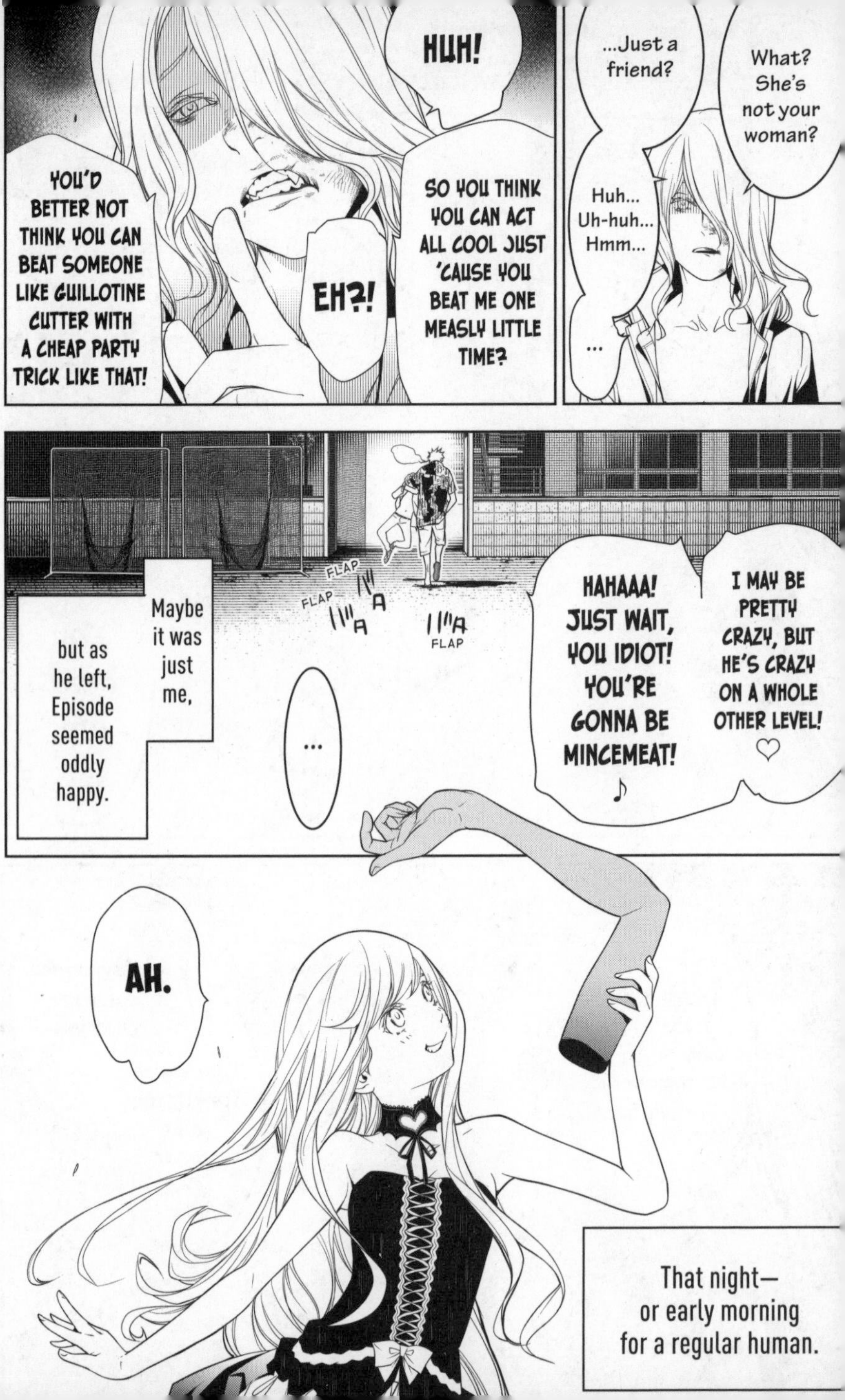
What? She's not your woman?
...Just a friend?
Huh... Uh-huh... Hmm...
...
HUH!
SO YOU THINK YOU CAN ACT ALL COOL JUST 'CAUSE YOU BEAT ME ONE MEASLY LITTLE TIME?
EH?!
YOU'D BETTER NOT THINK YOU CAN BEAT SOMEONE LIKE GUILLOTINE CUTTER WITH A CHEAP PARTY TRICK LIKE THAT!
I MAY BE PRETTY CRAZY, BUT HE'S CRAZY ON A WHOLE OTHER LEVEL! ♡
HAHAAA! JUST WAIT, YOU IDIOT! YOU'RE GONNA BE MINCEMEAT! ♪
FLAP
FLAP
FLAP
...
Maybe it was just me,
but as he left, Episode seemed oddly happy.
That night—or early morning for a regular human.
AH.

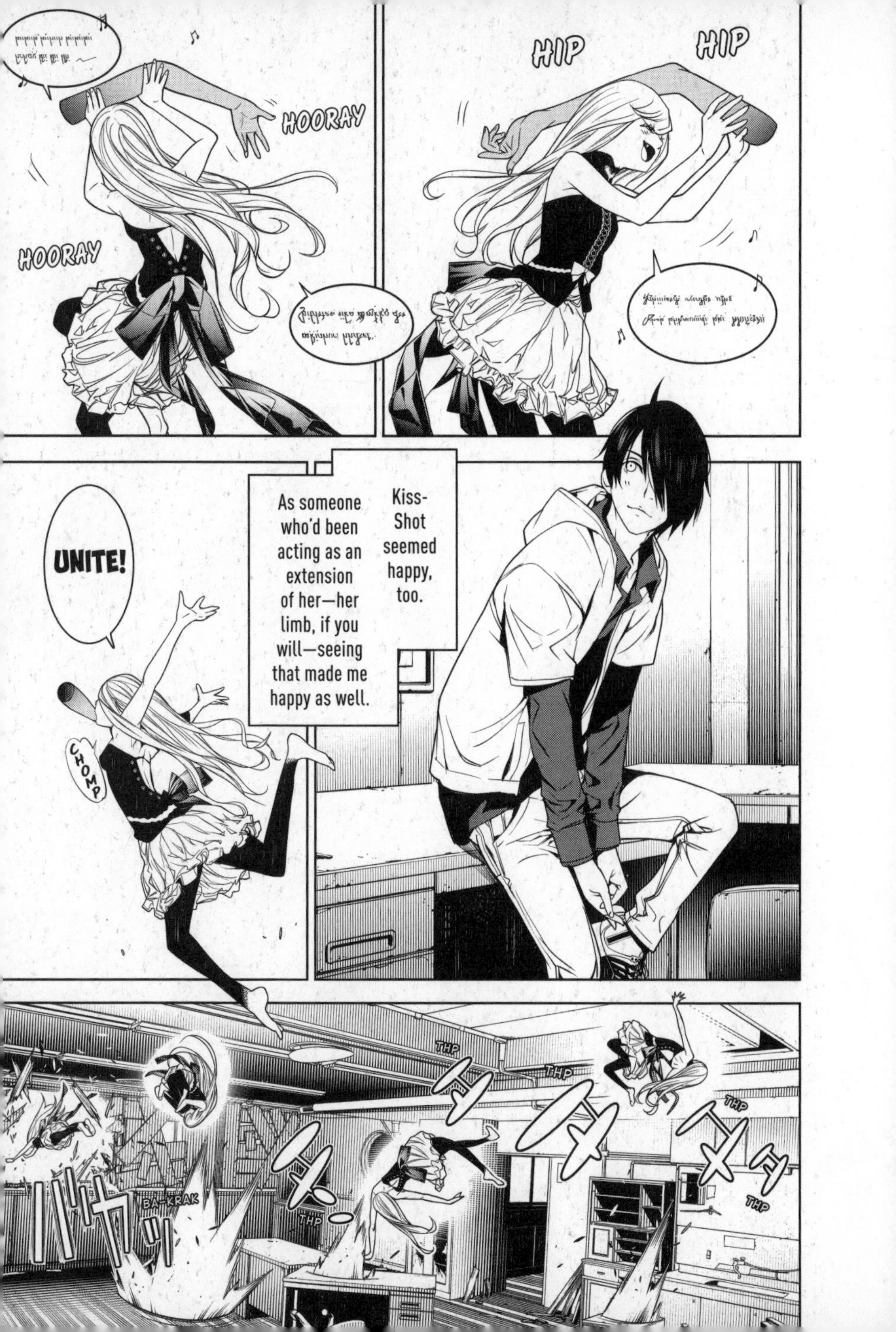
HIP HIP
HOORAY
HOORAY
Kiss-Shot seemed happy, too.
As someone who'd been acting as an extension of her—her limb, if you will—seeing that made me happy as well.
UNITE!
CHOMP
THP
THP
THP
THP
THP
BA-KRAK

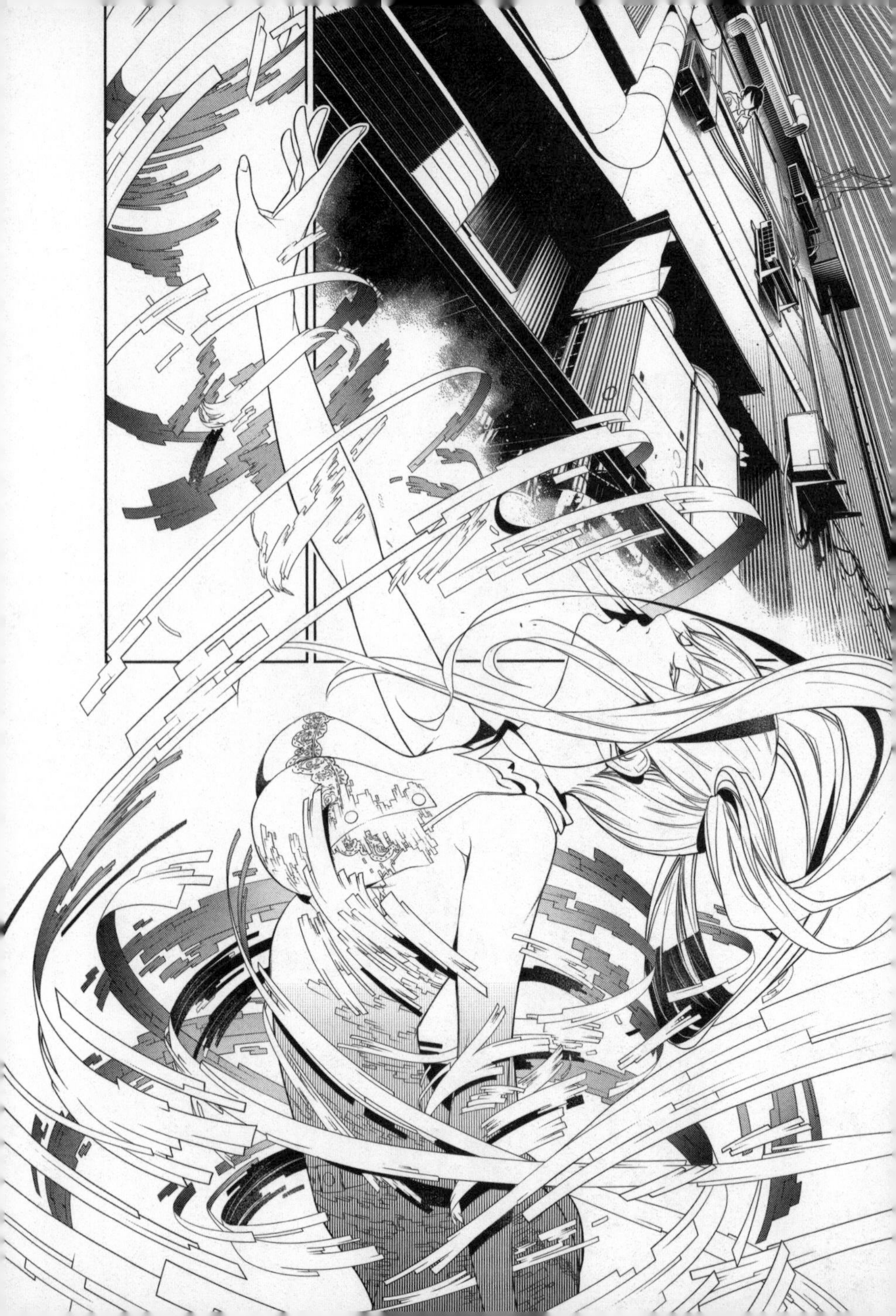

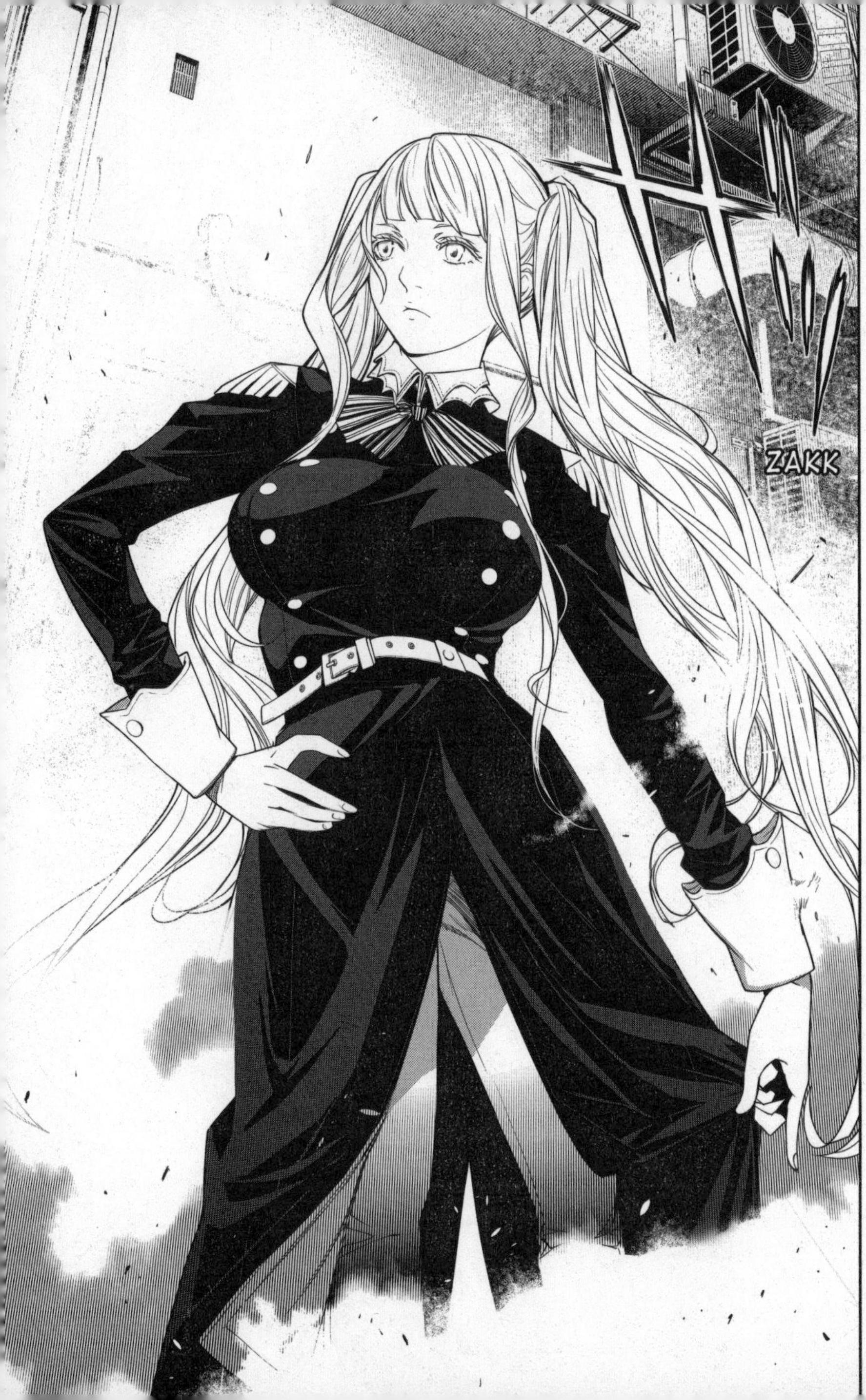
ZAKK

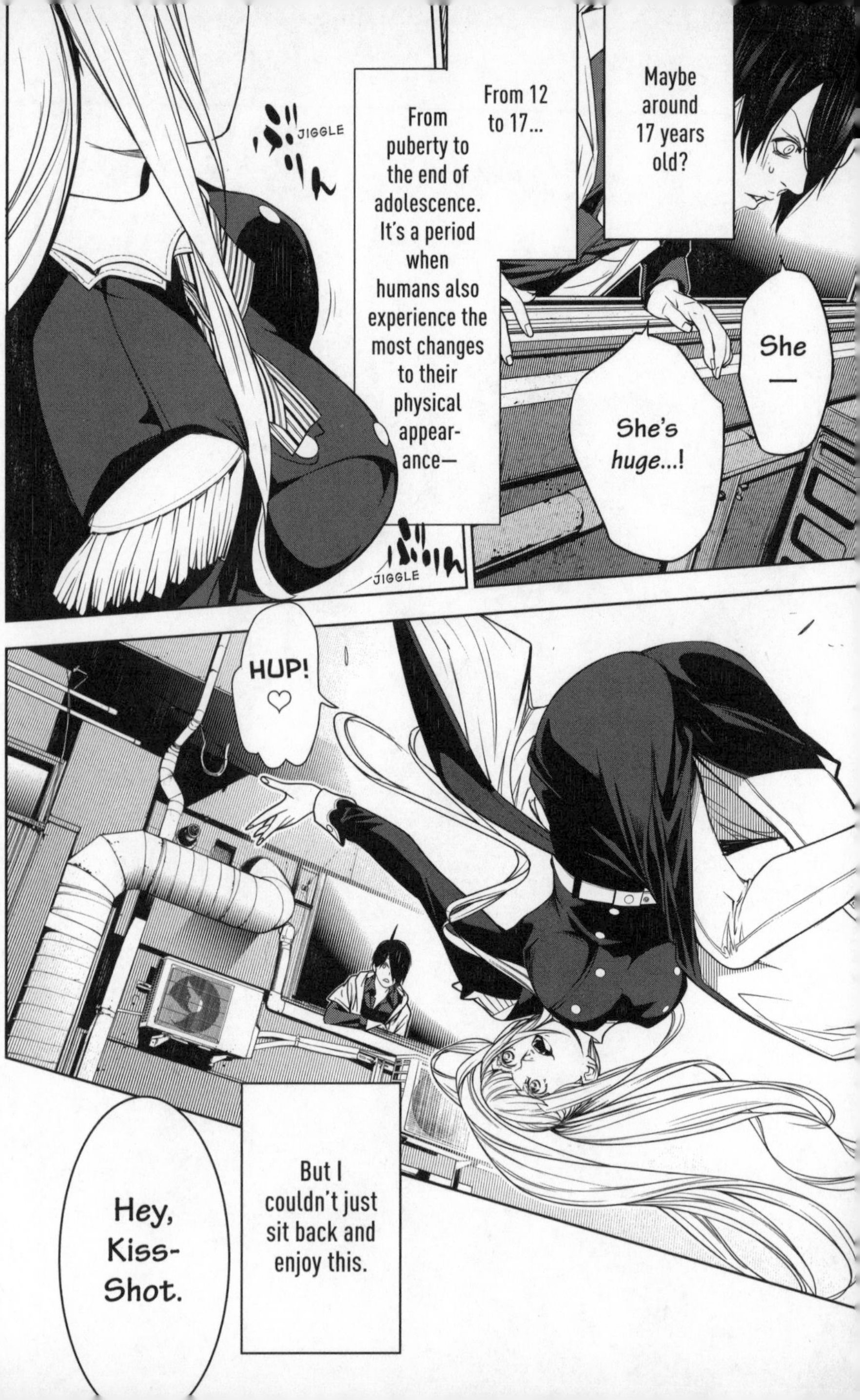
Maybe around 17 years old?
From 12 to 17...
She —
She's *huge*...!
JIGGLE
From puberty to the end of adolescence. It's a period when humans also experience the most changes to their physical appear-ance—
JIGGLE
HUP! ♡
But I couldn't just sit back and enjoy this.
Hey, Kiss-Shot.

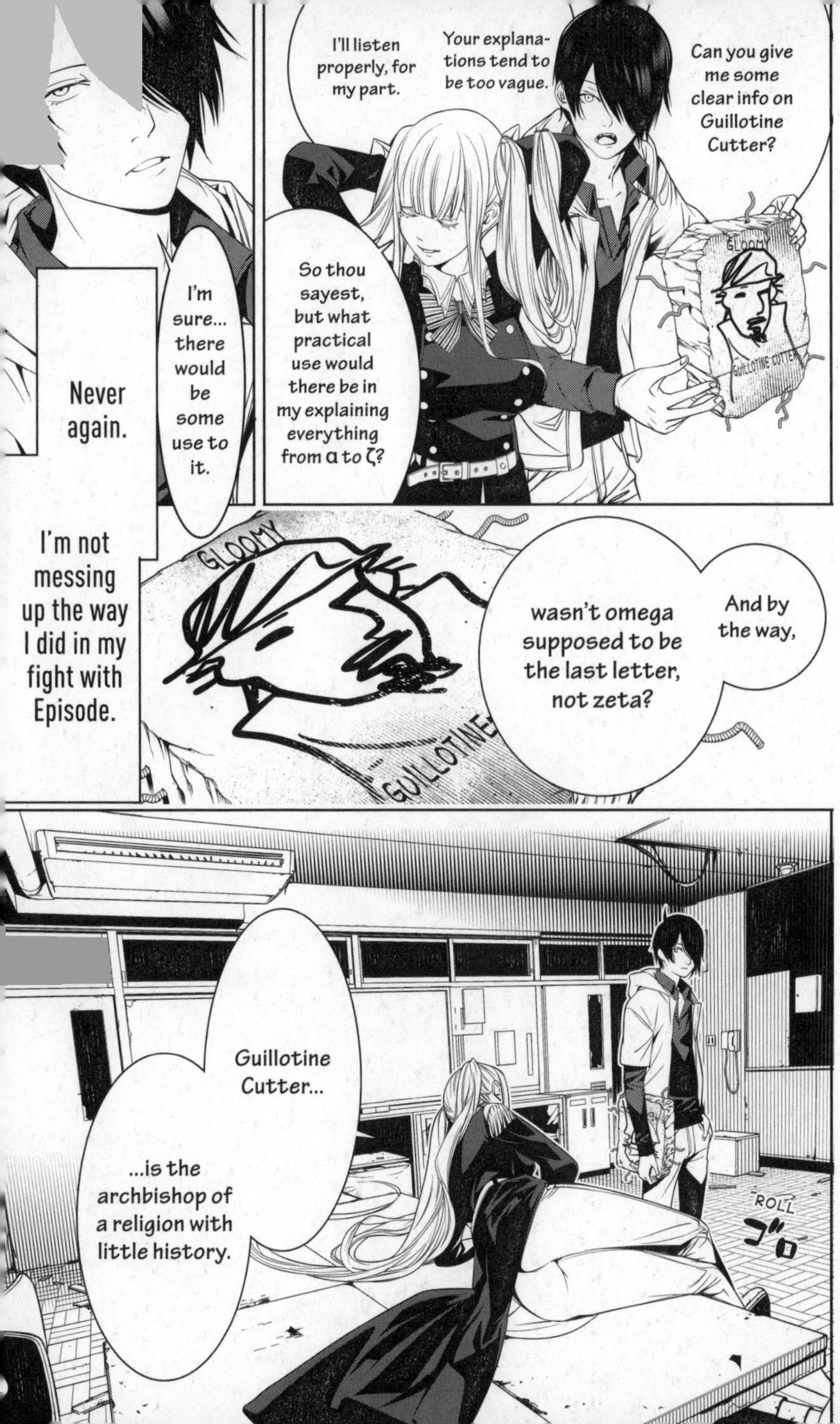

Can you give me some clear info on Guillotine Cutter?
Your explanations tend to be too vague.
I'll listen properly, for my part.
GLOOMY
GUILLOTINE CUTTER
So thou sayest, but what practical use would there be in my explaining everything from α to ζ?
I'm sure... there would be some use to it.
Never again.
And by the way,
wasn't omega supposed to be the last letter, not zeta?
GLOOMY
GUILLOTINE
I'm not messing up the way I did in my fight with Episode.
ROLL
ゴロ
Guillotine Cutter...
...is the archbishop of a religion with little history.

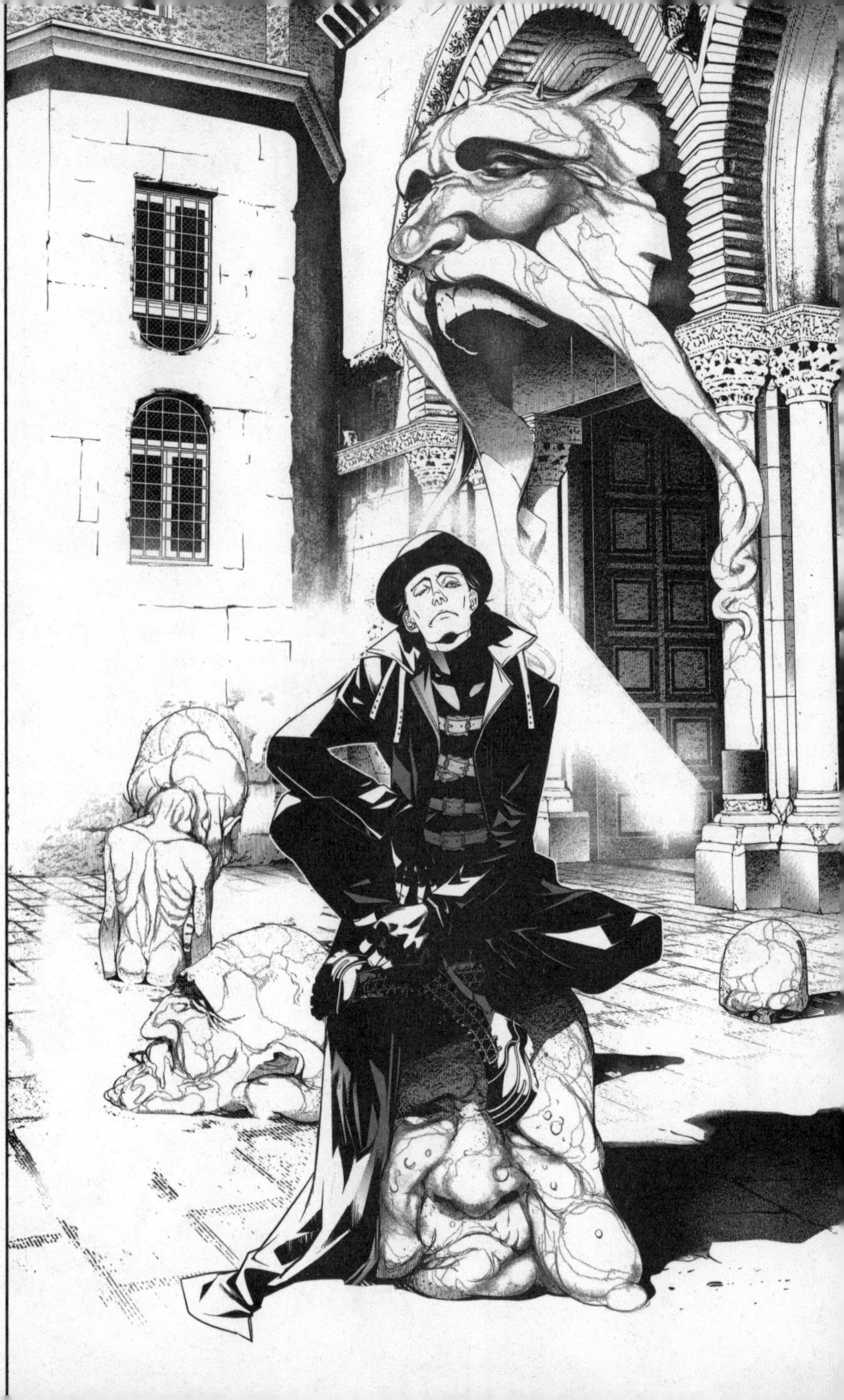

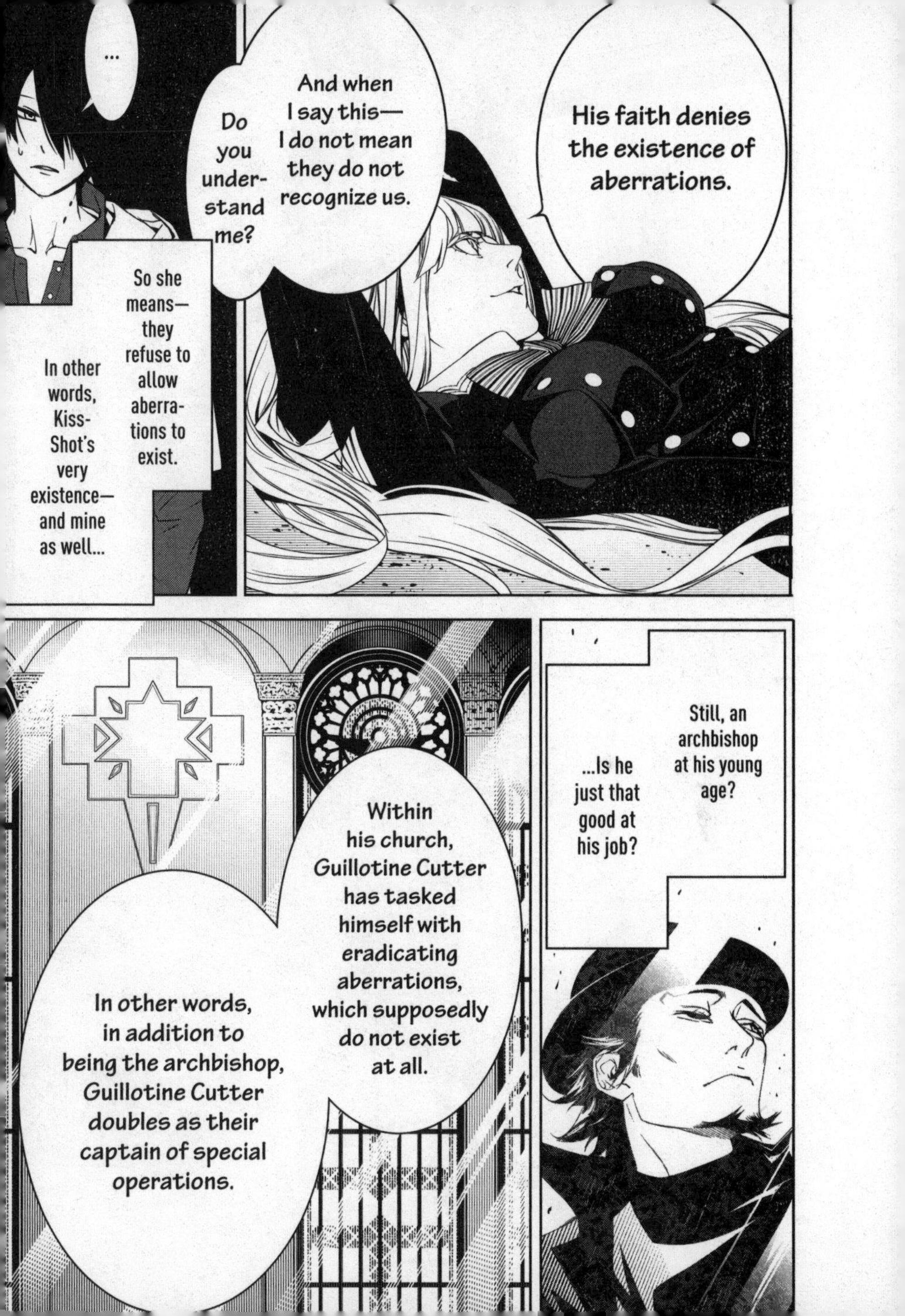
His faith denies the existence of aberrations.
And when I say this— I do not mean they do not recognize us.
Do you understand me?
...
So she means— they refuse to allow aberrations to exist.
In other words, Kiss-Shot's very existence— and mine as well...
Still, an archbishop at his young age?
...Is he just that good at his job?
Within his church, Guillotine Cutter has tasked himself with eradicating aberrations, which supposedly do not exist at all.
In other words, in addition to being the archbishop, Guillotine Cutter doubles as their captain of special operations.

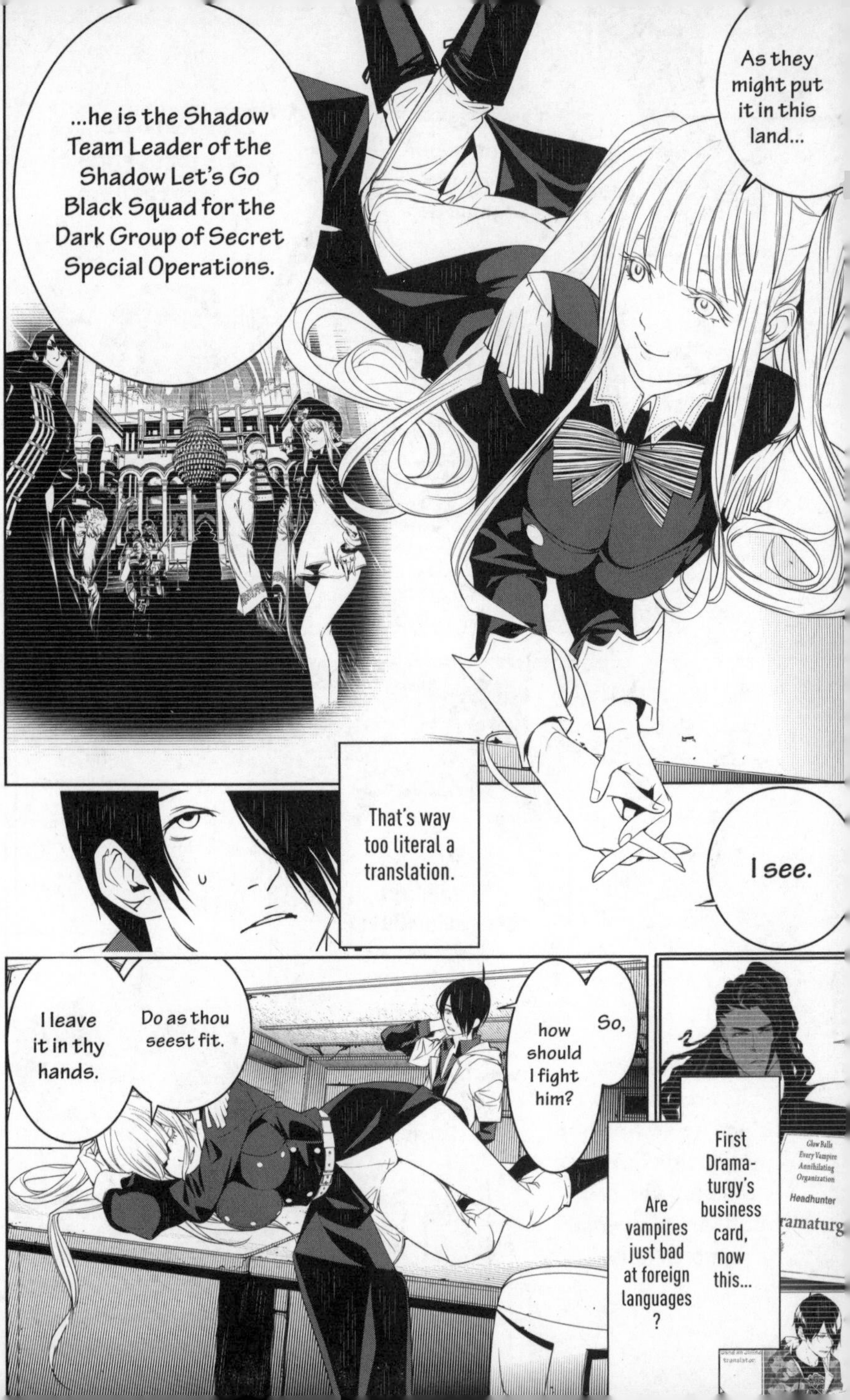
As they might put it in this land...
...he is the Shadow Team Leader of the Shadow Let's Go Black Squad for the Dark Group of Secret Special Operations.
I see.
That's way too literal a translation.
Glow Balls
Every Vampire
Annihilating
Organization
Headhunter
First Dramaturgy's business card, now this...
Are vampires just bad at foreign languages?
So, how should I fight him?
Do as thou seest fit.
I leave it in thy hands.

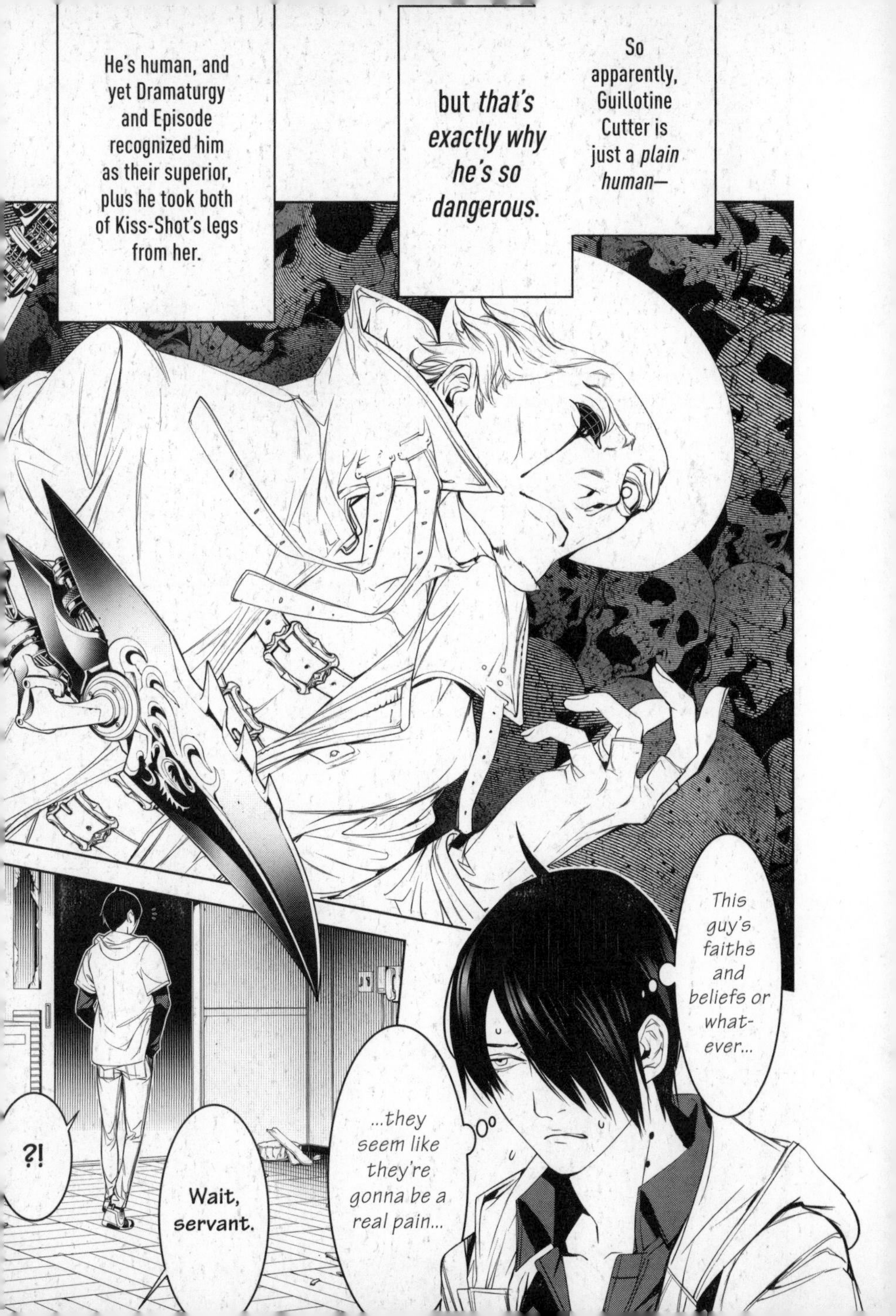
So apparently, Guillotine Cutter is just a *plain human*—
but *that's exactly why he's so dangerous.*
He's human, and yet Dramaturgy and Episode recognized him as their superior, plus he took both of Kiss-Shot's legs from her.
This guy's faiths and beliefs or what-ever...
...they seem like they're gonna be a real pain...
Wait, servant.
?!

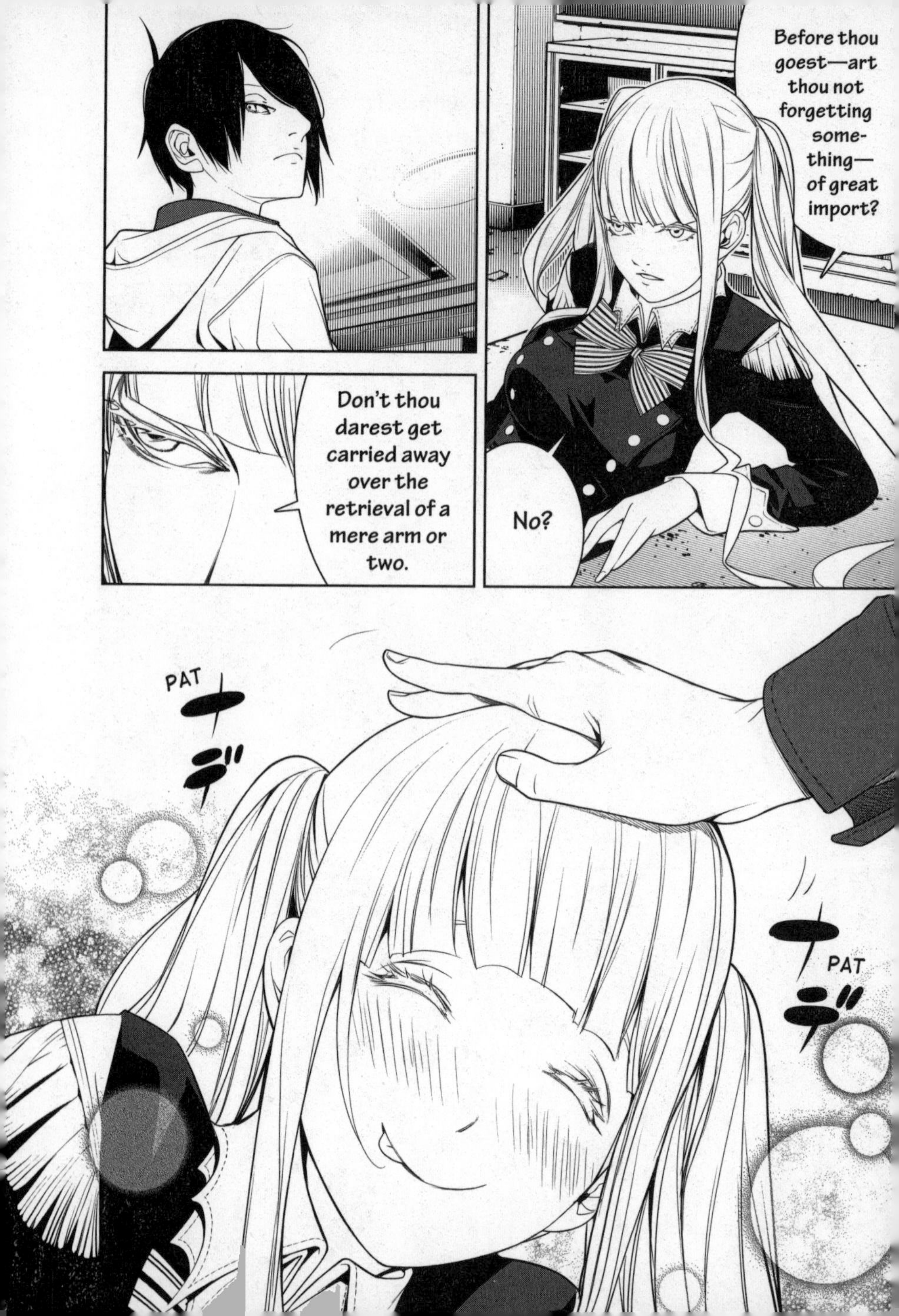
Before thou goest—art thou not forgetting some-thing—of great import?
No?
Don't thou darest get carried away over the retrieval of a mere arm or two.
PAT
PAT

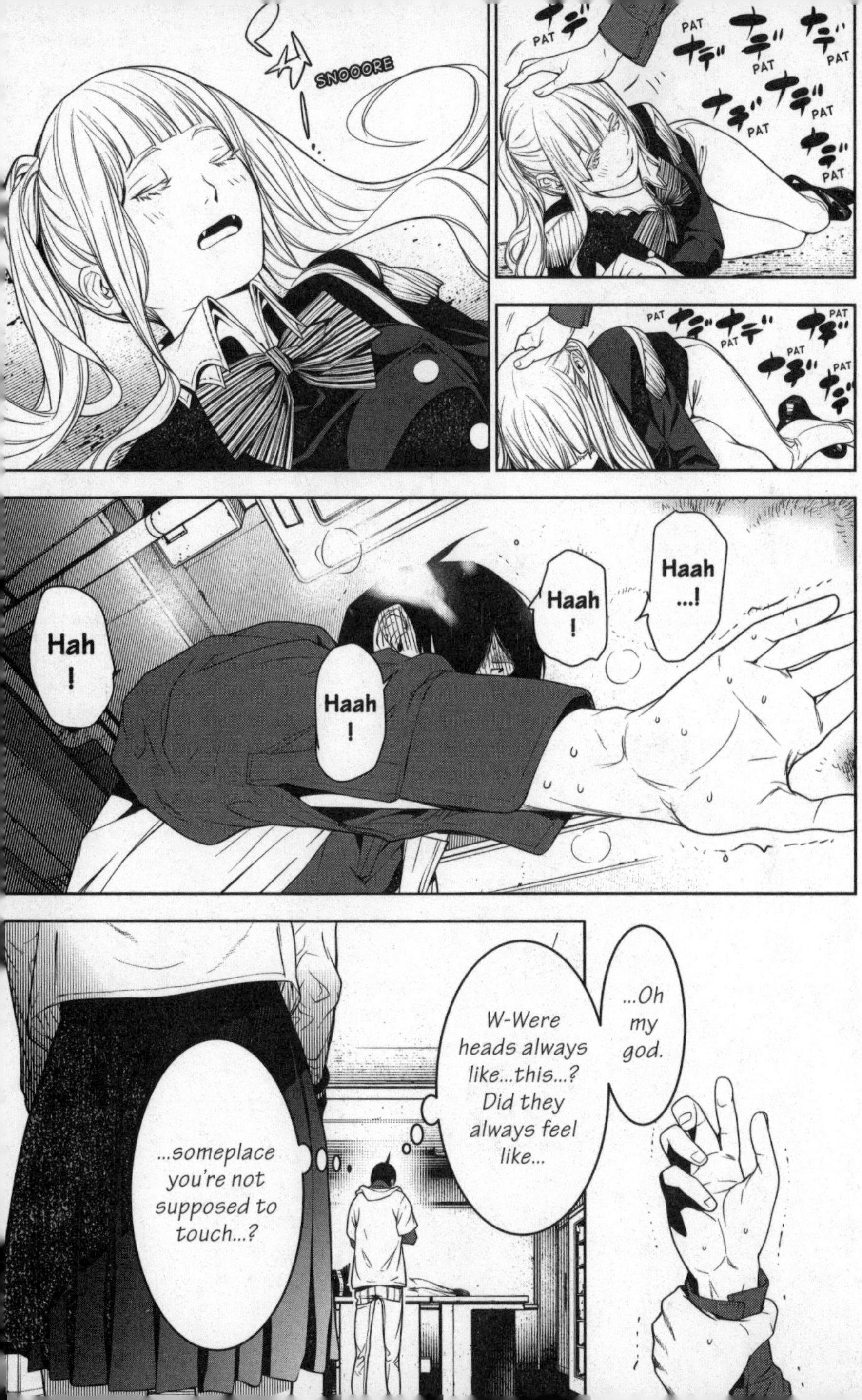
PAT PAT PAT PAT PAT PAT PAT
PAT PAT PAT PAT PAT
SNOOORE
Haah ...!
Haah !
Haah !
Hah !
...Oh my god.
W-Were heads always like...this...? Did they always feel like...
...someplace you're not supposed to touch...?

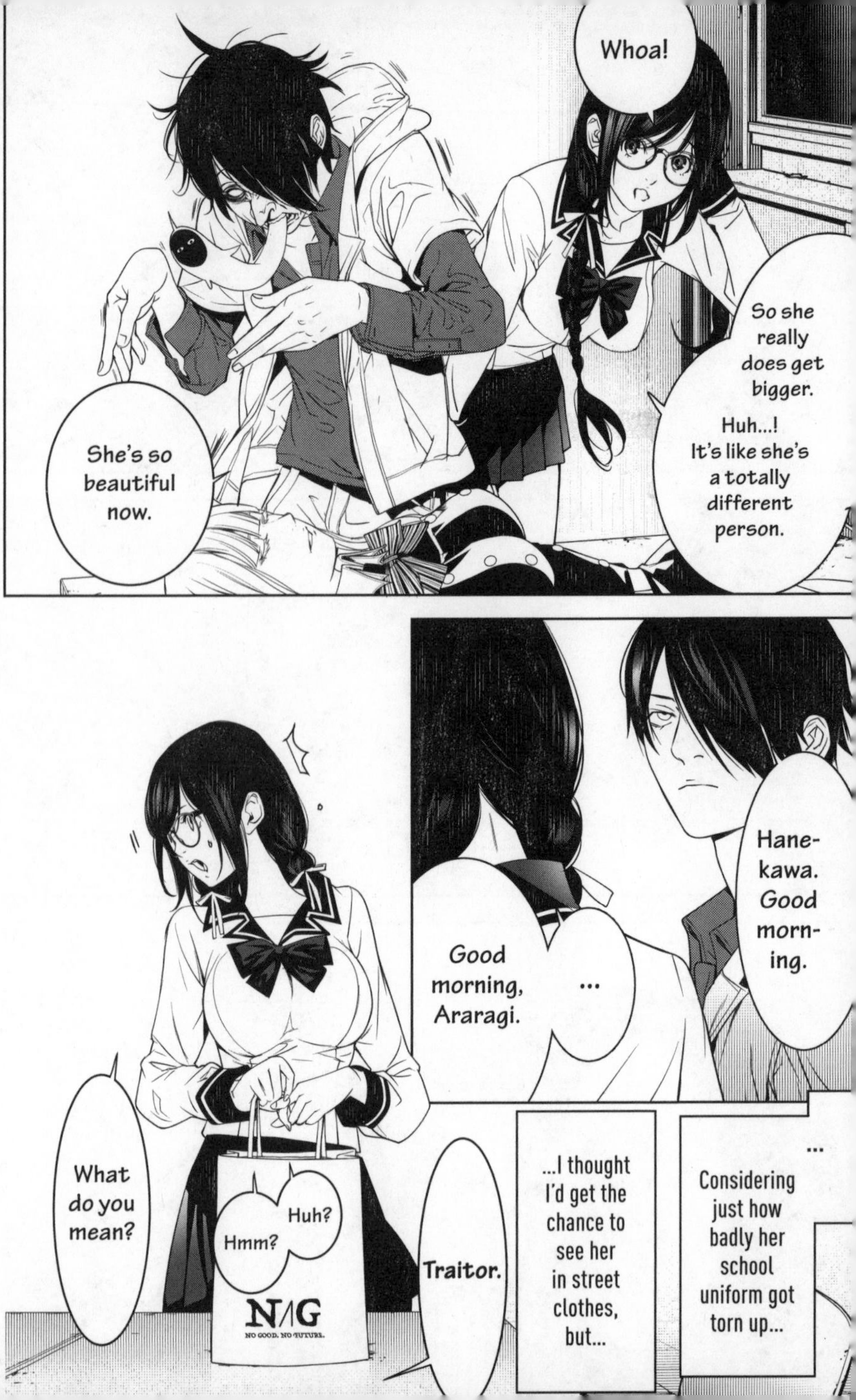
Whoa!
So she really does get bigger.
Huh...! It's like she's a totally different person.
She's so beautiful now.
Hane-kawa. Good morn-ing.
...
Good morning, Araragi.
...
Considering just how badly her school uniform got torn up...
...I thought I'd get the chance to see her in street clothes, but...
Traitor.
Huh?
Hmm?
N/G
NO GOOD. NO FUTURE.
What do you mean?

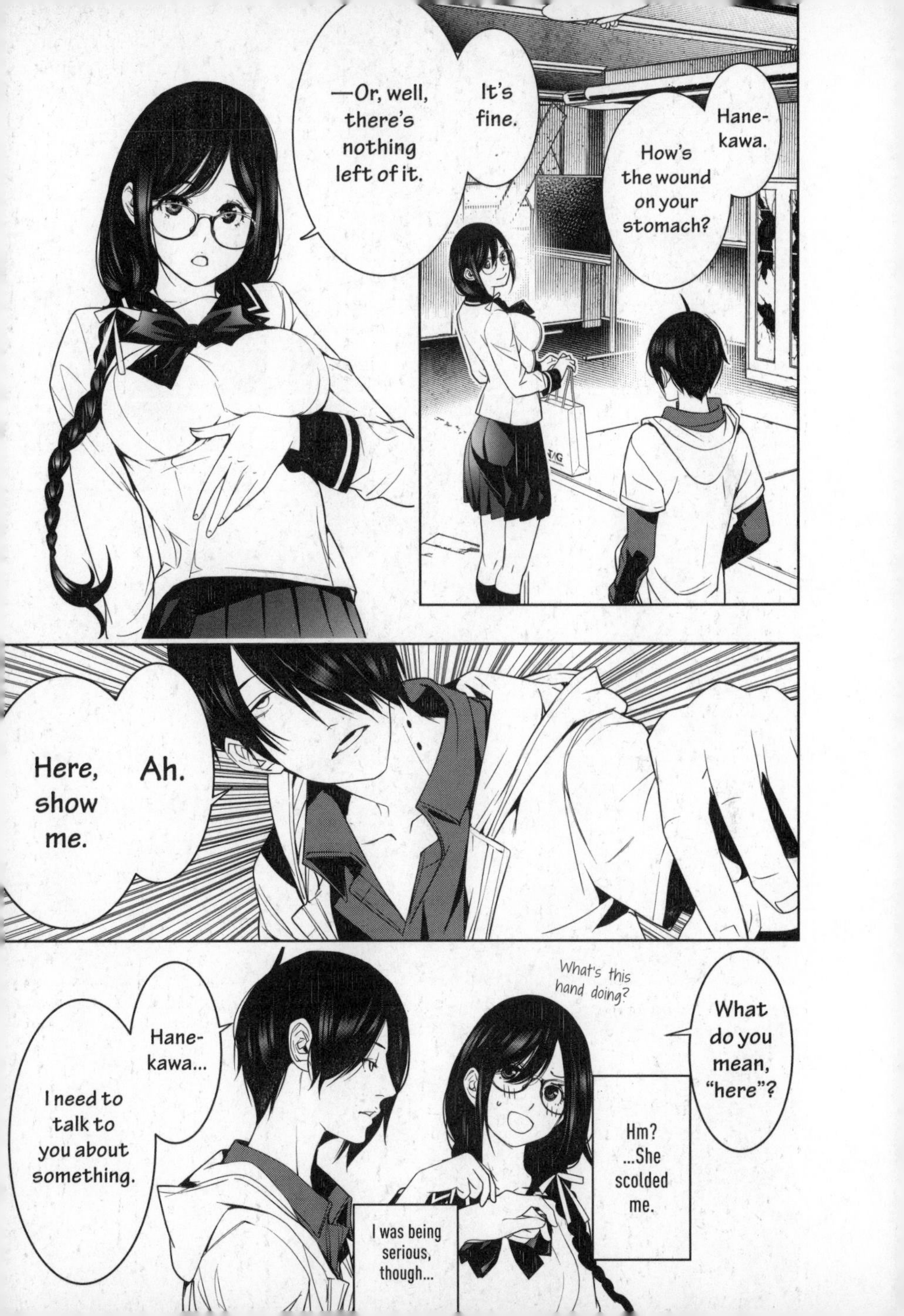
Hane-kawa.
How's the wound on your stomach?
It's fine.
—Or, well, there's nothing left of it.
Ah.
Here, show me.
What do you mean, "here"?
What's this hand doing?
Hm? ...She scolded me.
I was being serious, though...
Hane-kawa...
I need to talk to you about something.

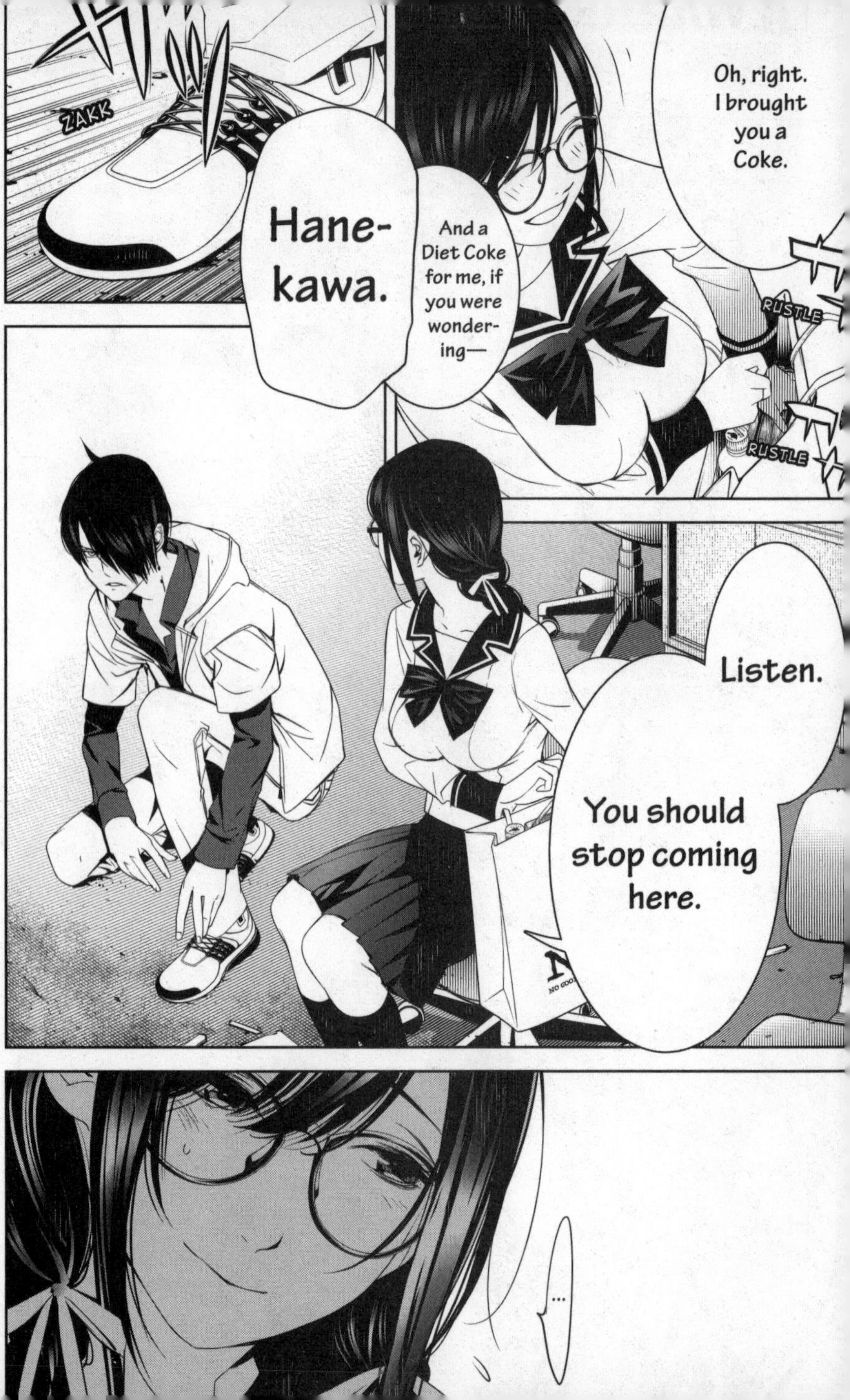
Oh, right. I brought you a Coke.
RUSTLE
RUSTLE
And a Diet Coke for me, if you were wondering—
ZAKK
Hane-kawa.
Listen.
You should stop coming here.
...

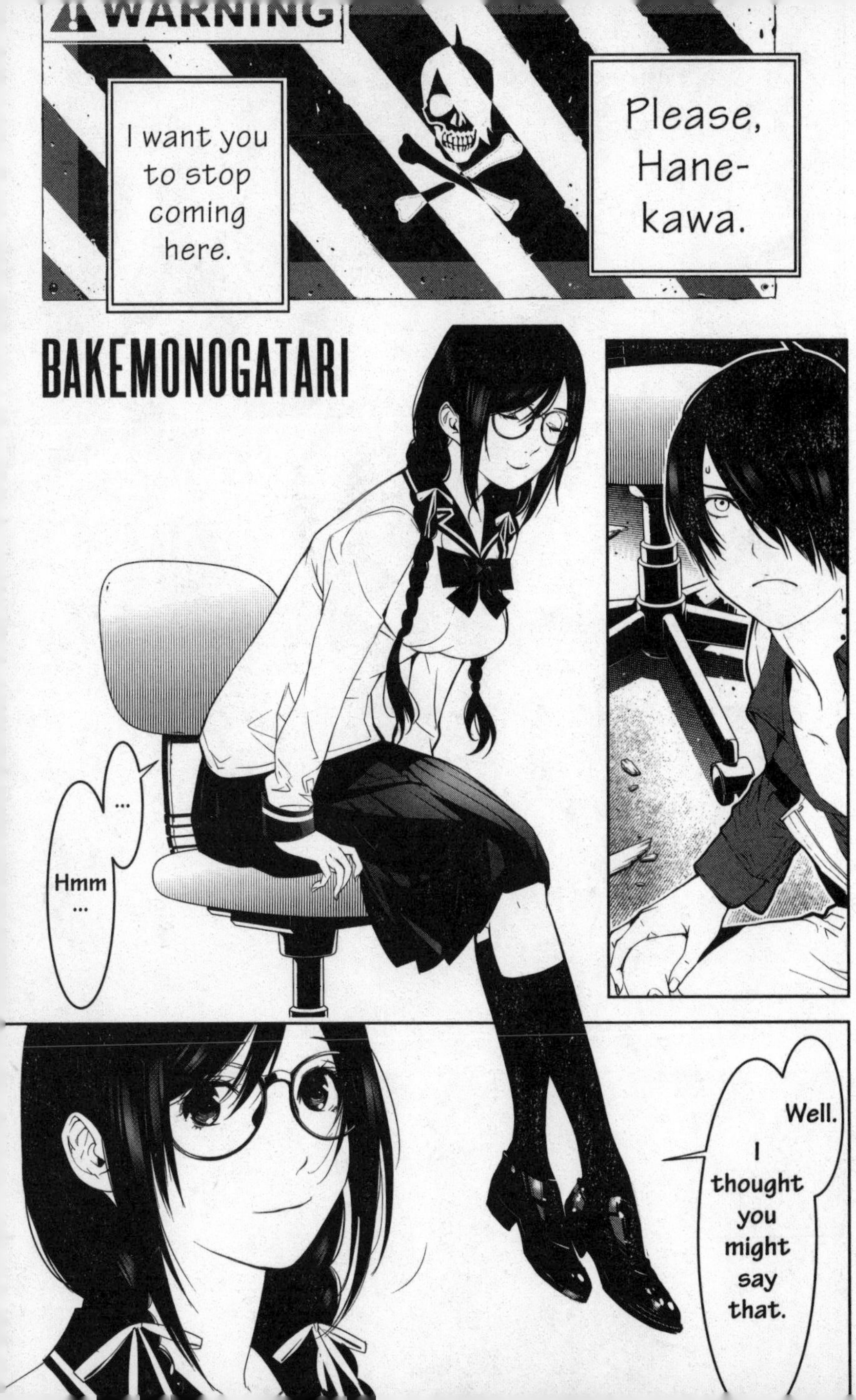
WARNING
Please, Hane-kawa.
I want you to stop coming here.
BAKEMONOGATARI
... Hmm ...
Well. I thought you might say that.

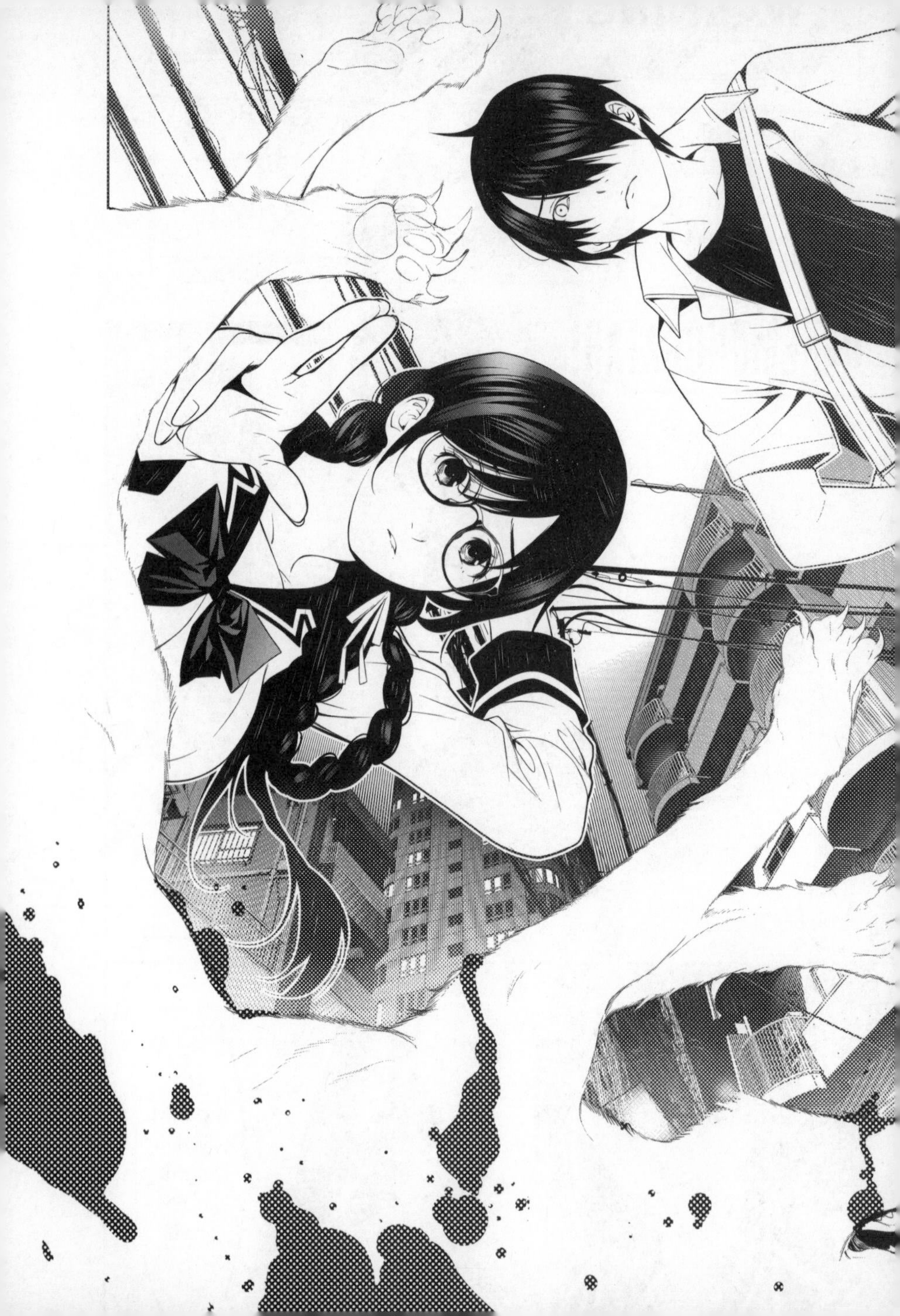

Please don't take this the wrong way—

It's not like last time.

I was only after your fortune.

I do still want to avoid getting you mixed up in this, but— this time is different.

... How's it different?

...

Yesterday.

When Episode's cross took a chunk out of your side...

I lost myself...

SBLORCH

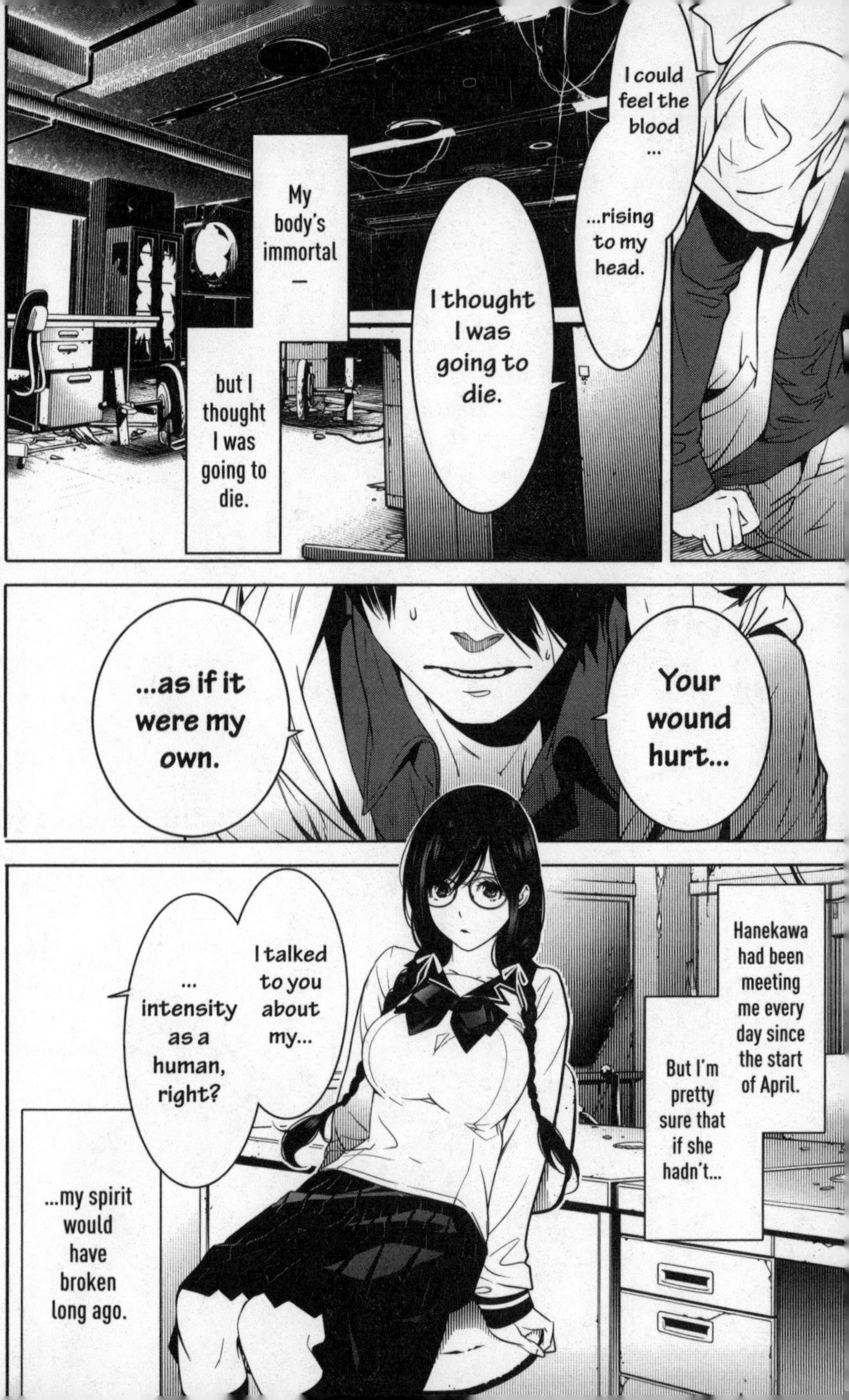
I could feel the blood ...
...rising to my head.
I thought I was going to die.
My body's immortal —
but I thought I was going to die.
Your wound hurt...
...as if it were my own.
Hanekawa had been meeting me every day since the start of April.
But I'm pretty sure that if she hadn't...
I talked to you about my...
... intensity as a human, right?
...my spirit would have broken long ago.

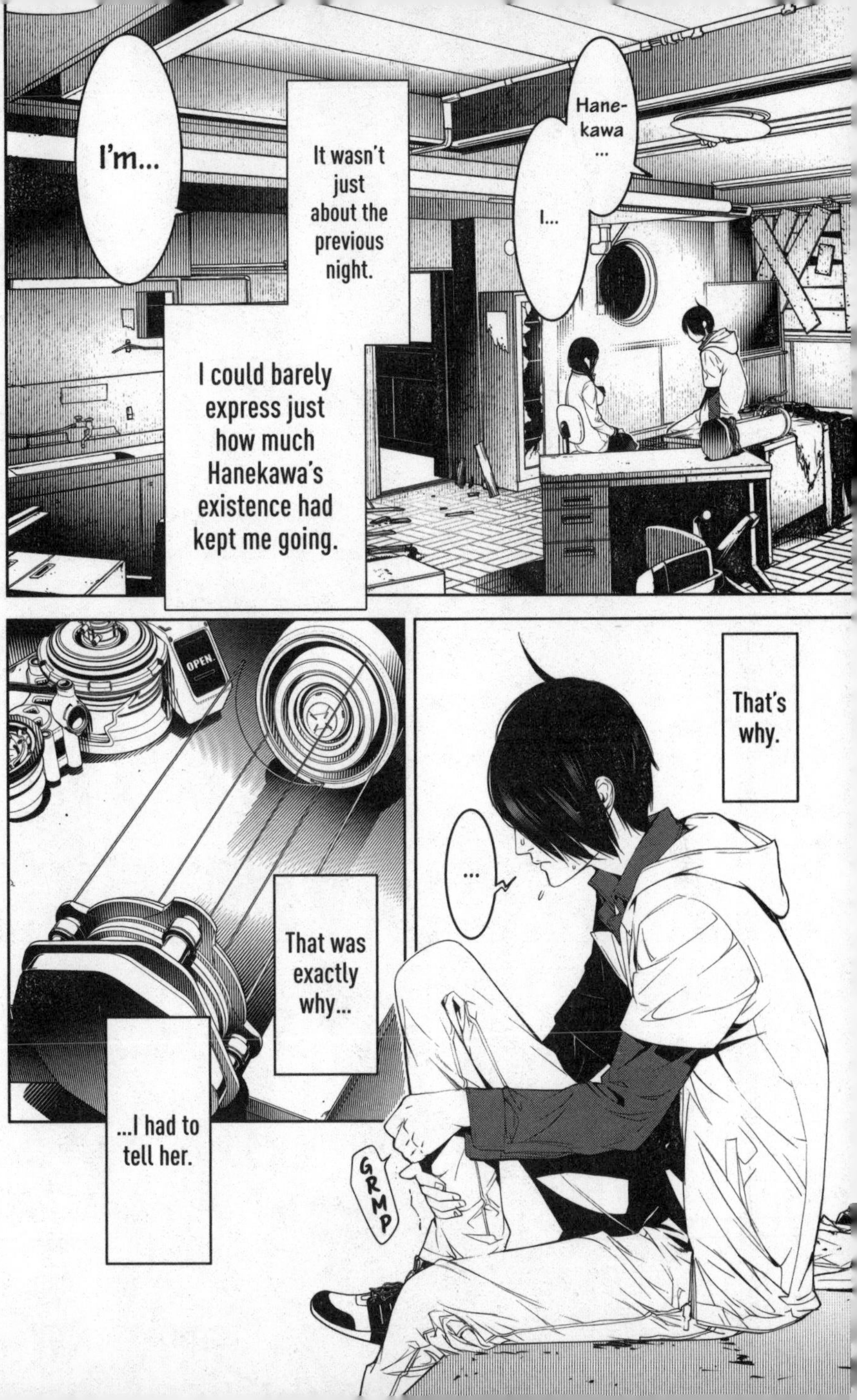
Hane-kawa...
I...
It wasn't just about the previous night.
I'm...
I could barely express just how much Hanekawa's existence had kept me going.
That's why.
...
GRMP
That was exactly why...
...I had to tell her.

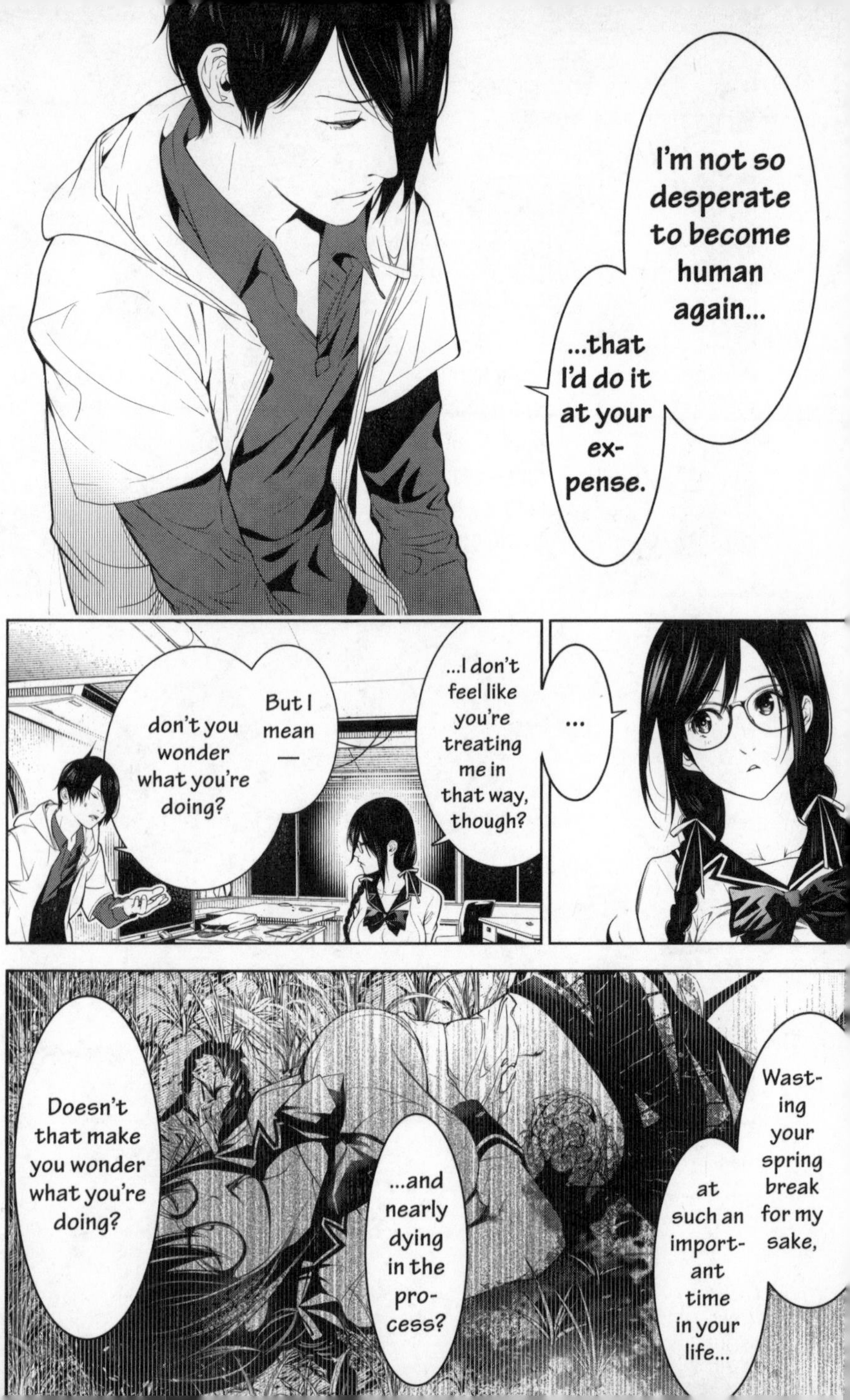
I'm not so desperate to become human again...
...that I'd do it at your expense.
...
...I don't feel like you're treating me in that way, though?
But I mean—
don't you wonder what you're doing?
Wasting your spring break for my sake,
at such an important time in your life...
...and nearly dying in the process?
Doesn't that make you wonder what you're doing?

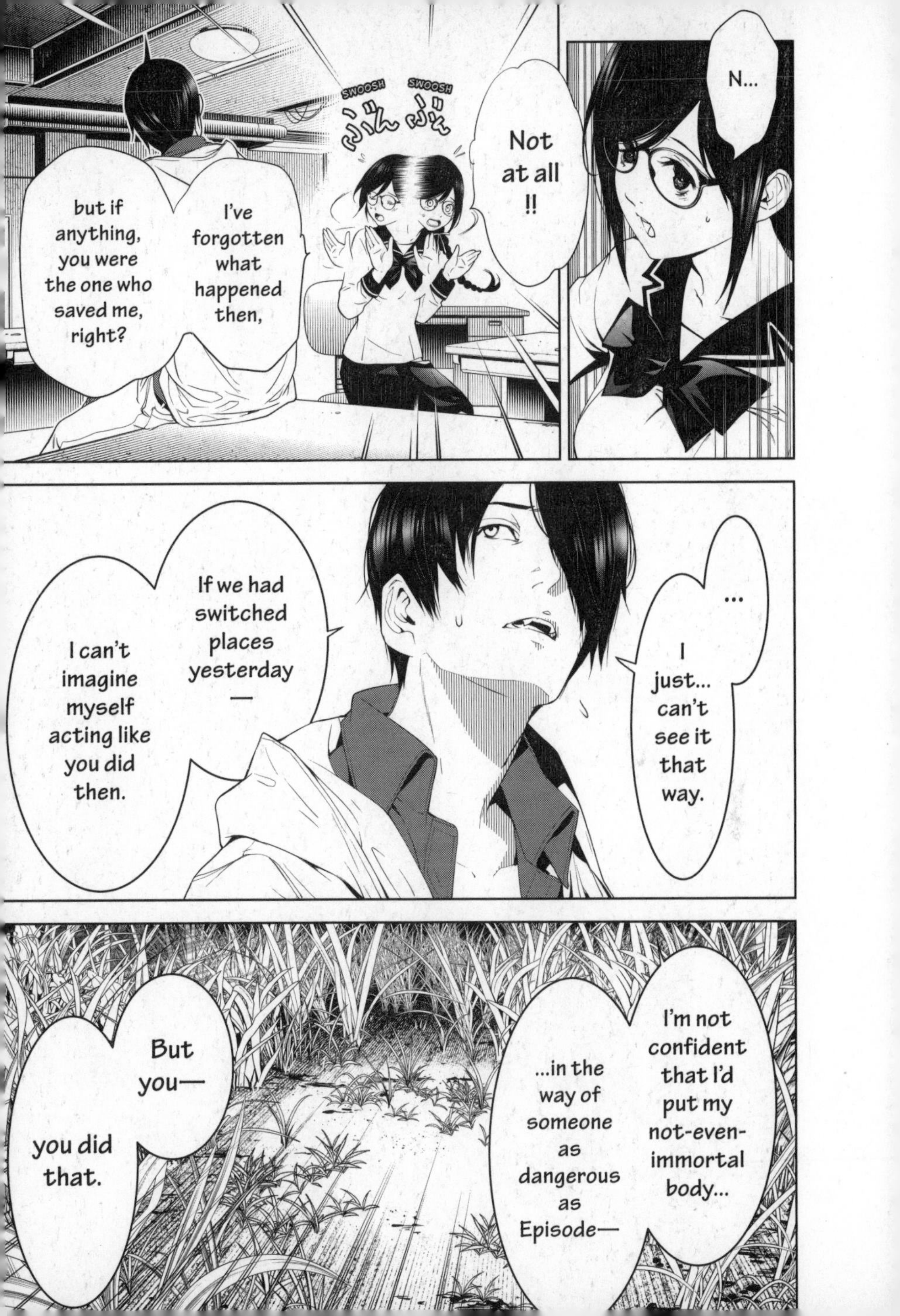
N...
Not at all !!
SWOOSH SWOOSH
ぶん ぶん
I've forgotten what happened then,
but if anything, you were the one who saved me, right?
...
I just... can't see it that way.
If we had switched places yesterday —
I can't imagine myself acting like you did then.
I'm not confident that I'd put my not-even-immortal body...
...in the way of someone as dangerous as Episode—
But you—
you did that.

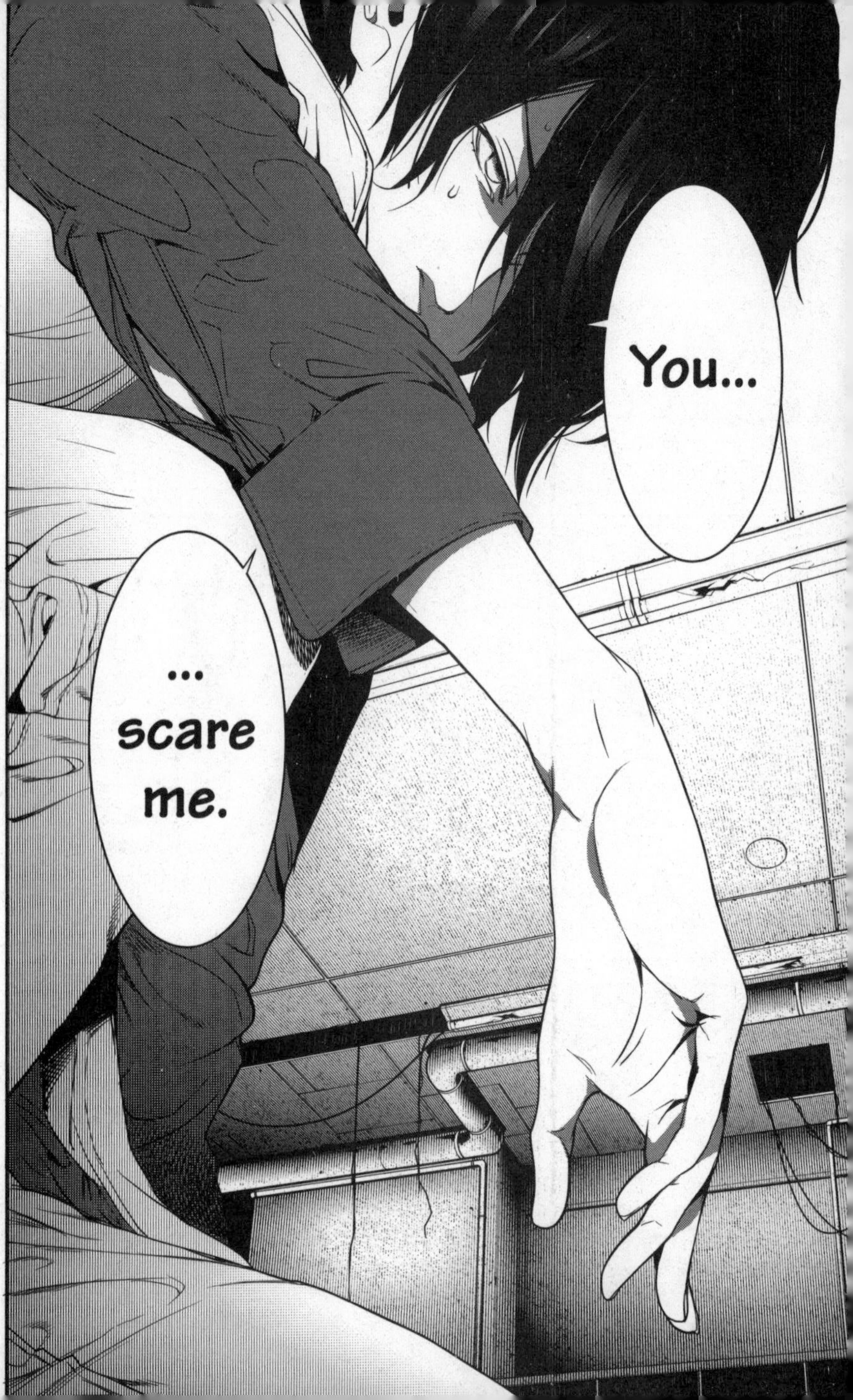
You...
... scare me.

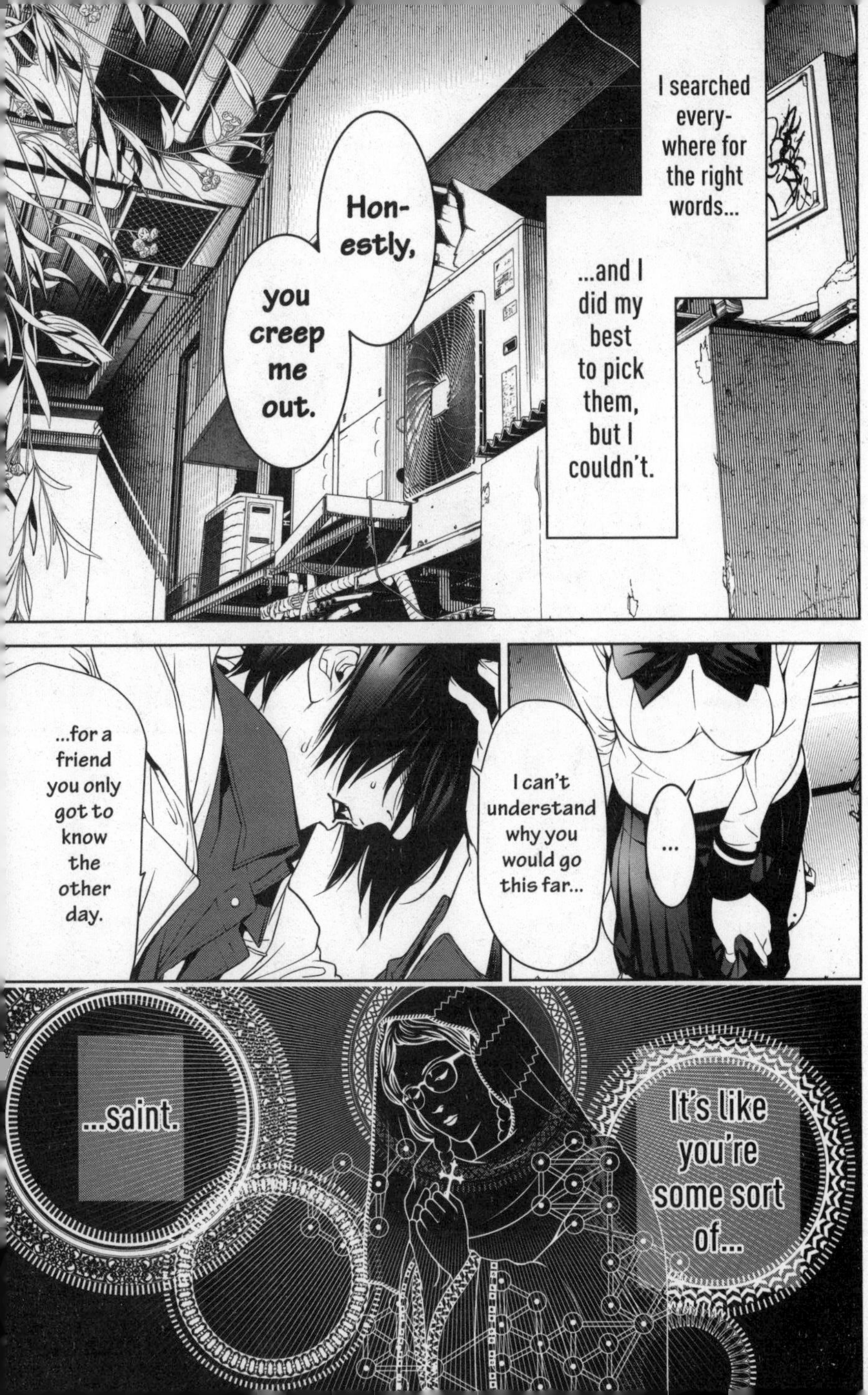
I searched every-where for the right words...
...and I did my best to pick them, but I couldn't.
Hon-estly, you creep me out.
...
I can't understand why you would go this far...
...for a friend you only got to know the other day.
It's like you're some sort of...
...saint.

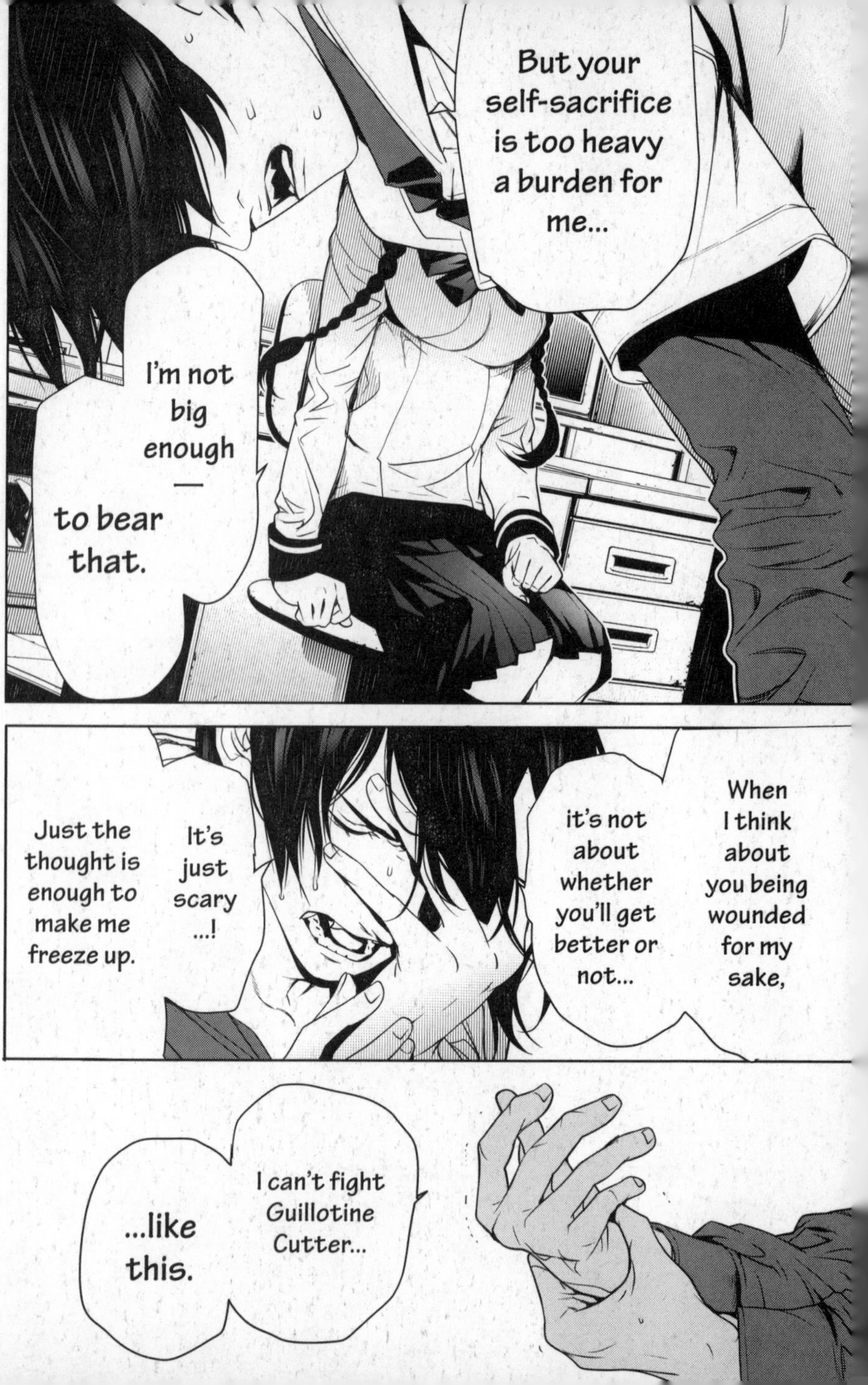
But your self-sacrifice is too heavy a burden for me...
I'm not big enough — to bear that.
When I think about you being wounded for my sake,
it's not about whether you'll get better or not...
It's just scary ...!
Just the thought is enough to make me freeze up.
I can't fight Guillotine Cutter...
...like this.

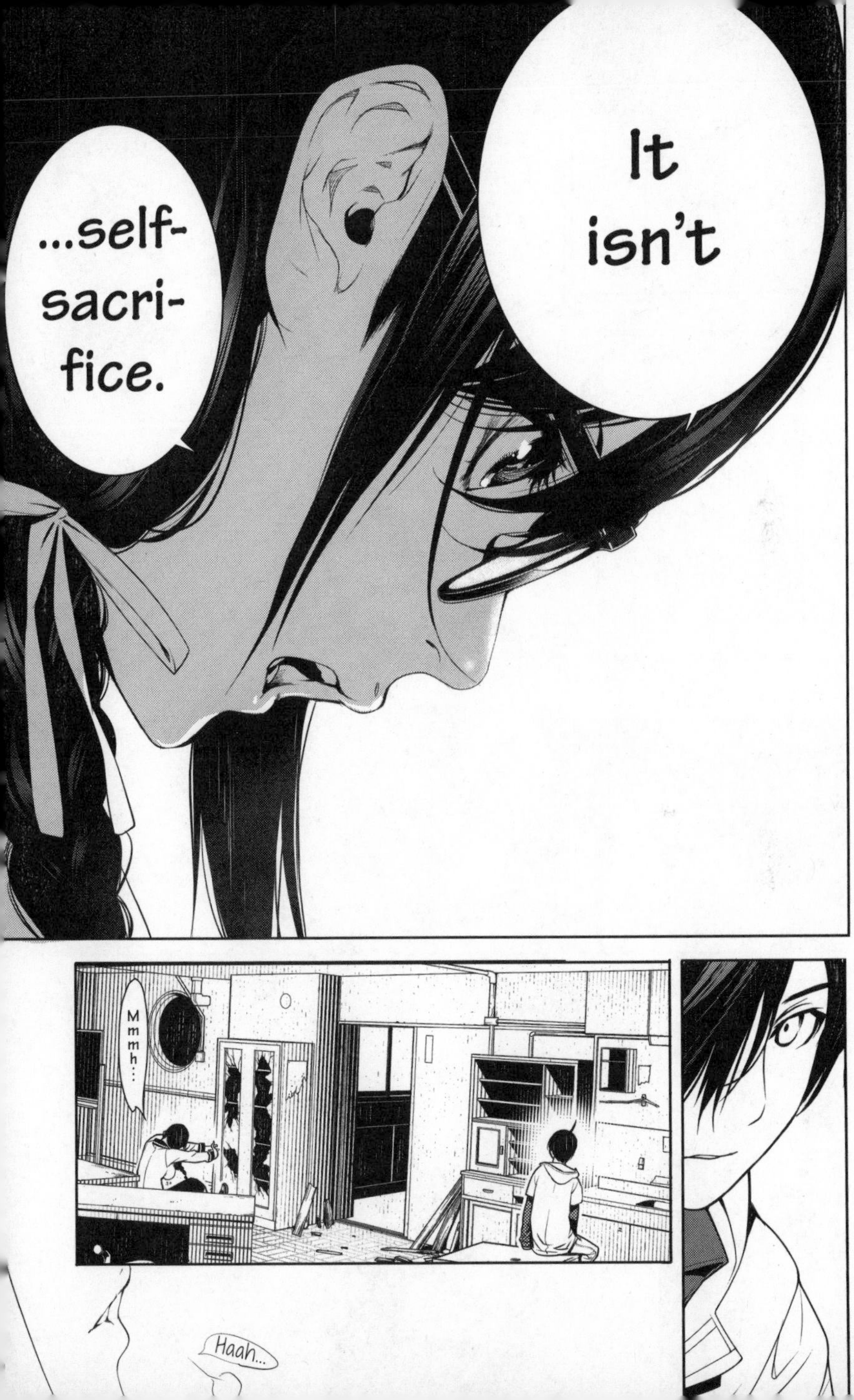
It isn't
...self-sacrifice.
Mmmh...
Haah...

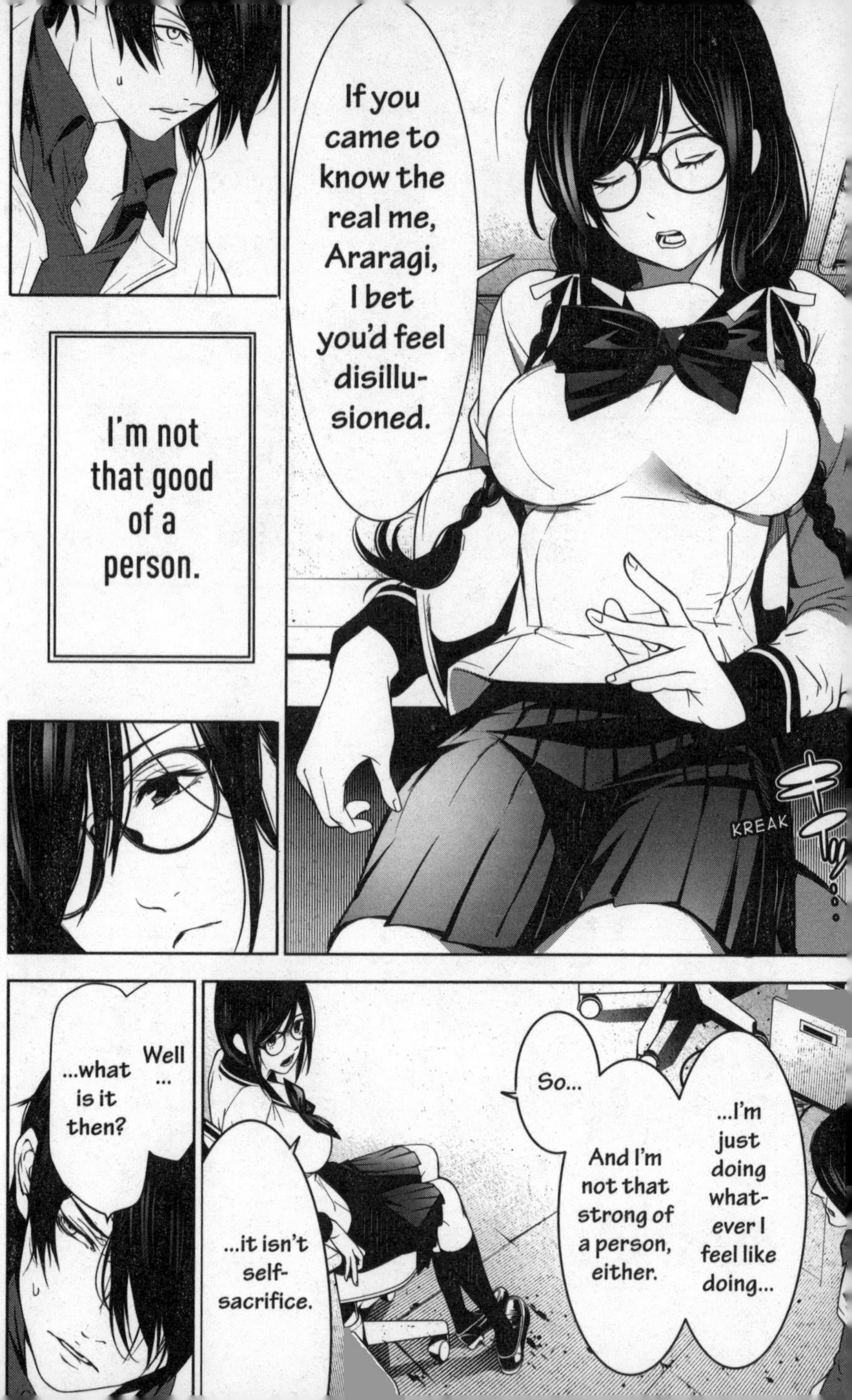
If you came to know the real me, Araragi, I bet you'd feel disillusioned.
KREAK
I'm not that good of a person.
And I'm not that strong of a person, either.
So...
...I'm just doing whatever I feel like doing...
...it isn't self-sacrifice.
Well...
...what is it then?

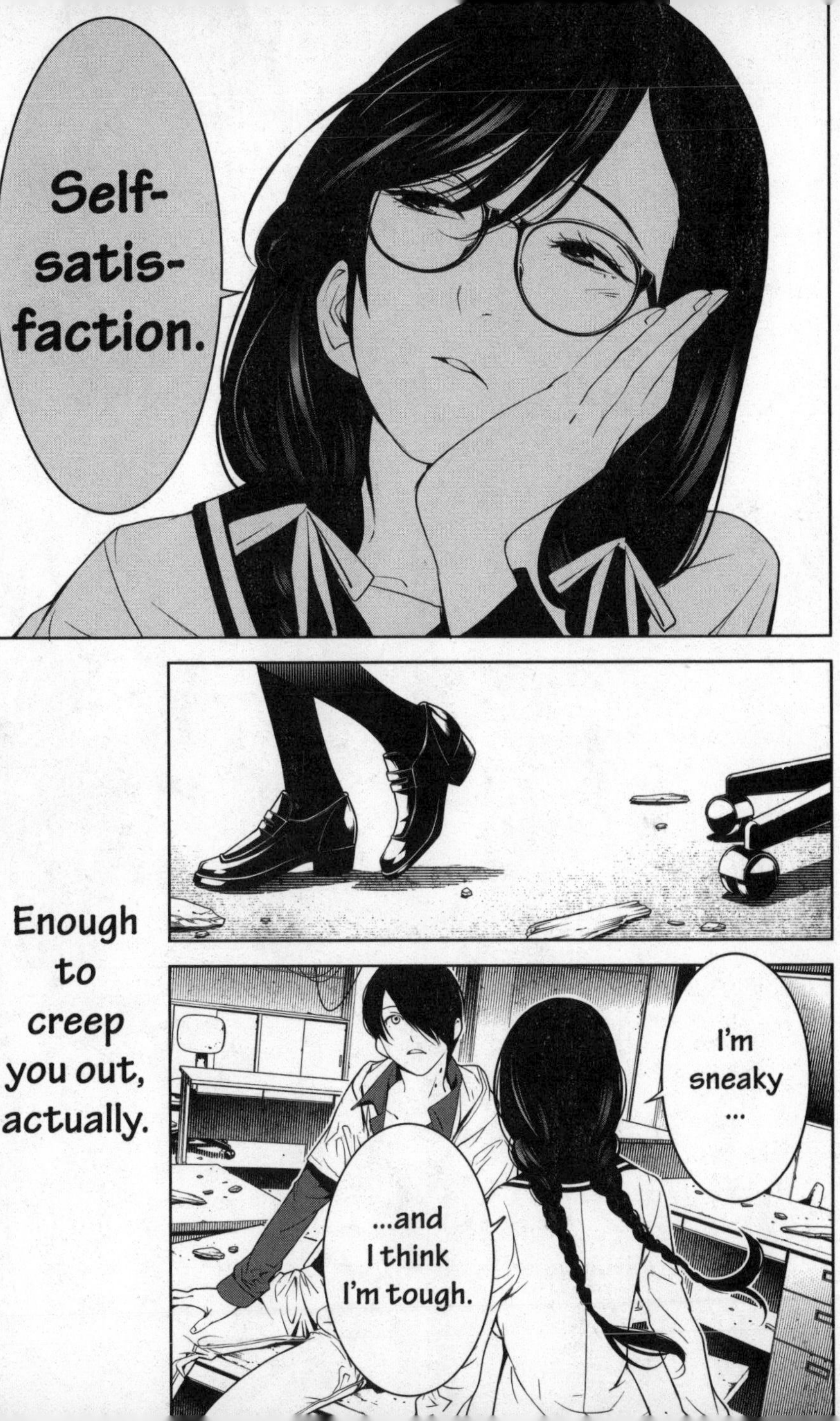
Self-satisfaction.
I'm sneaky...
...and I think I'm tough.
Enough to creep you out, actually.

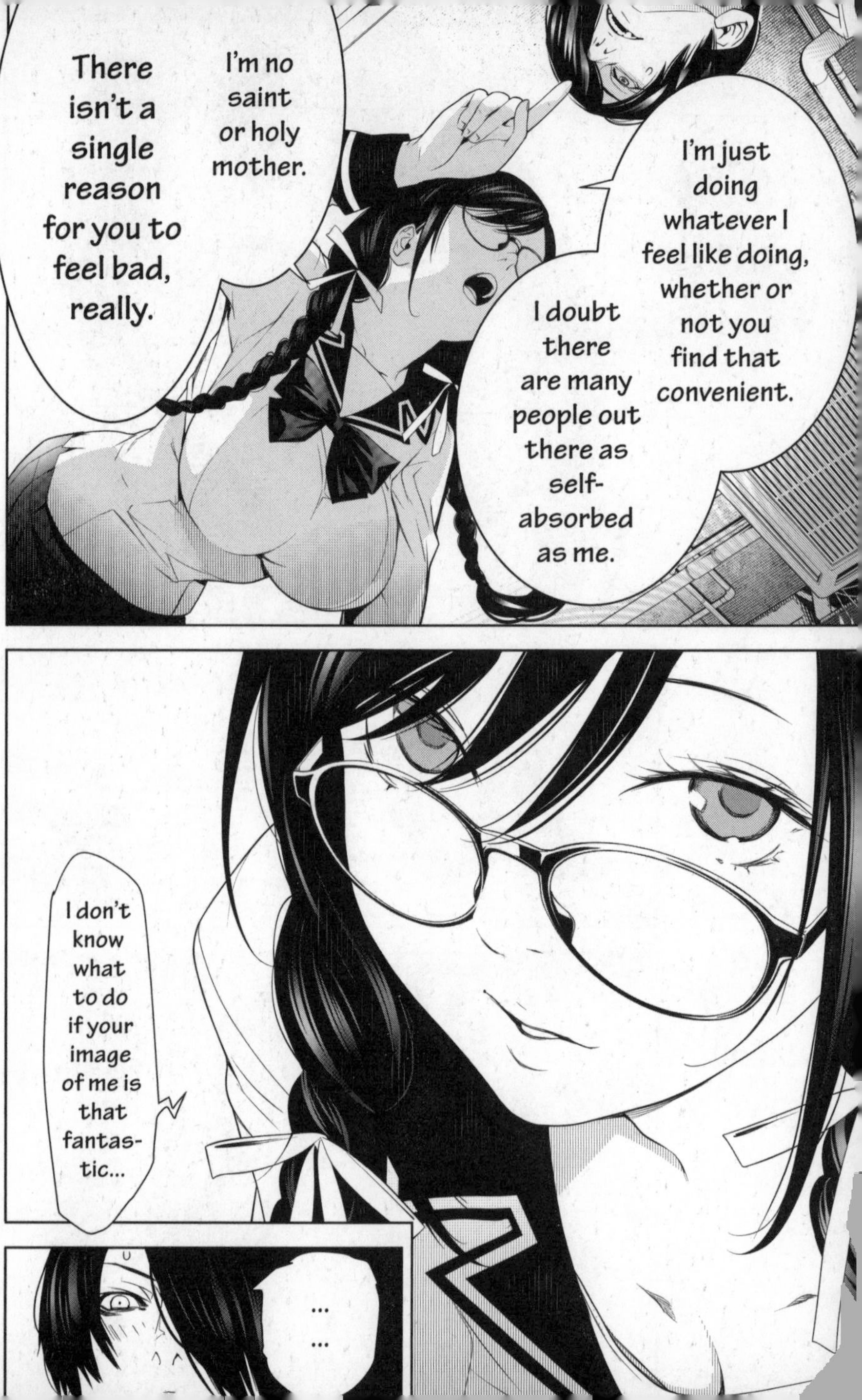
I'm just doing whatever I feel like doing, whether or not you find that convenient.
I doubt there are many people out there as self-absorbed as me.
I'm no saint or holy mother.
There isn't a single reason for you to feel bad, really.
I don't know what to do if your image of me is that fantastic...
...
...

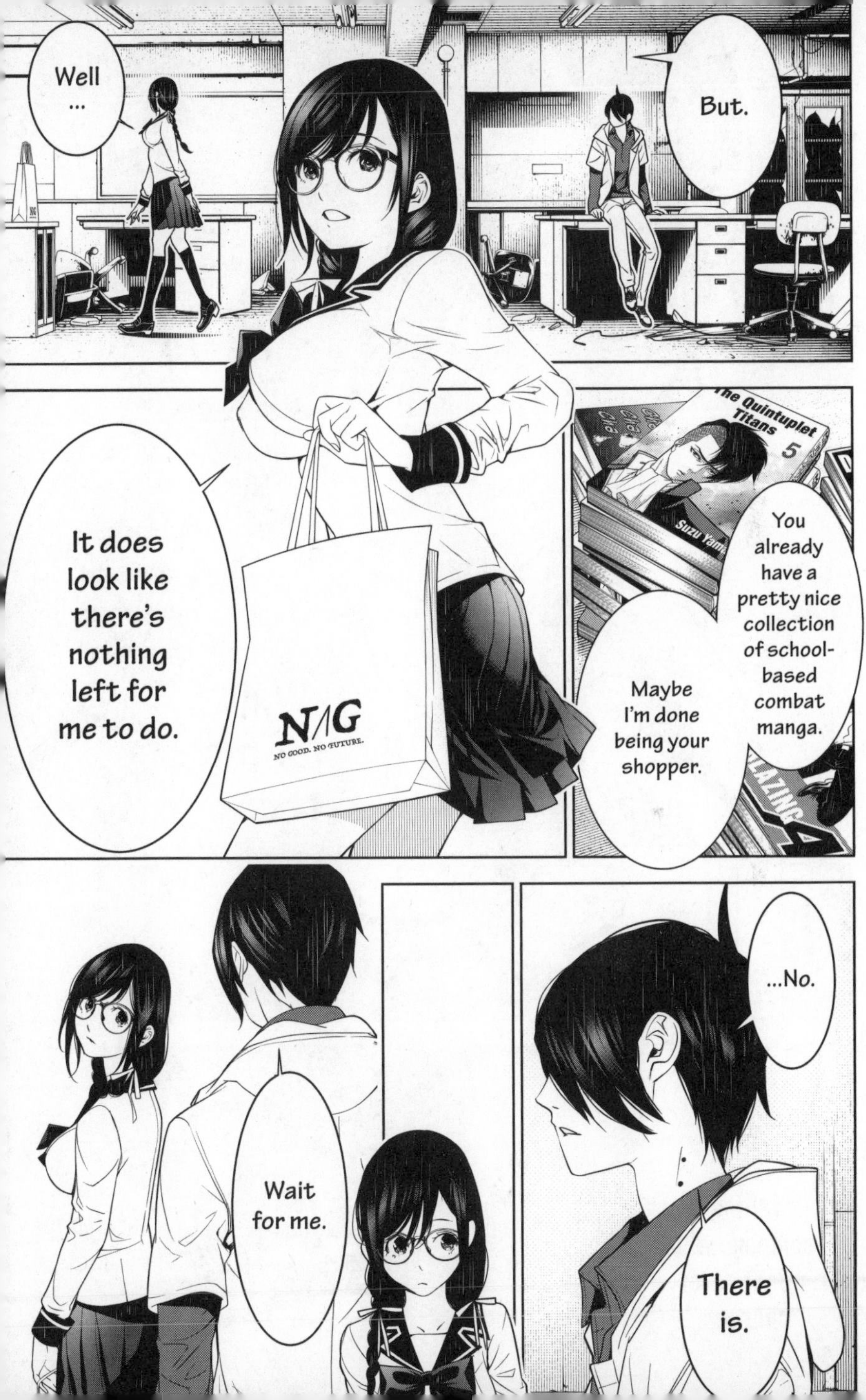
But.
Well ...
The Quintuplet Titans
5
You already have a pretty nice collection of school-based combat manga.
Maybe I'm done being your shopper.
It does look like there's nothing left for me to do.
N/G
NO GOOD. NO FUTURE.
...No.
There is.
Wait for me.

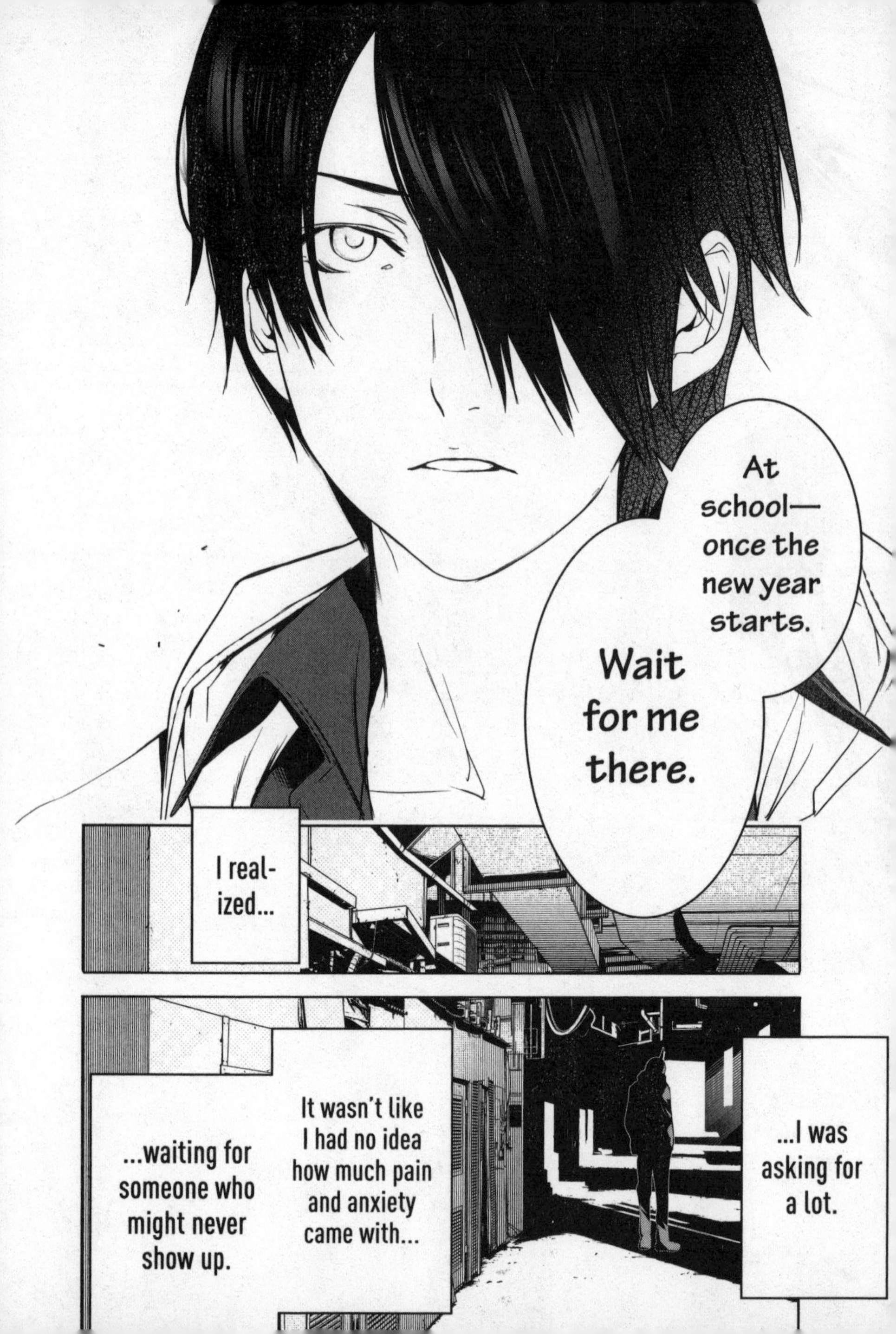
At school—once the new year starts.
Wait for me there.
I realized...
...I was asking for a lot.
It wasn't like I had no idea how much pain and anxiety came with...
...waiting for someone who might never show up.

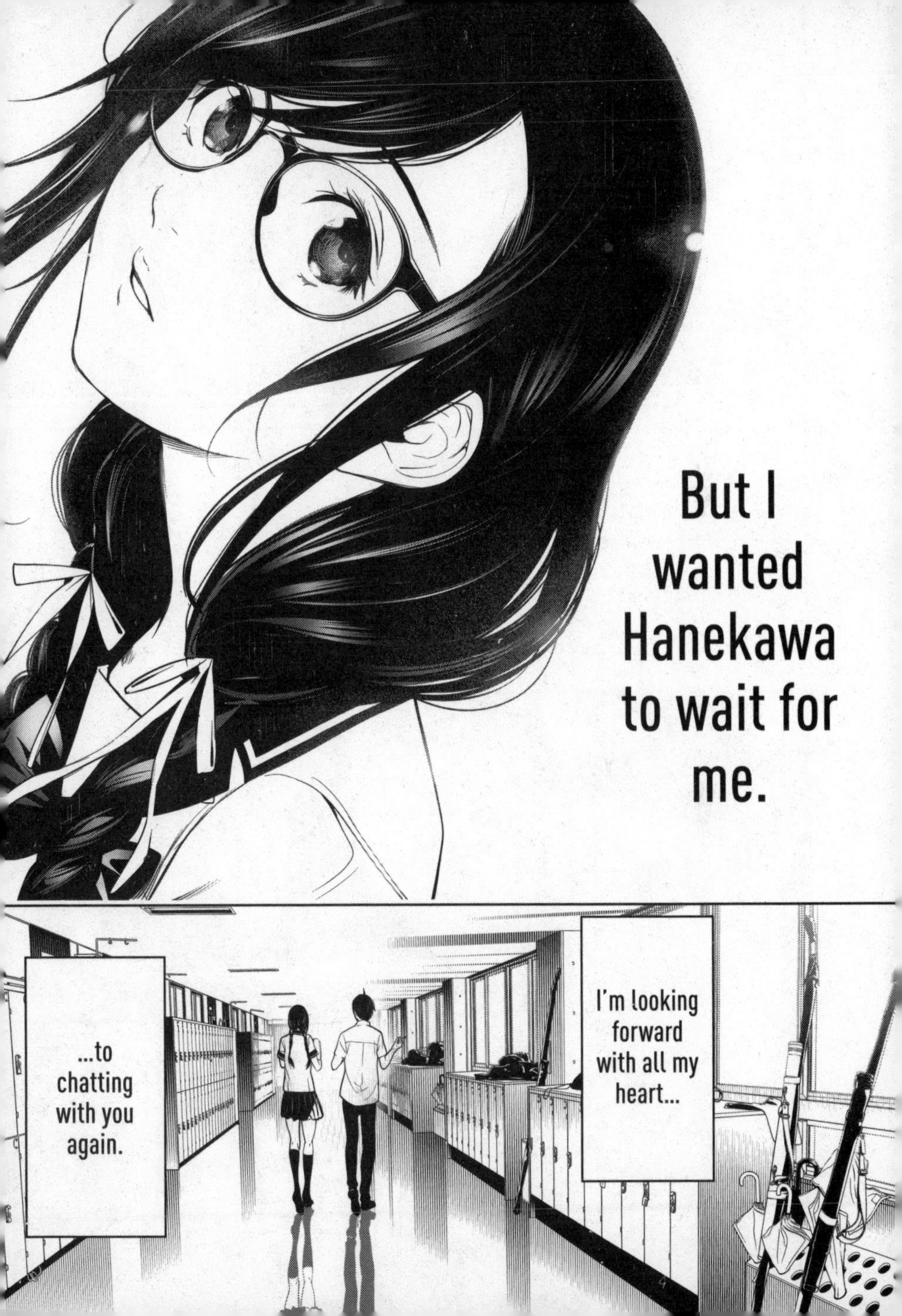
But I wanted Hanekawa to wait for me.
I'm looking forward with all my heart...
...to chatting with you again.

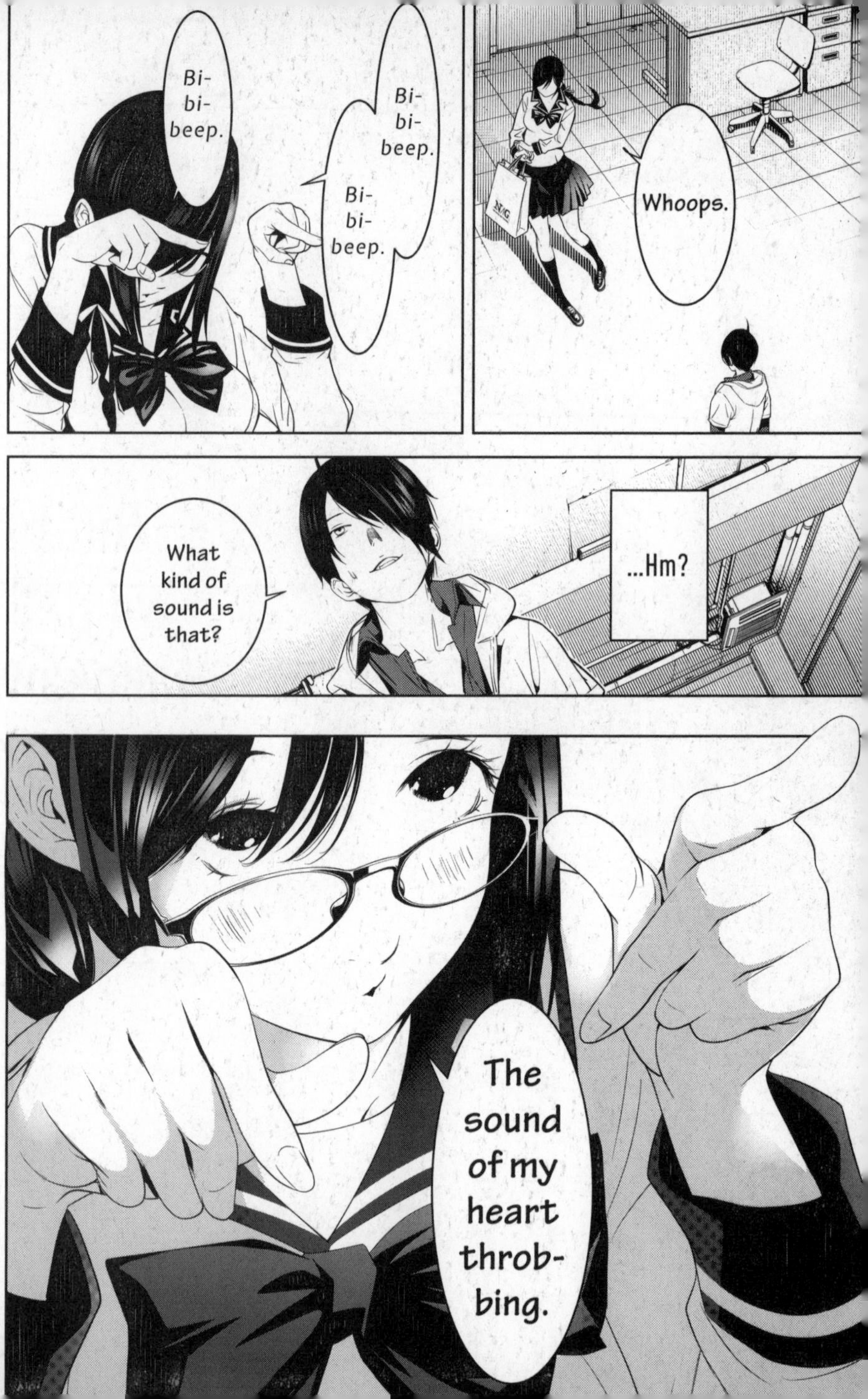
Whoops.
Bi-bi-beep.
Bi-bi-beep.
Bi-bi-beep.
...Hm?
What kind of sound is that?
The sound of my heart throbbing.

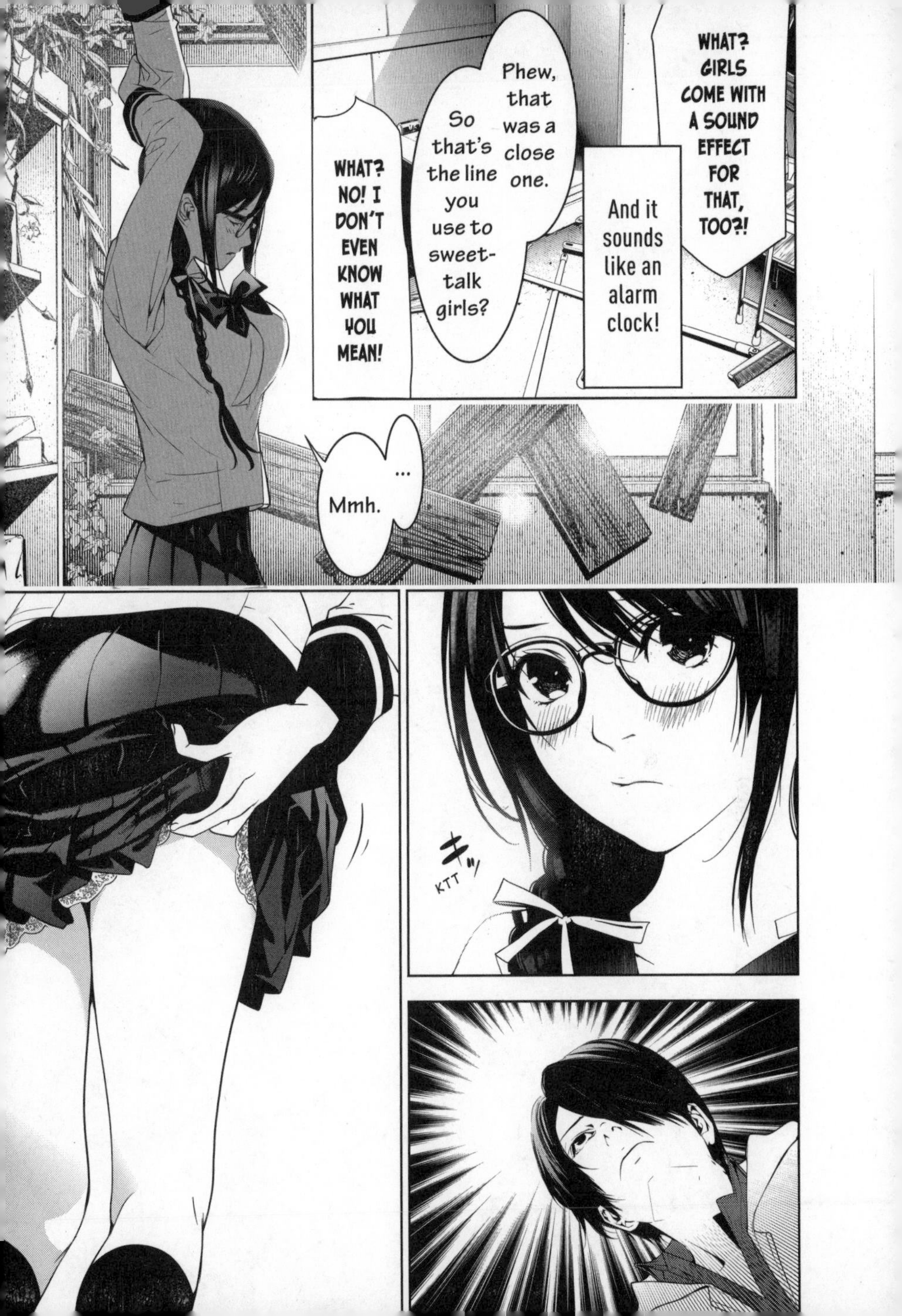
WHAT? GIRLS COME WITH A SOUND EFFECT FOR THAT, TOO?!
And it sounds like an alarm clock!
Phew, that was a close one.
So that's the line you use to sweet-talk girls?
WHAT? NO! I DON'T EVEN KNOW WHAT YOU MEAN!
... Mmh.
KTT

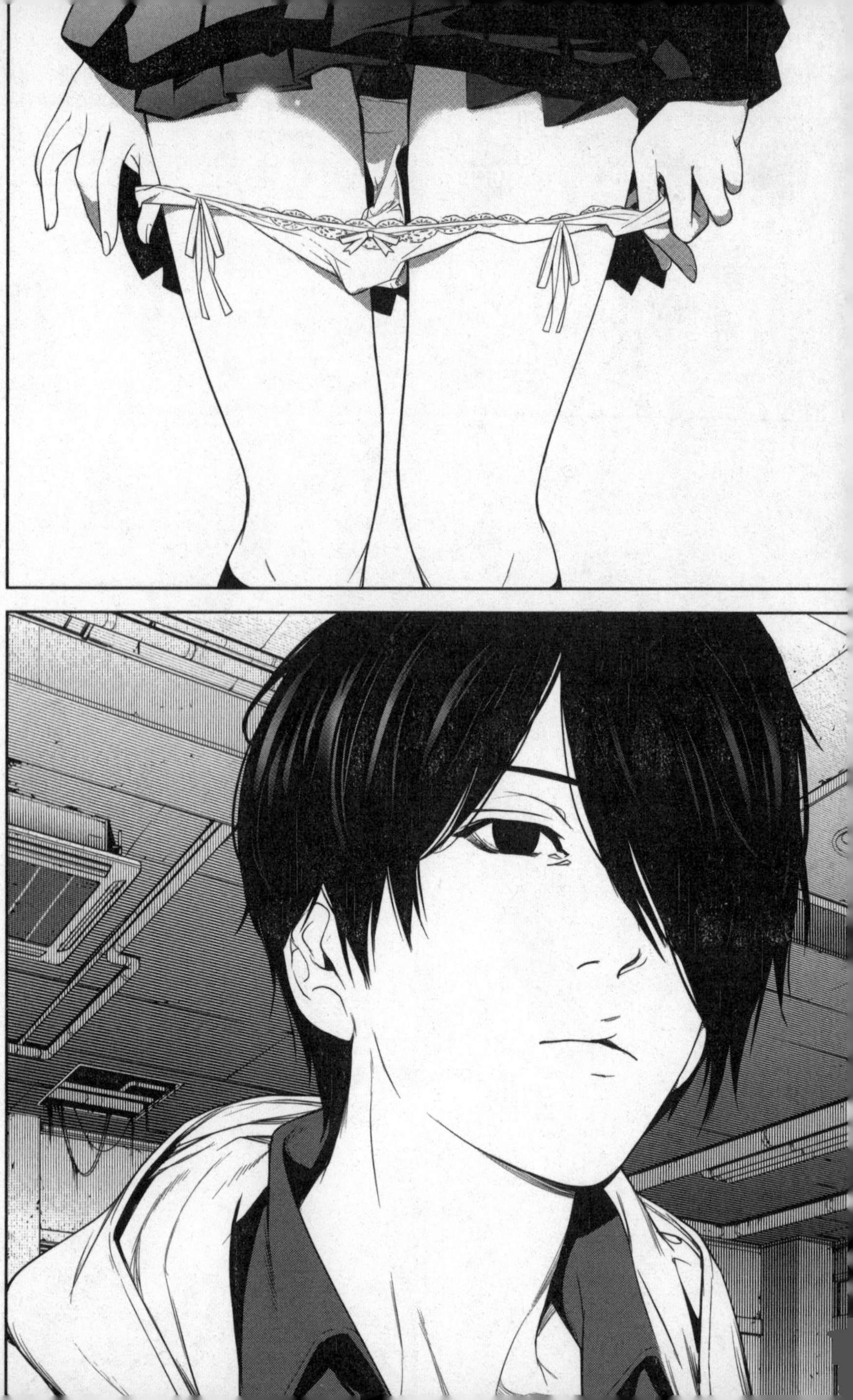

After giving her body an exaggerated stretch and putting on a determined look, she thrust both of her hands underneath the hem of her school uniform's pleated skirt. I thought she was going to pull up her skirt again, but no, Hanekawa wouldn't do something so illogical.

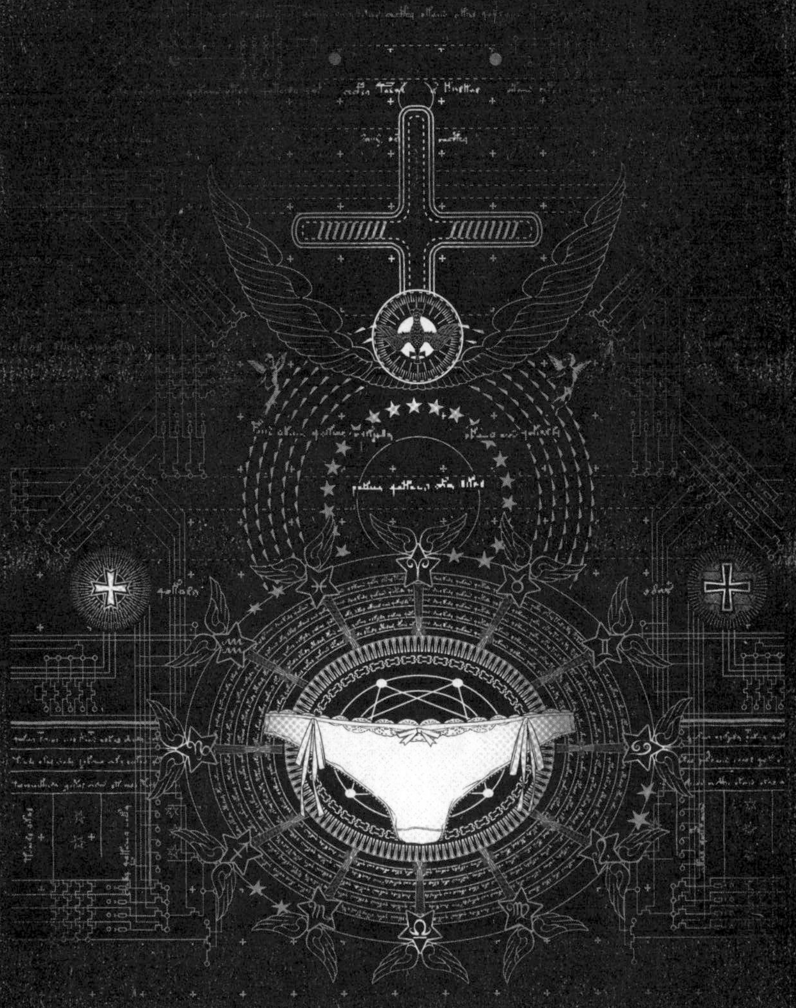

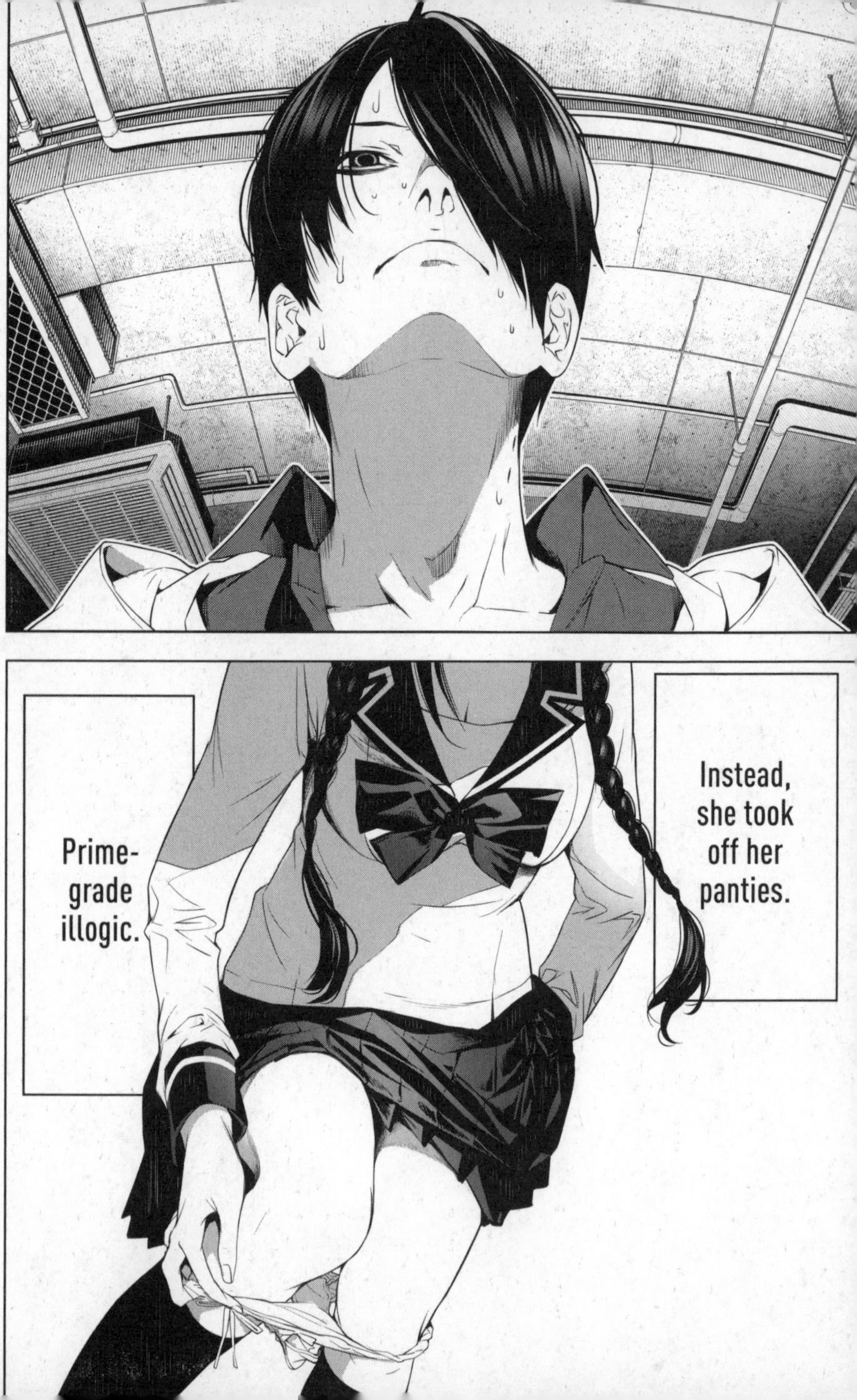
Instead, she took off her panties.
Prime-grade illogic.

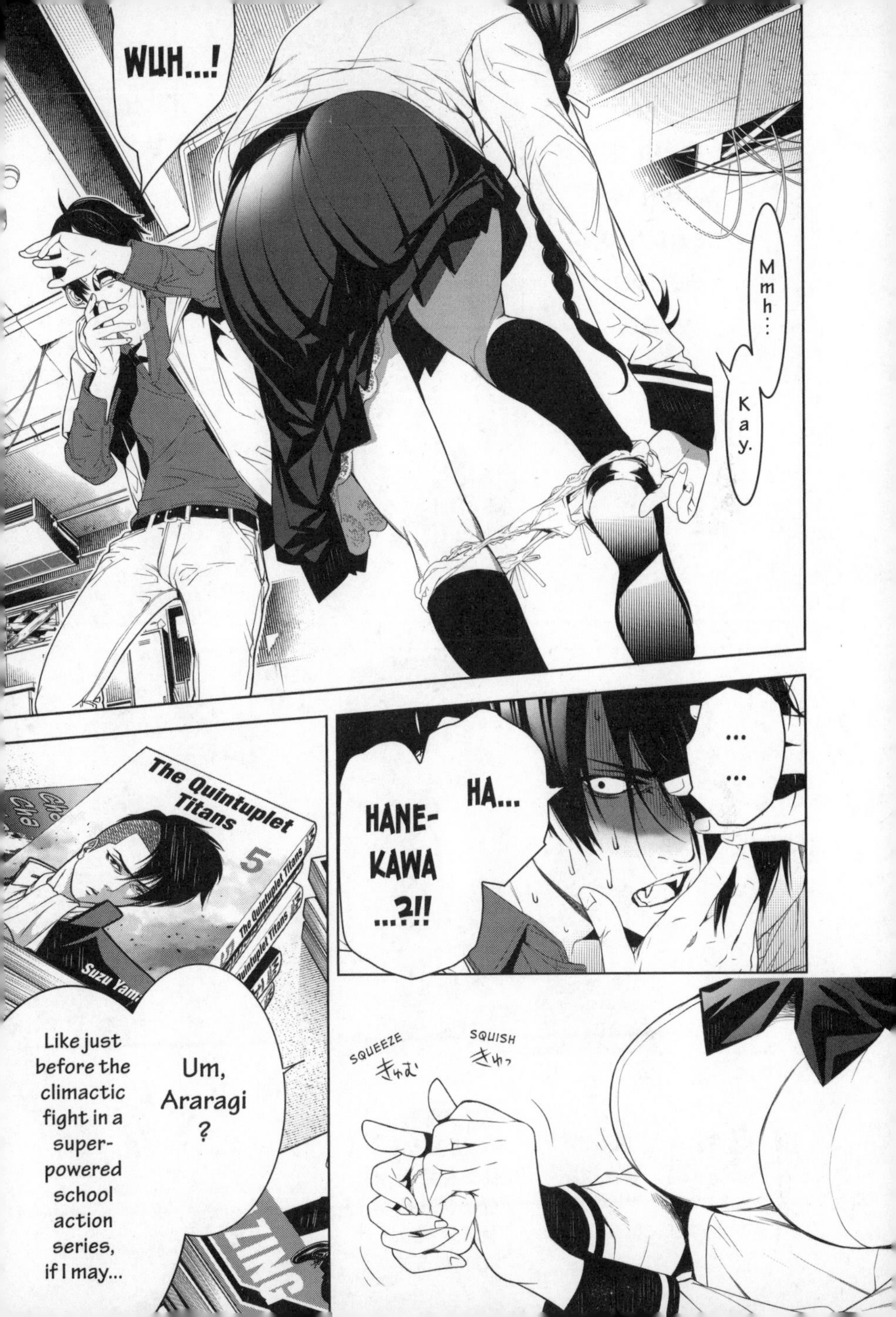

Mmh… Kay.
WUH...!
... ...
HA... HANE-KAWA ...?!!
The Quintuplet Titans
5
The Quintuplet Titans
The Quintuplet Titans
Suzu Yam
SQUISH
きゅっ
SQUEEZE
きゅむ
Um, Araragi?
Like just before the climactic fight in a super-powered school action series, if I may...

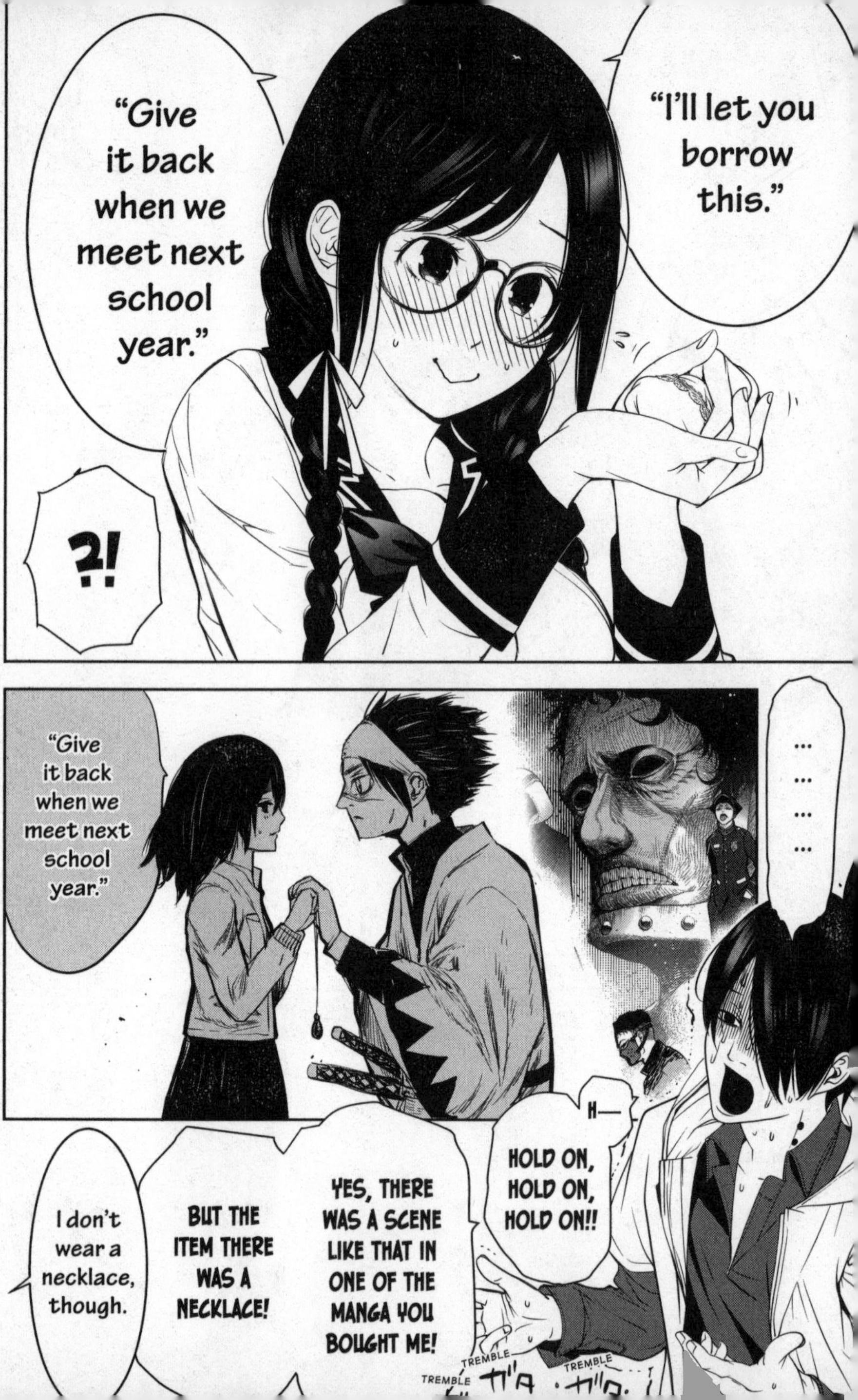
"I'll let you borrow this."
"Give it back when we meet next school year."
?!
... ...
"Give it back when we meet next school year."
H—
HOLD ON, HOLD ON, HOLD ON!!
TREMBLE
TREMBLE
TREMBLE
YES, THERE WAS A SCENE LIKE THAT IN ONE OF THE MANGA YOU BOUGHT ME!
BUT THE ITEM THERE WAS A NECKLACE!
I don't wear a necklace, though.

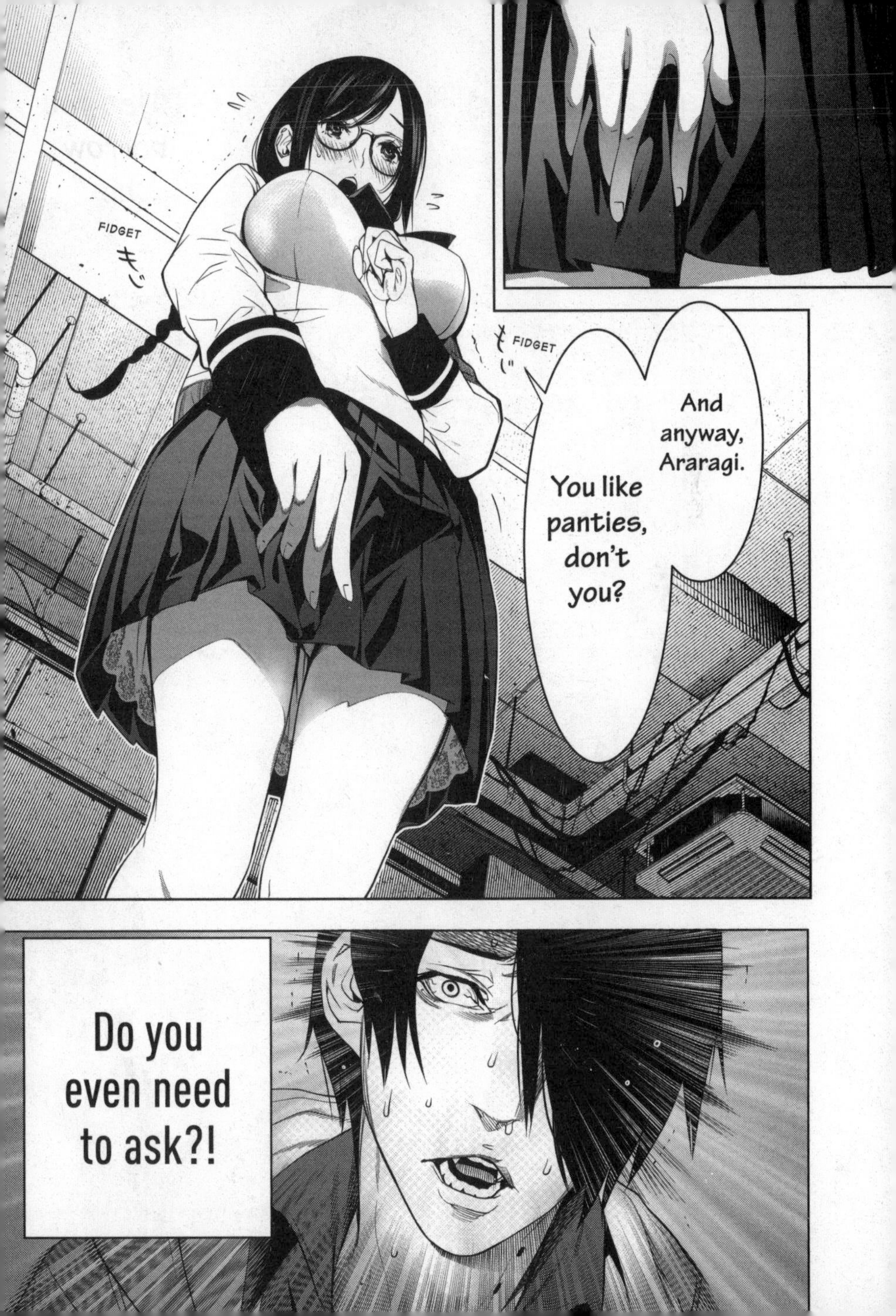
FIDGET
FIDGET
And anyway, Araragi.
You like panties, don't you?
Do you even need to ask?!

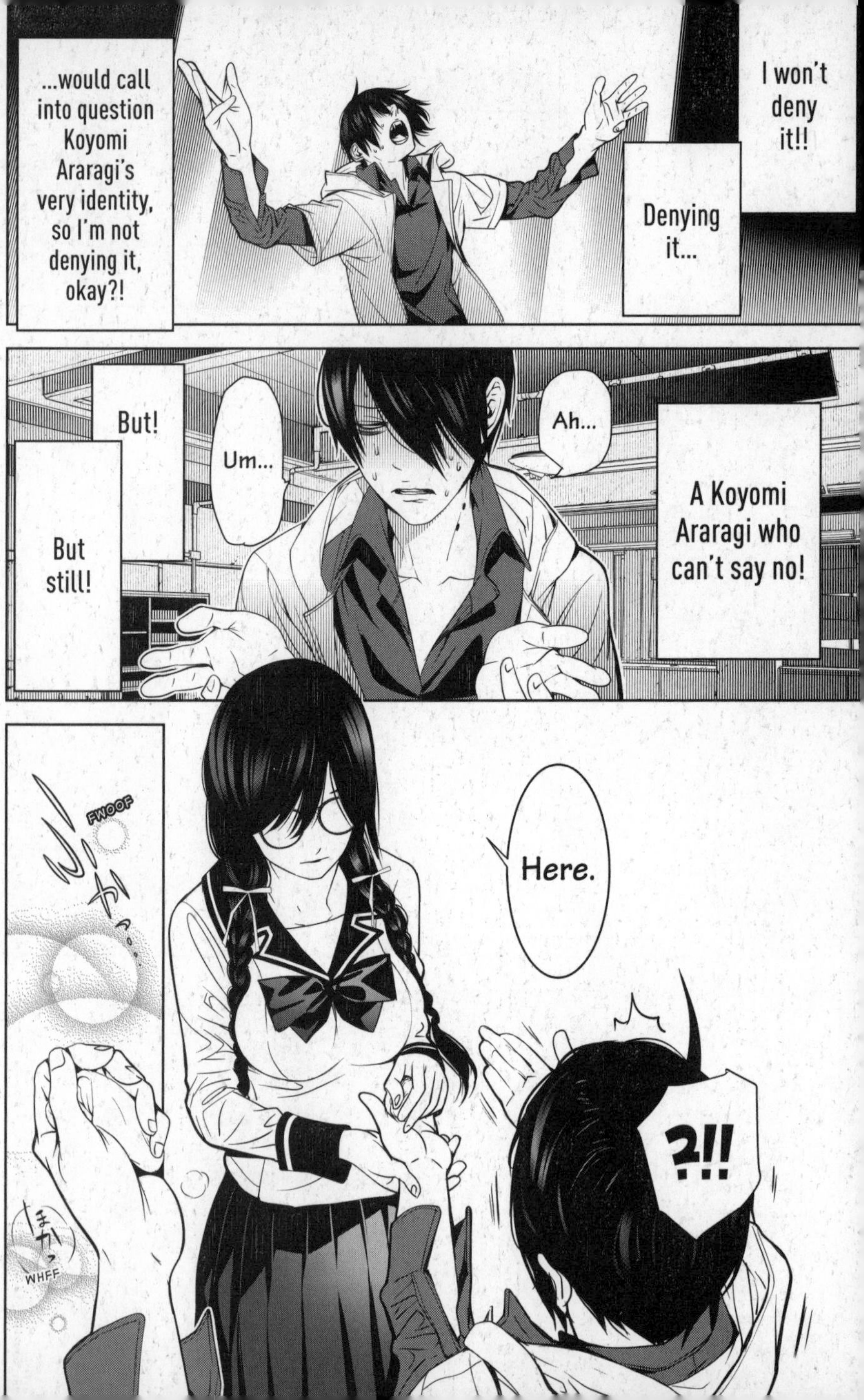
I won't deny it!!
Denying it...
...would call into question Koyomi Araragi's very identity, so I'm not denying it, okay?!
A Koyomi Araragi who can't say no!
Ah...
Um...
But!
But still!
Here.
FWOOF
?!!
WHFF

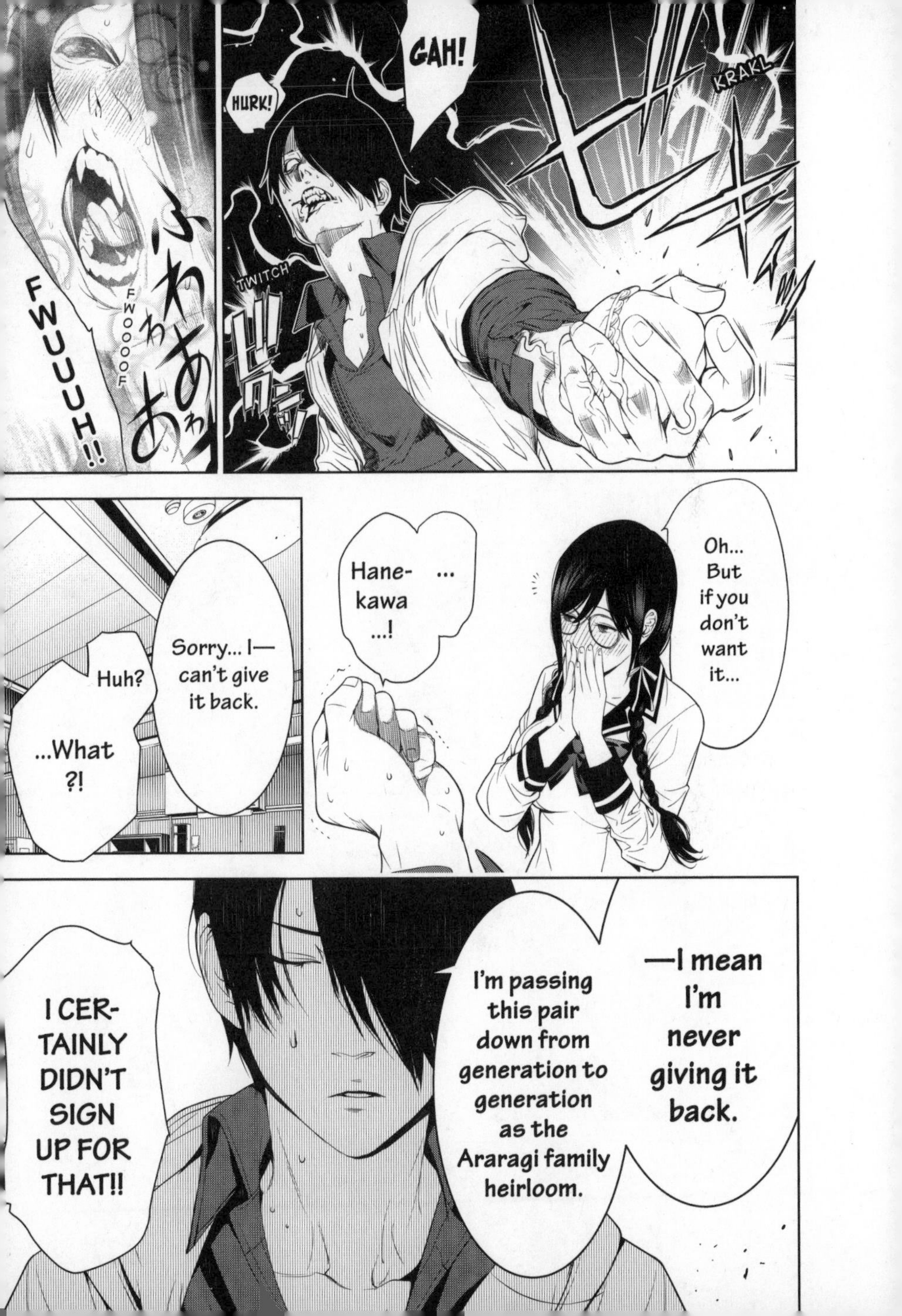
KRAKL
GAH!
HURK!
TWITCH
FWOOOOF
FWUUUH!!
Oh... But if you don't want it...
Hane- kawa ...!
...
Sorry... I— can't give it back.
Huh?
...What ?!
—I mean I'm never giving it back.
I'm passing this pair down from generation to generation as the Araragi family heirloom.
I CERTAINLY DIDN'T SIGN UP FOR THAT!!

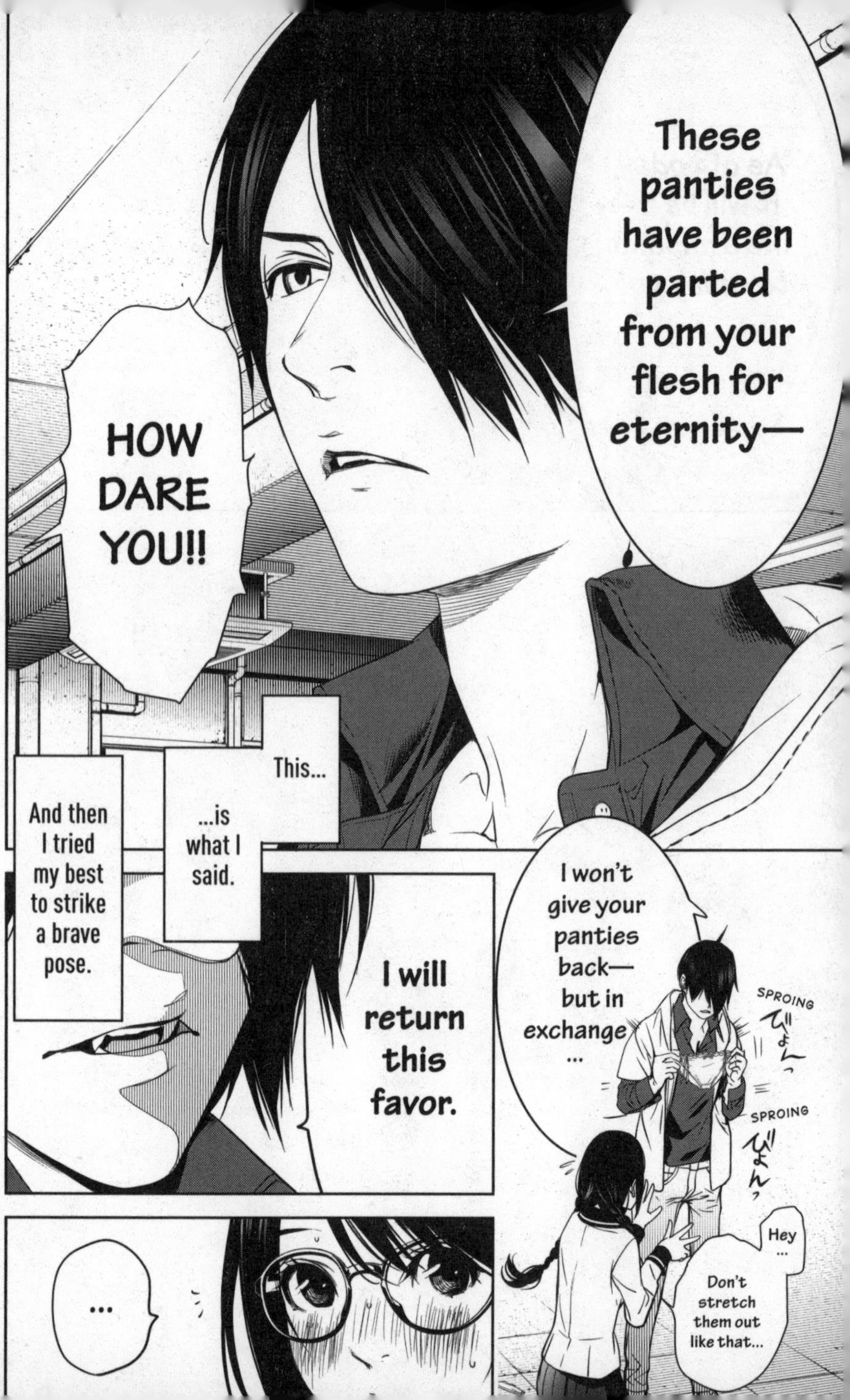
These panties have been parted from your flesh for eternity—
HOW DARE YOU!!
This...
...is what I said.
And then I tried my best to strike a brave pose.
I won't give your panties back—but in exchange...
SPROING
SPROING
Hey...
Don't stretch them out like that...
I will return this favor.
...

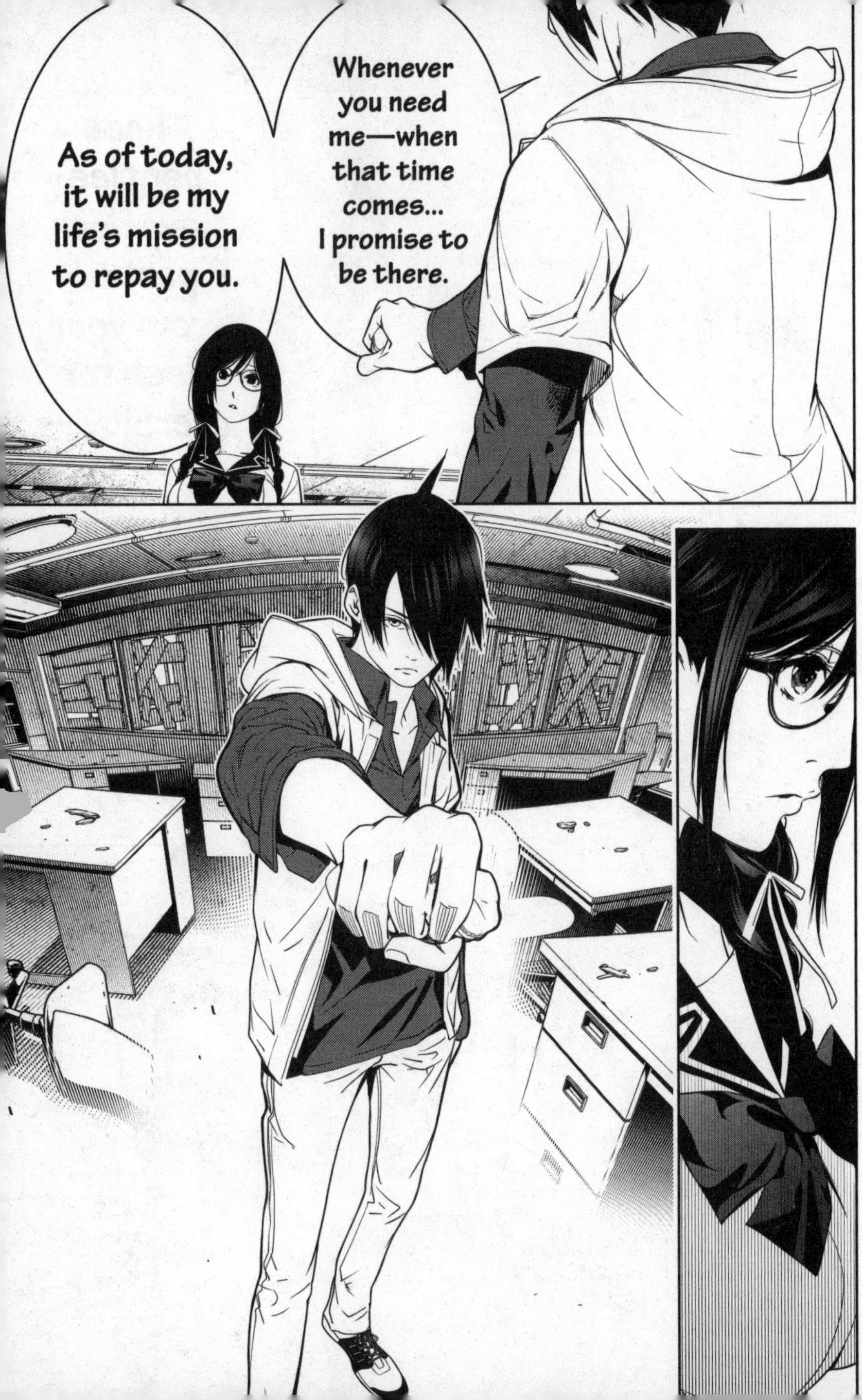
Whenever you need me—when that time comes... I promise to be there.
As of today, it will be my life's mission to repay you.

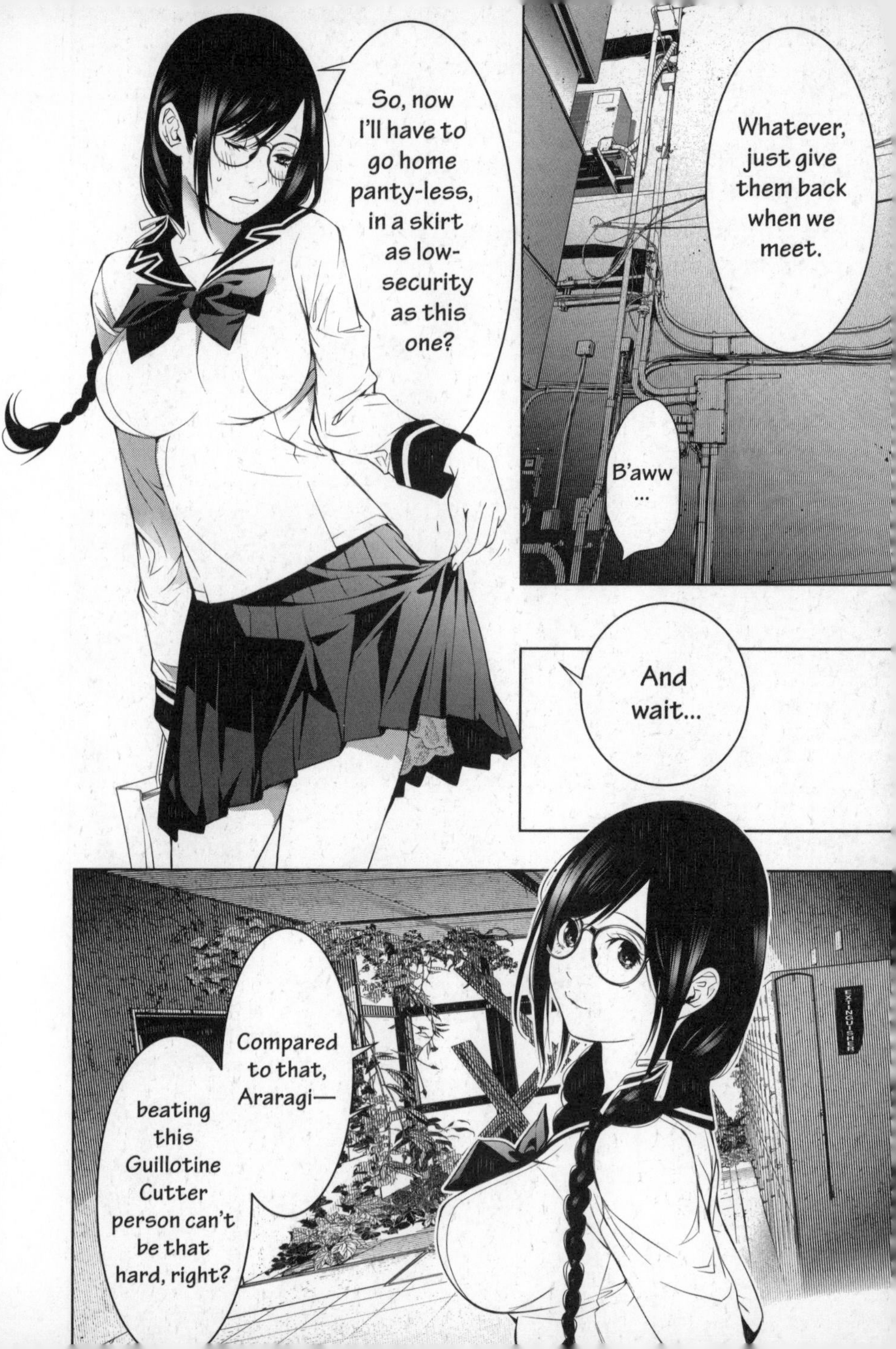
Whatever, just give them back when we meet.
B'aww ...
So, now I'll have to go home panty-less, in a skirt as low-security as this one?
And wait...
Compared to that, Araragi—
beating this Guillotine Cutter person can't be that hard, right?
EXTINGUISHER

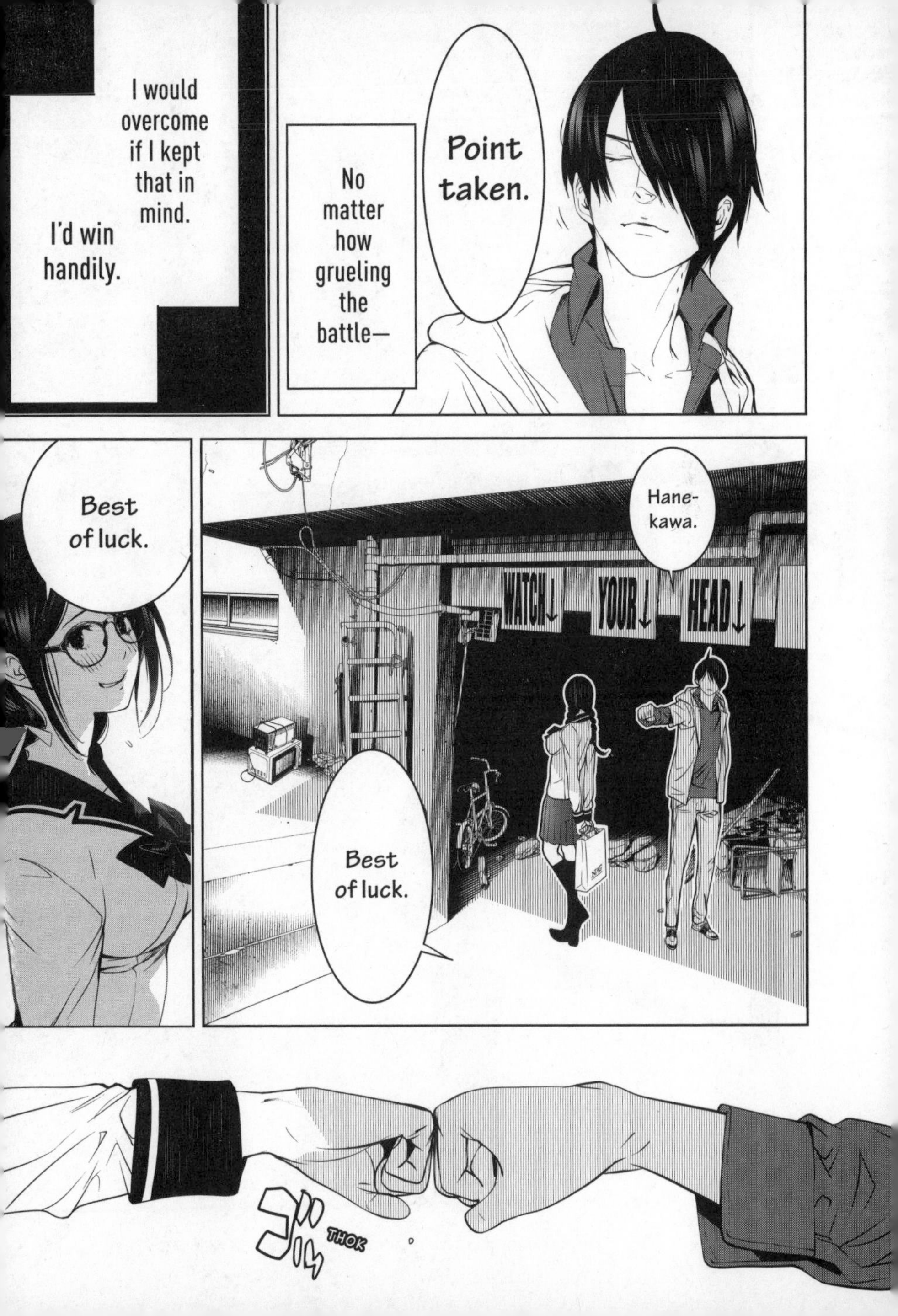
Point taken.
No matter how grueling the battle—
I would overcome if I kept that in mind.
I'd win handily.
Hane-kawa.
WATCH↓ YOUR↓ HEAD↓
Best of luck.
Best of luck.
THOK

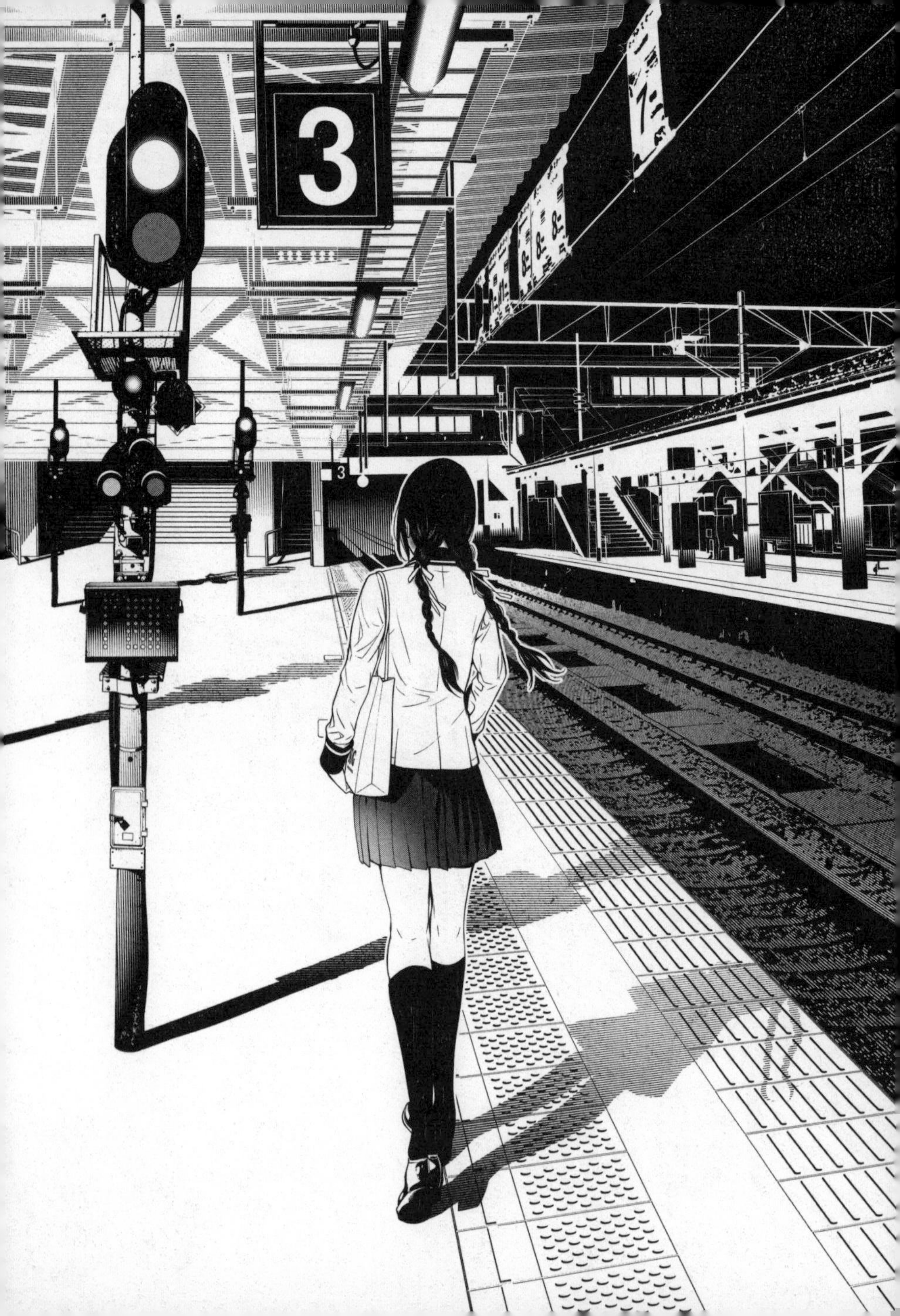
3

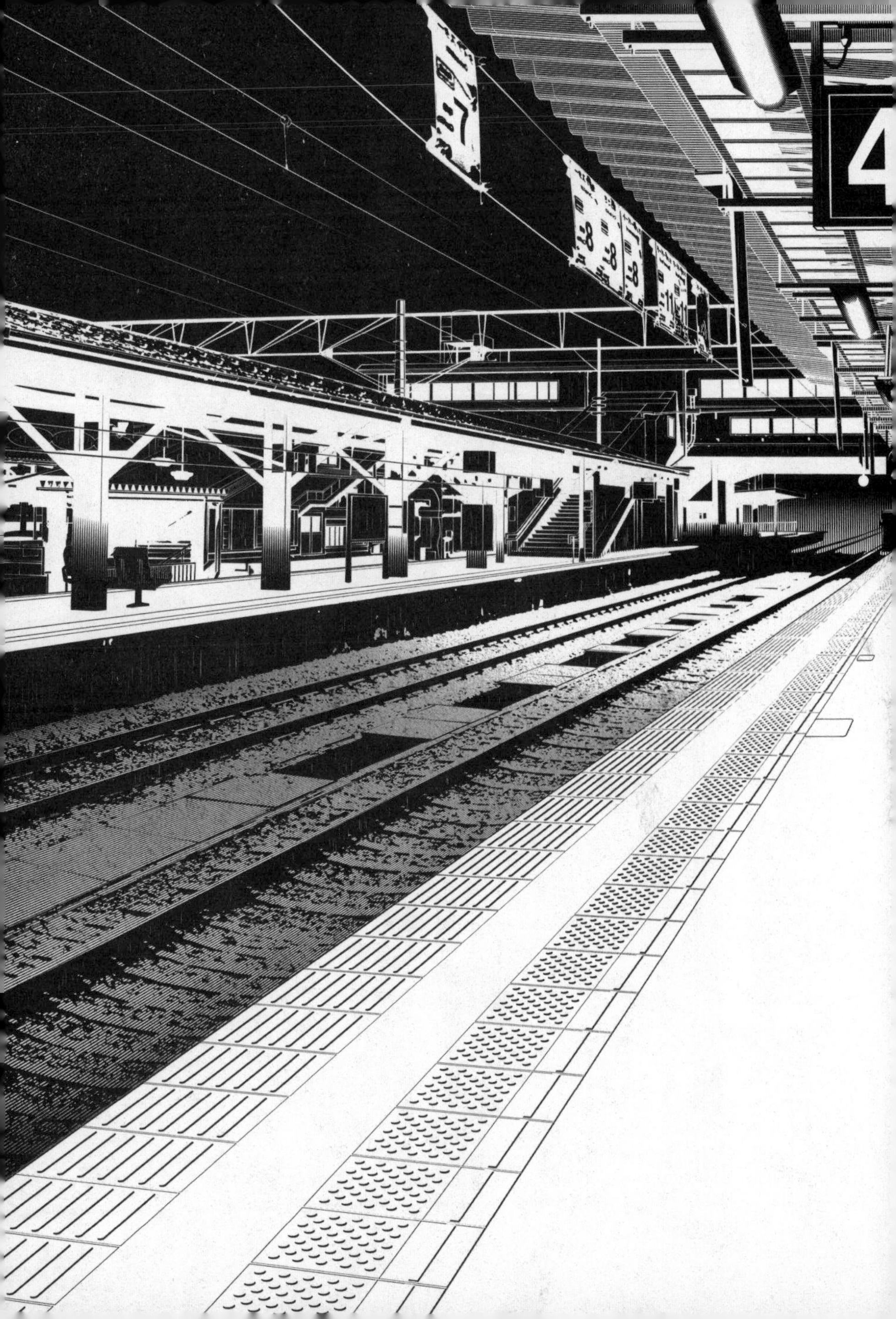
4

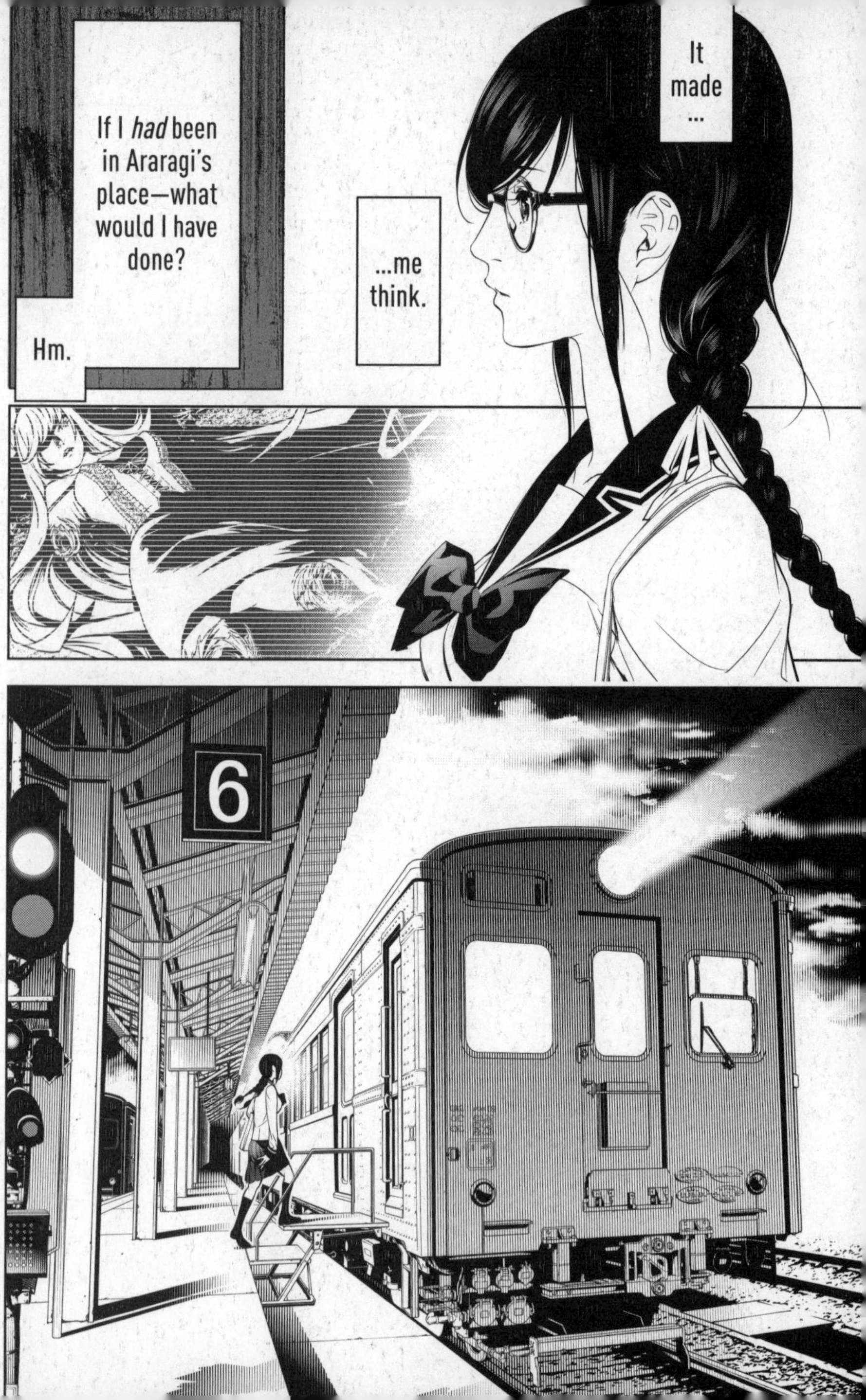
It made …
…me think.
If I *had* been in Araragi's place—what would I have done?
Hm.
6

It's the kind of question that I can't see ending...

...in a very pleasant way.

Hmm... Perhaps I'd be like, "It's too bad, but this is just the way of the world."

Would I just give up like that?

Who knows, maybe I would've abandoned her without hesitation.

Watch

Maybe I would've taken the stress from it and the awful taste it left in my mouth and tossed it all away somewhere—

without even considering what could happen if a stray cat ate some litter like that.

her

die

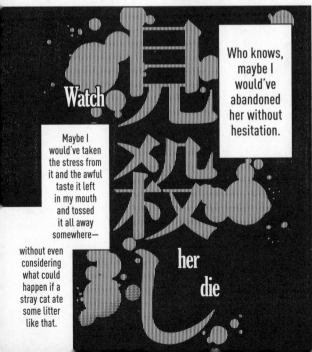

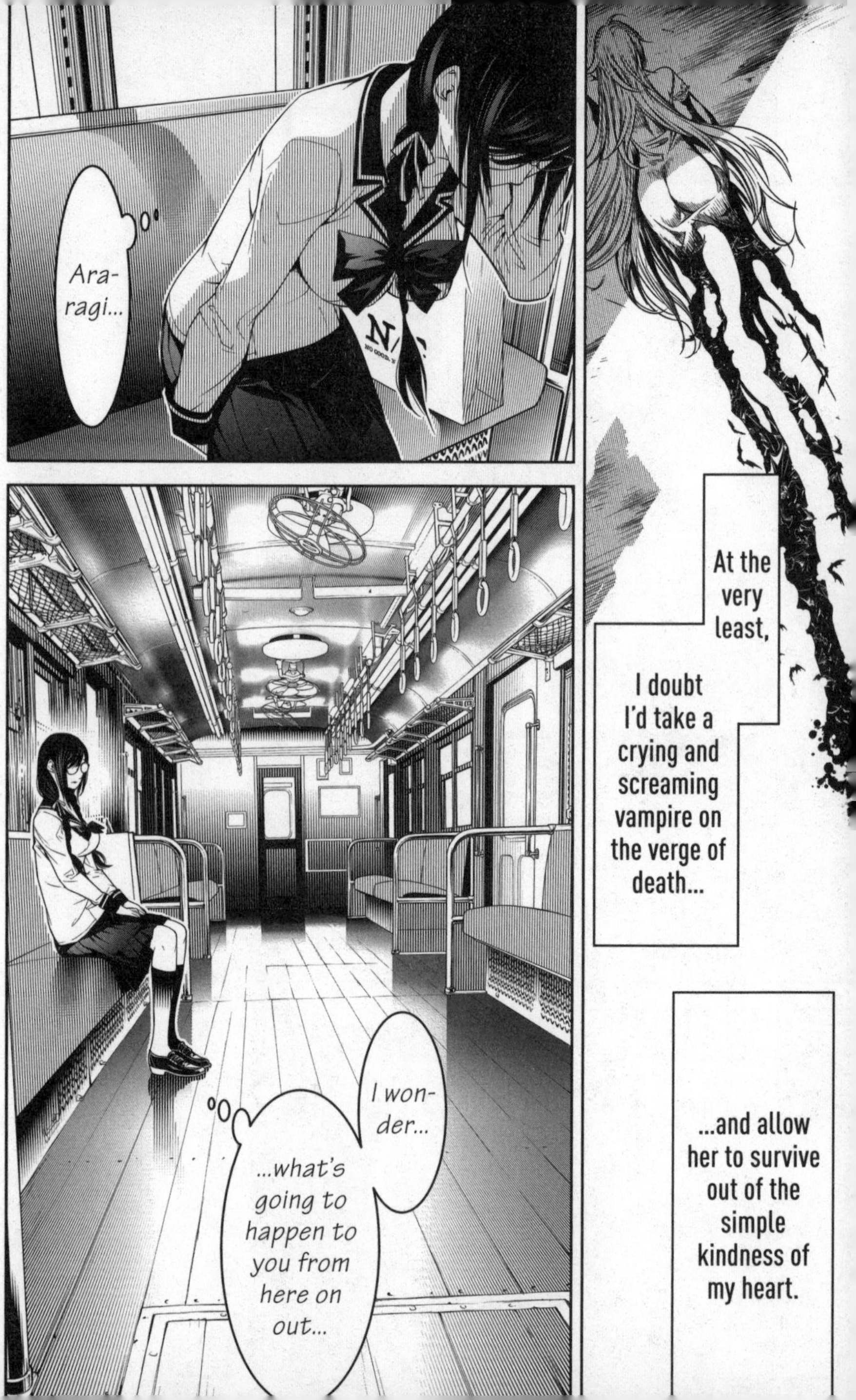
At the very least,
I doubt I'd take a crying and screaming vampire on the verge of death...
...and allow her to survive out of the simple kindness of my heart.
Ara-ragi...
I won-der...
...what's going to happen to you from here on out...

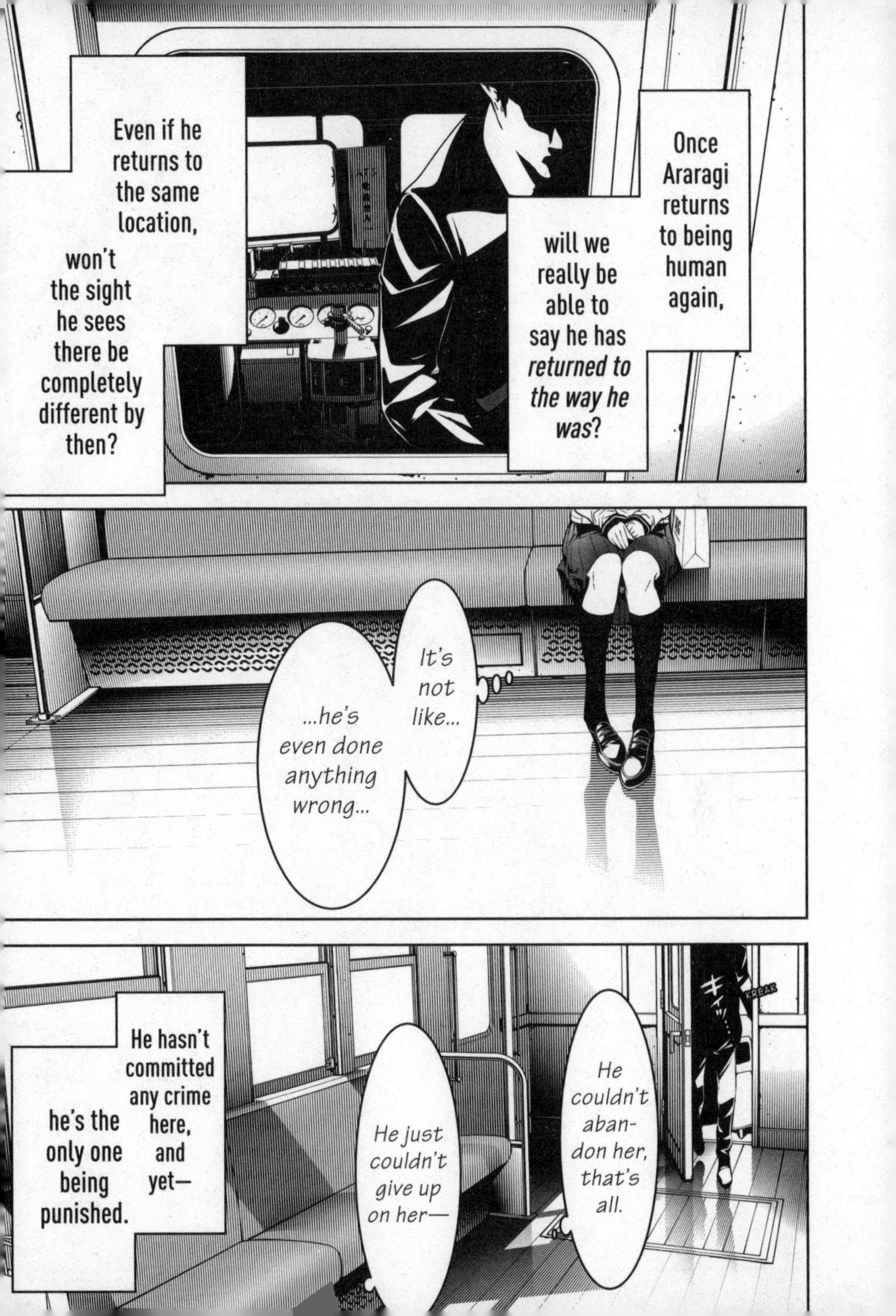
Once Araragi returns to being human again,
will we really be able to say he has *returned to the way he was*?
Even if he returns to the same location,
won't the sight he sees there be completely different by then?
It's not like...
...he's even done anything wrong...
KREAK
He couldn't abandon her, that's all.
He just couldn't give up on her—
He hasn't committed any crime here, and yet—
he's the only one being punished.

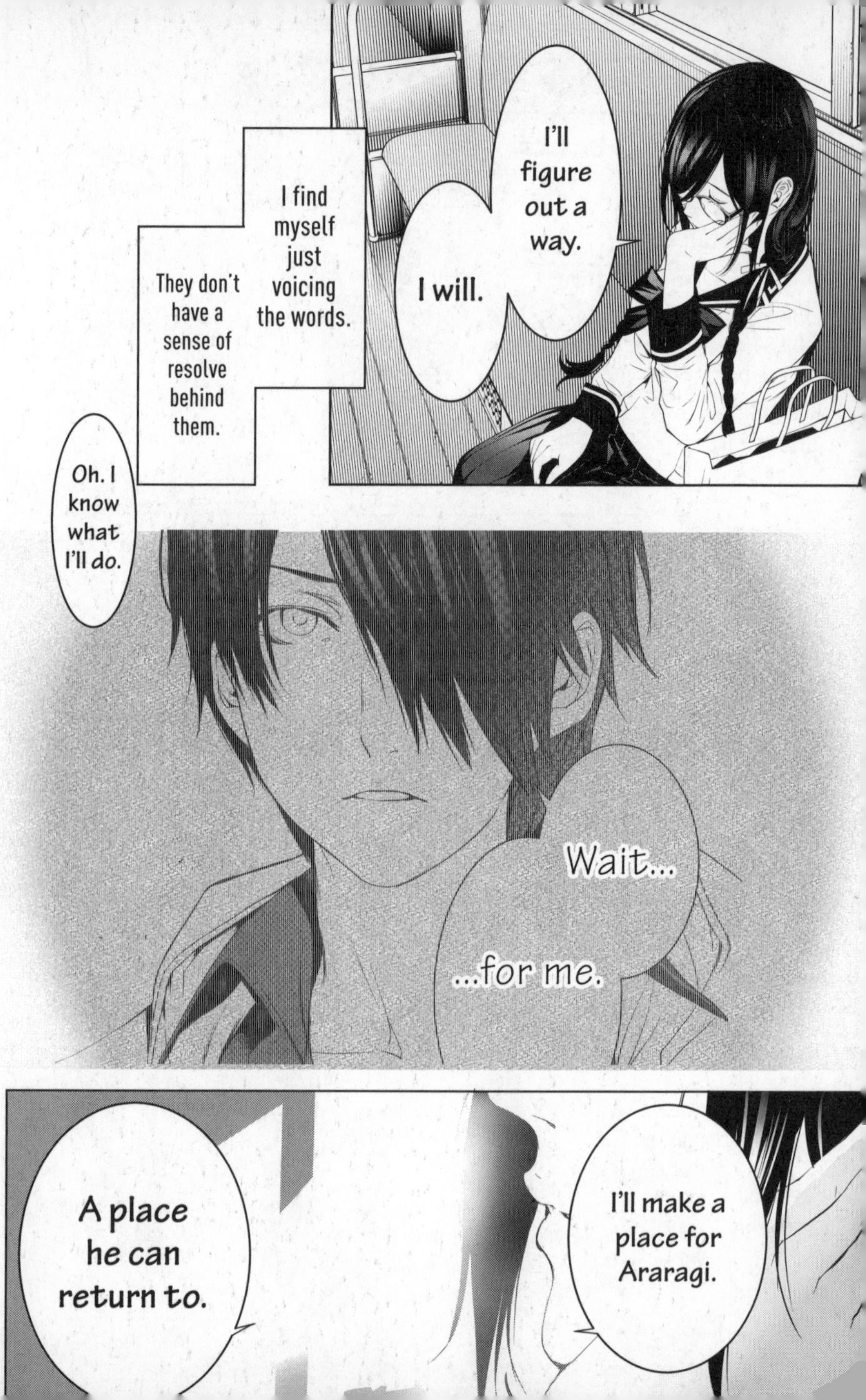
I'll figure out a way.
I will.
I find myself just voicing the words.
They don't have a sense of resolve behind them.
Oh. I know what I'll do.
Wait...
...for me.
I'll make a place for Araragi.
A place he can return to.

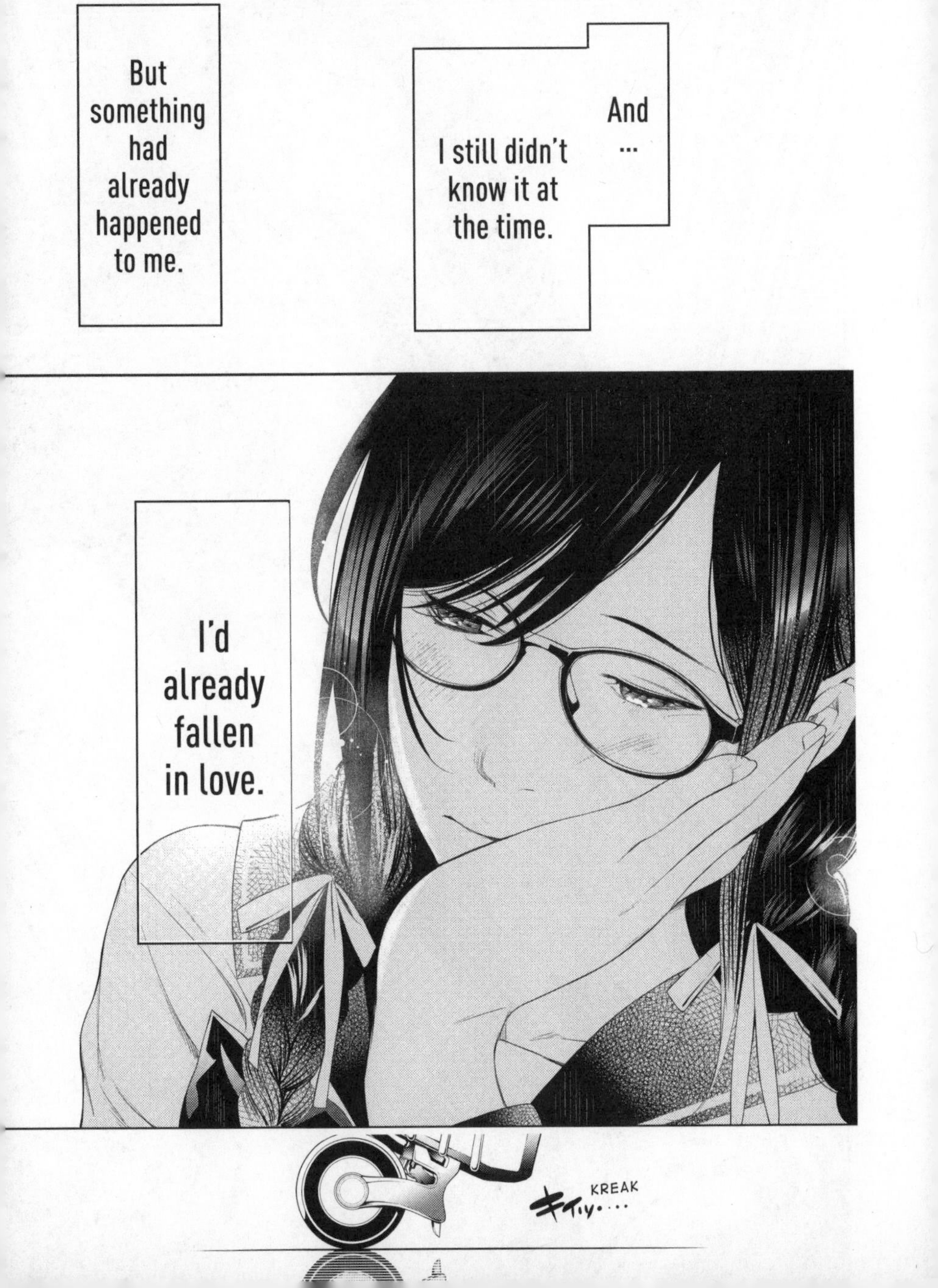
And ...
I still didn't know it at the time.
But something had already happened to me.
I'd already fallen in love.
KREAK

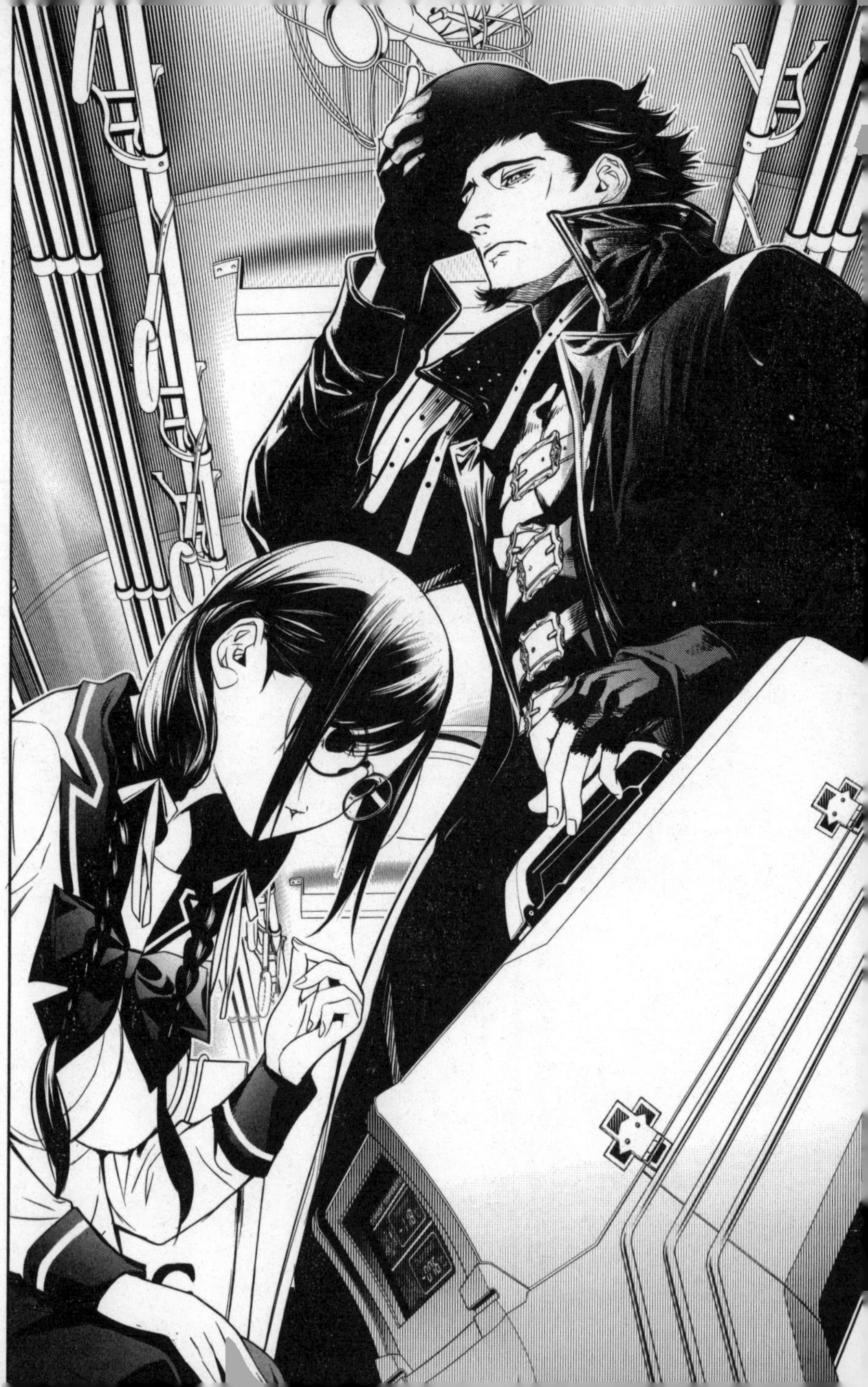

語 *gatari*

物 *mono*

KOYOMIvamp 12

化 *bake*

化 bake

物 mono

語 gatari

KOYOMIvamp

12

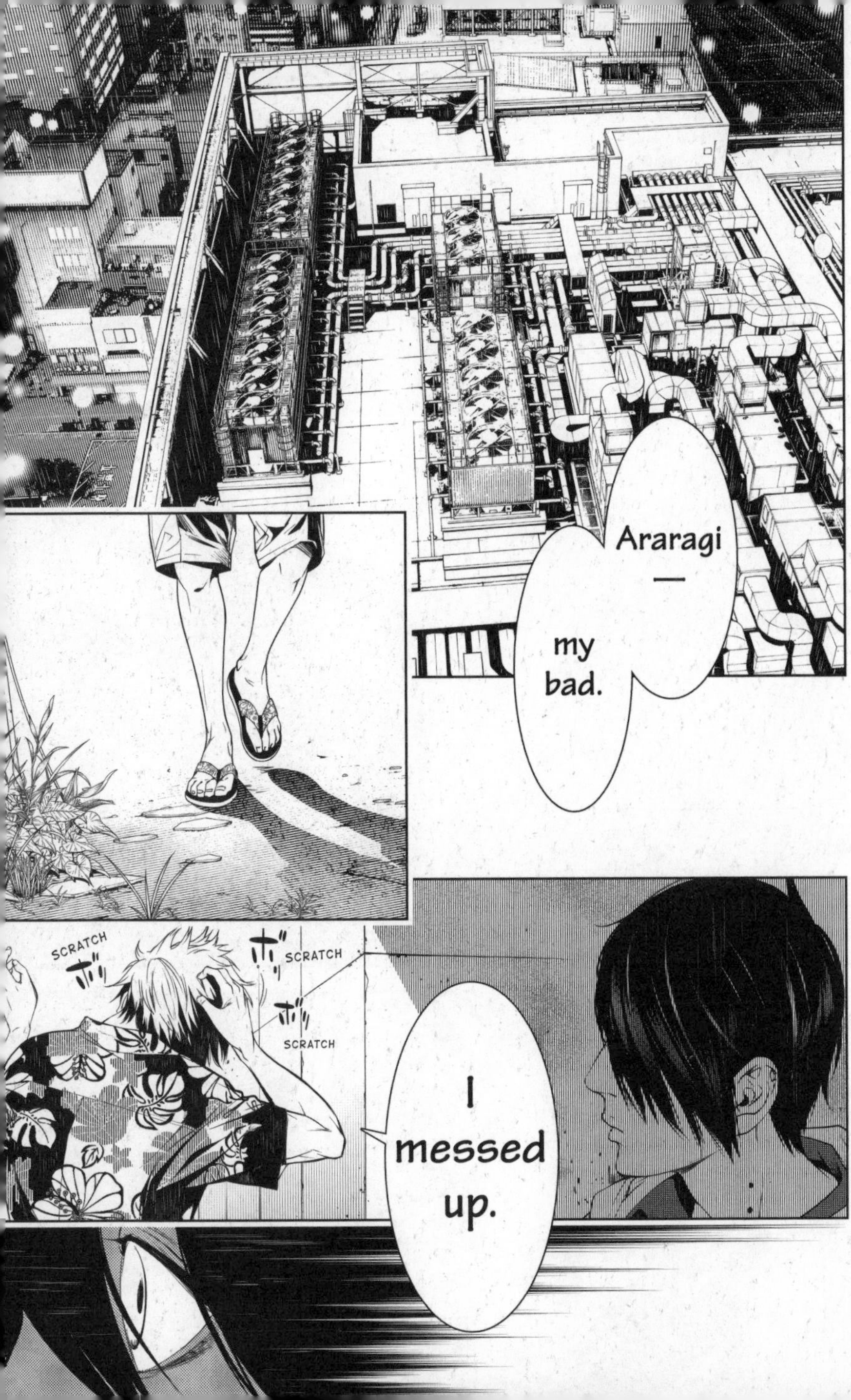
Araragi — my bad.
SCRATCH
SCRATCH
SCRATCH
I messed up.

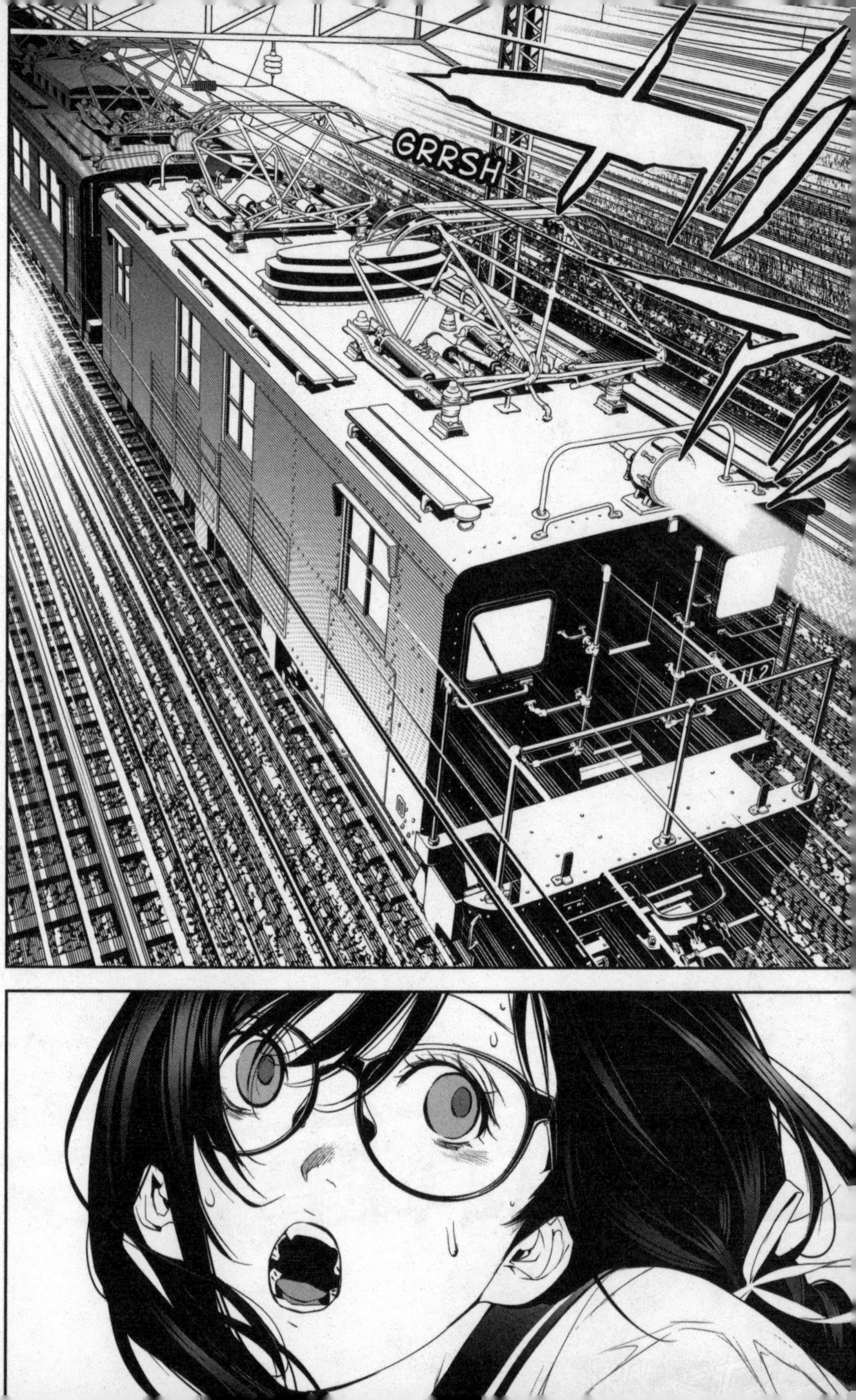
GRRSH

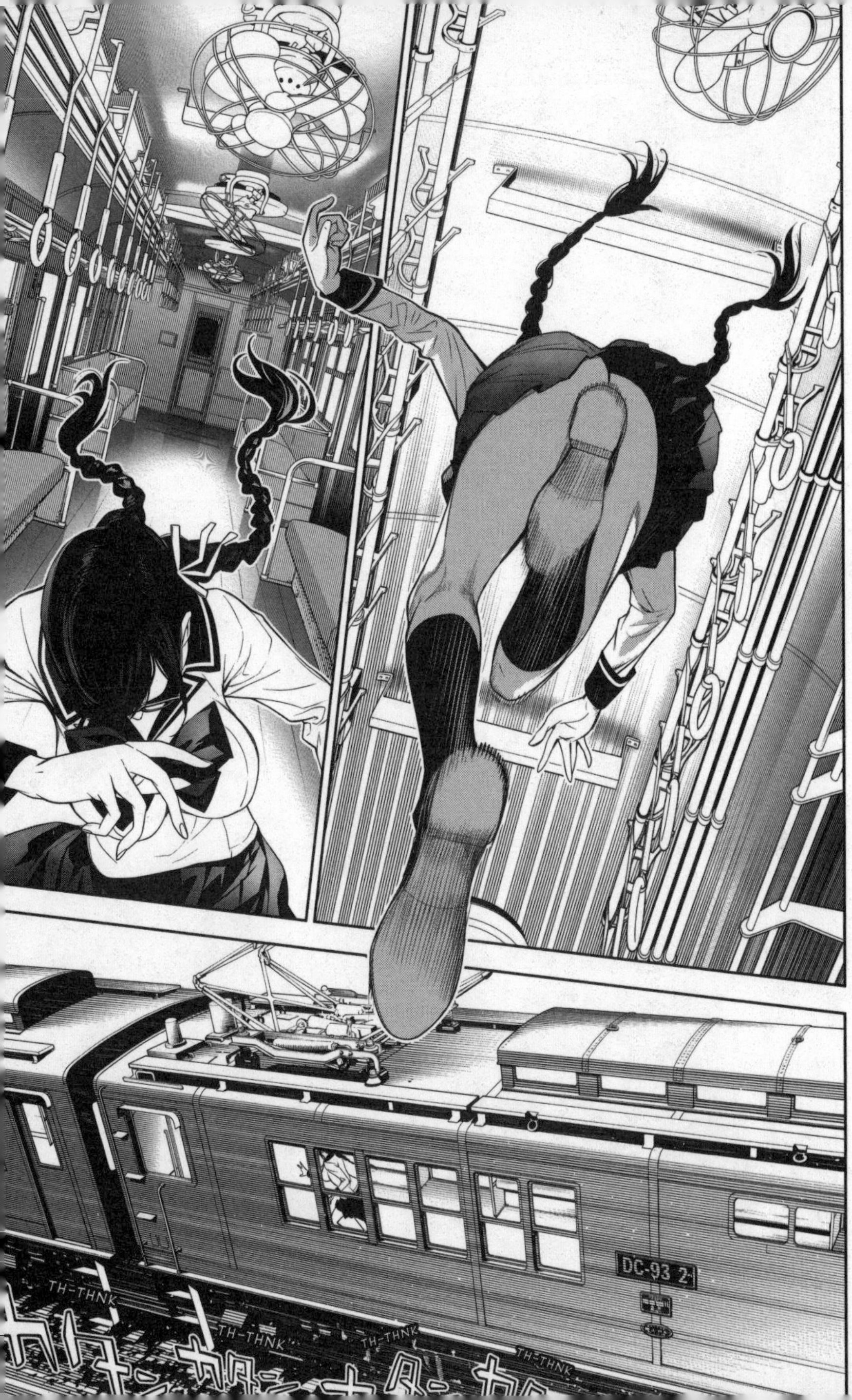
DC-93 2
TH-THNK
TH-THNK
TH-THNK
TH-THNK

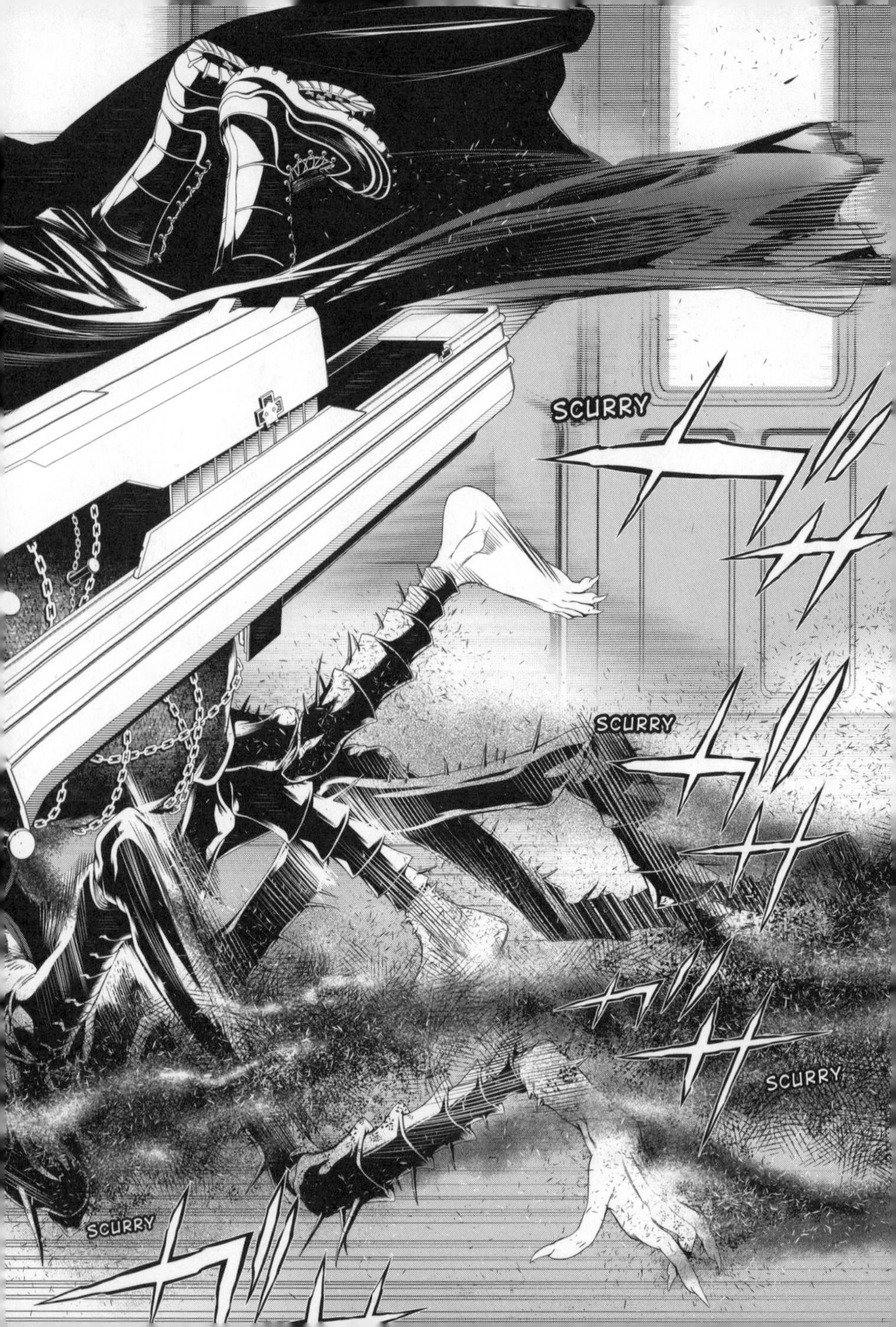

SCURRY
SCURRY
SCURRY
SCURRY

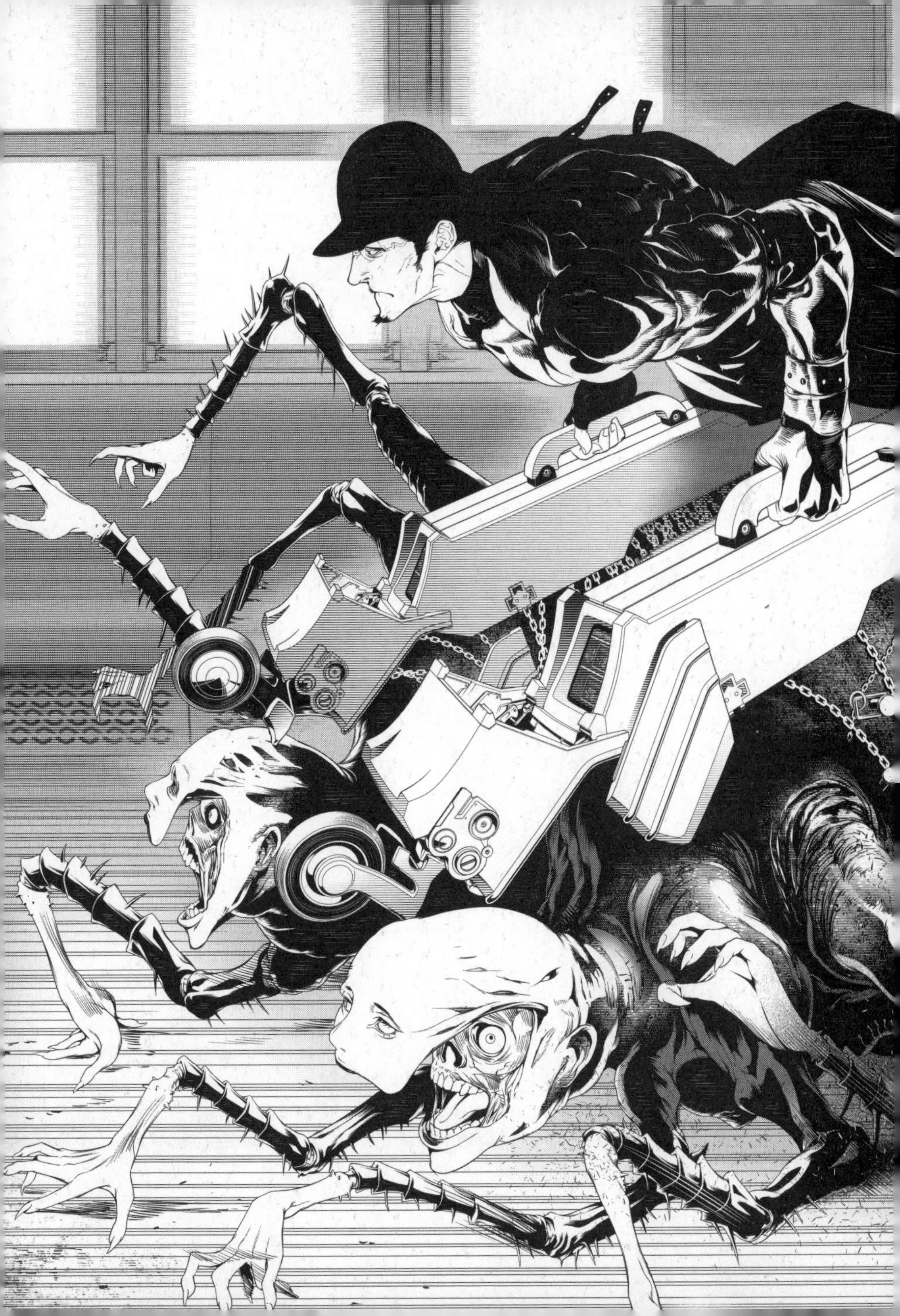

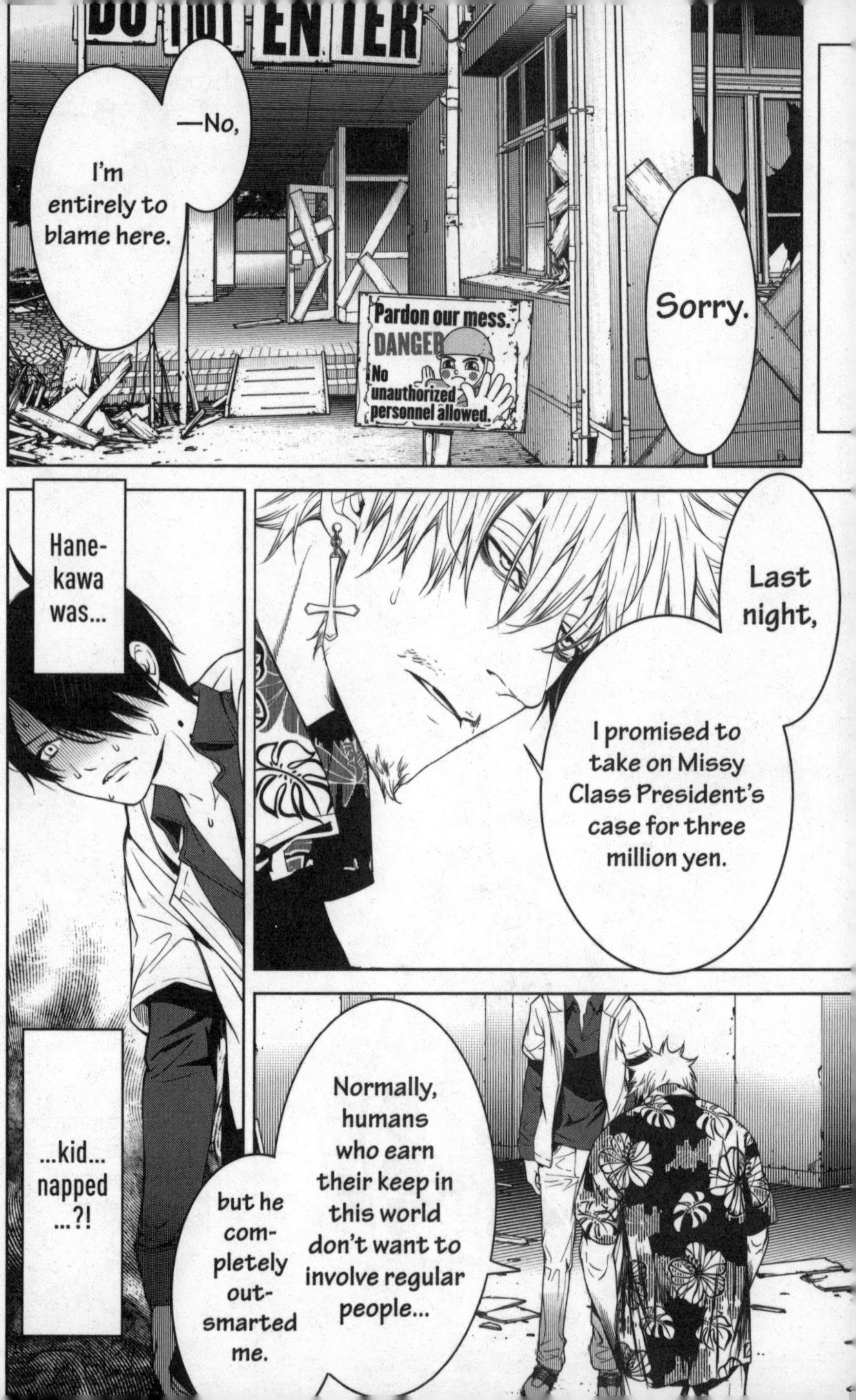
ENTER
Sorry.
—No, I'm entirely to blame here.
Pardon our mess. DANGER No unauthorized personnel allowed.
Last night, I promised to take on Missy Class President's case for three million yen.
Hane-kawa was...
Normally, humans who earn their keep in this world don't want to involve regular people...
but he com-pletely out-smarted me.
...kid... napped ...?!

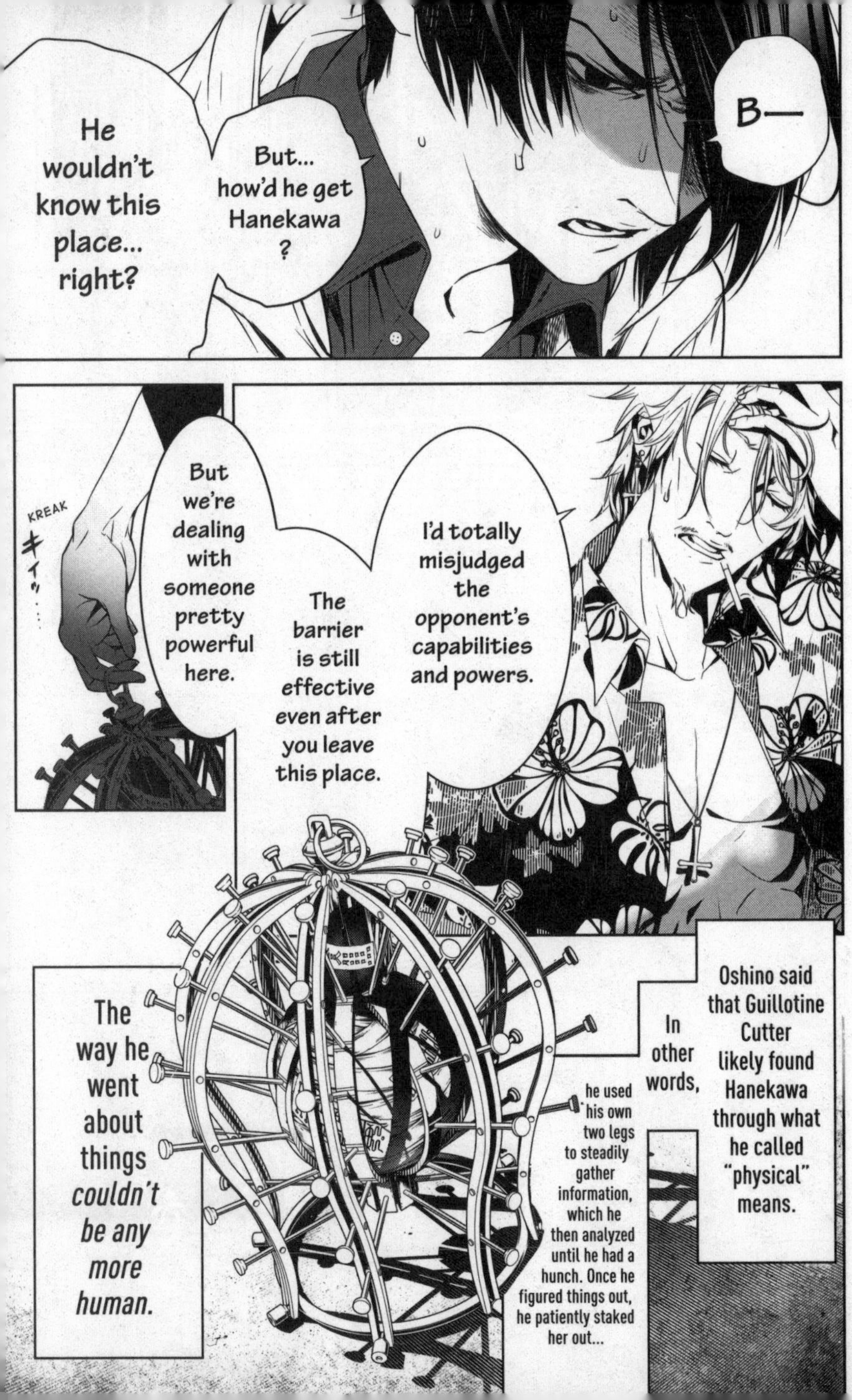
B—
But... how'd he get Hanekawa?
He wouldn't know this place... right?
I'd totally misjudged the opponent's capabilities and powers.
The barrier is still effective even after you leave this place.
But we're dealing with someone pretty powerful here.
KREAK
Oshino said that Guillotine Cutter likely found Hanekawa through what he called "physical" means.
In other words,
he used his own two legs to steadily gather information, which he then analyzed until he had a hunch. Once he figured things out, he patiently staked her out...
The way he went about things *couldn't be any more human.*

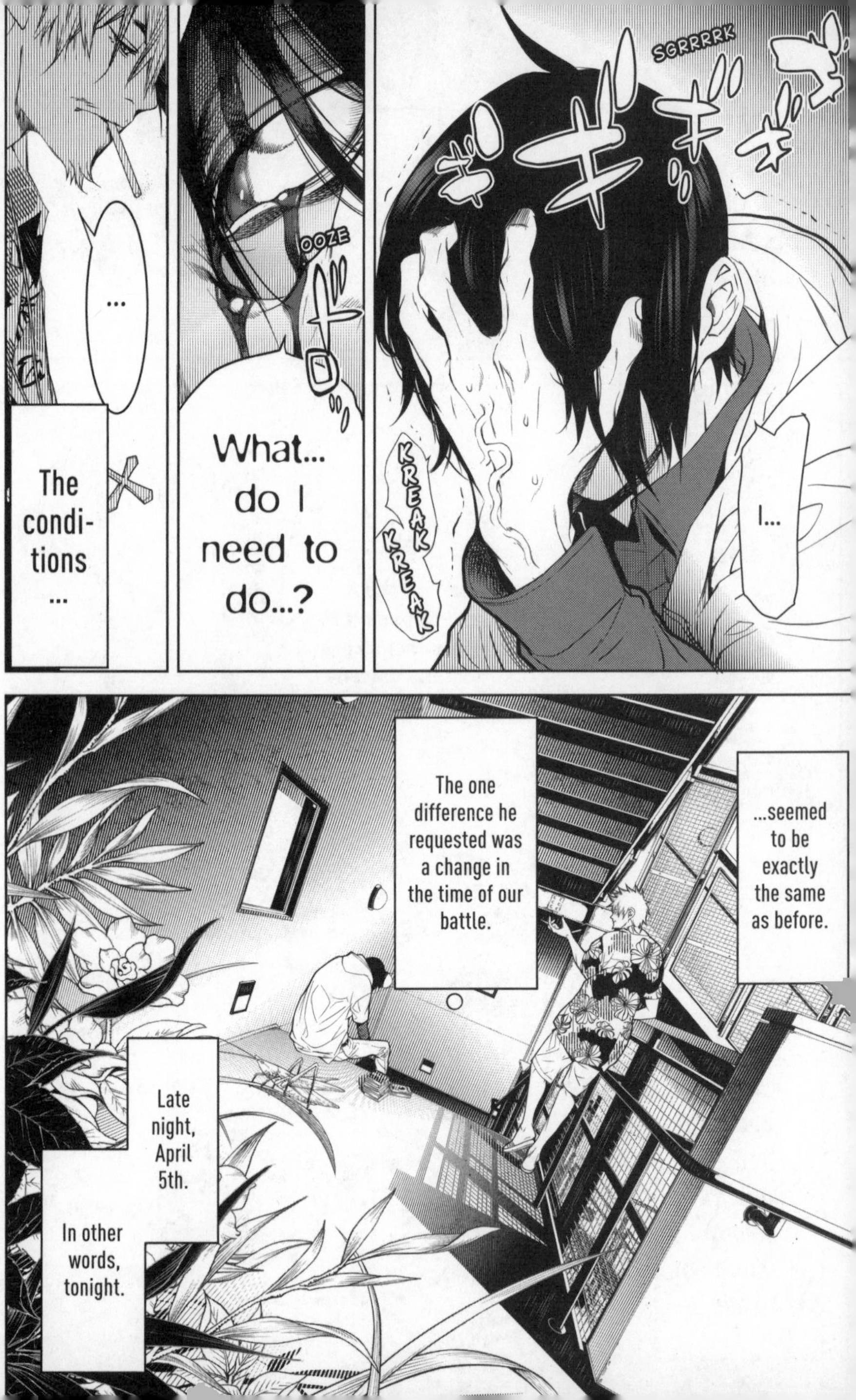
SGRRRRK
I...
KREAK KREAK
OOZE
What... do I need to do...?
...
The condi-tions ...
...seemed to be exactly the same as before.
The one difference he requested was a change in the time of our battle.
Late night, April 5th.
In other words, tonight.

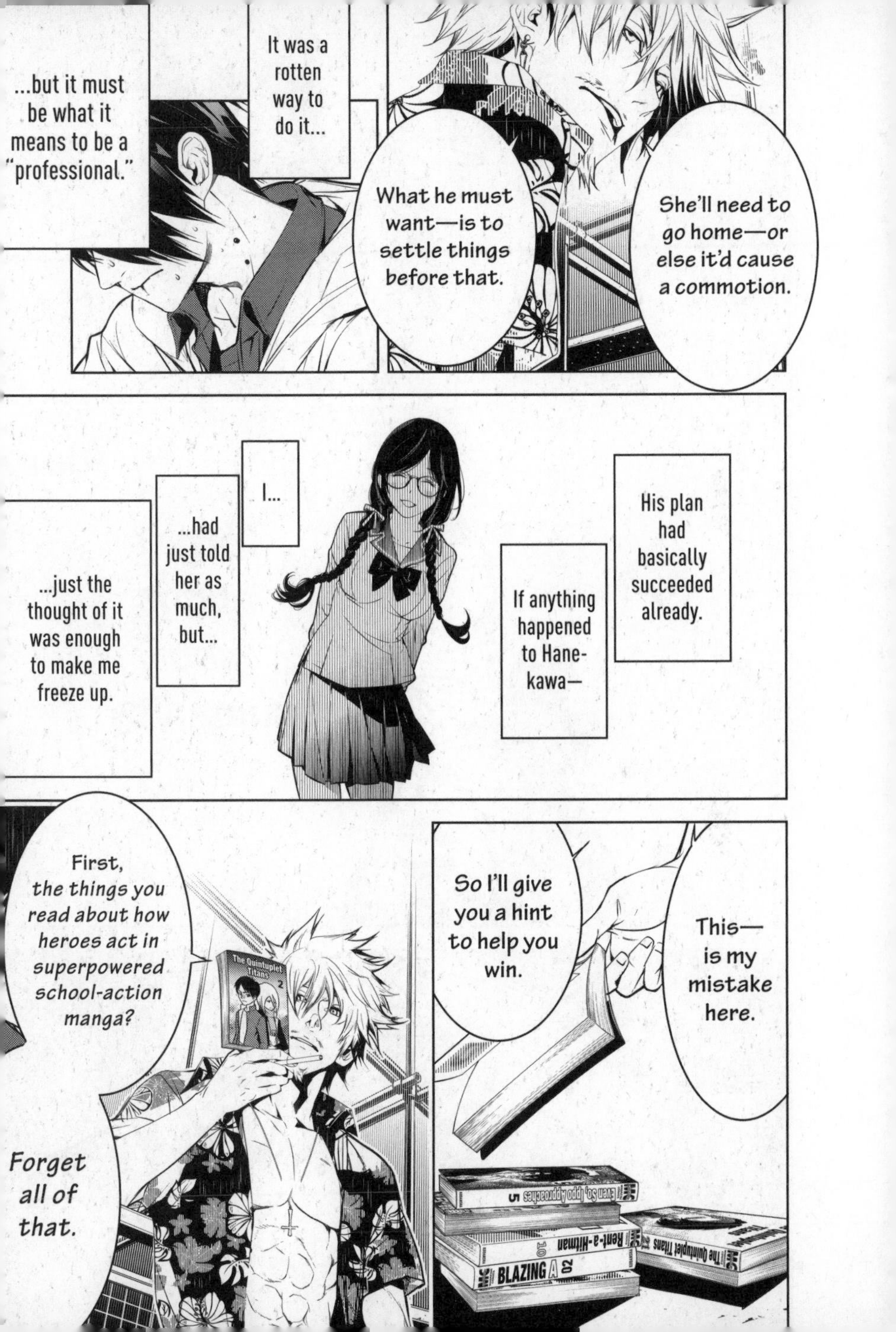
She'll need to go home—or else it'd cause a commotion.
What he must want—is to settle things before that.
It was a rotten way to do it...
...but it must be what it means to be a "professional."
His plan had basically succeeded already.
If anything happened to Hane-kawa—
I...
...had just told her as much, but...
...just the thought of it was enough to make me freeze up.
This—is my mistake here.
So I'll give you a hint to help you win.
First, the things you read about how heroes act in superpowered school-action manga?
The Quintuplet Titans 2
Forget all of that.
Even So, Ippo Approaches 5
Rent-a-Hitman 10
BLAZING A 13
The Quintuplet Titans

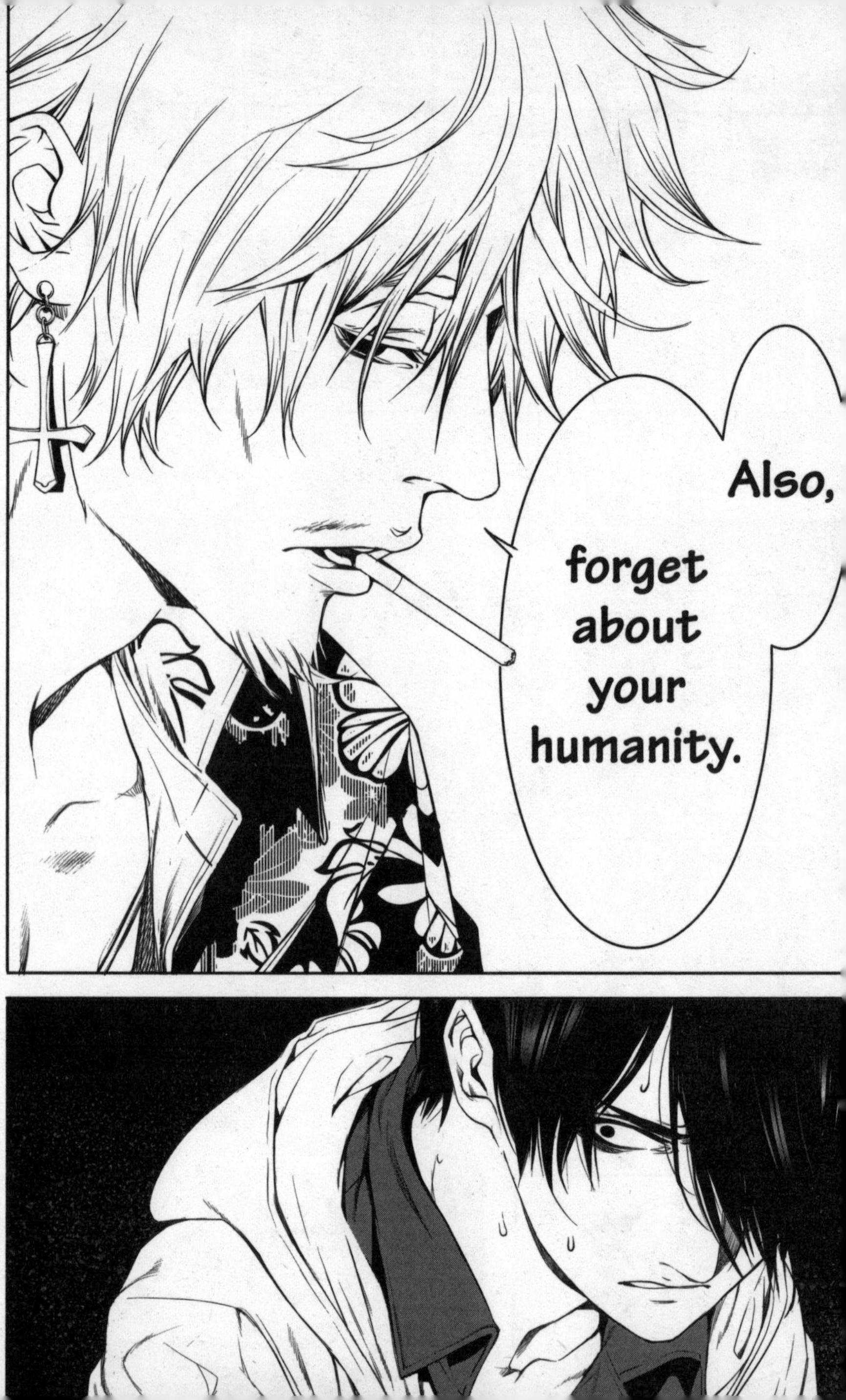
Also,
forget about your humanity.

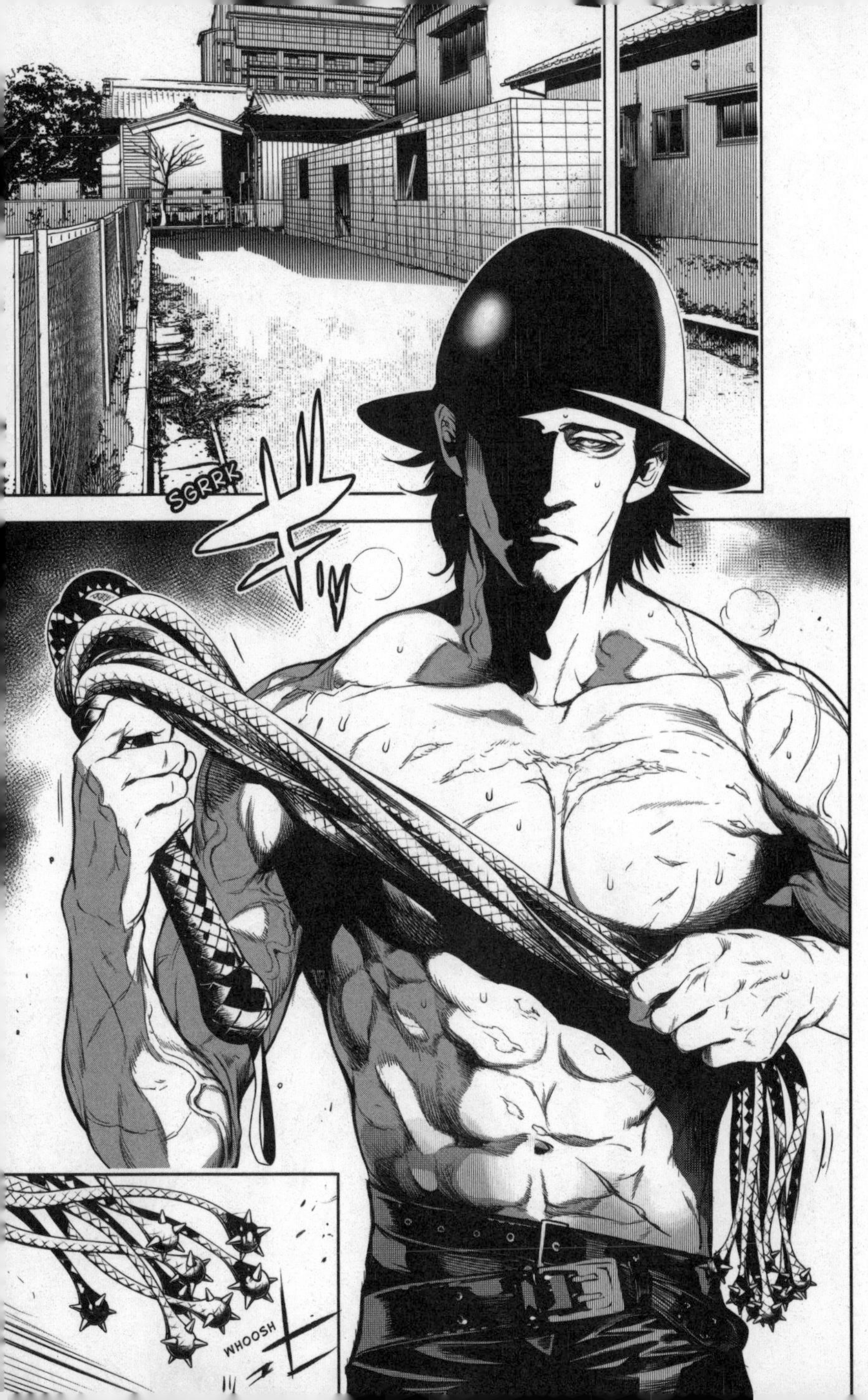
SGRRK
WHOOSH

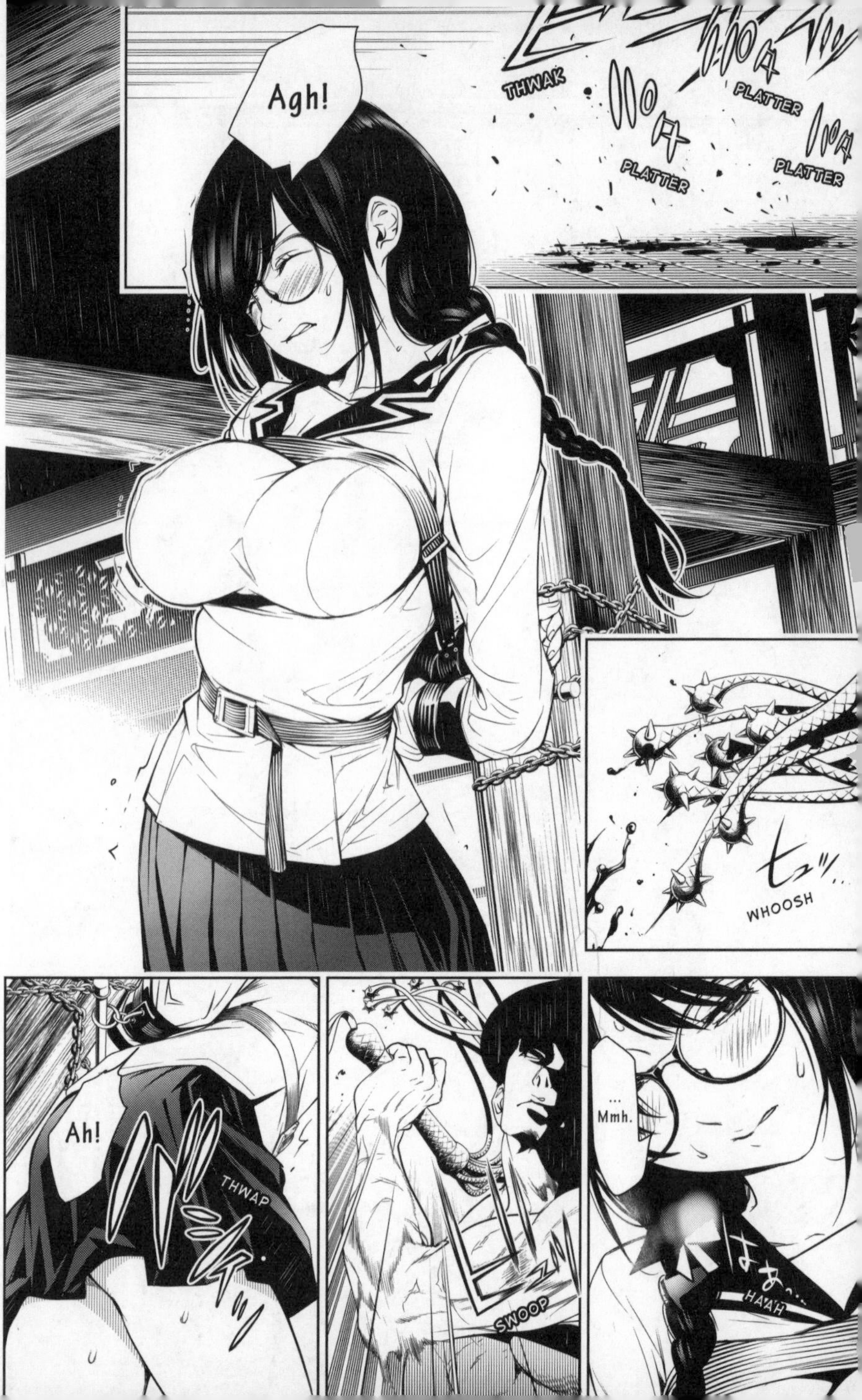
THWAK
PLATTER
PLATTER
PLATTER
WHOOSH
Agh!
...Mmh.
HAAH
SWOOP
Ah!
THWAP

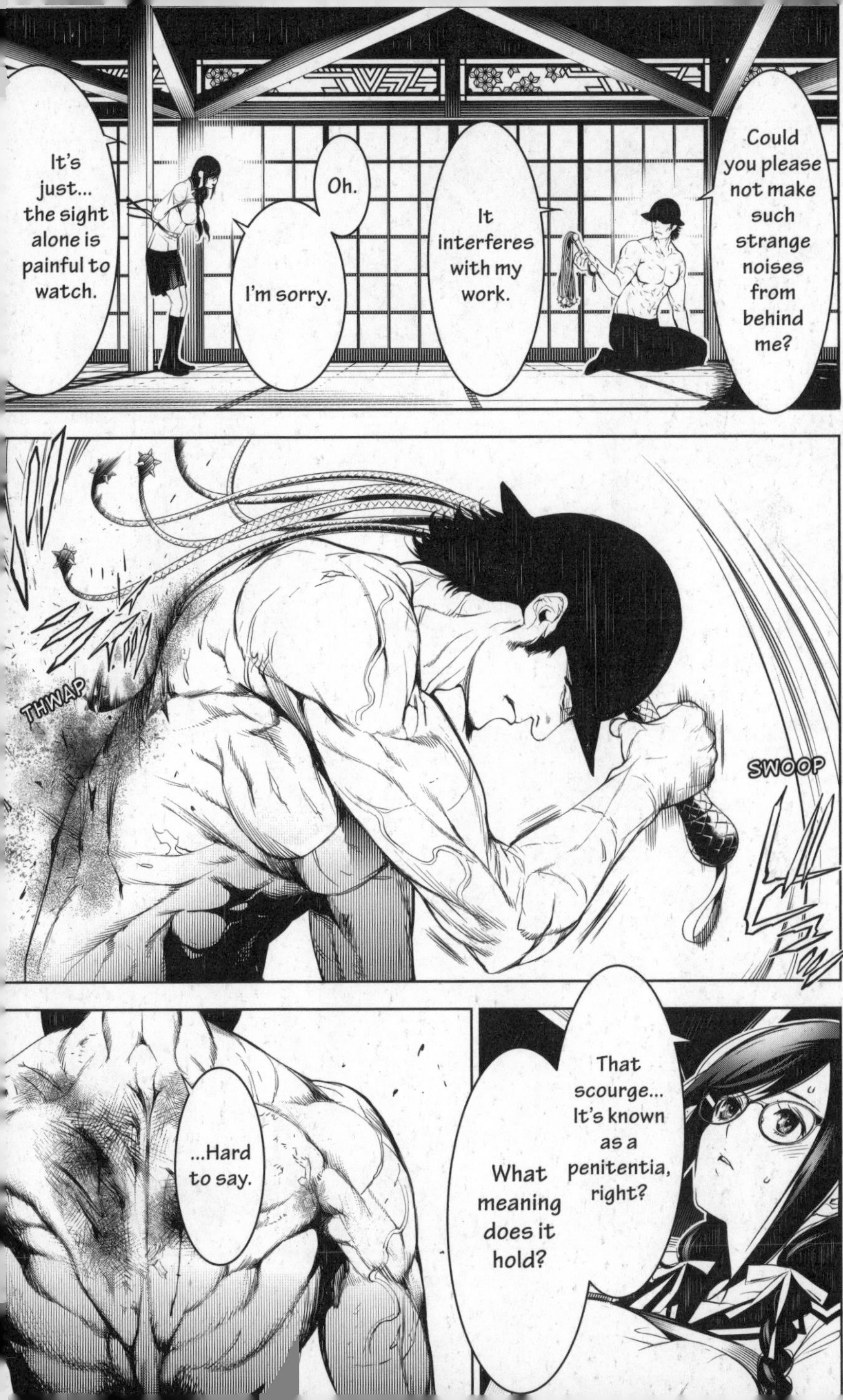
Could you please not make such strange noises from behind me?
It interferes with my work.
Oh.
I'm sorry.
It's just... the sight alone is painful to watch.
SWOOP
THWAP
That scourge... It's known as a penitentia, right?
What meaning does it hold?
...Hard to say.

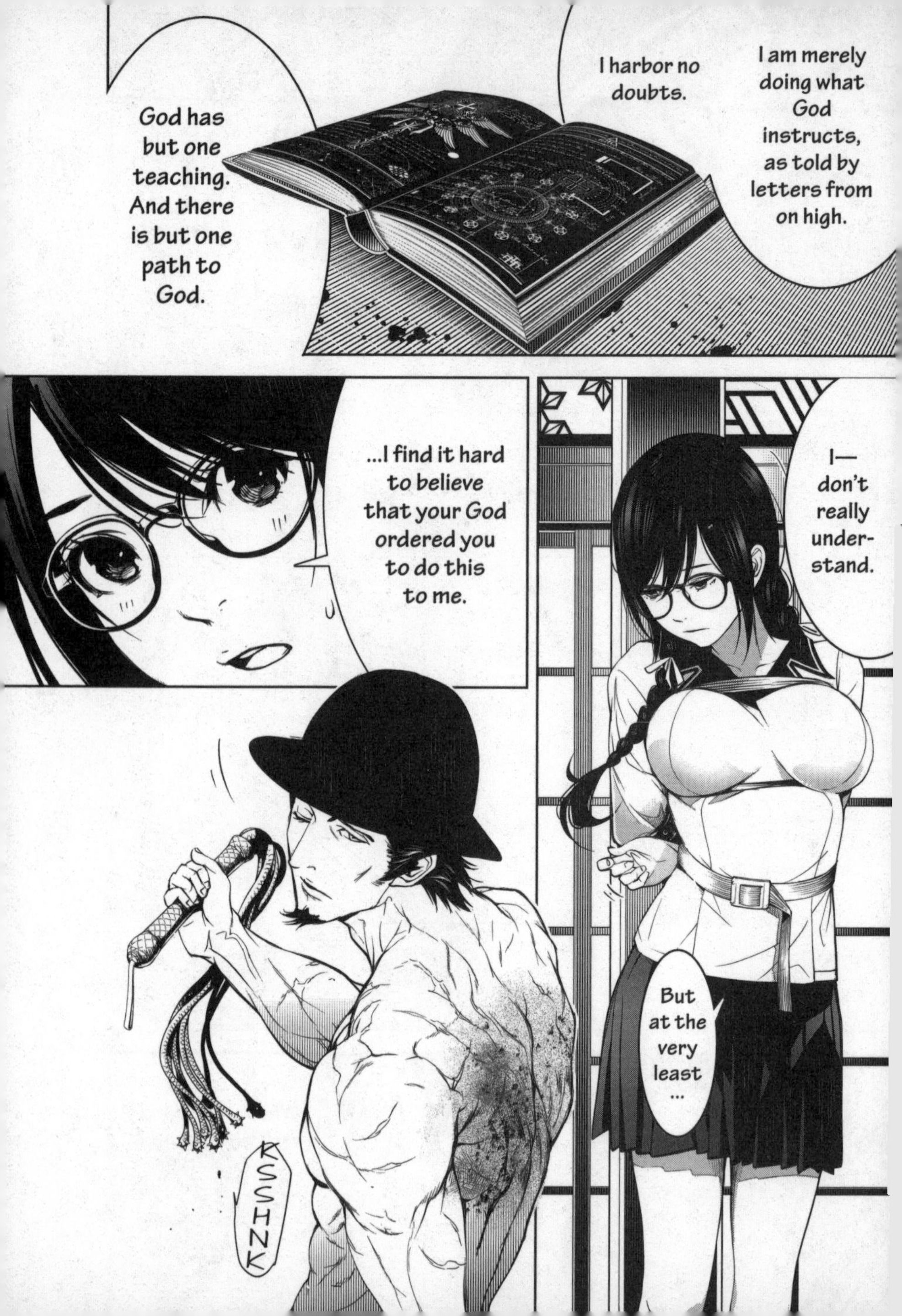
I am merely doing what God instructs, as told by letters from on high.
I harbor no doubts.
God has but one teaching. And there is but one path to God.
I— don't really under-stand.
But at the very least ...
...I find it hard to believe that your God ordered you to do this to me.
KSSHNK

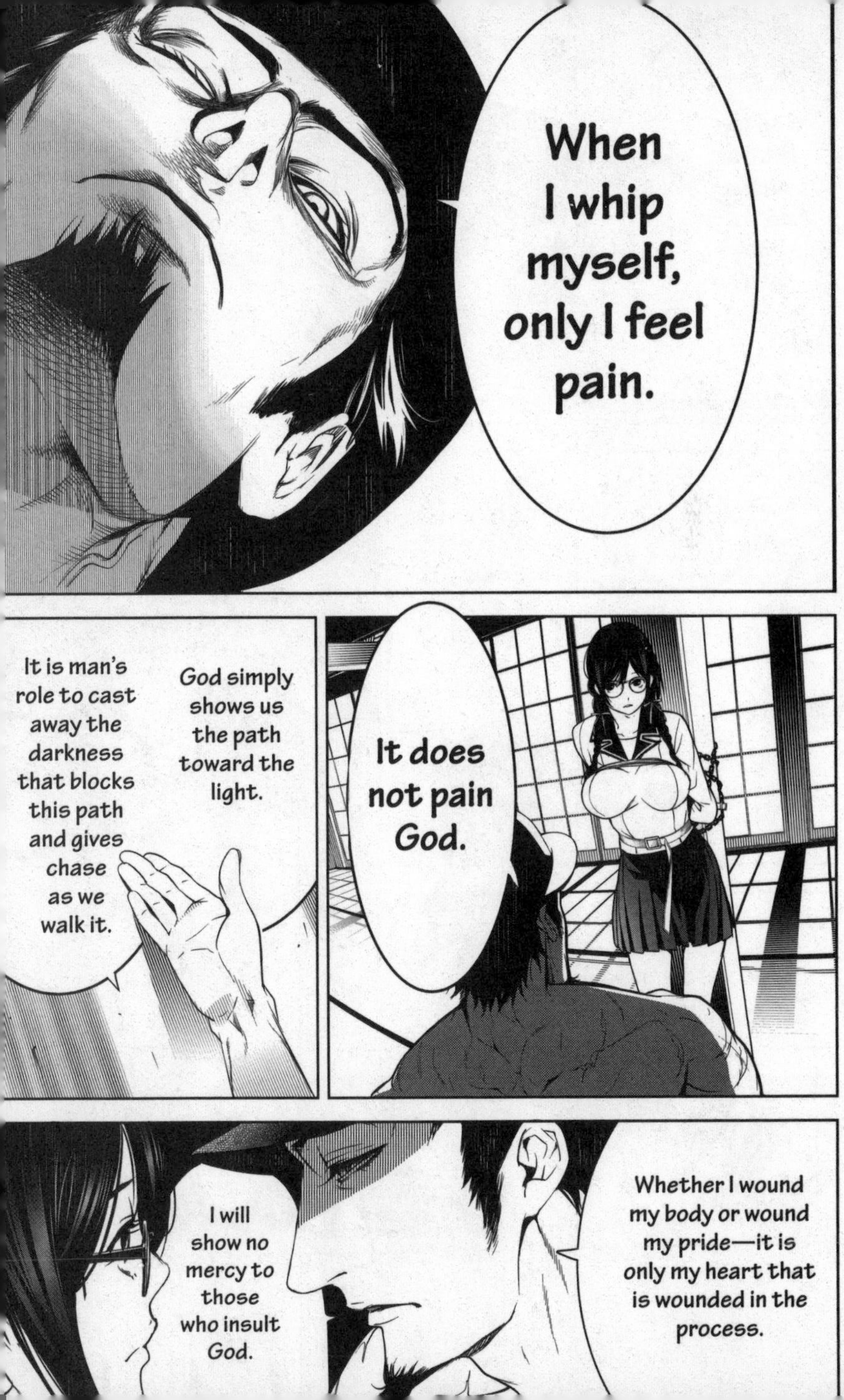
When I whip myself, only I feel pain.
It does not pain God.
God simply shows us the path toward the light.
It is man's role to cast away the darkness that blocks this path and gives chase as we walk it.
Whether I wound my body or wound my pride—it is only my heart that is wounded in the process.
I will show no mercy to those who insult God.

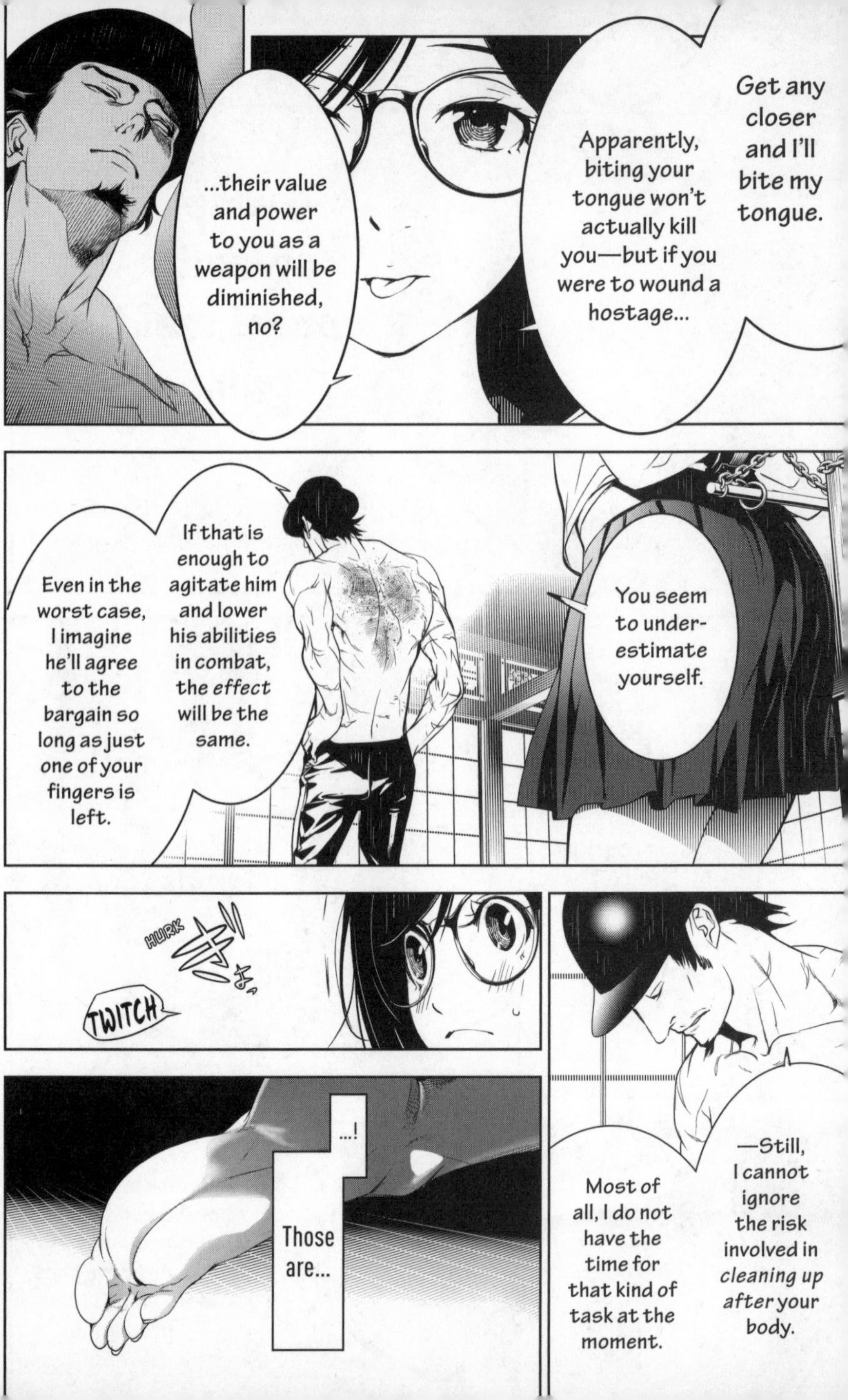
Get any closer and I'll bite my tongue.
Apparently, biting your tongue won't actually kill you—but if you were to wound a hostage...
...their value and power to you as a weapon will be diminished, no?
You seem to under-estimate yourself.
If that is enough to agitate him and lower his abilities in combat, the *effect* will be the same.
Even in the worst case, I imagine he'll agree to the bargain so long as just one of your fingers is left.
HURK
TWITCH
—Still, I cannot ignore the risk involved in *cleaning up after* your body.
Most of all, I do not have the time for that kind of task at the moment.
...!
Those are...

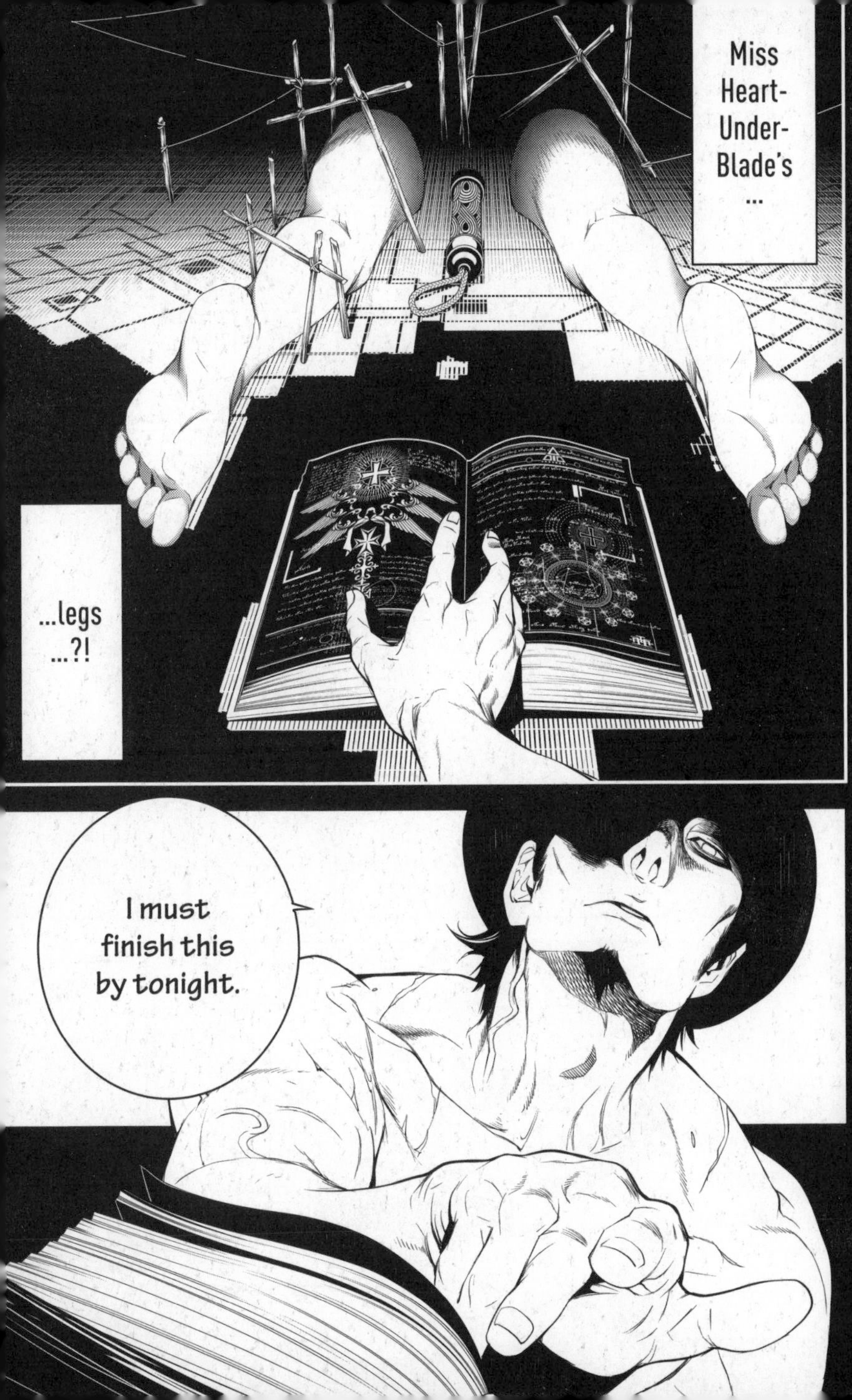
Miss Heart-Under-Blade's ...
...legs ...?!
I must finish this by tonight.

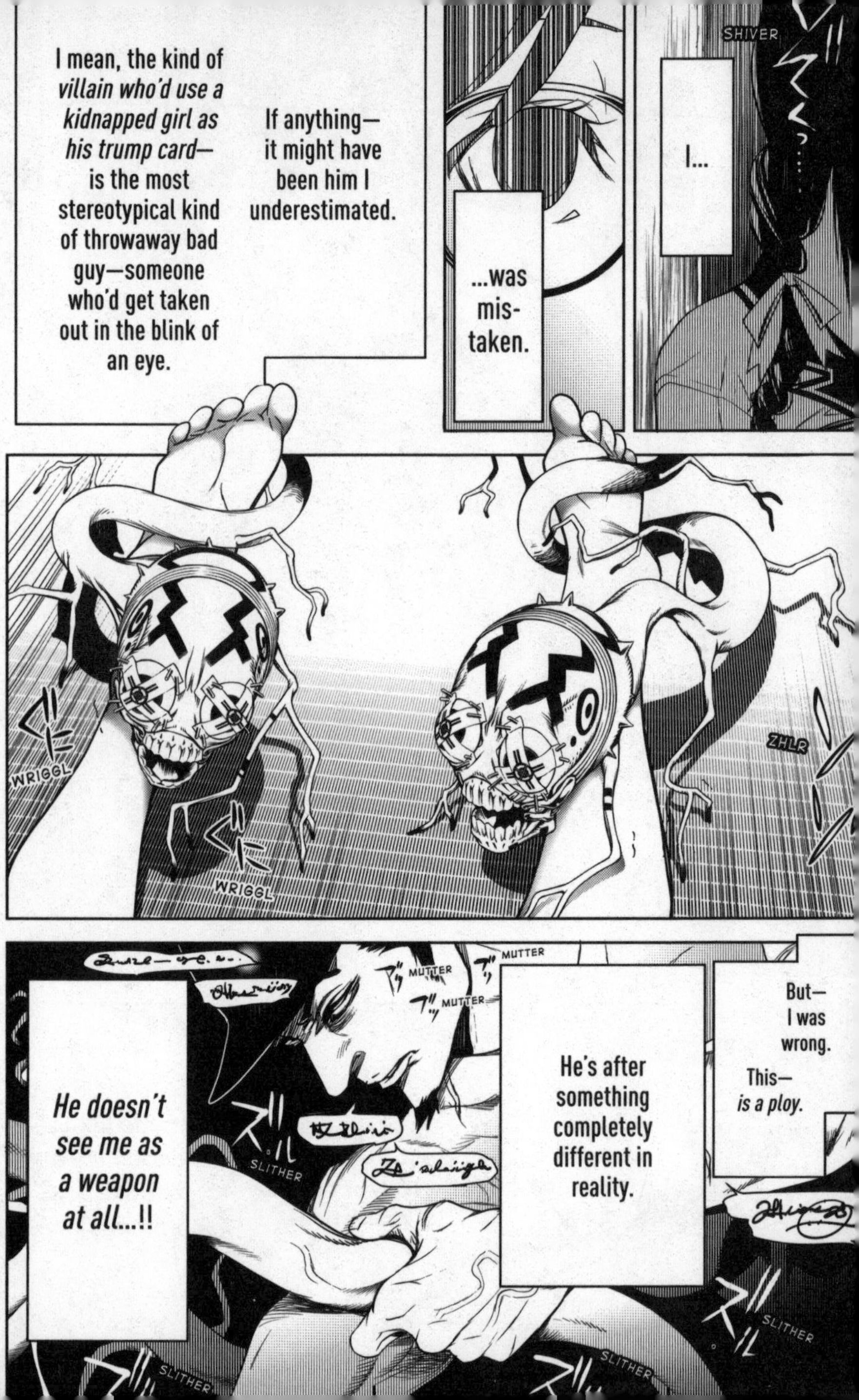
SHIVER
I...
...was mis-taken.
If anything— it might have been him I underestimated.
I mean, the kind of *villain who'd use a kidnapped girl as his trump card*— is the most stereotypical kind of throwaway bad guy—someone who'd get taken out in the blink of an eye.
ZHLR
WRIGGL
WRIGGL
But— I was wrong.
This— *is a ploy.*
MUTTER
MUTTER
MUTTER
He's after something completely different in reality.
He doesn't see me as a weapon at all...!!
SLITHER
SLITHER
SLITHER
SLITHER

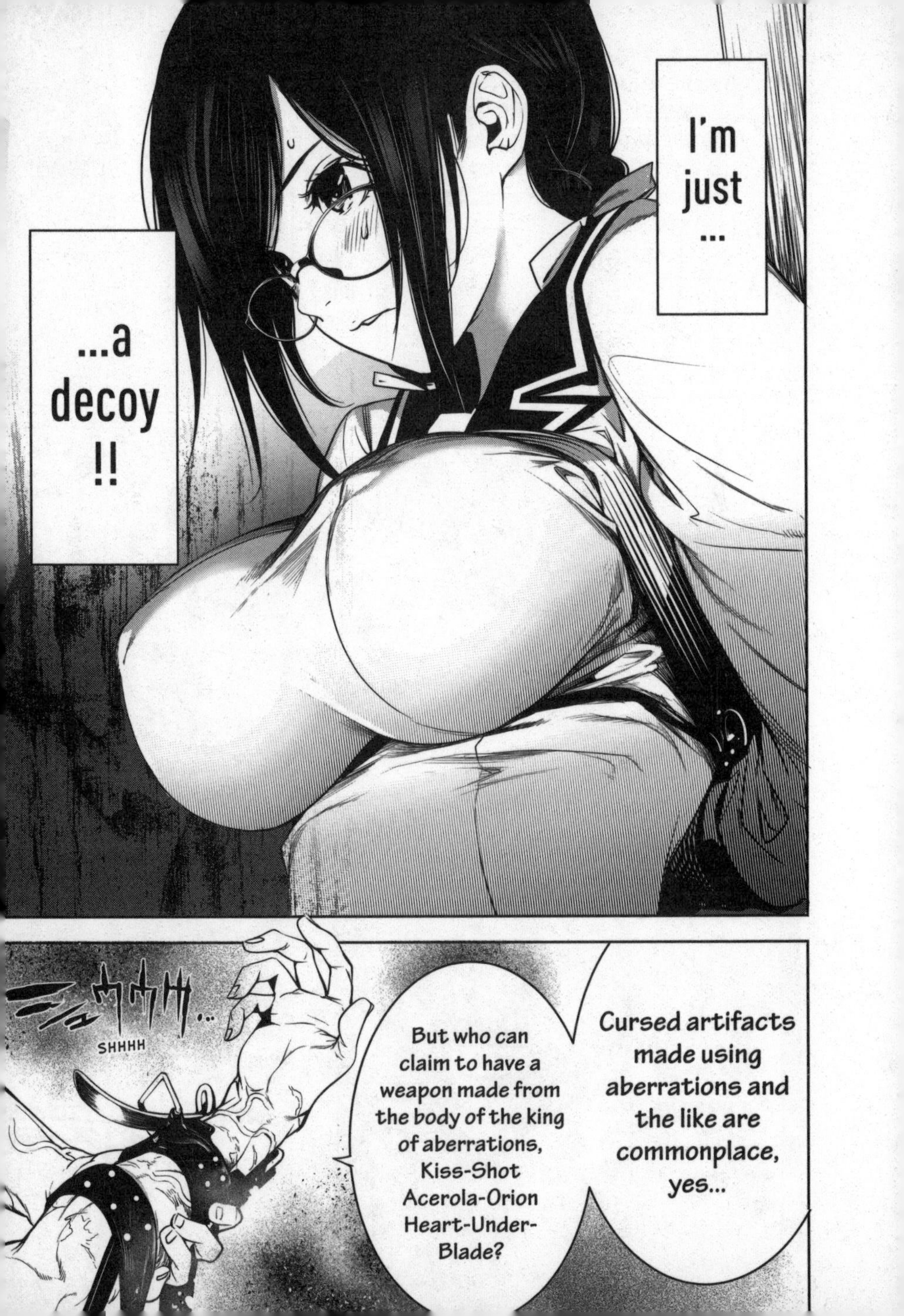
I'm just ...
...a decoy !!
Cursed artifacts made using aberrations and the like are commonplace, yes...
But who can claim to have a weapon made from the body of the king of aberrations, Kiss-Shot Acerola-Orion Heart-Under-Blade?
SHHHH

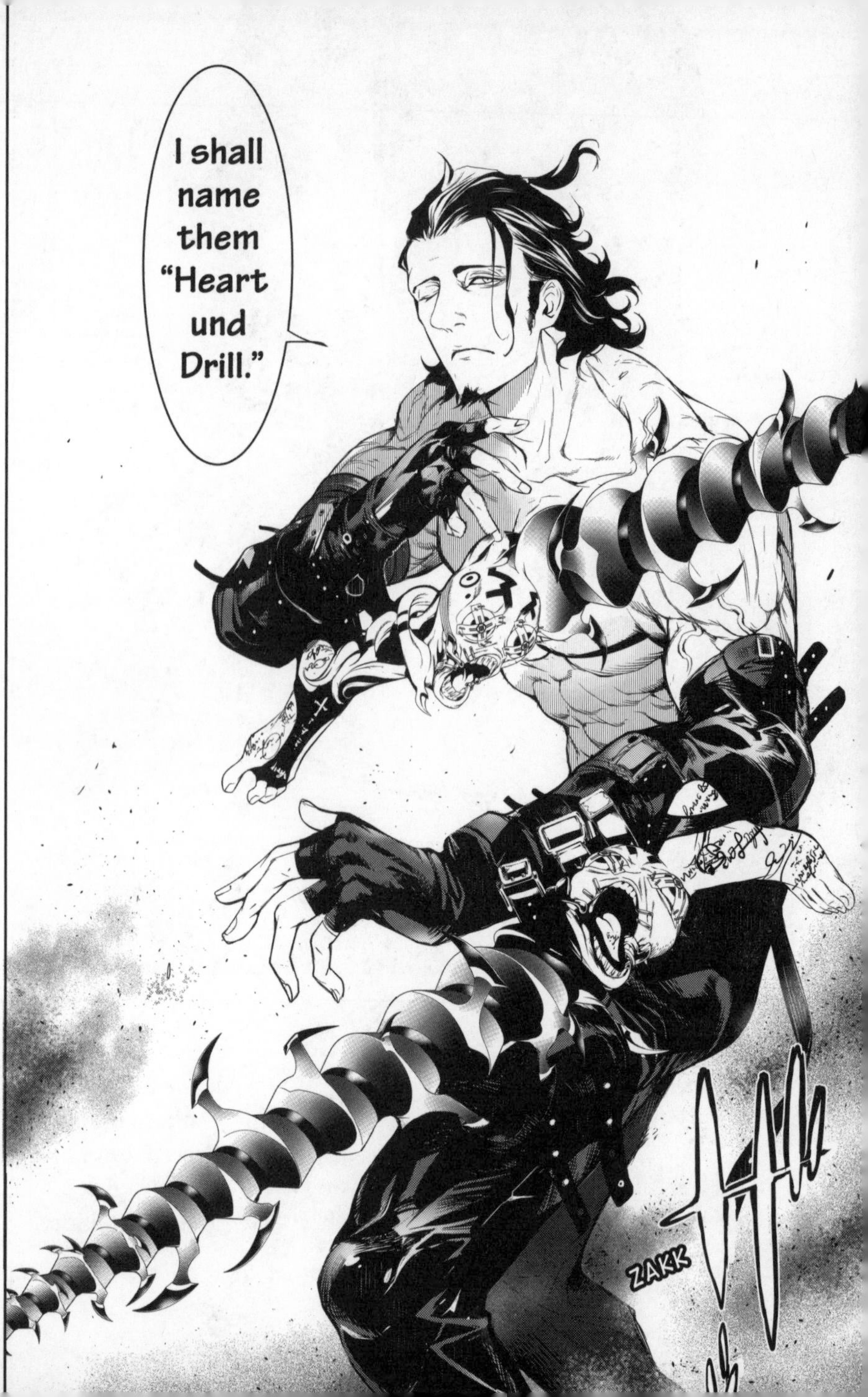
I shall name them "Heart und Drill."
ZAKK

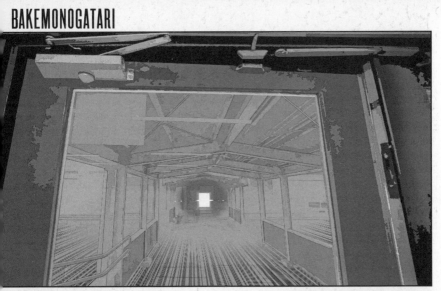

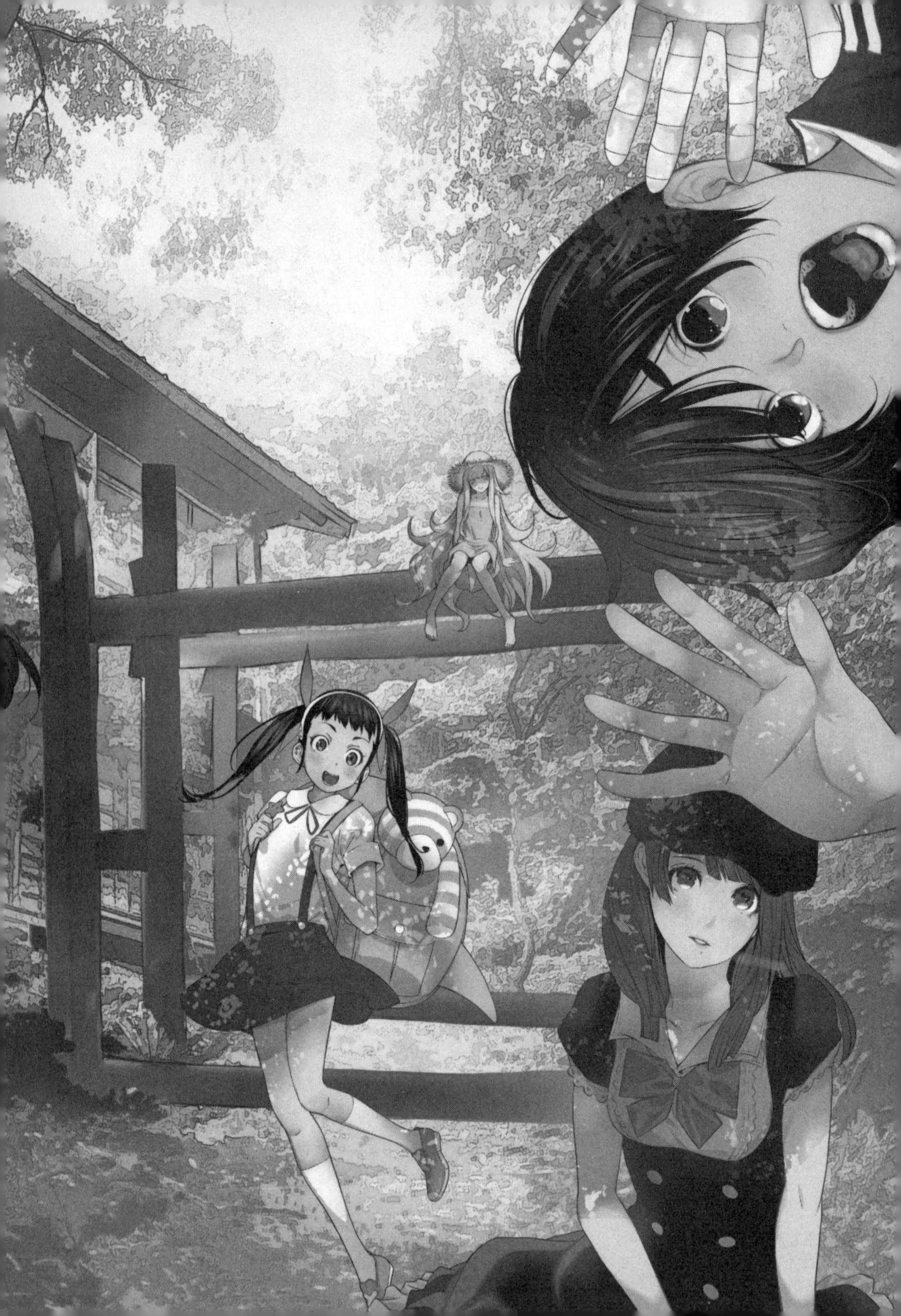

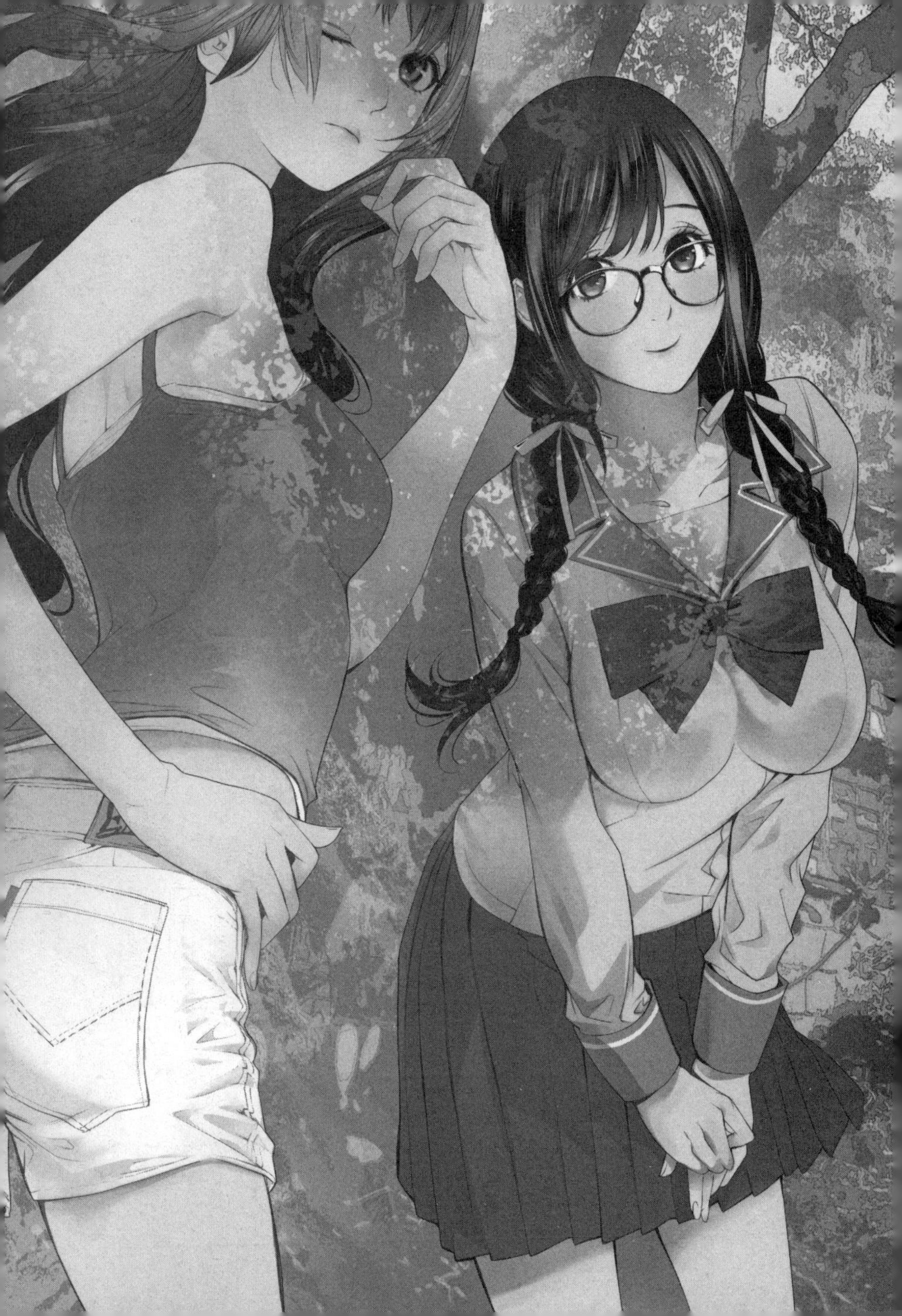

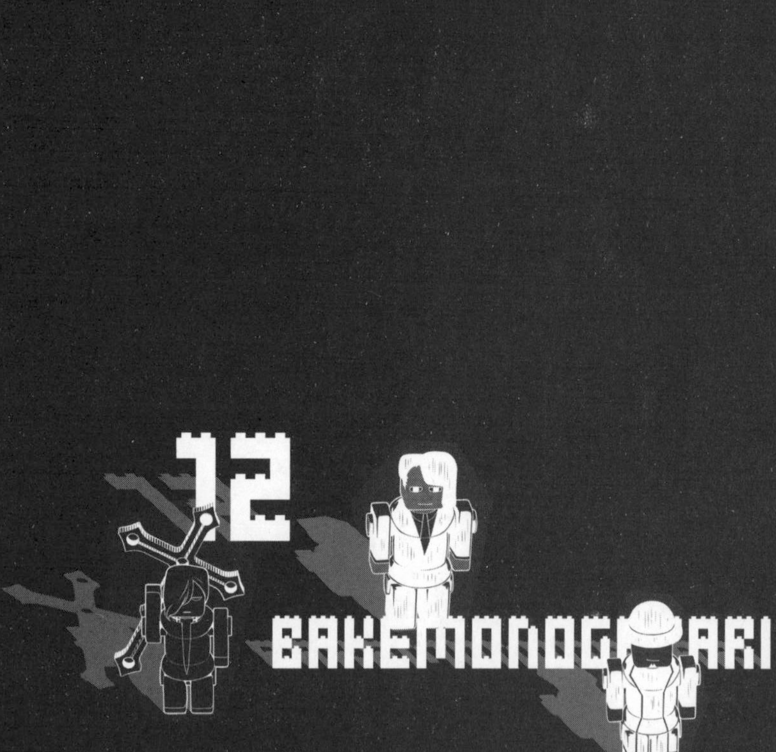
12
BAKEMONOG ARI

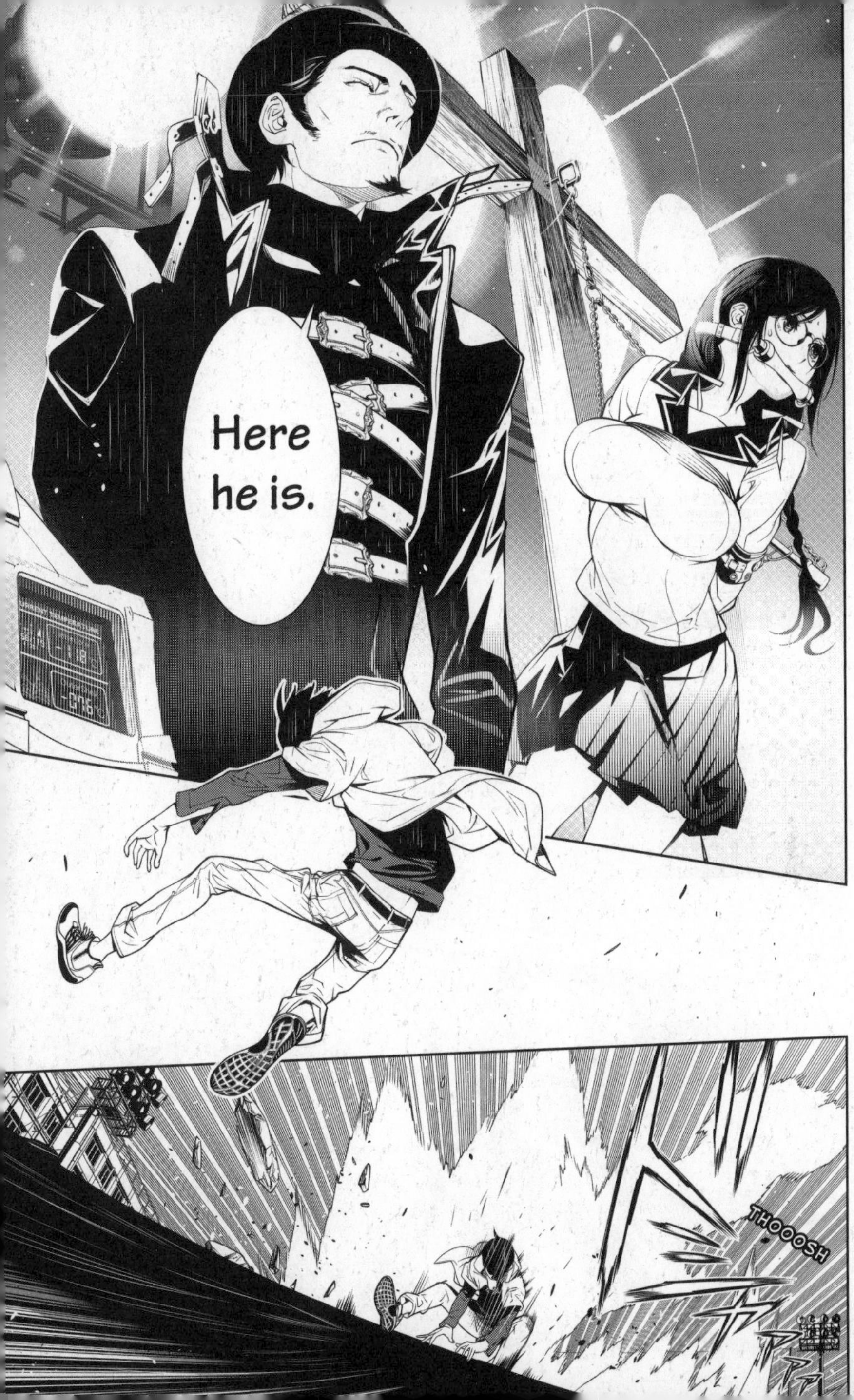
Here he is.
THOOOSH

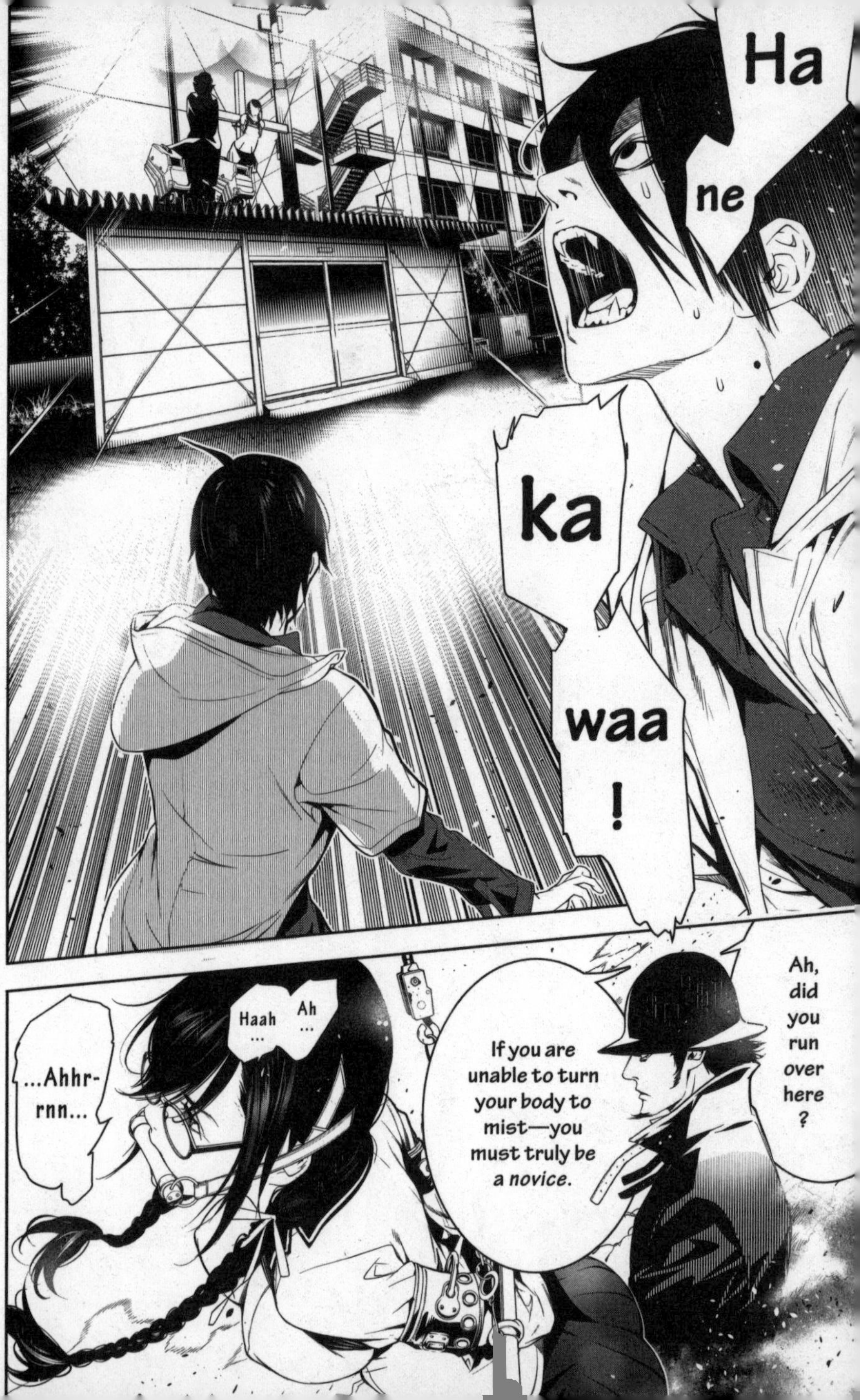
Ha
ne
ka
waa
!
Ah, did you run over here?
If you are unable to turn your body to mist—you must truly be a *novice*.
Ah ...
Haah ...
...Ahhr-rnn...

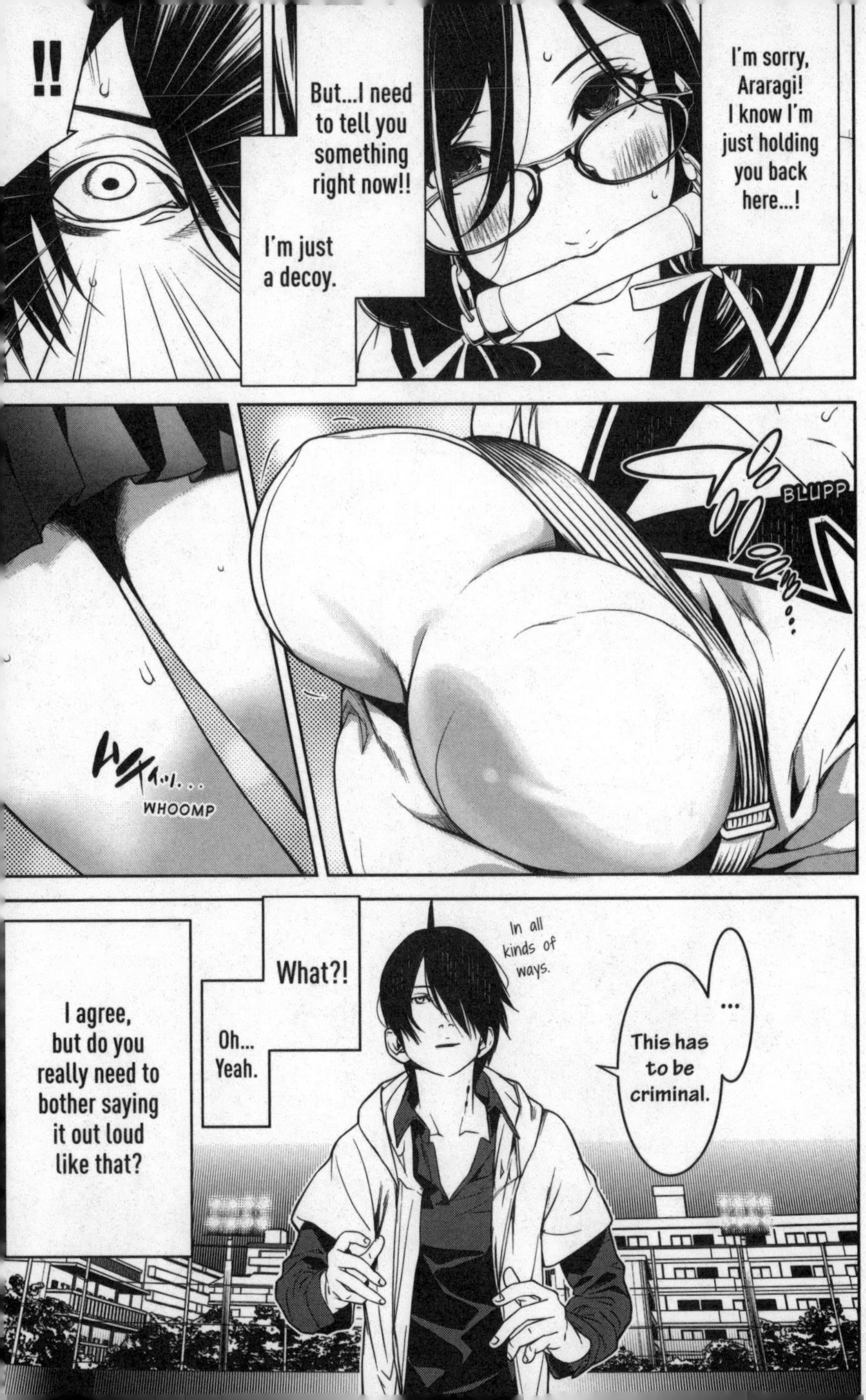
I'm sorry, Araragi! I know I'm just holding you back here...!
But...I need to tell you something right now!!
I'm just a decoy.
!!
BLUPP
WHOOMP
...
This has to be criminal.
In all kinds of ways.
What?!
Oh... Yeah.
I agree, but do you really need to bother saying it out loud like that?

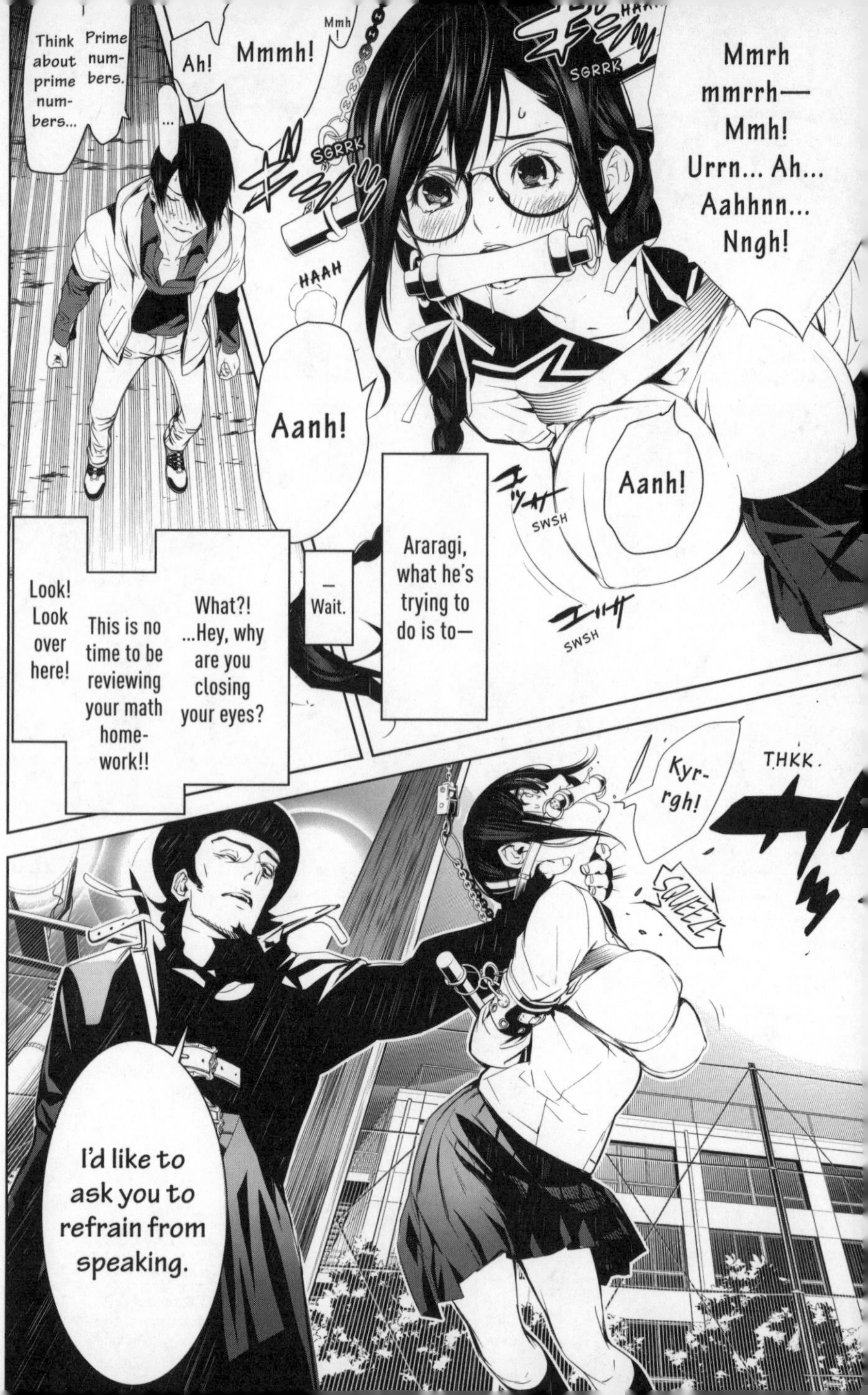

SGRRK
Mmrh mmrrh— Mmh! Urrn... Ah... Aahhnn... Nngh!
SGRRK
Mmh !
Mmmh!
Ah!
...
Prime numbers.
Think about prime numbers...
HAAH
Aanh!
Aanh!
SWSH
SWSH
Araragi, what he's trying to do is to—
—Wait.
What?! ...Hey, why are you closing your eyes?
This is no time to be reviewing your math homework!!
Look! Look over here!
THKK.
Kyr-rgh!
SQUEEZE
I'd like to ask you to refrain from speaking.

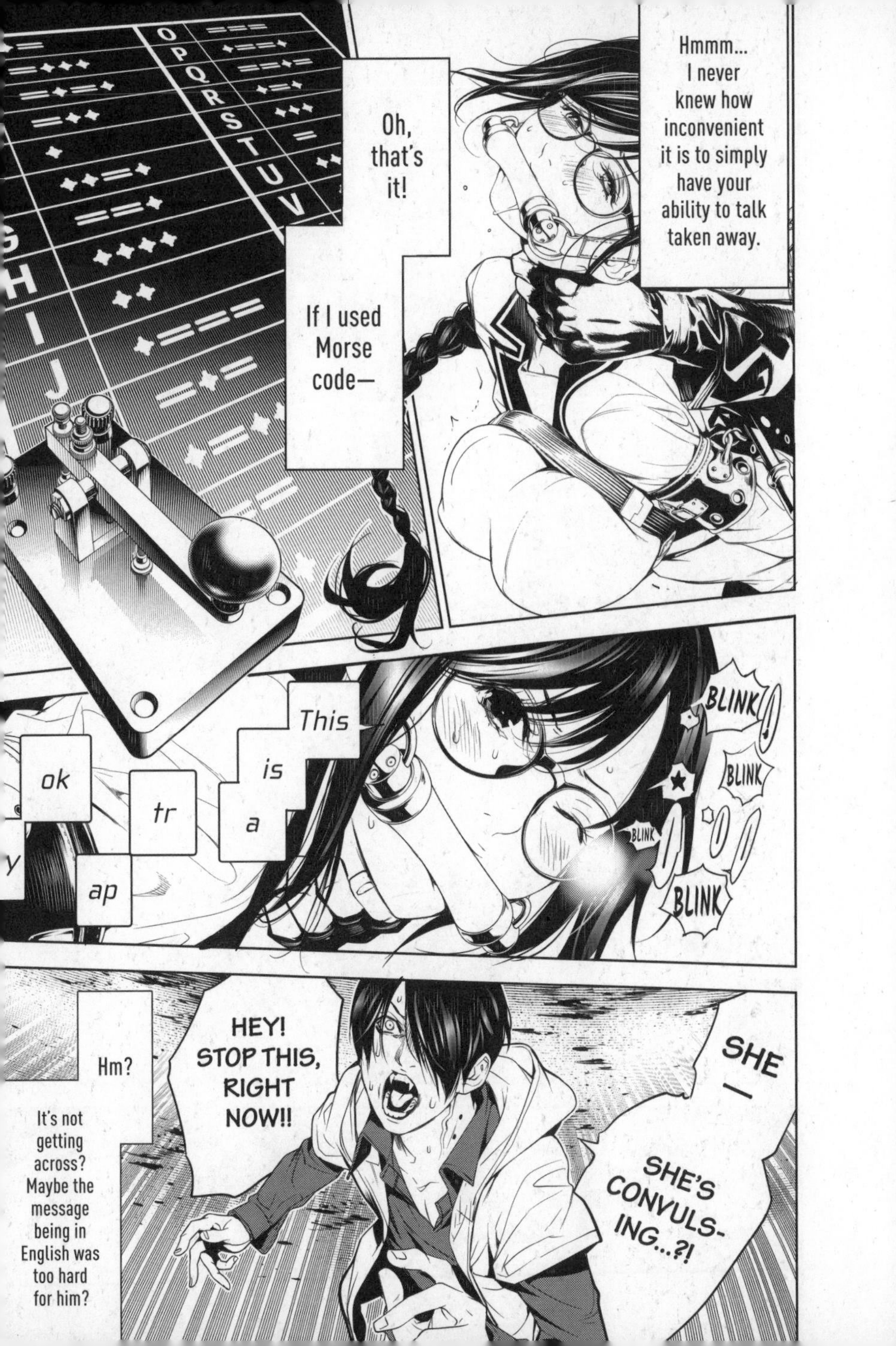
Hmmm... I never knew how inconvenient it is to simply have your ability to talk taken away.
Oh, that's it!
If I used Morse code—
BLINK
BLINK
BLINK
BLINK
This
is
a
tr
ap
ok
y
SHE—
SHE'S CONVULS-ING...?!
HEY! STOP THIS, RIGHT NOW!!
Hm?
It's not getting across? Maybe the message being in English was too hard for him?

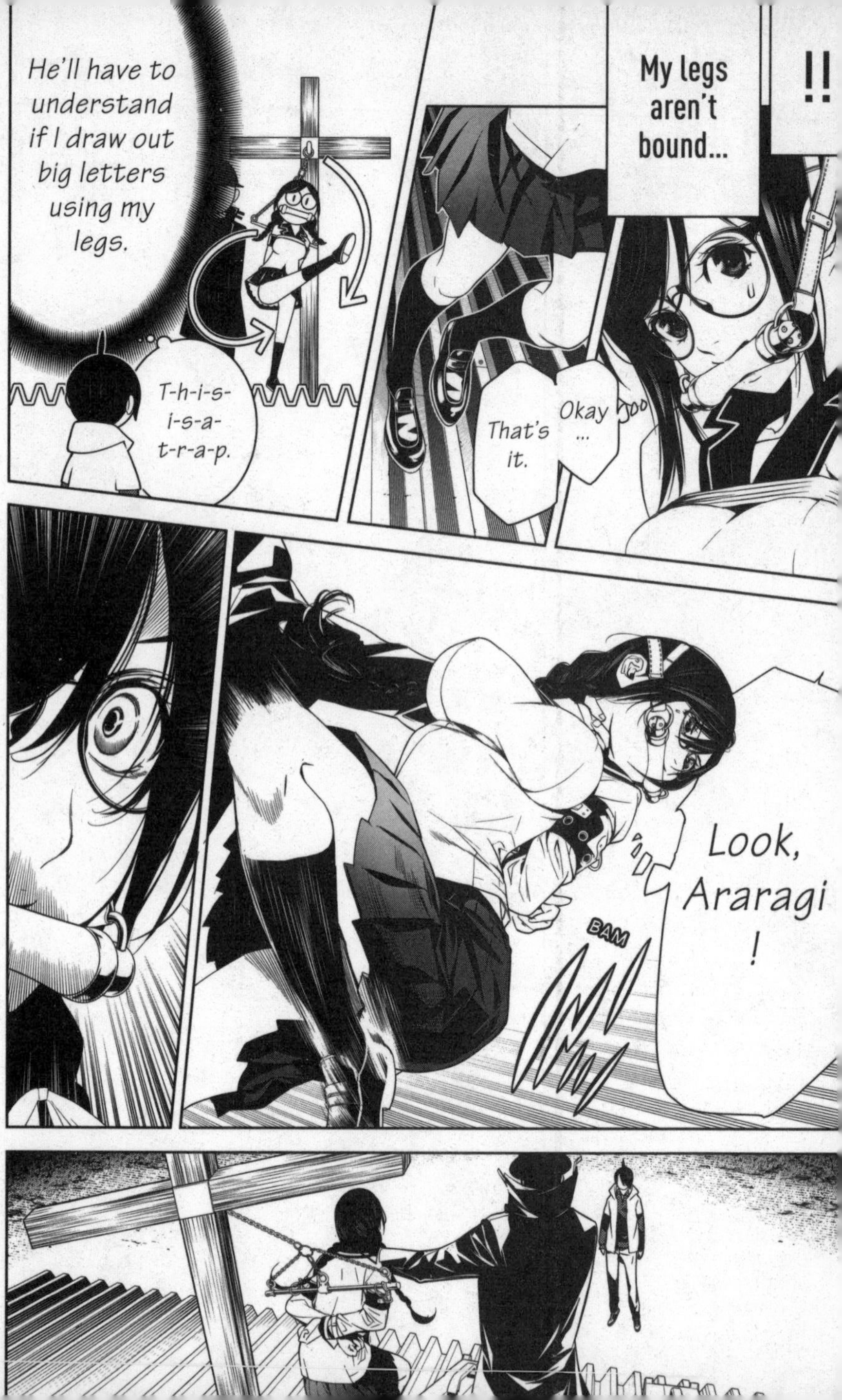
!!
My legs aren't bound...
Okay...
That's it.
He'll have to understand if I draw out big letters using my legs.
T-h-i-s-i-s-a-t-r-a-p.
Look, Araragi!
BAM

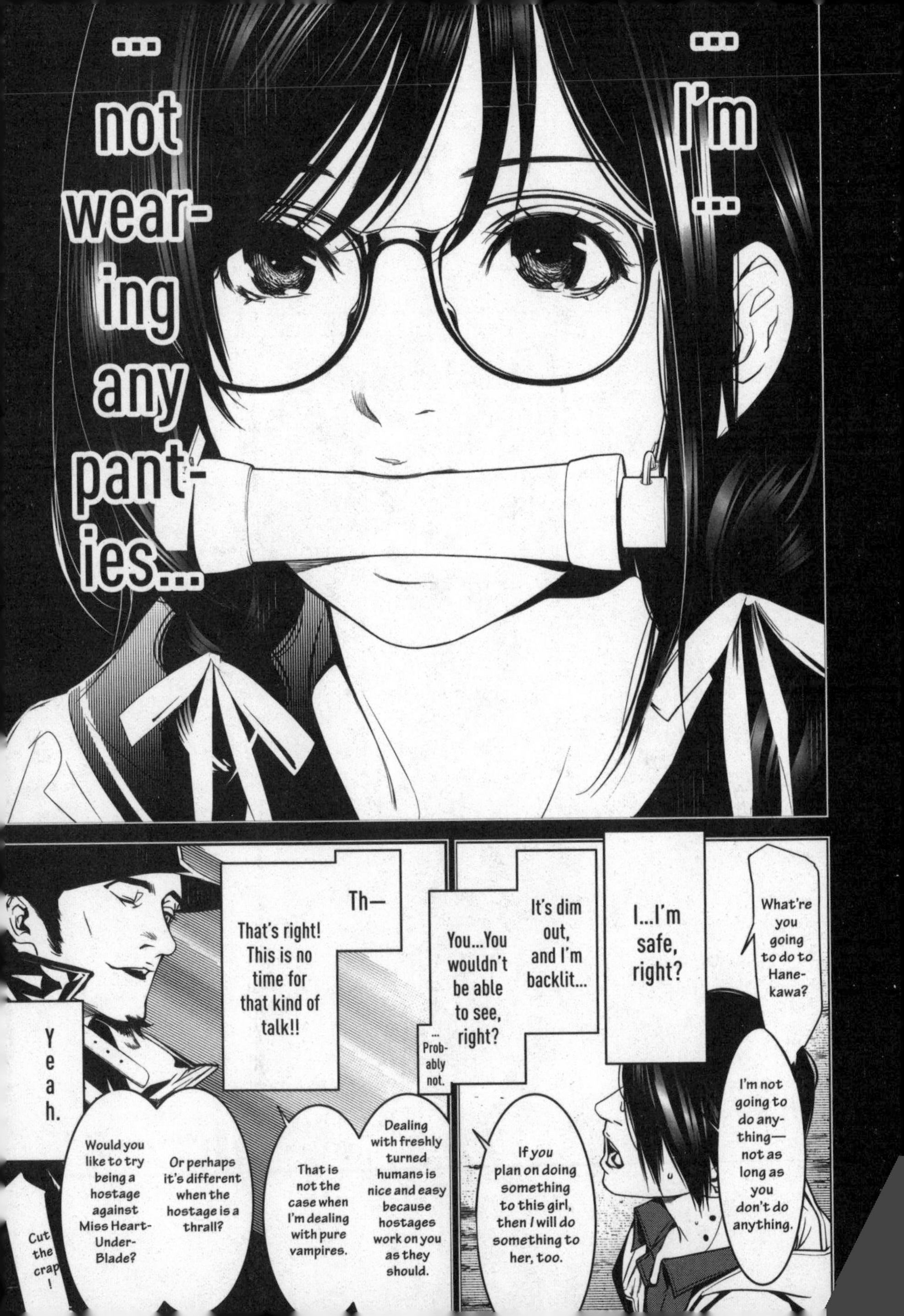

...I'm...
...not wear-ing any pant-ies...
What're you going to do to Hane-kawa?
I...I'm safe, right?
It's dim out, and I'm backlit...
You...You wouldn't be able to see, right?
...Prob-ably not.
I'm not going to do any-thing—not as long as you don't do anything.
If *you* plan on doing something to this girl, then *I* will do something to her, too.
Th—
That's right! This is no time for that kind of talk!!
Yeah.
Dealing with freshly turned humans is nice and easy because hostages work on you as they should.
That is not the case when I'm dealing with pure vampires.
Or perhaps it's different when the hostage is a thrall?
Would you like to try being a hostage against Miss Heart-Under-Blade?
Cut the crap!

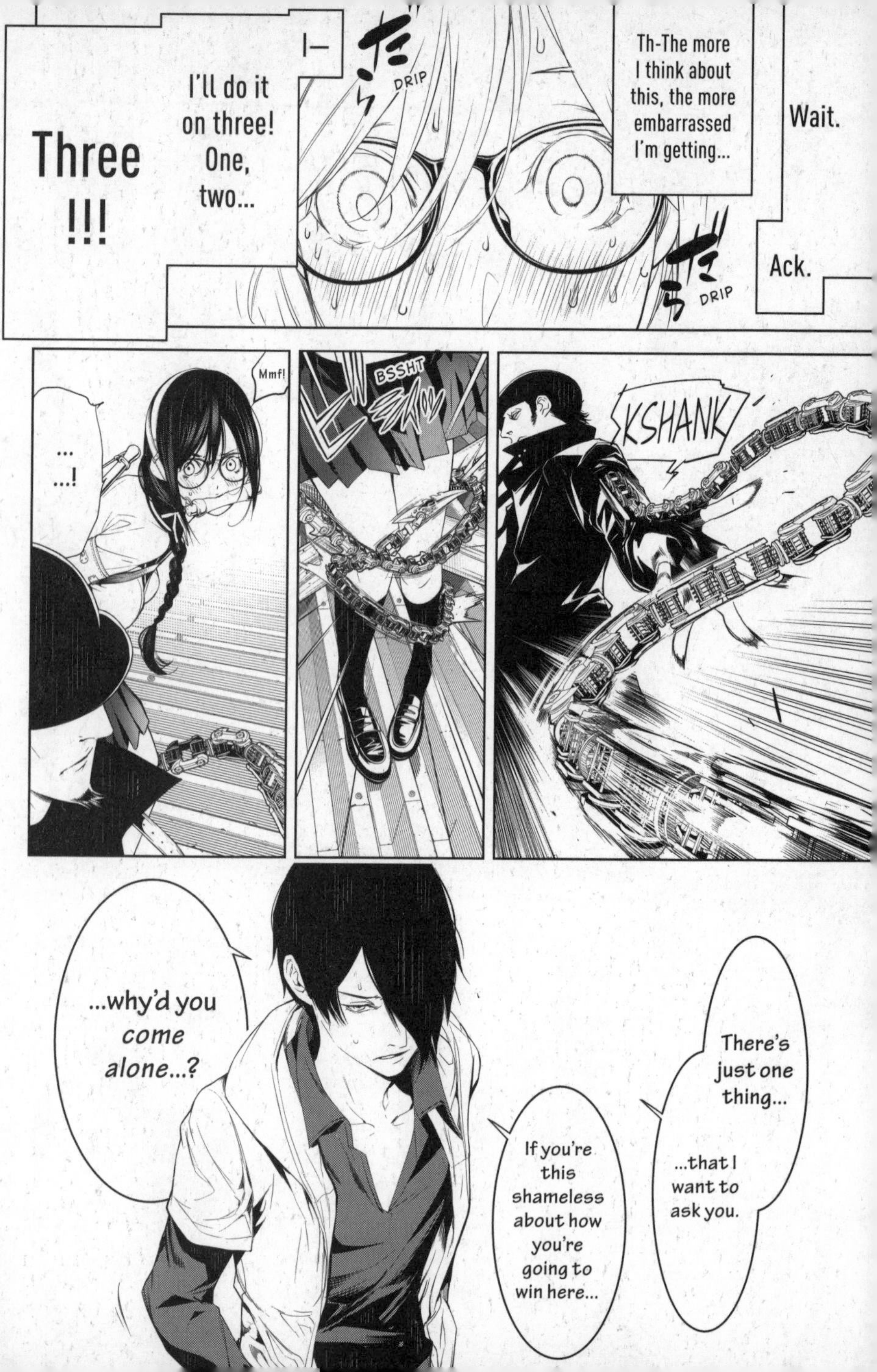
Wait.
Ack.
Th-The more I think about this, the more embarrassed I'm getting...
DRIP
DRIP
I—
I'll do it on three! One, two...
Three!!!
KSHANK
BSSHT
Mmf!
... ...!
There's just one thing...
...that I want to ask you.
If you're this shameless about how you're going to win here...
...why'd you come alone...?

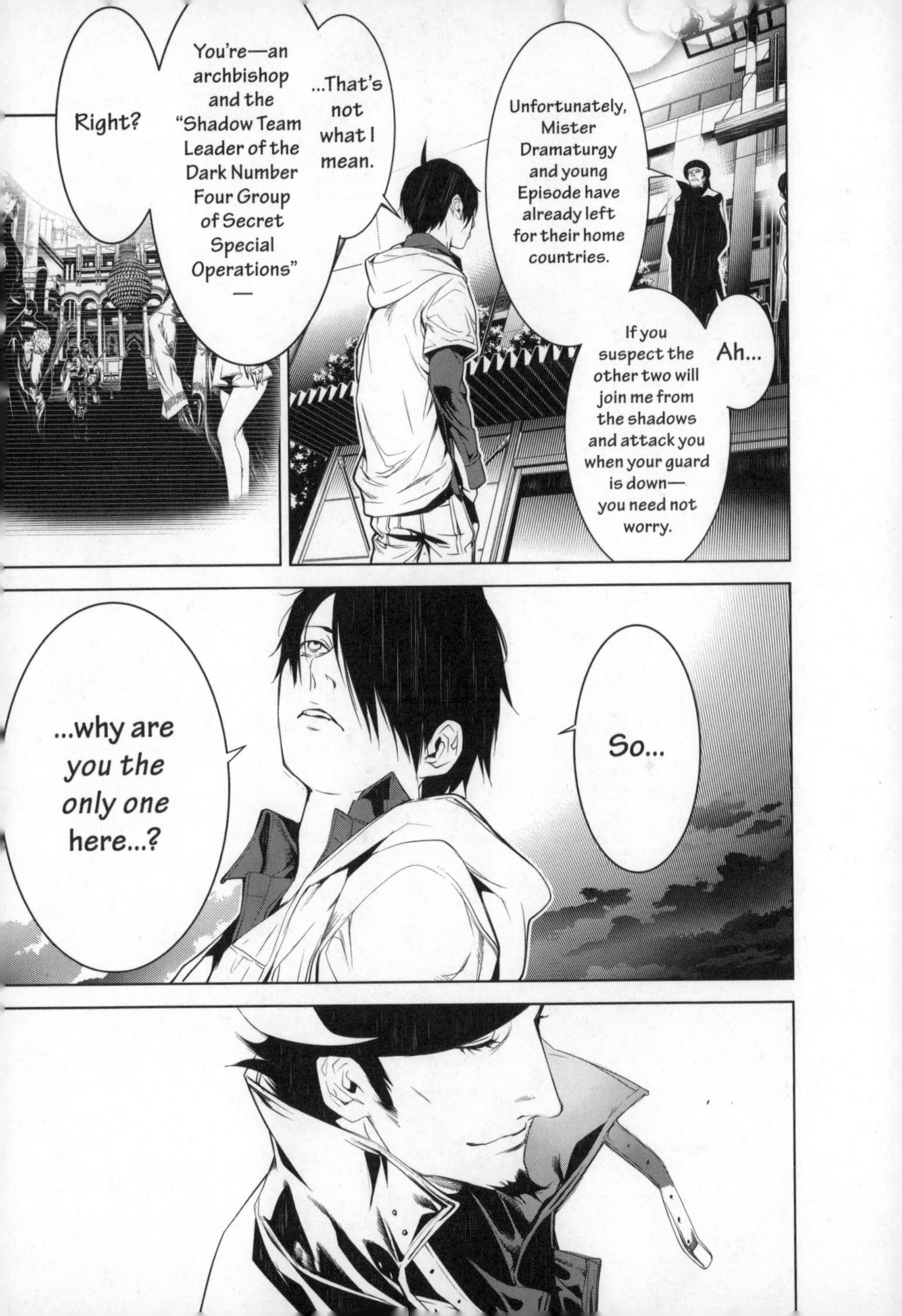
Unfortunately, Mister Dramaturgy and young Episode have already left for their home countries.
Ah...
If you suspect the other two will join me from the shadows and attack you when your guard is down—you need not worry.
...That's not what I mean.
You're—an archbishop and the "Shadow Team Leader of the Dark Number Four Group of Secret Special Operations"—
Right?
So...
...why are you the only one here...?

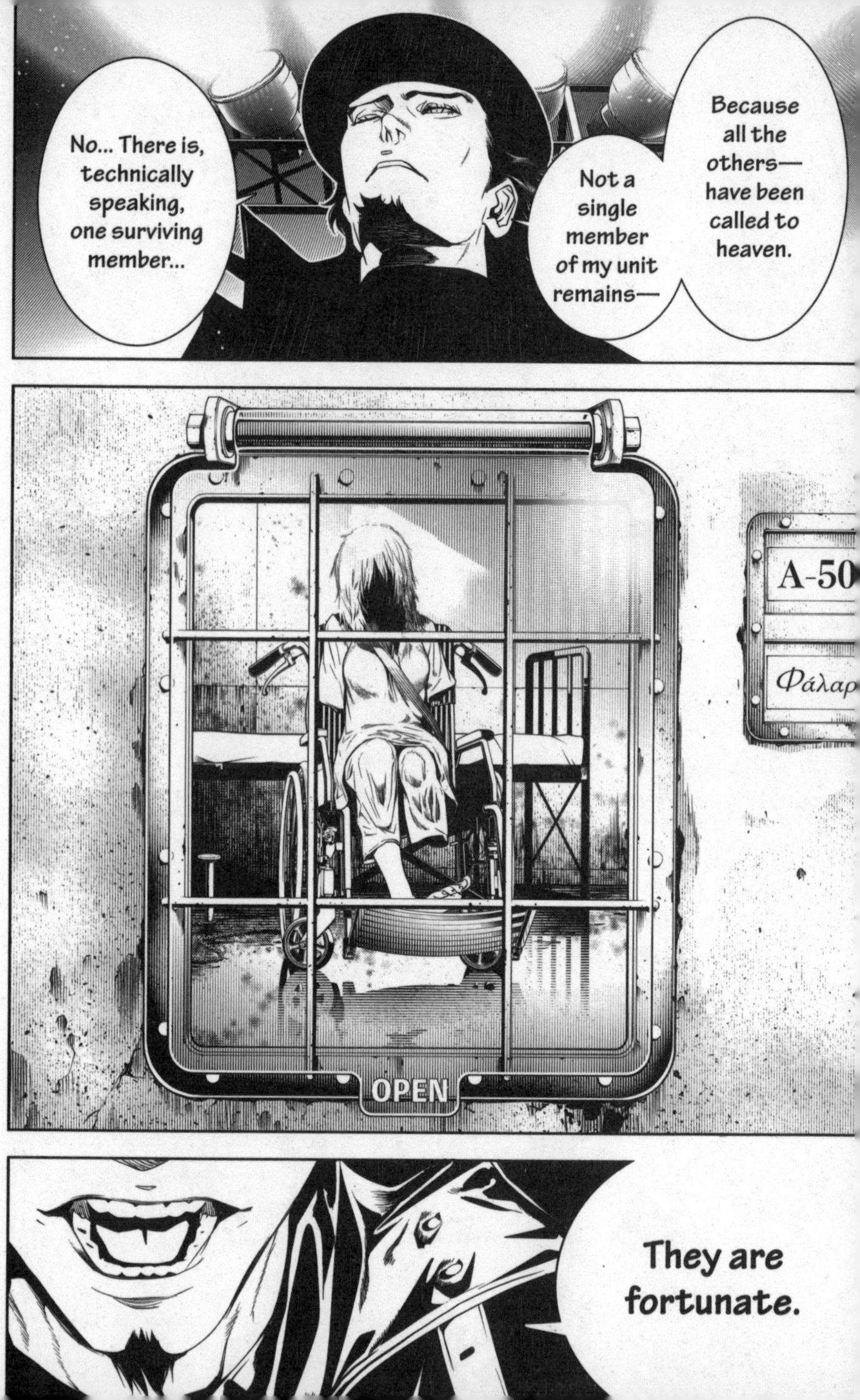
Because all the others— have been called to heaven.
Not a single member of my unit remains—
No... There is, technically speaking, one surviving member...
A-50
OPEN
They are fortunate.

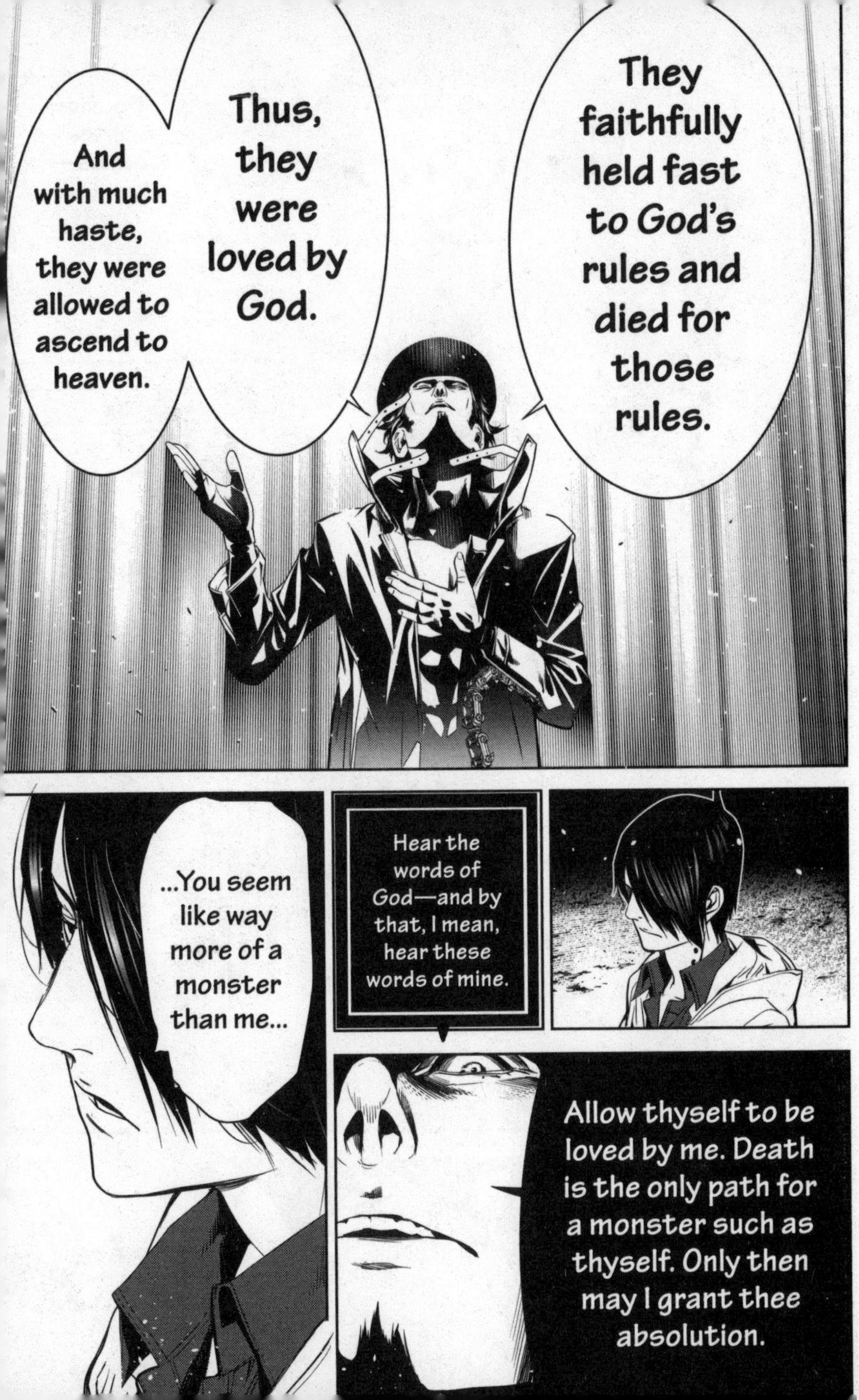
They faithfully held fast to God's rules and died for those rules.
Thus, they were loved by God.
And with much haste, they were allowed to ascend to heaven.
Hear the words of God—and by that, I mean, hear these words of mine.
Allow thyself to be loved by me. Death is the only path for a monster such as thyself. Only then may I grant thee absolution.
...You seem like way more of a monster than me...

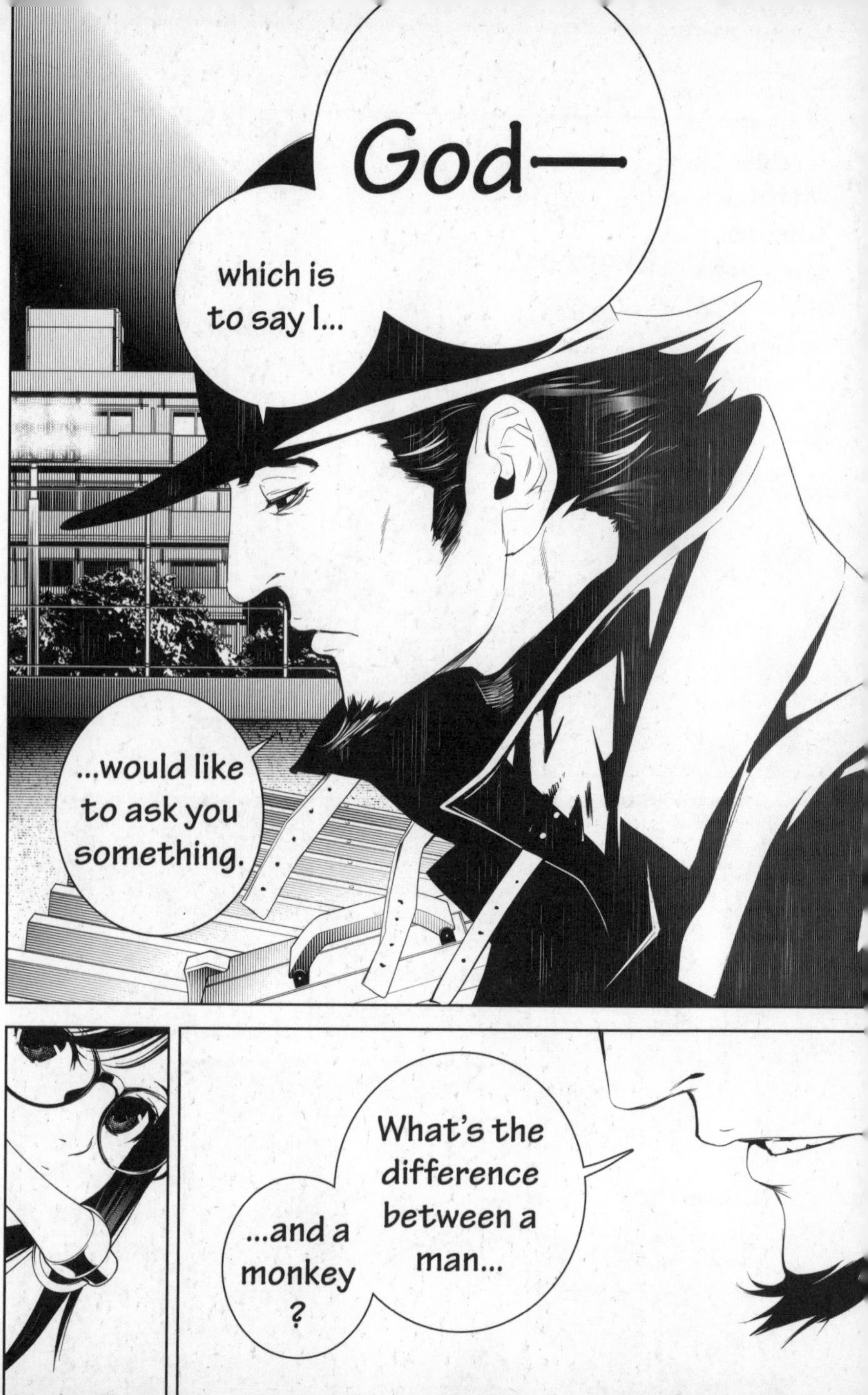
God—
which is to say I...
...would like to ask you something.
What's the difference between a man...
...and a monkey ?

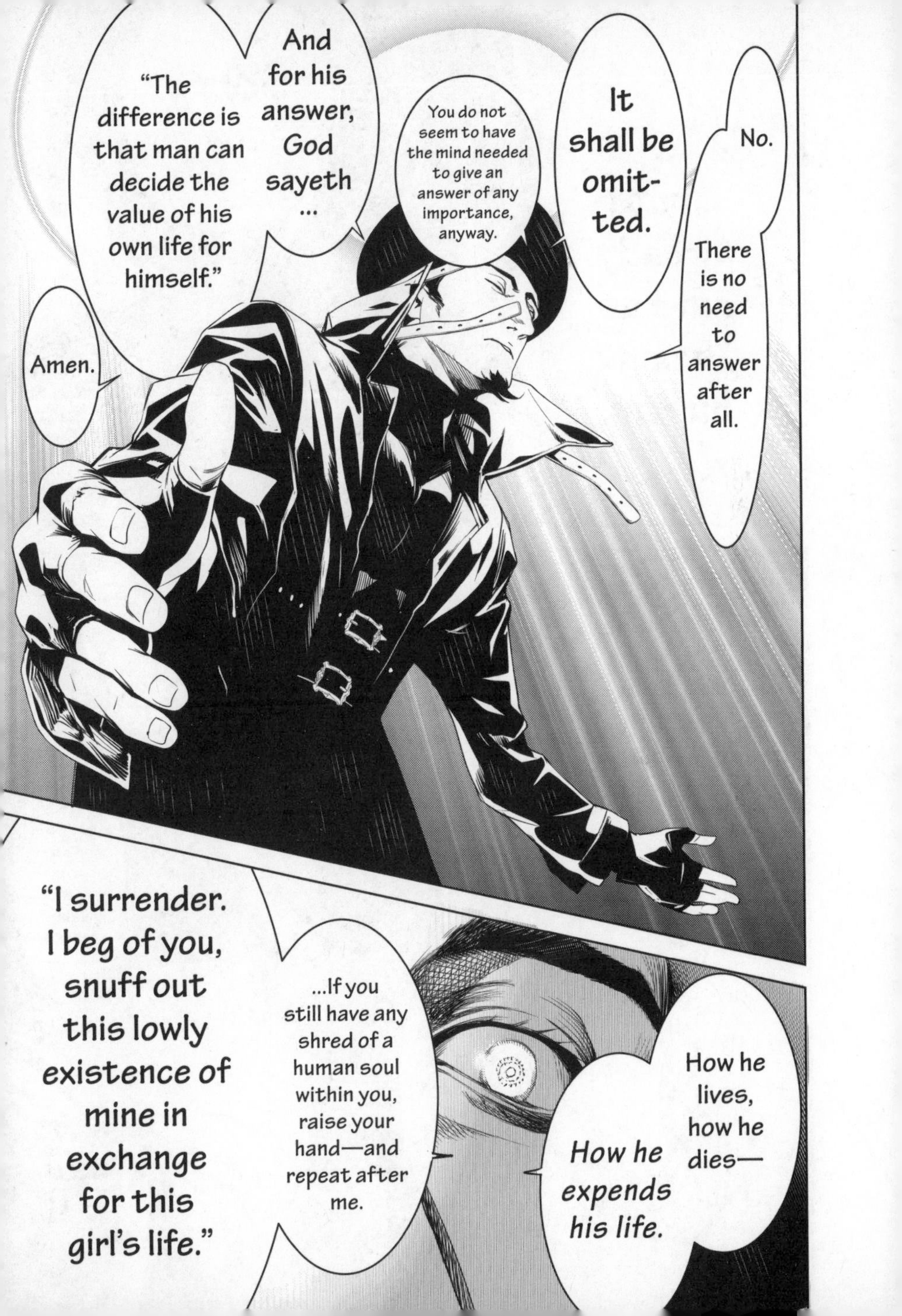
No.
There is no need to answer after all.
It shall be omitted.
You do not seem to have the mind needed to give an answer of any importance, anyway.
And for his answer, God sayeth ...
"The difference is that man can decide the value of his own life for himself."
Amen.
How he lives, how he dies—
How he expends his life.
...If you still have any shred of a human soul within you, raise your hand—and repeat after me.
"I surrender. I beg of you, snuff out this lowly existence of mine in exchange for this girl's life."

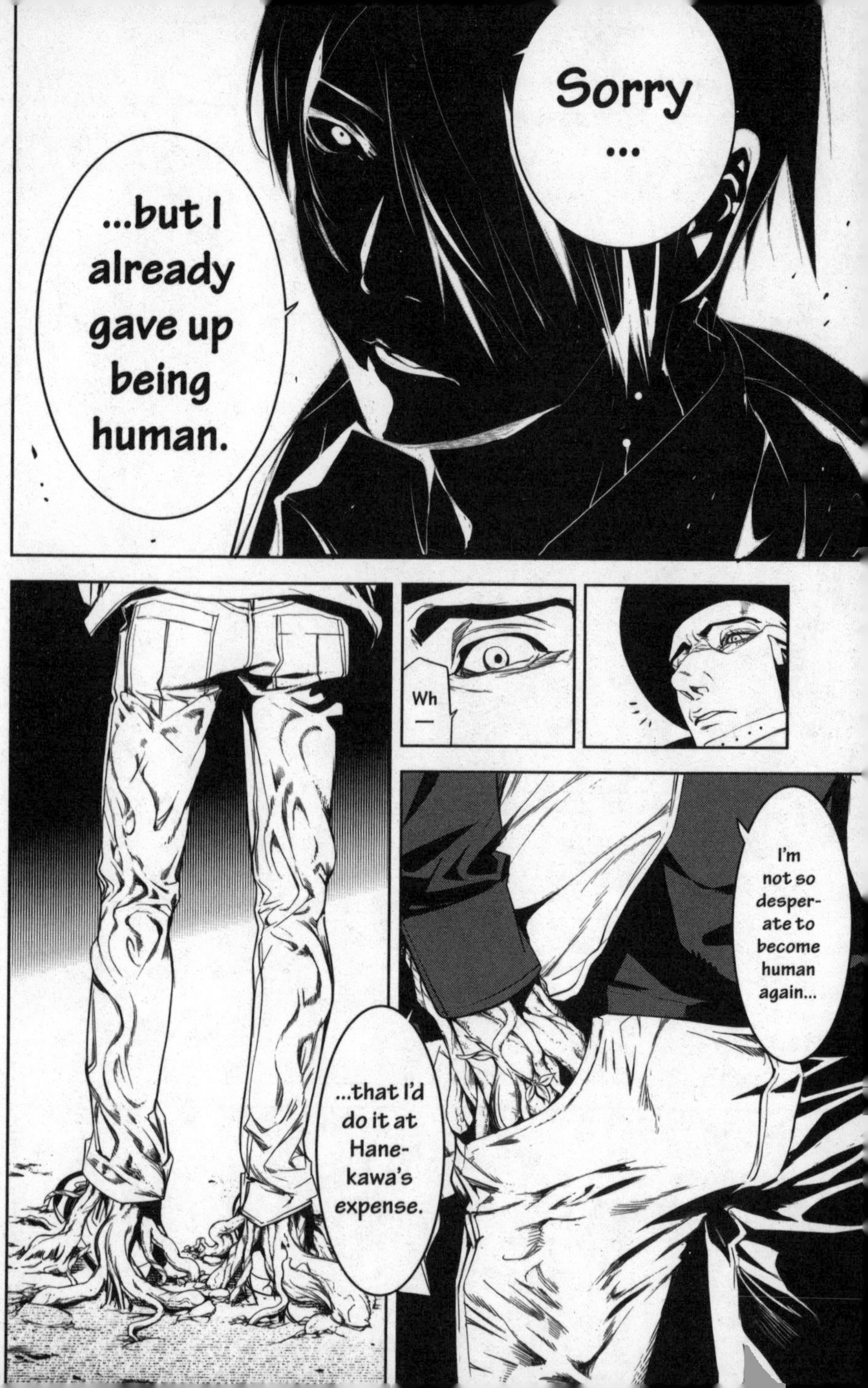
Sorry ...
...but I already gave up being human.
Wh—
I'm not so desperate to become human again...
...that I'd do it at Hanekawa's expense.

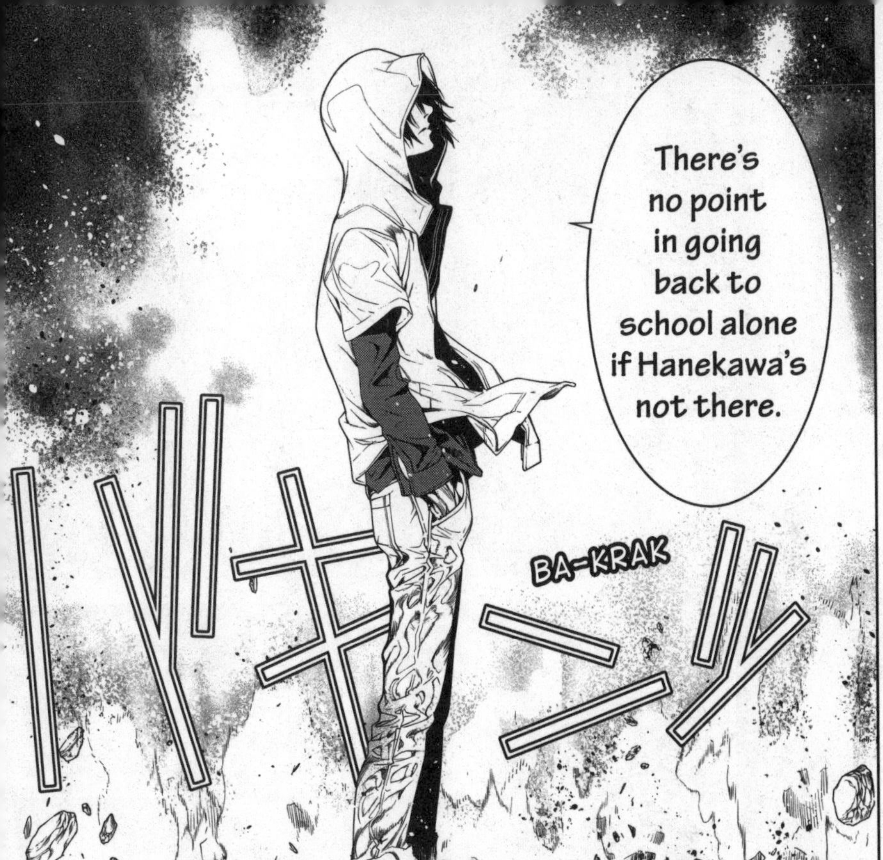
There's no point in going back to school alone if Hanekawa's not there.
バキーンッ
BA-KRAK
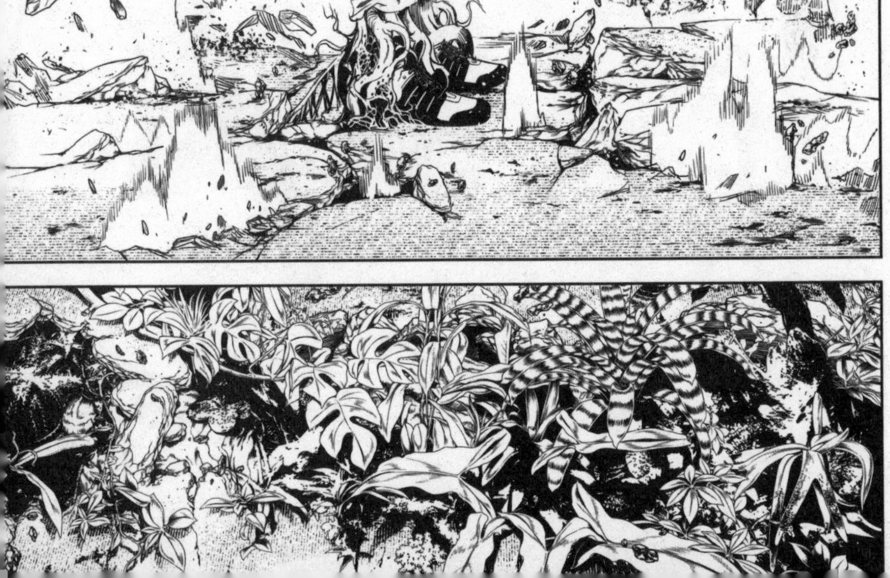

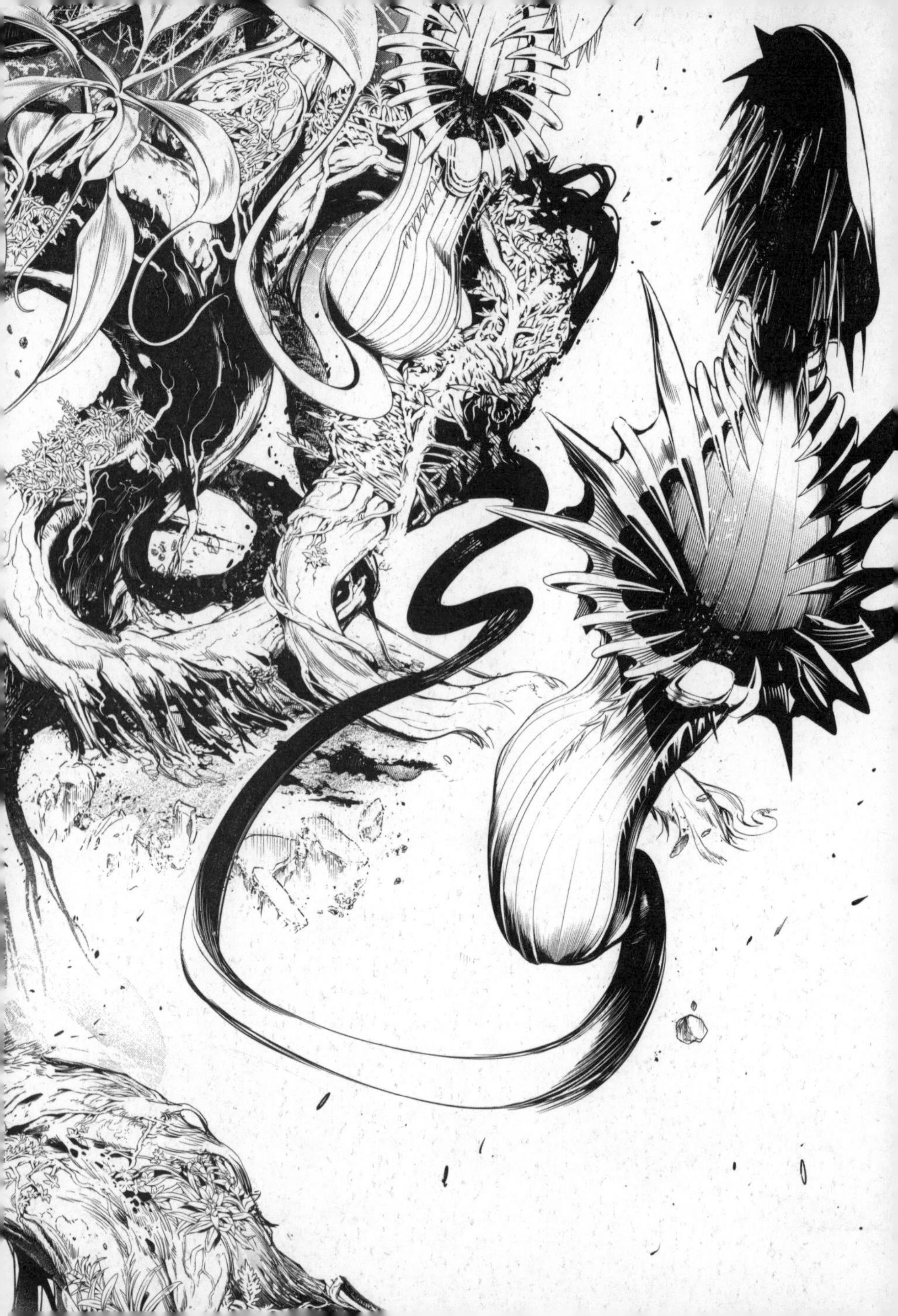

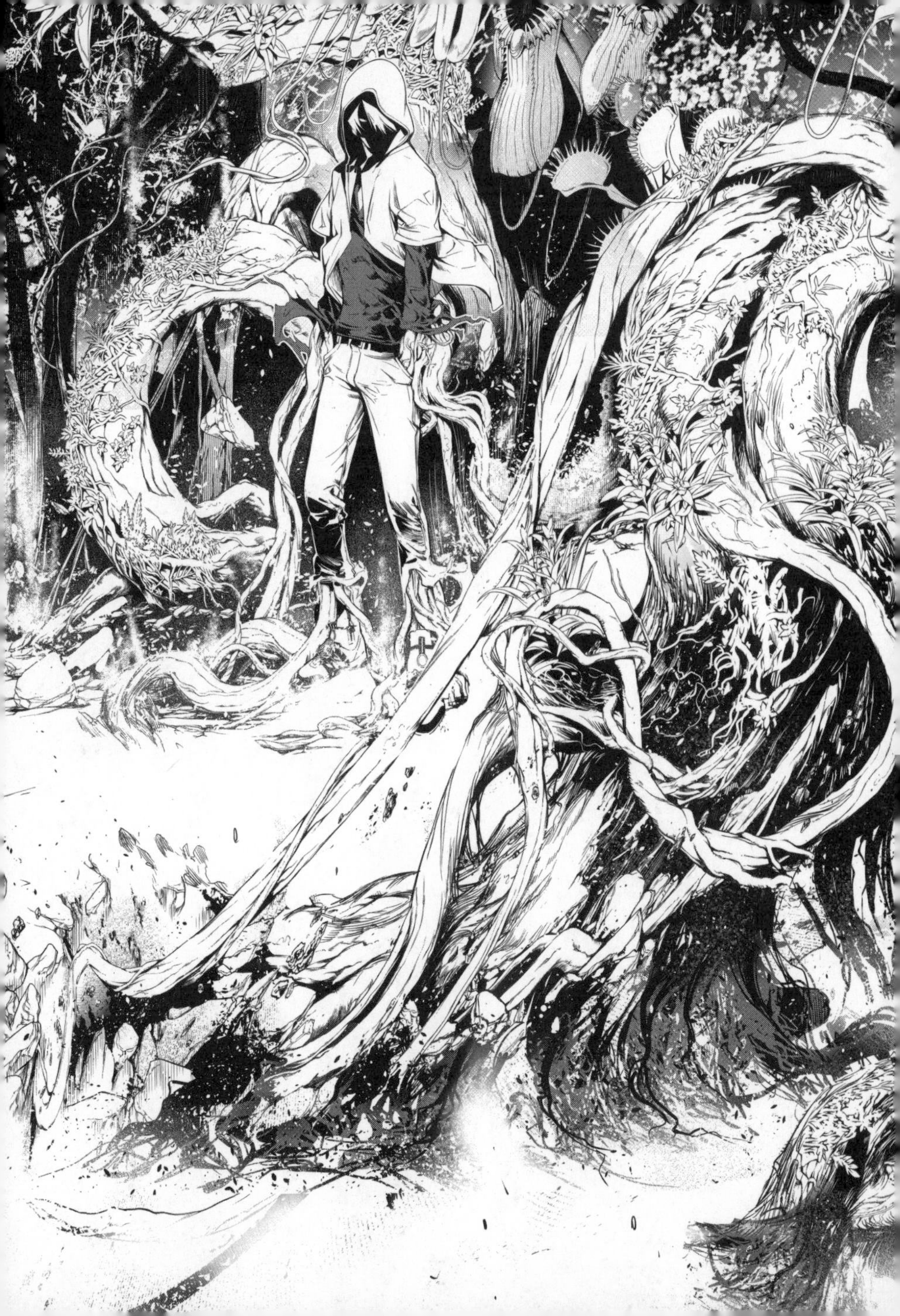

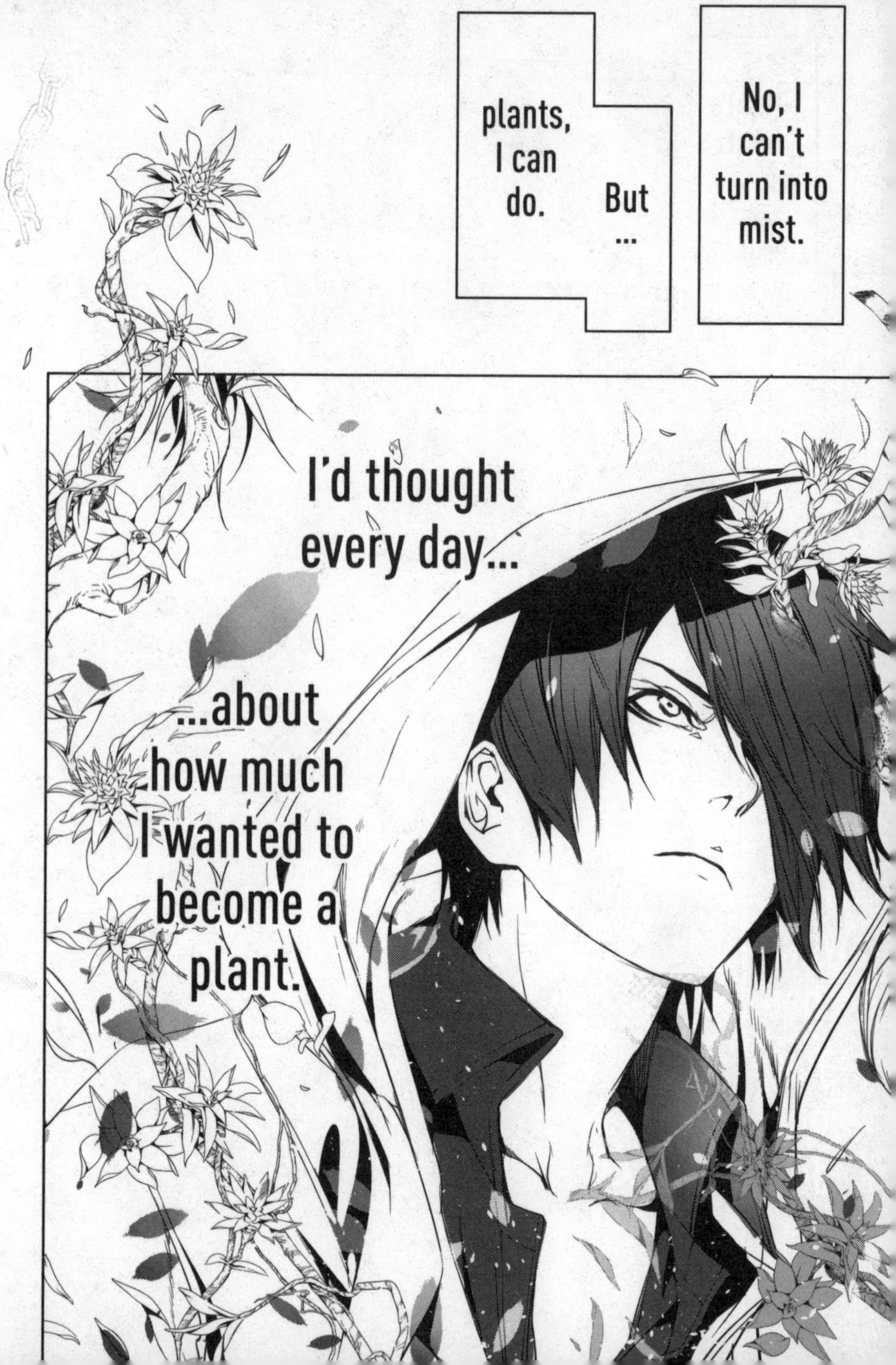
No, I can't turn into mist.
But ...
plants, I can do.
I'd thought every day...
...about how much I wanted to become a plant.

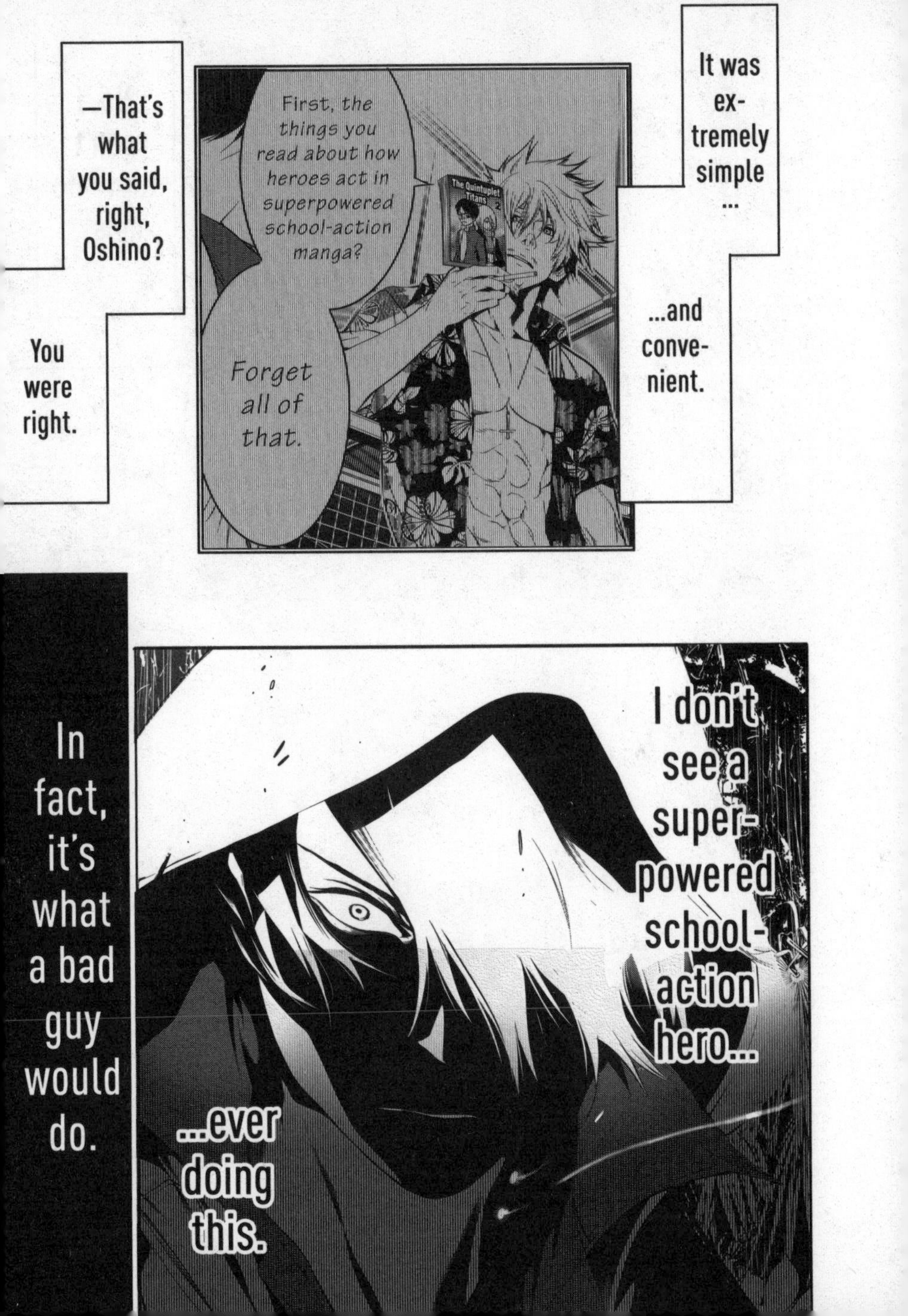
It was extremely simple...
...and convenient.
First, the things you read about how heroes act in superpowered school-action manga?
The Quintuplet Titans 2
Forget all of that.
—That's what you said, right, Oshino?
You were right.
I don't see a super-powered school-action hero...
...ever doing this.
In fact, it's what a bad guy would do.

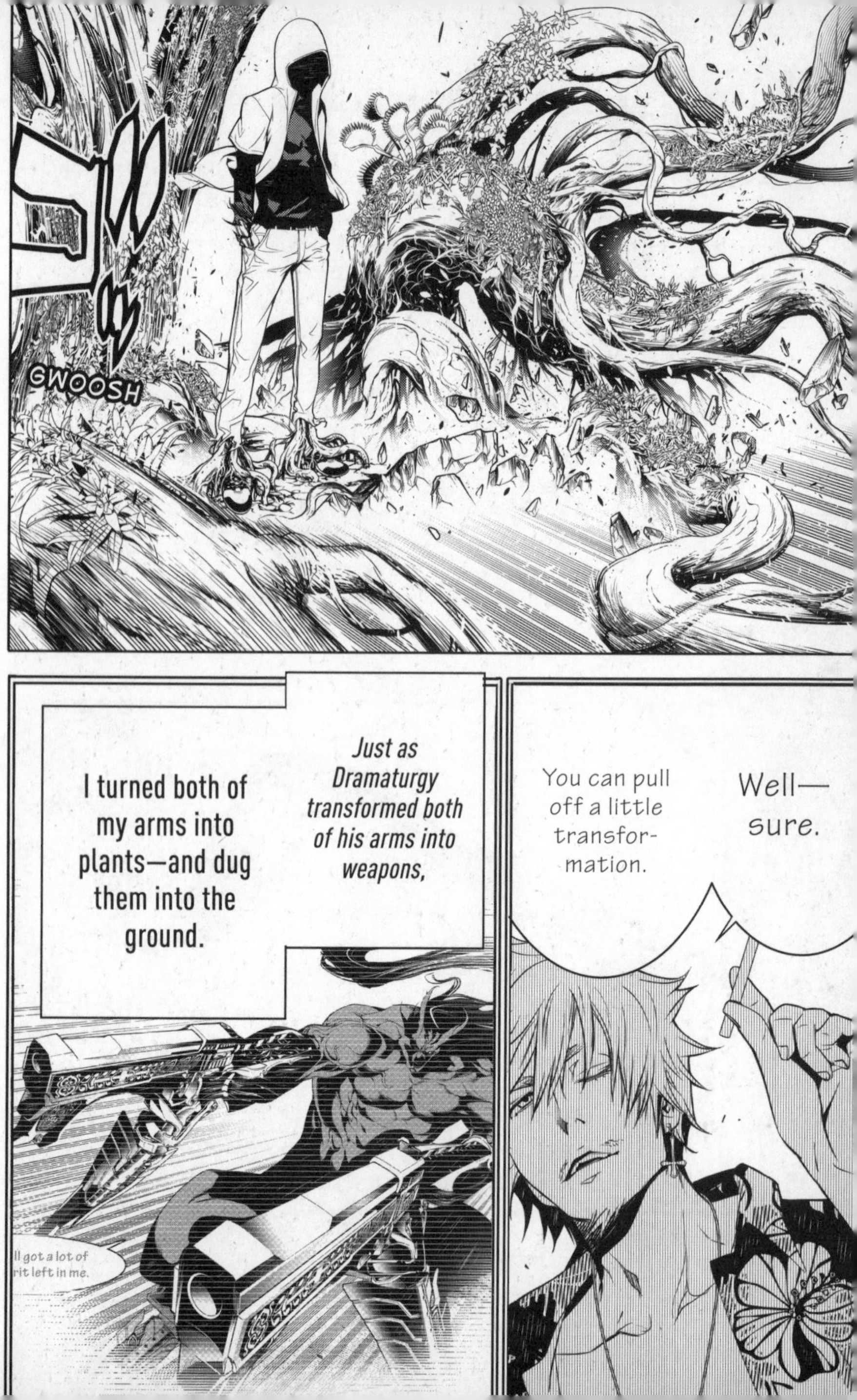
GWOOSH
Well— sure.
You can pull off a little transformation.
Just as Dramaturgy transformed both of his arms into weapons,
I turned both of my arms into plants—and dug them into the ground.
ll got a lot of rit left in me.

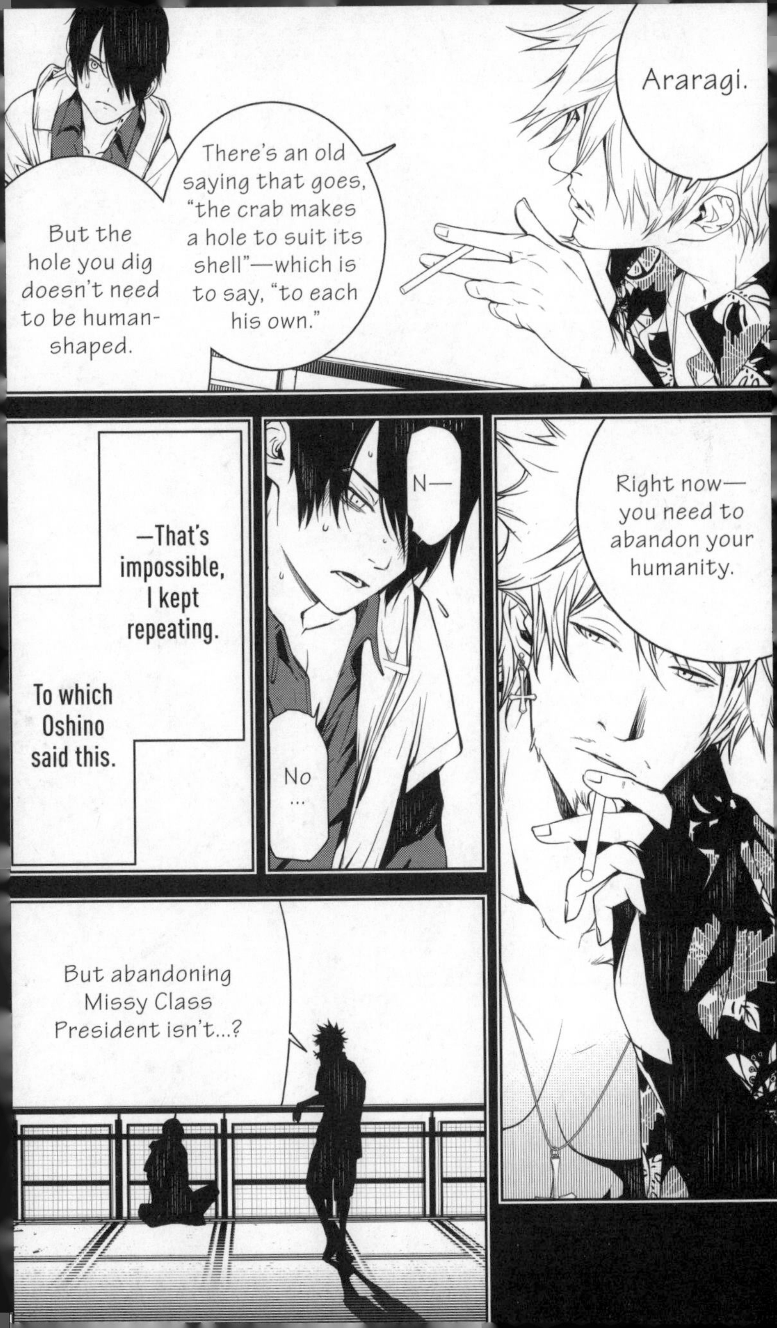
Araragi.
There's an old saying that goes, "the crab makes a hole to suit its shell"—which is to say, "to each his own."
But the hole you dig doesn't need to be human-shaped.
Right now—you need to abandon your humanity.
N—
No ...
—That's impossible, I kept repeating.
To which Oshino said this.
But abandoning Missy Class President isn't...?

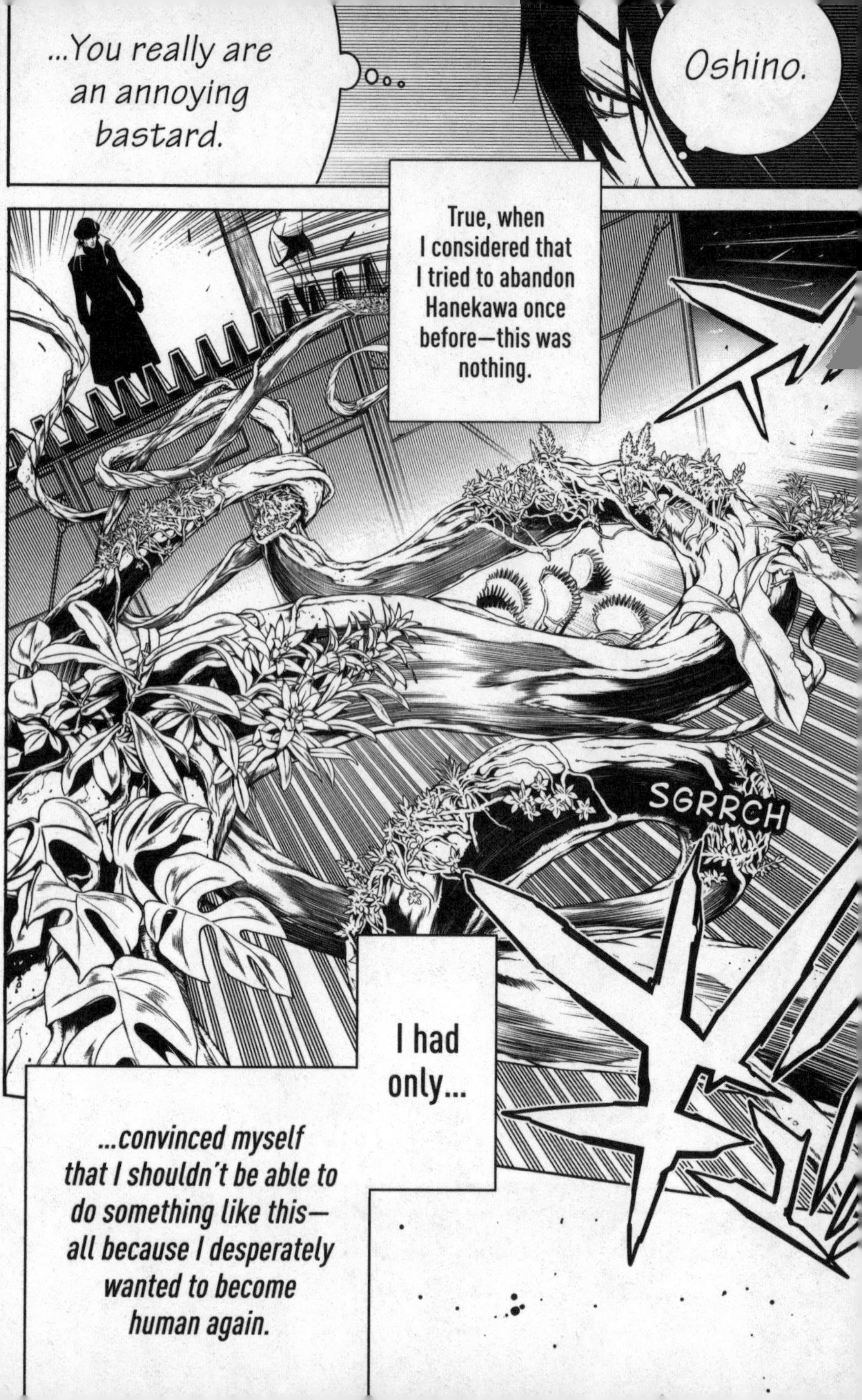
Oshino.
...You really are an annoying bastard.
True, when I considered that I tried to abandon Hanekawa once before—this was nothing.
SGRRCH
I had only...
...convinced myself that I shouldn't be able to do something like this—all because I desperately wanted to become human again.

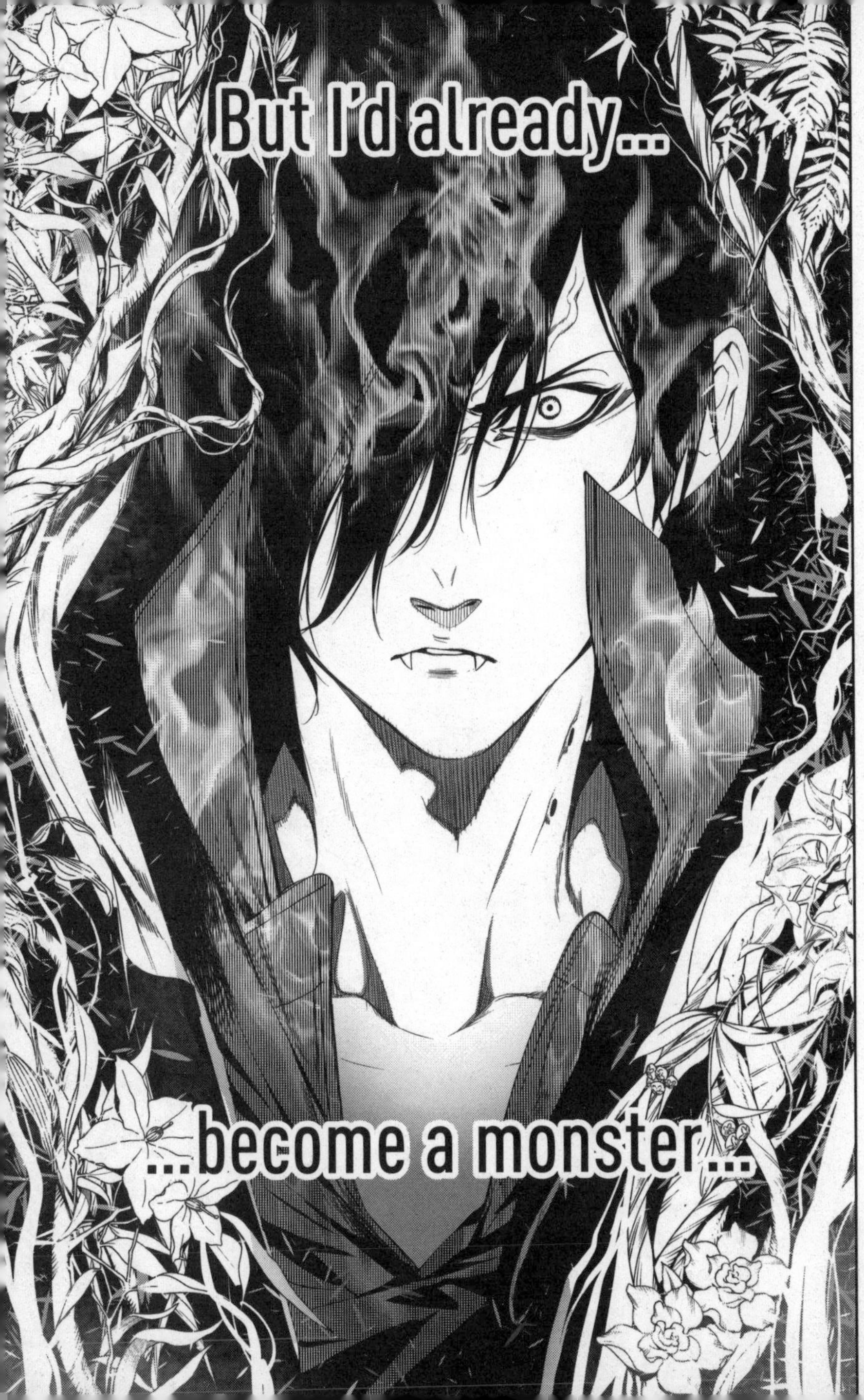
But I'd already...
...become a monster...

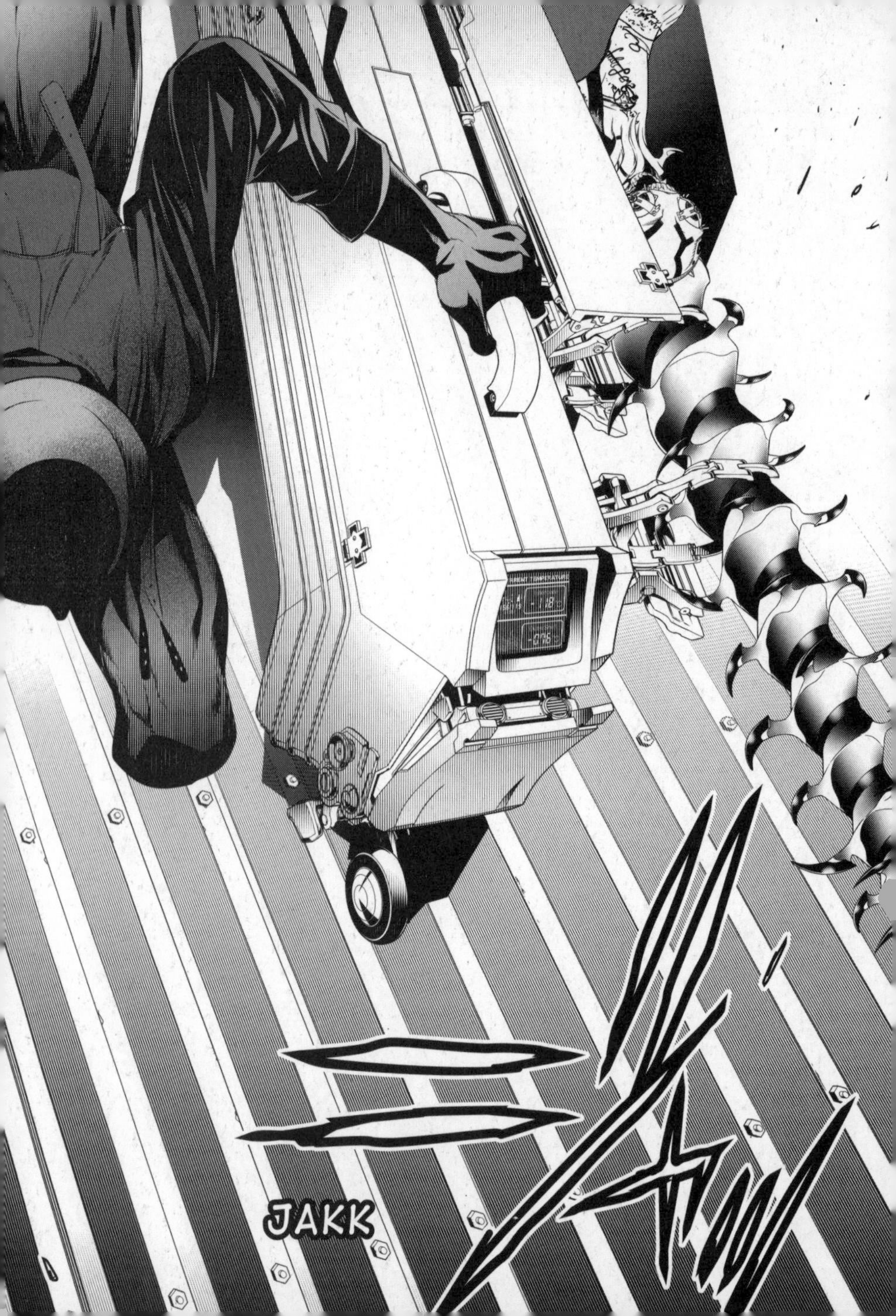
JAKK

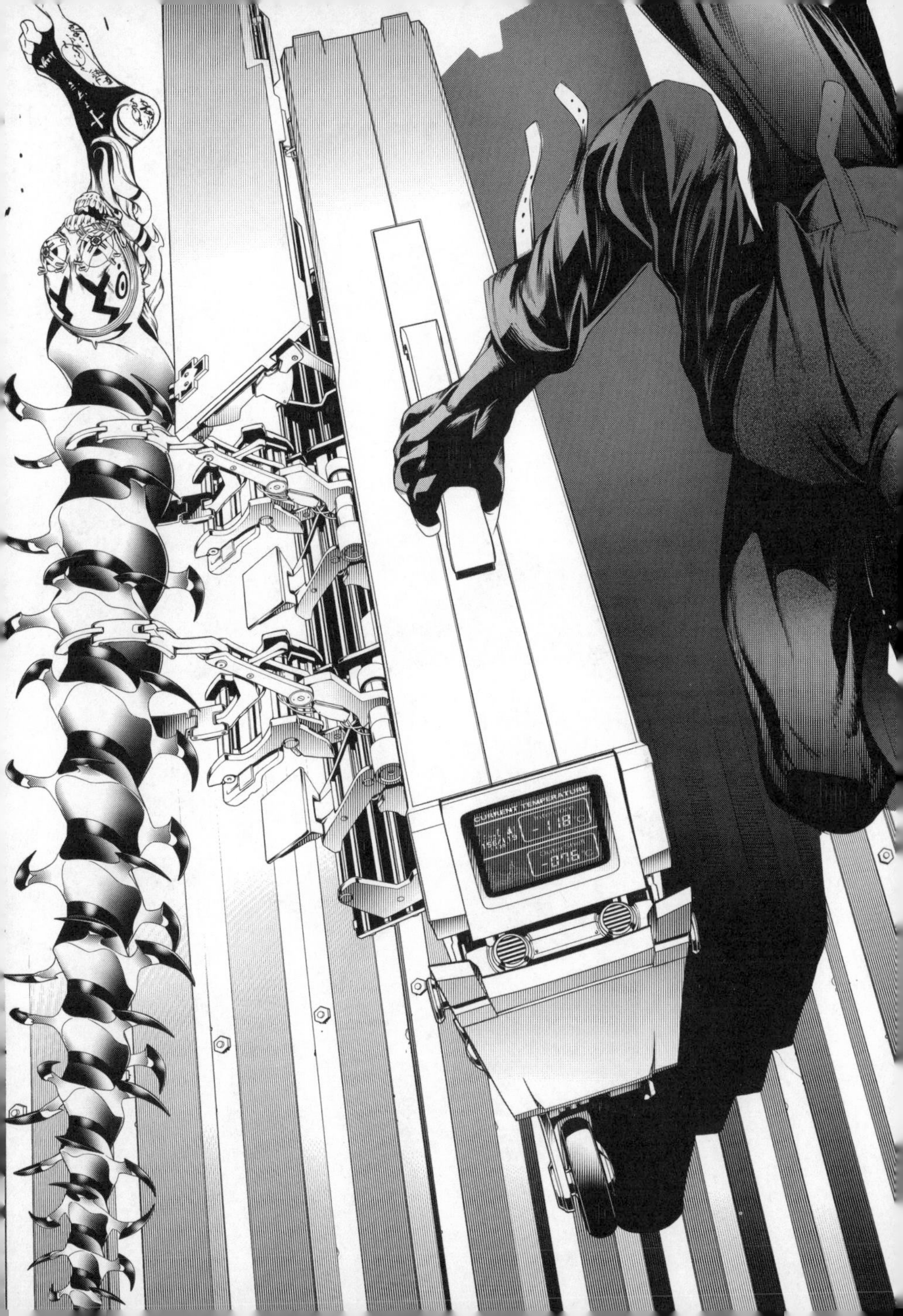

CURRENT TEMPERATURE
-118
-076

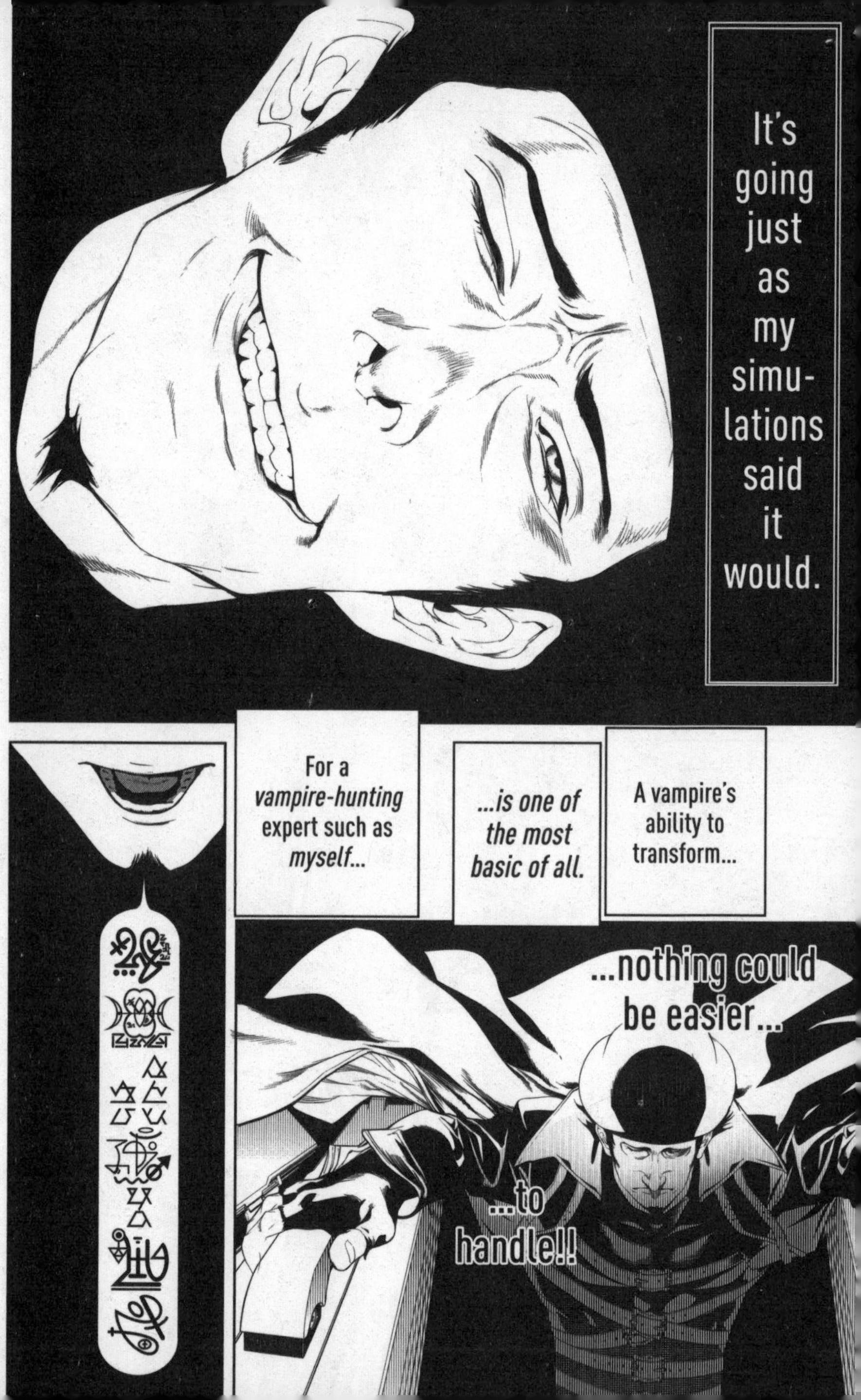
It's going just as my simu-lations said it would.
A vampire's ability to transform...
...is one of the most basic of all.
For a *vampire-hunting* expert such as *myself*...
...nothing could be easier...
...to handle!!

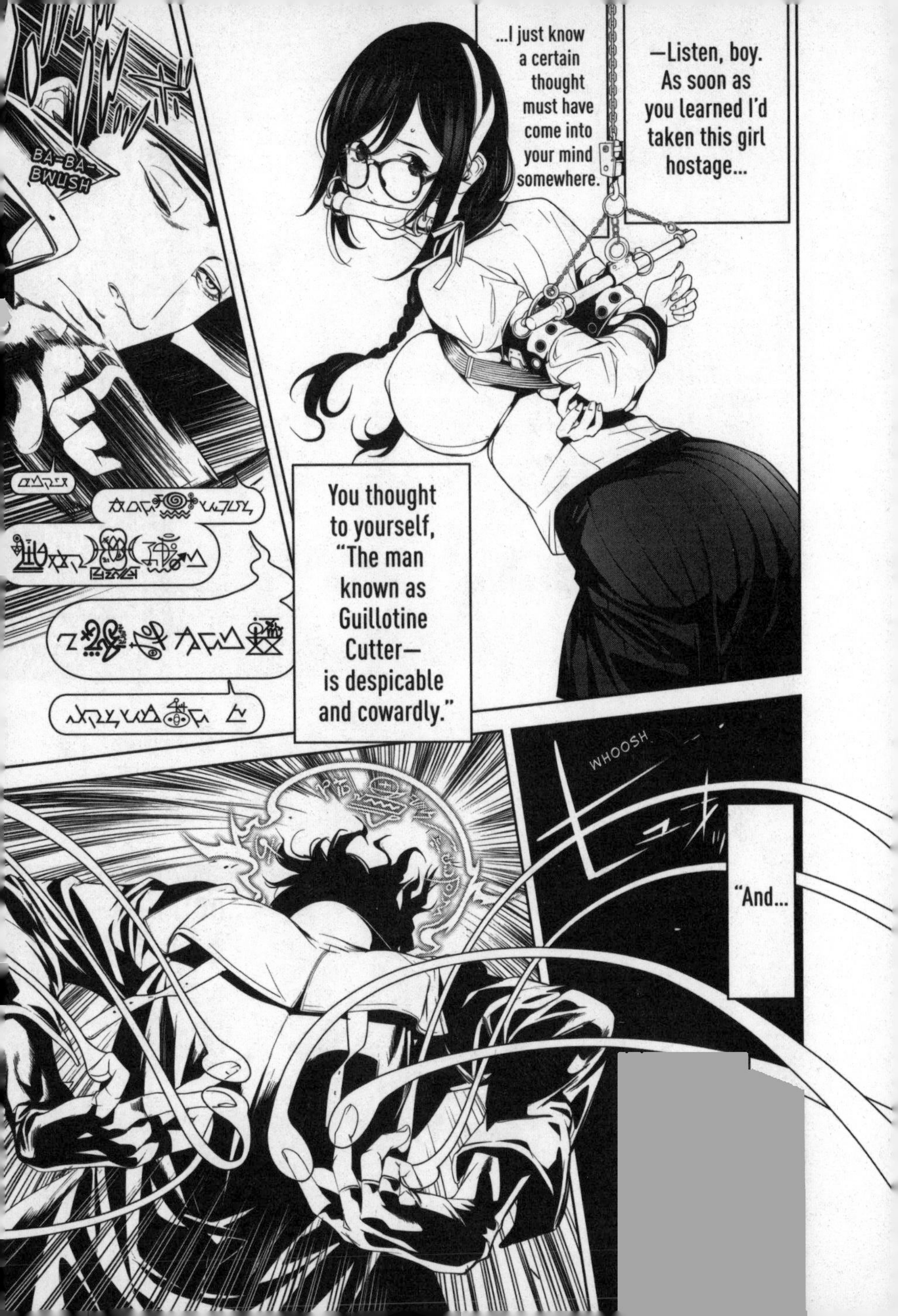
—Listen, boy. As soon as you learned I'd taken this girl hostage...
...I just know a certain thought must have come into your mind somewhere.
You thought to yourself, "The man known as Guillotine Cutter—is despicable and cowardly."
BA-BA-BWUSH
WHOOSH
"And...

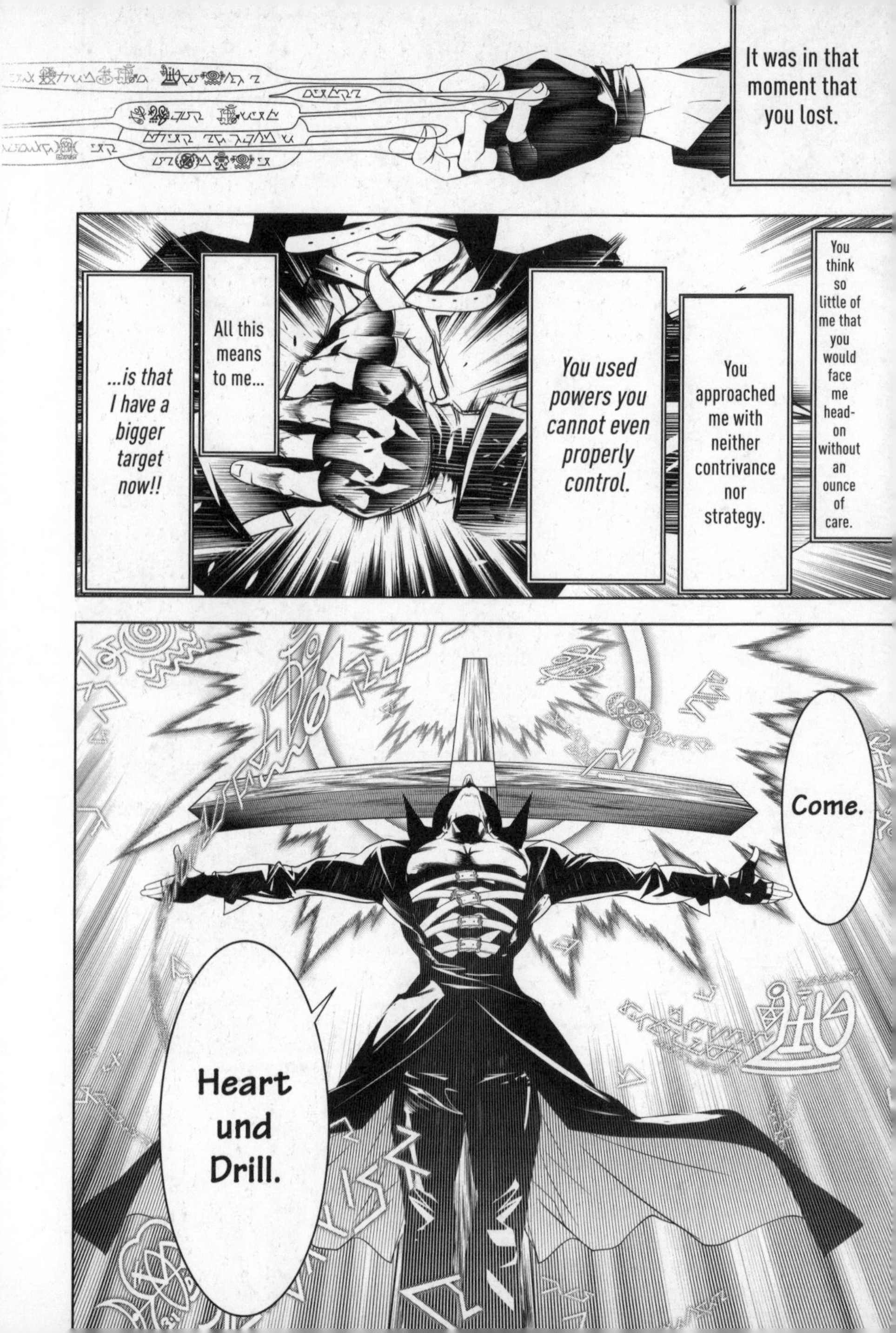
It was in that moment that you lost.
You think so little of me that you would face me head-on without an ounce of care.
You approached me with neither contrivance nor strategy.
You used powers you cannot even properly control.
All this means to me...
...is that I have a bigger target now!!
Come.
Heart und Drill.

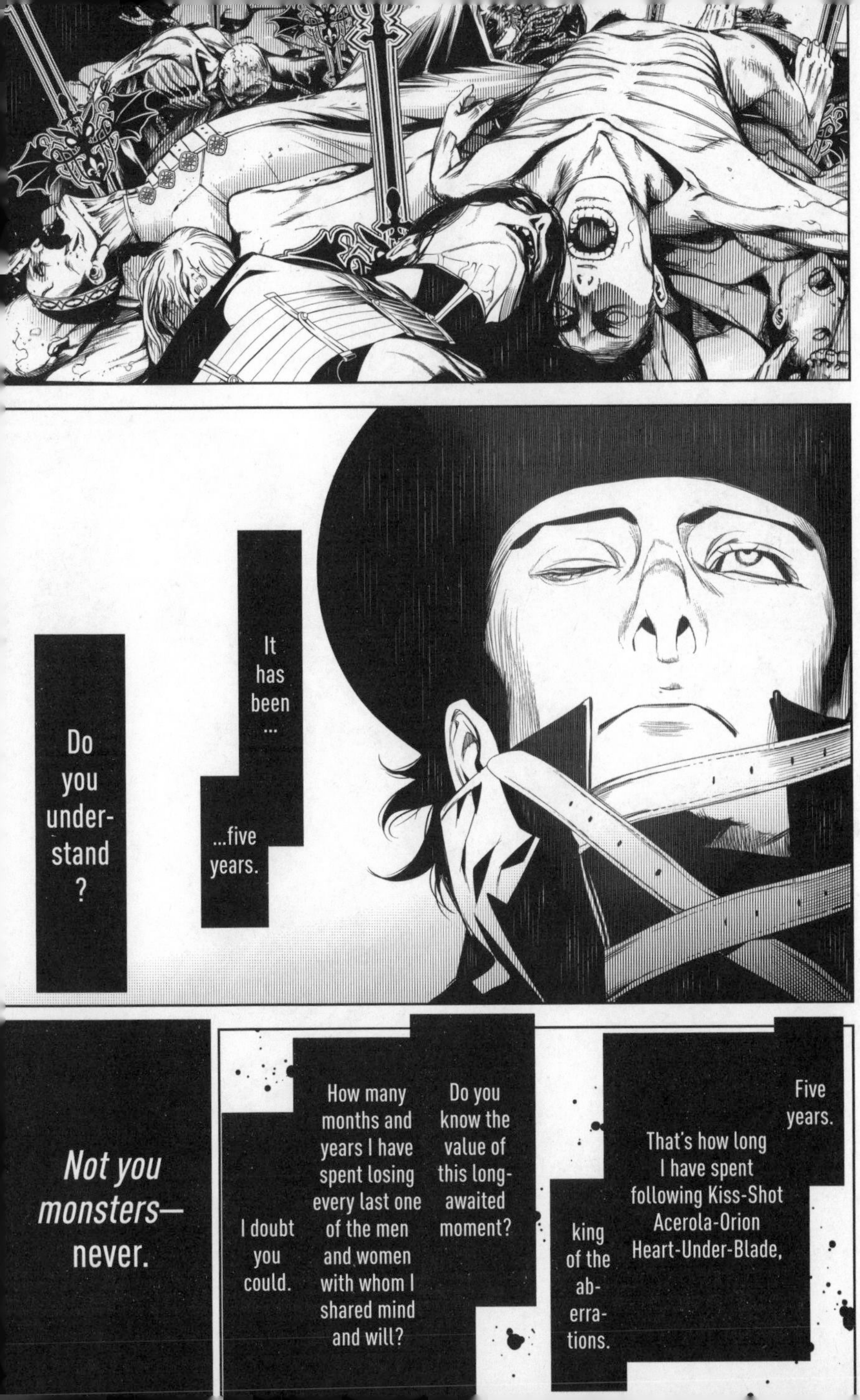
It has been...
...five years.
Do you understand?
Five years.
That's how long I have spent following Kiss-Shot Acerola-Orion Heart-Under-Blade,
king of the aberrations.
Do you know the value of this long-awaited moment?
How many months and years I have spent losing every last one of the men and women with whom I shared mind and will?
I doubt you could.
Not you monsters—
never.

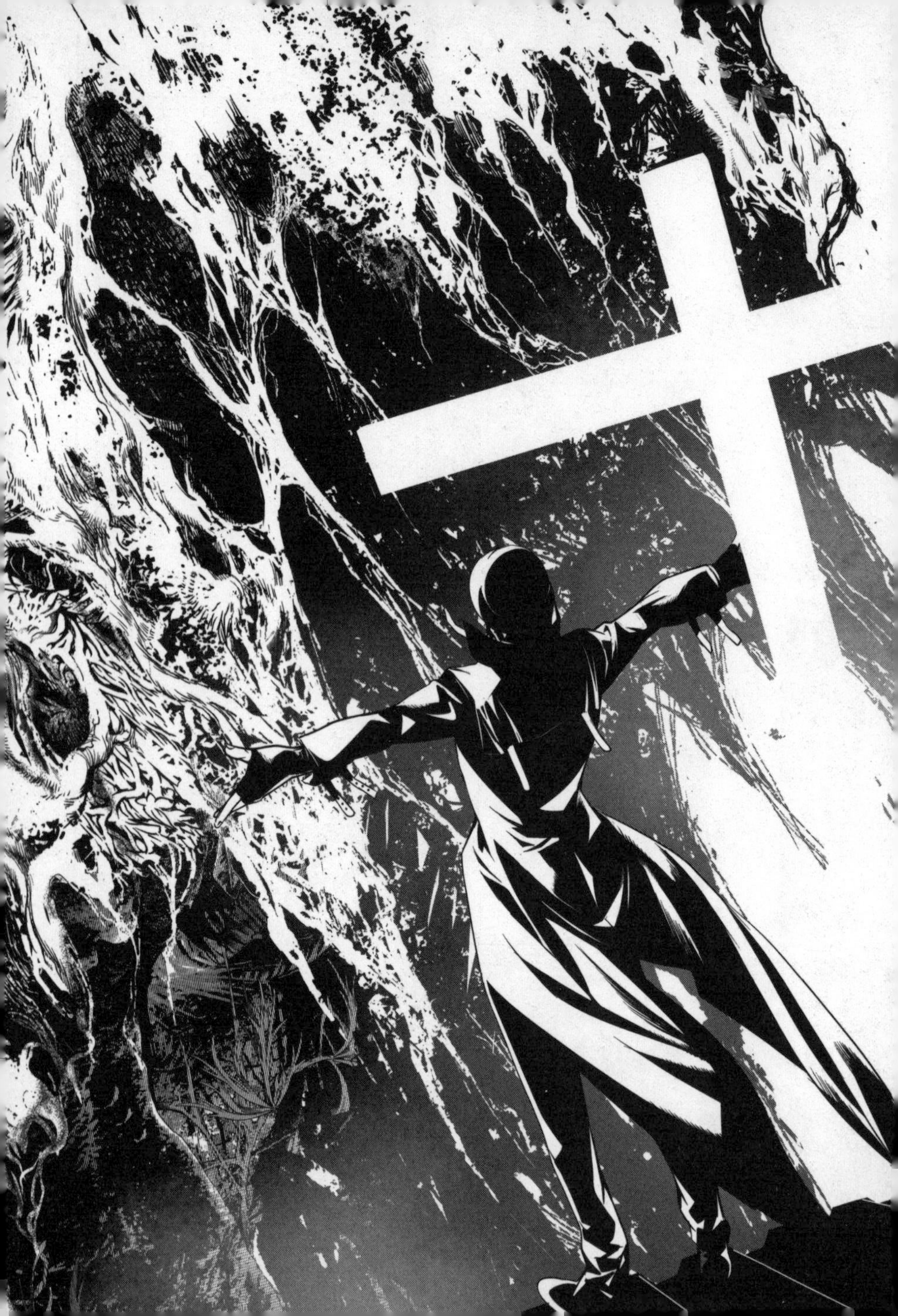

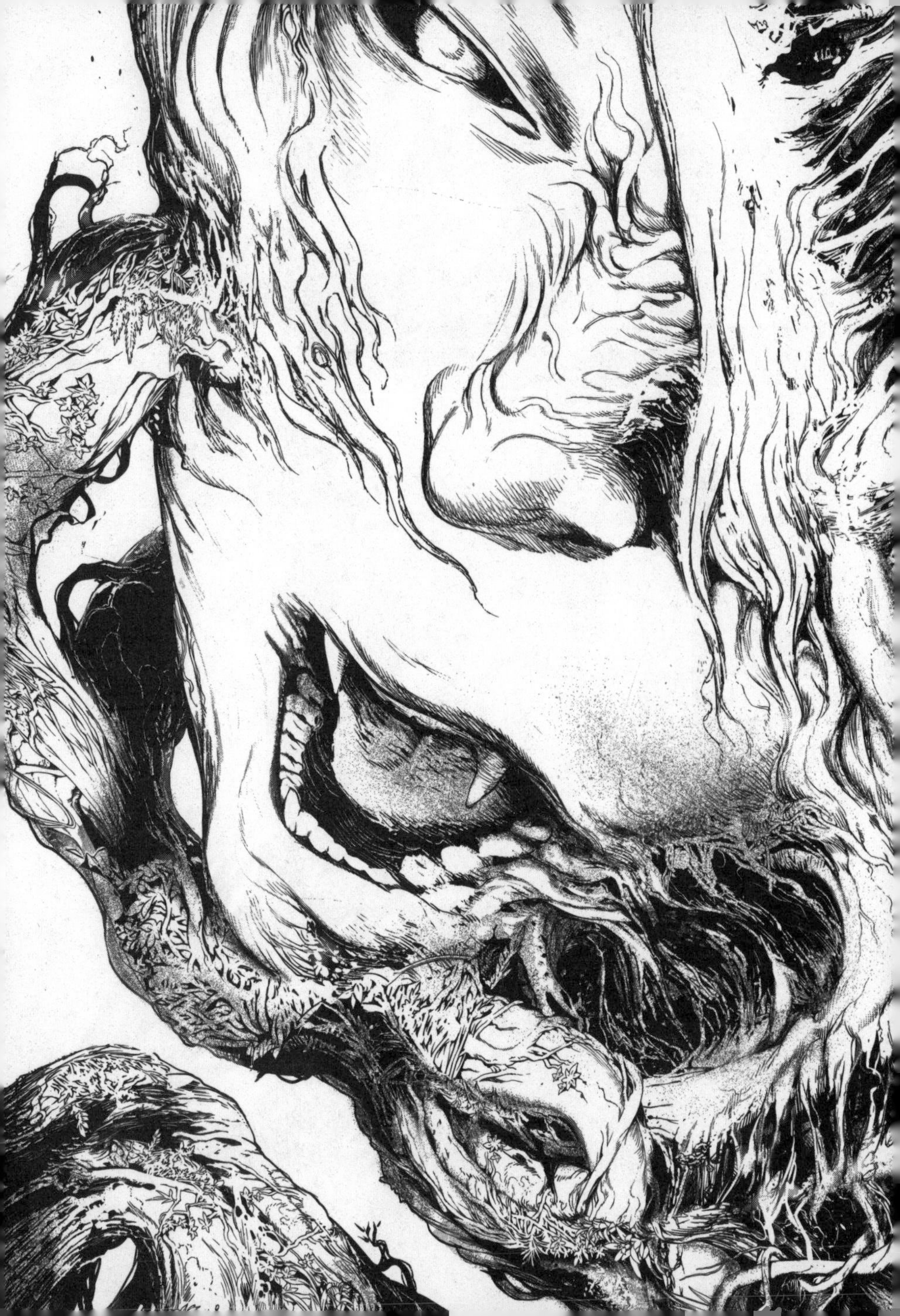

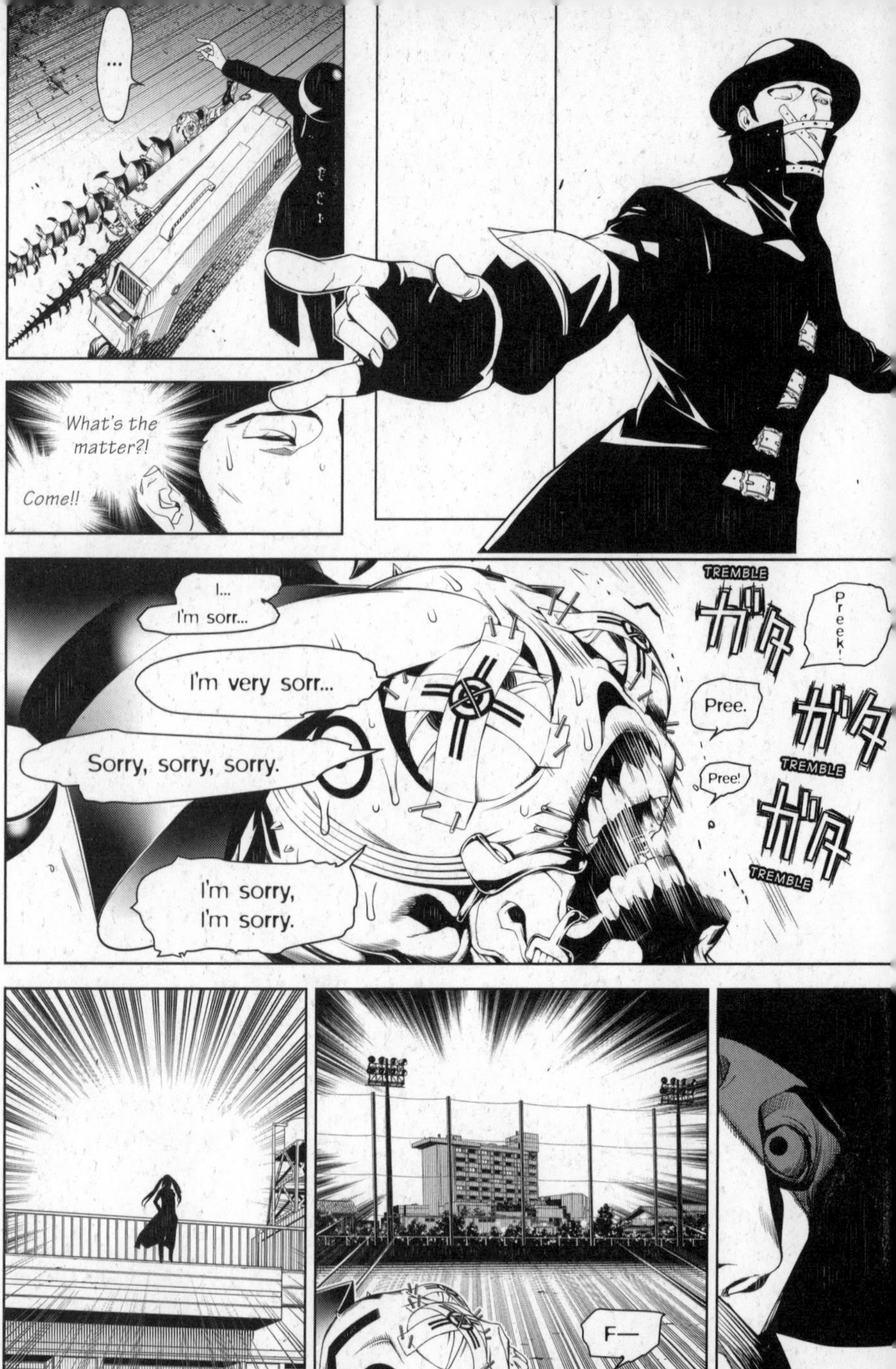
...
What's the matter?!
Come!!
TREMBLE
ガタ
Preek!
Pree.
ガタ
TREMBLE
Pree!
ガタ
TREMBLE
I...
I'm sorr...
I'm very sorr...
Sorry, sorry, sorry.
I'm sorry,
I'm sorry.
F—
Forgive me...!

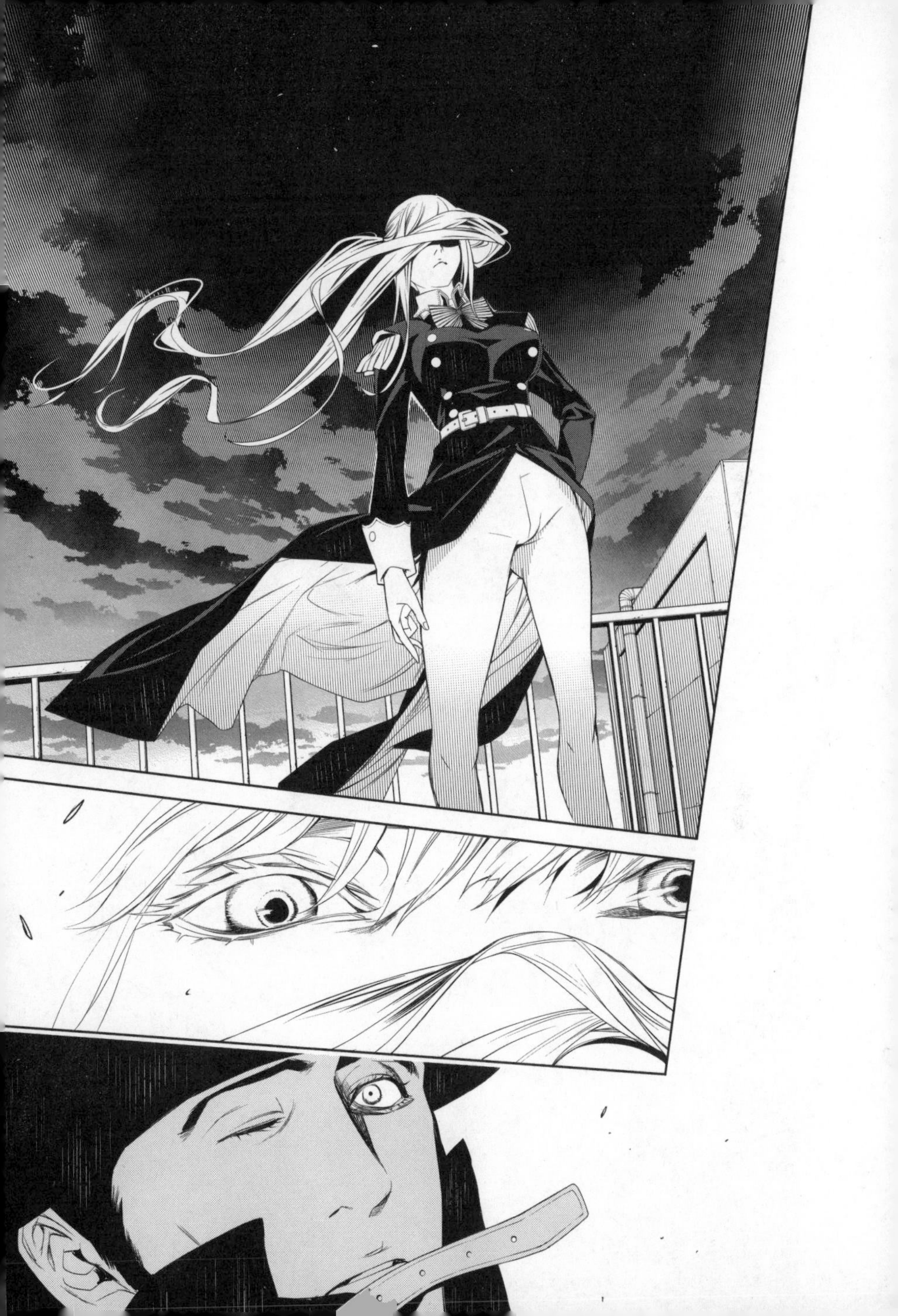

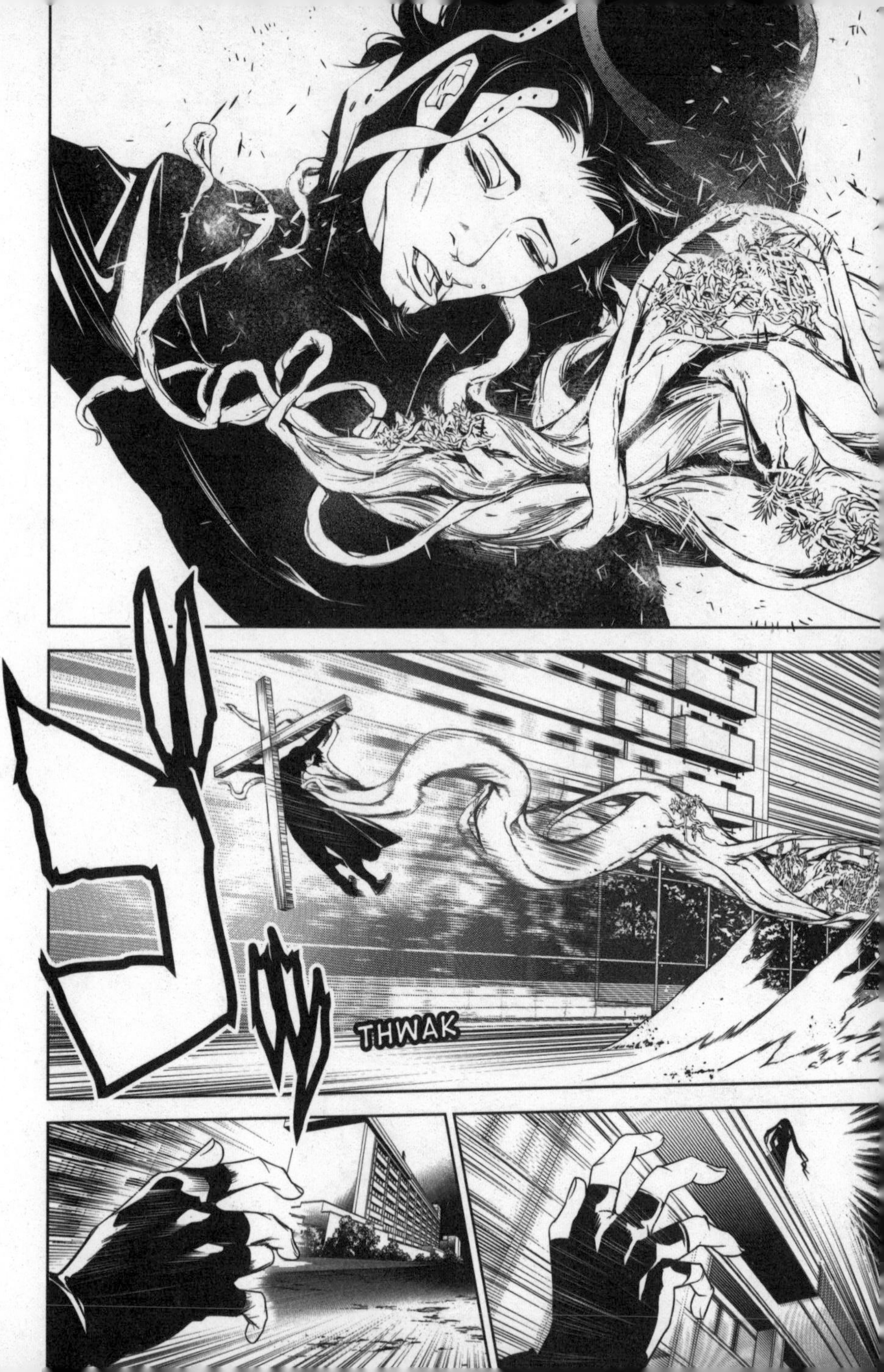
THWAK

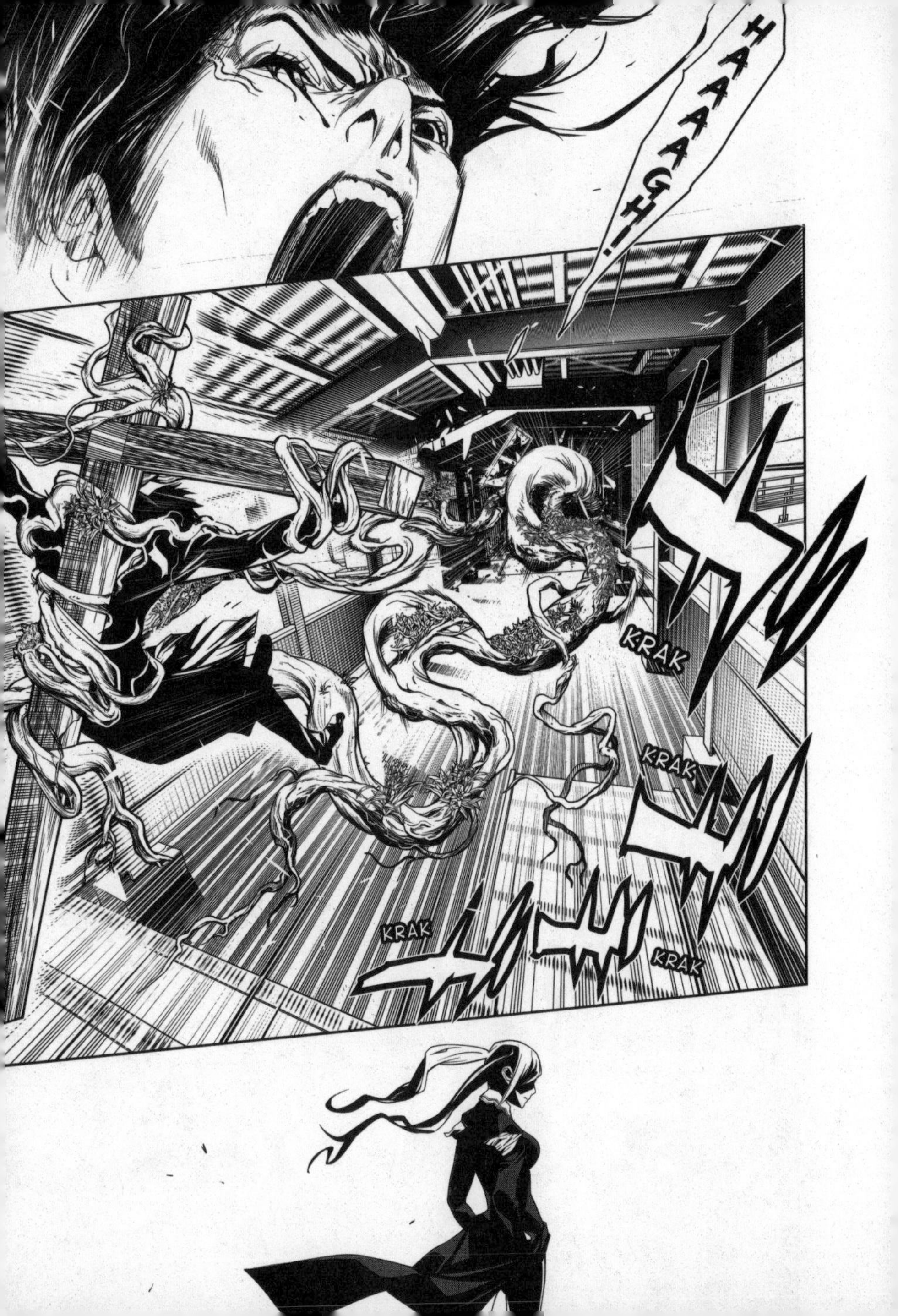
HAAAAGH!!
KRAK
KRAK
KRAK
KRAK

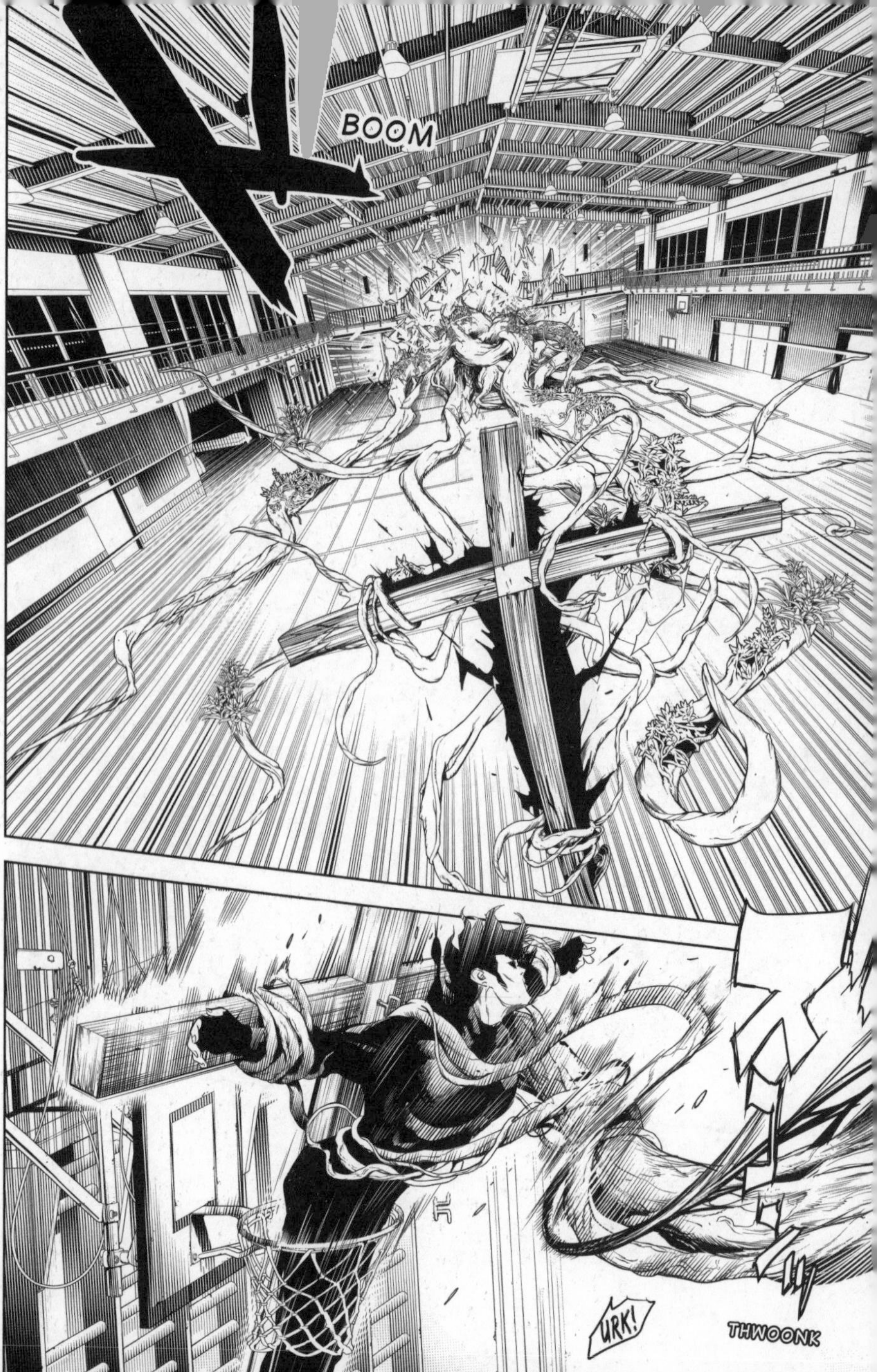
BOOM
THWOONK
URK!

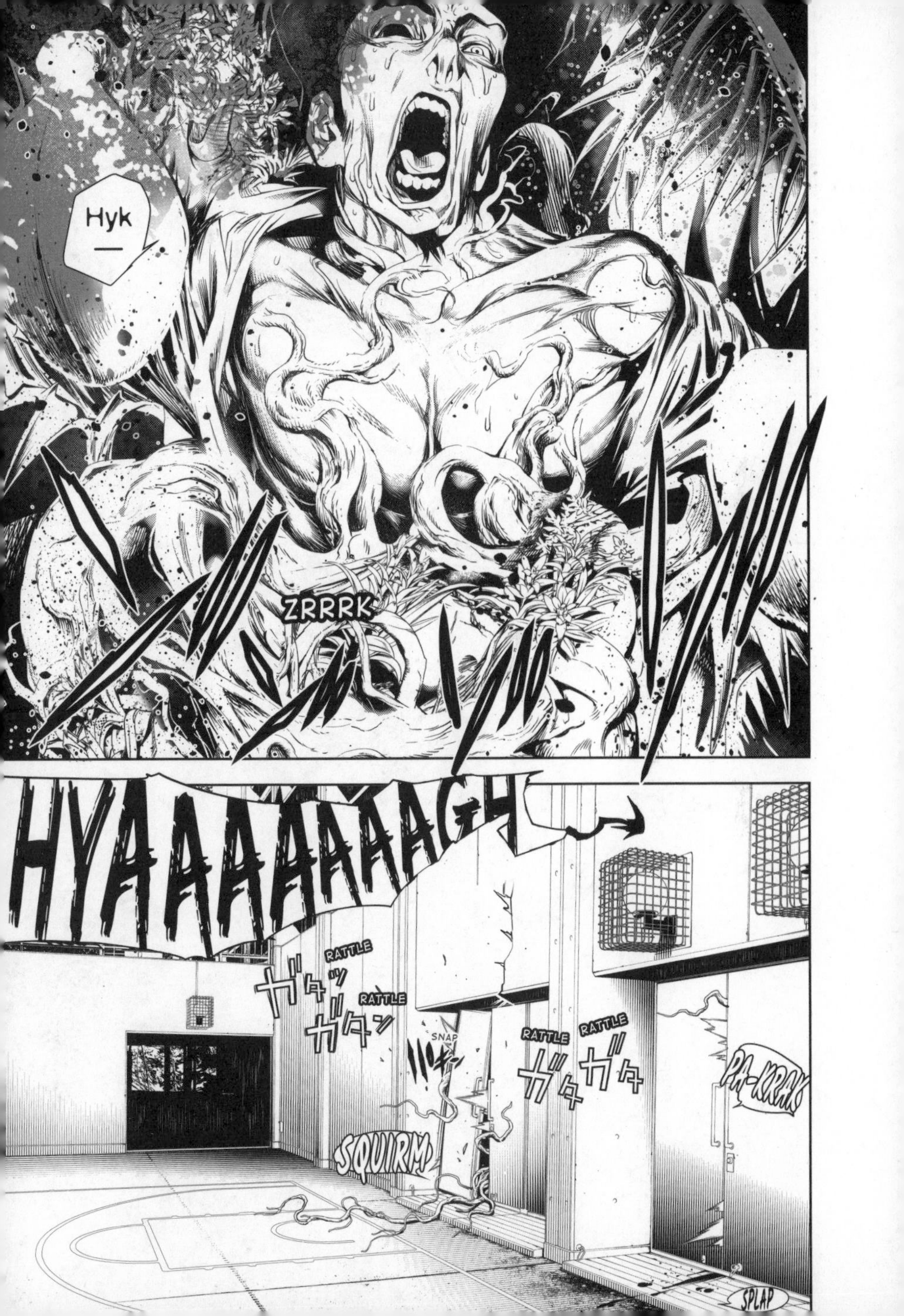
Hyk
—
ZRRRK
HYAAAAAAAGH
PA-KRAK
RATTLE
RATTLE
ガタガタ
SNAP
RATTLE
ガタン
RATTLE
ガタッ
SQUIRM
SPLAP

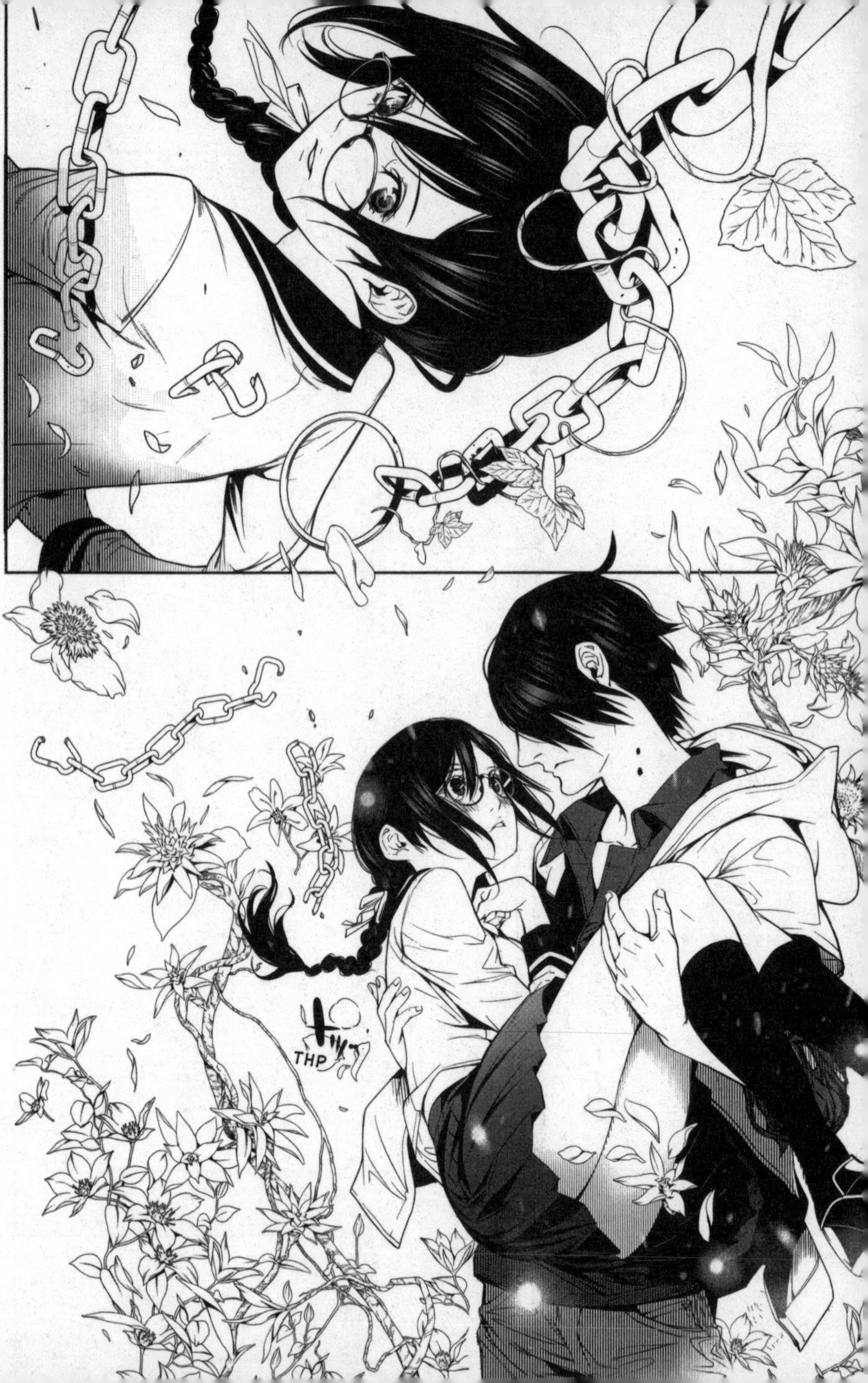
THP

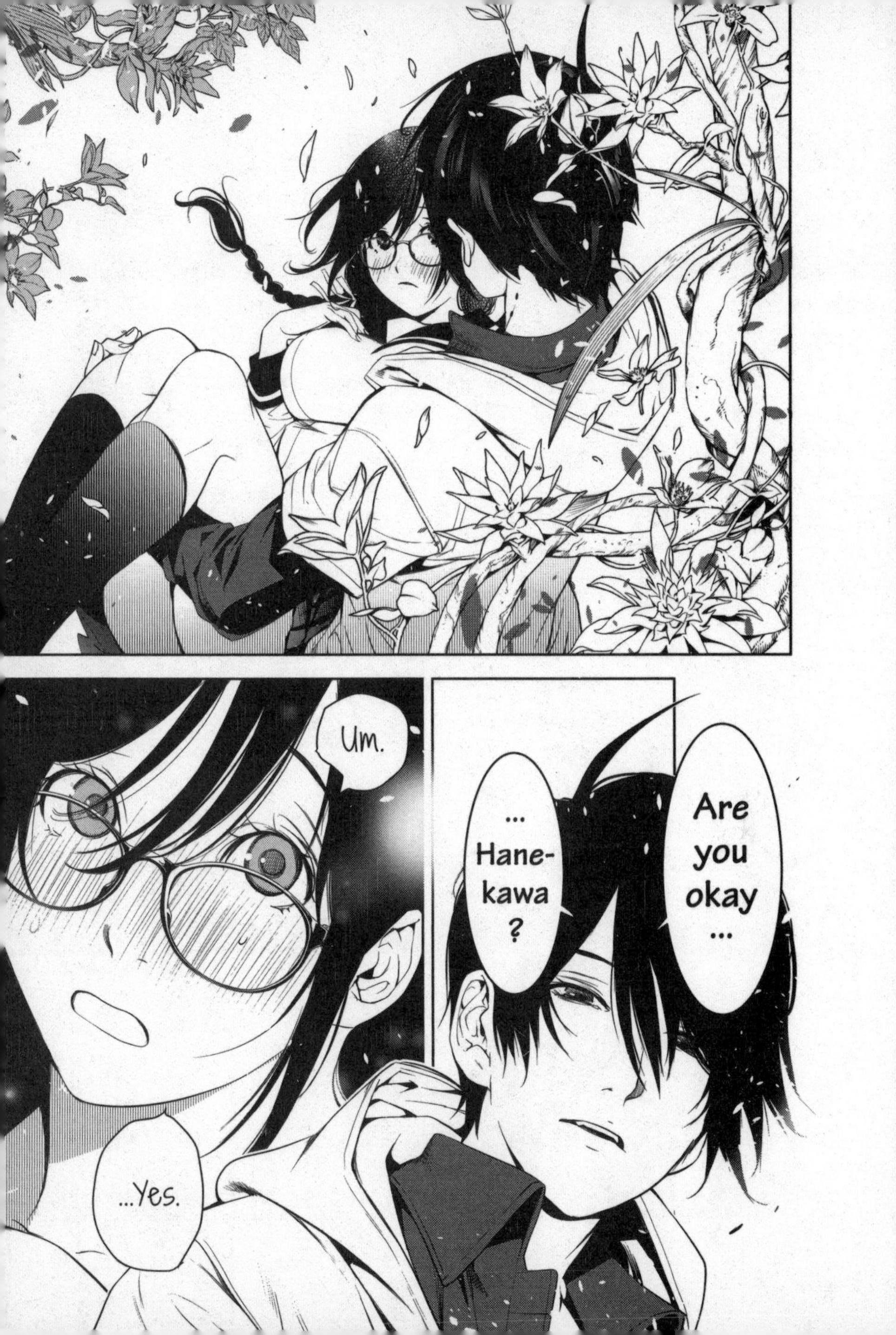
Are you okay ...
... Hanekawa ?
Um.
...Yes.

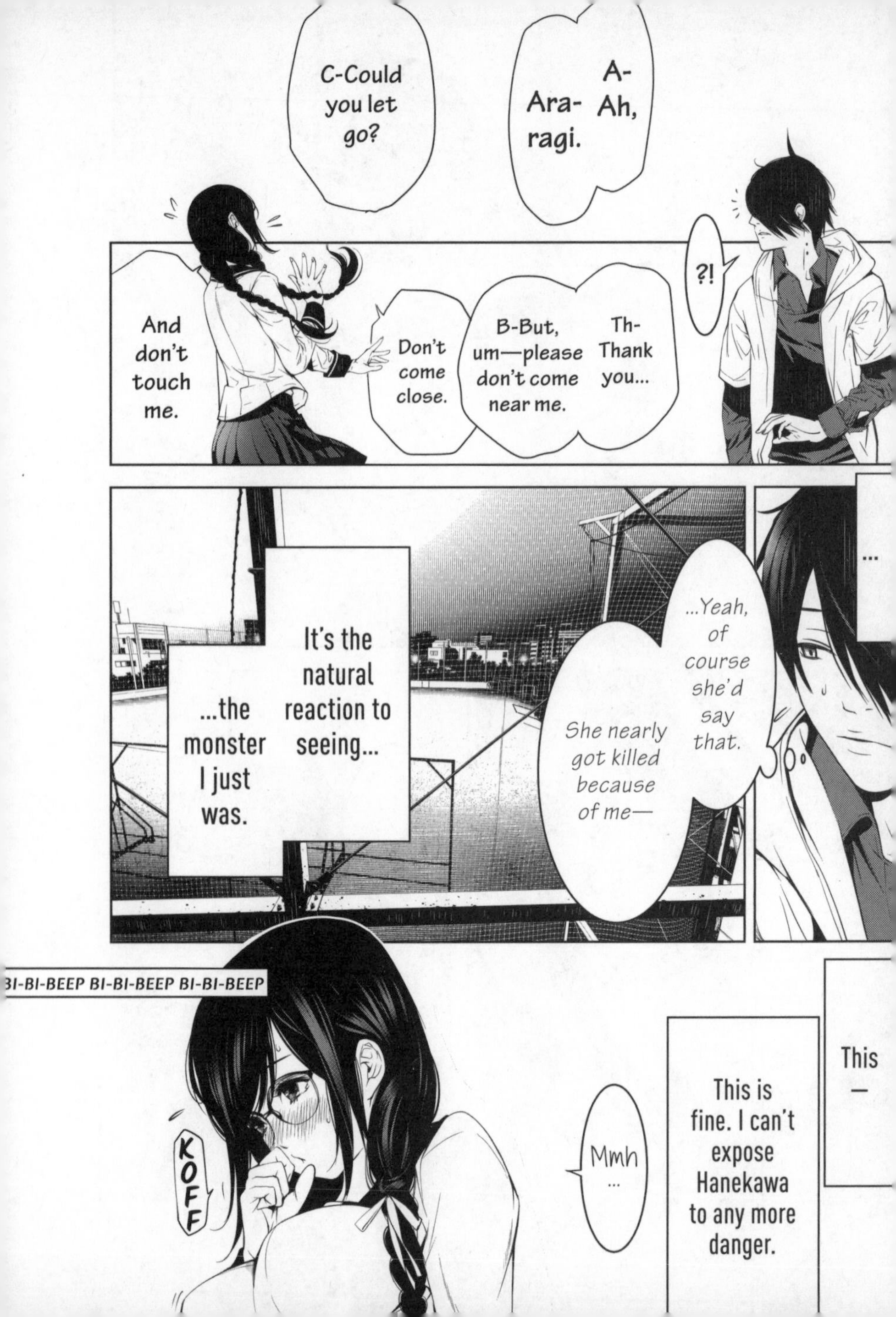
A- Ah, Ara-ragi.
C-Could you let go?
?!
Th- Thank you...
B-But, um—please don't come near me.
Don't come close.
And don't touch me.
...
...Yeah, of course she'd say that.
She nearly got killed because of me—
It's the natural reaction to seeing...
...the monster I just was.
This—
This is fine. I can't expose Hanekawa to any more danger.
Mmh...
KOFF
BI-BI-BEEP BI-BI-BEEP BI-BI-BEEP

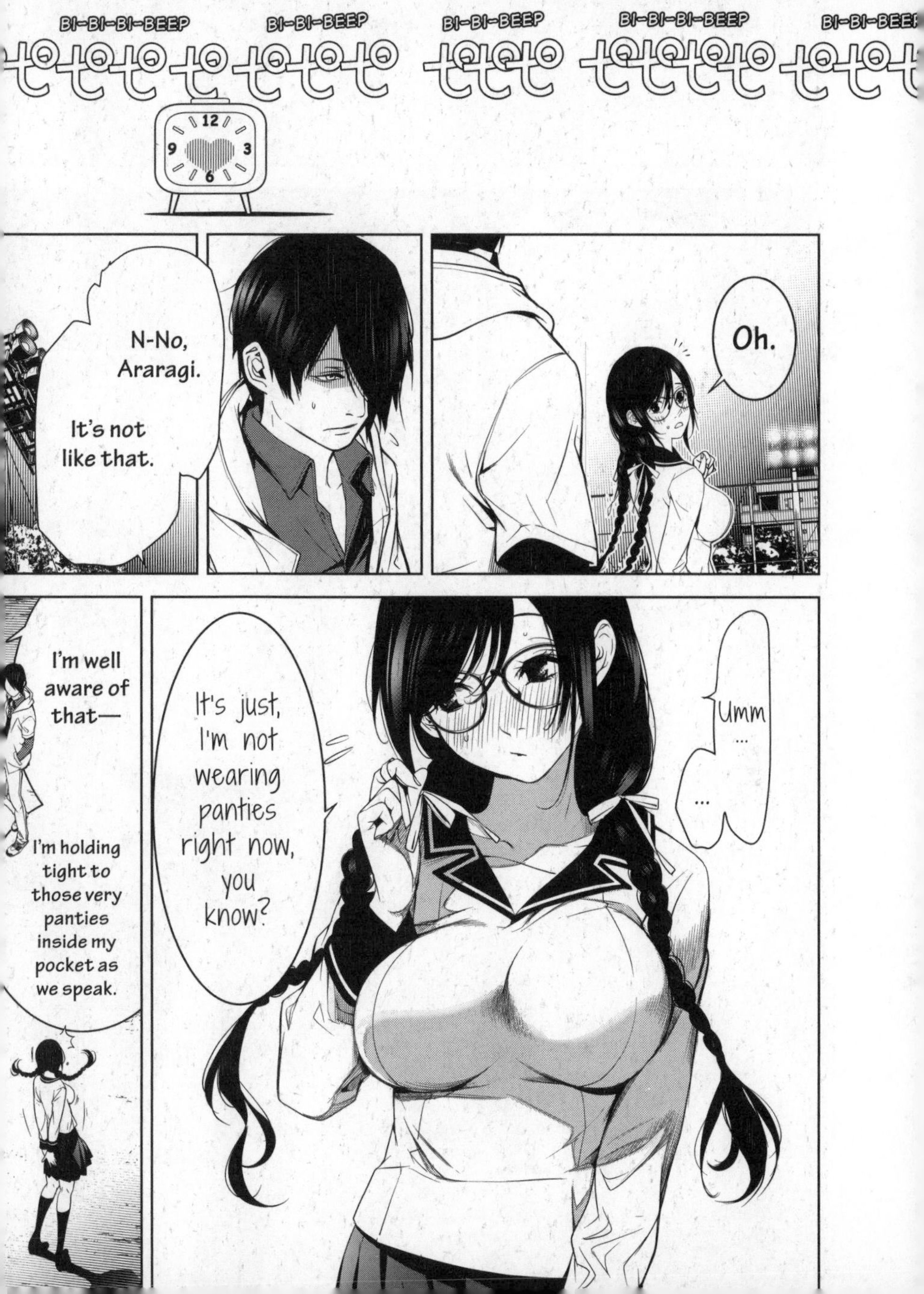

BI-BI-BEEP
BI-BI-BI-BEEP
BI-BI-BEEP
BI-BI-BEEP
BI-BI-BI-BEEP
12 3 6 9
Oh.
N-No, Araragi.
It's not like that.
Umm... ...
It's just, I'm not wearing panties right now, you know?
I'm well aware of that—
I'm holding tight to those very panties inside my pocket as we speak.

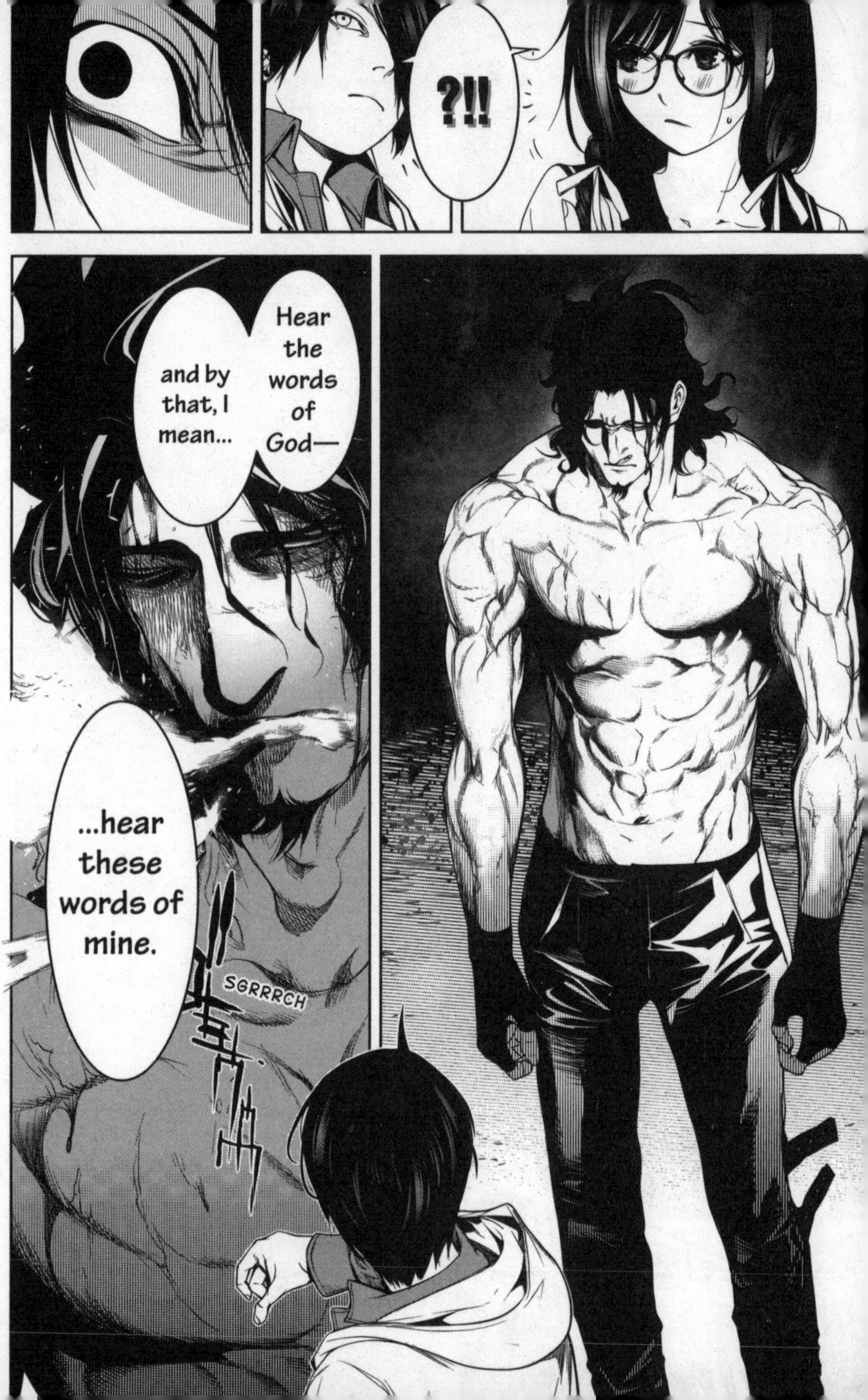
?!!
Hear the words of God—
and by that, I mean...
...hear these words of mine.
SGRRRCH

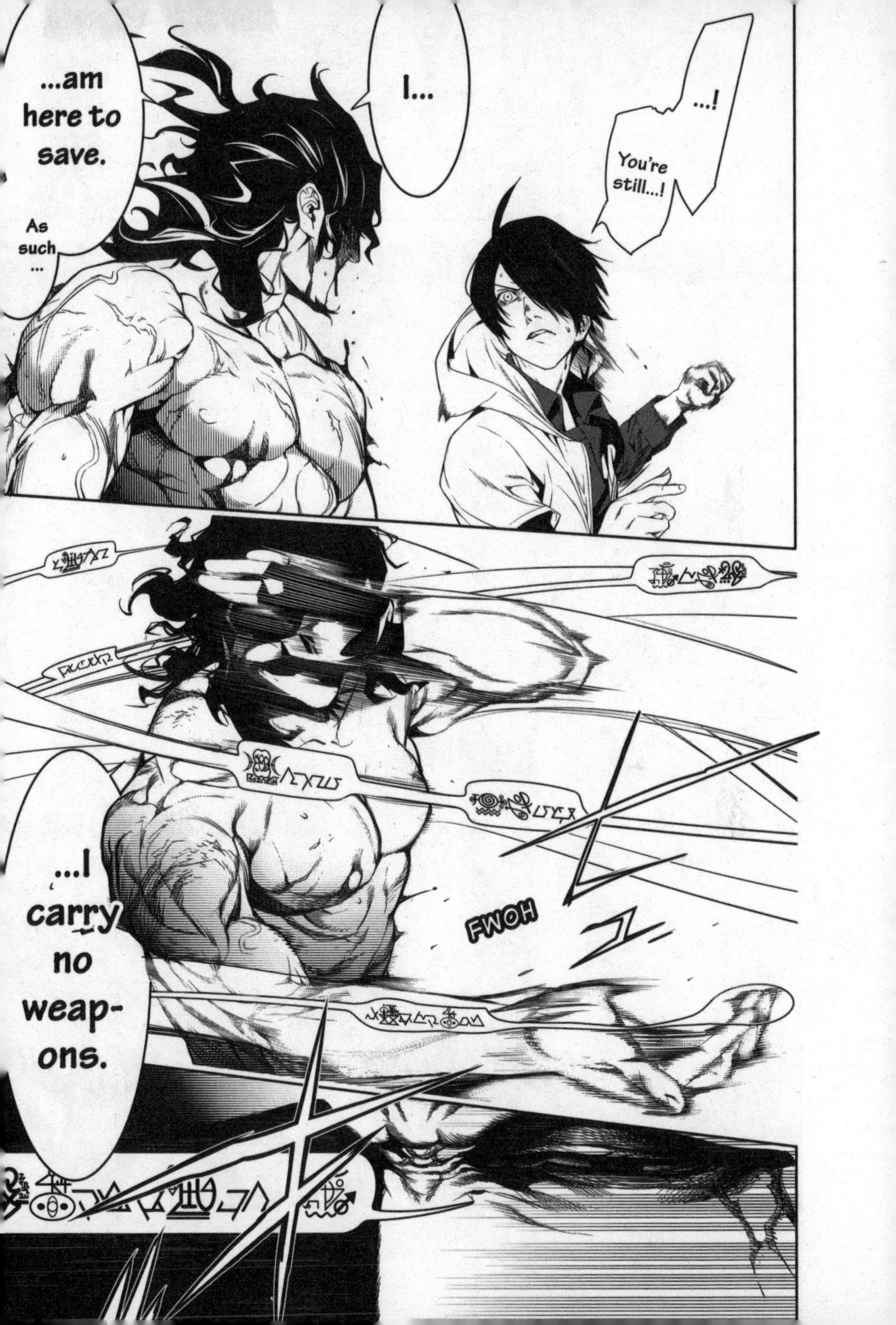
...!
You're still...!
I...
...am here to save.
As such ...
...I carry no weap-ons.
FWOH

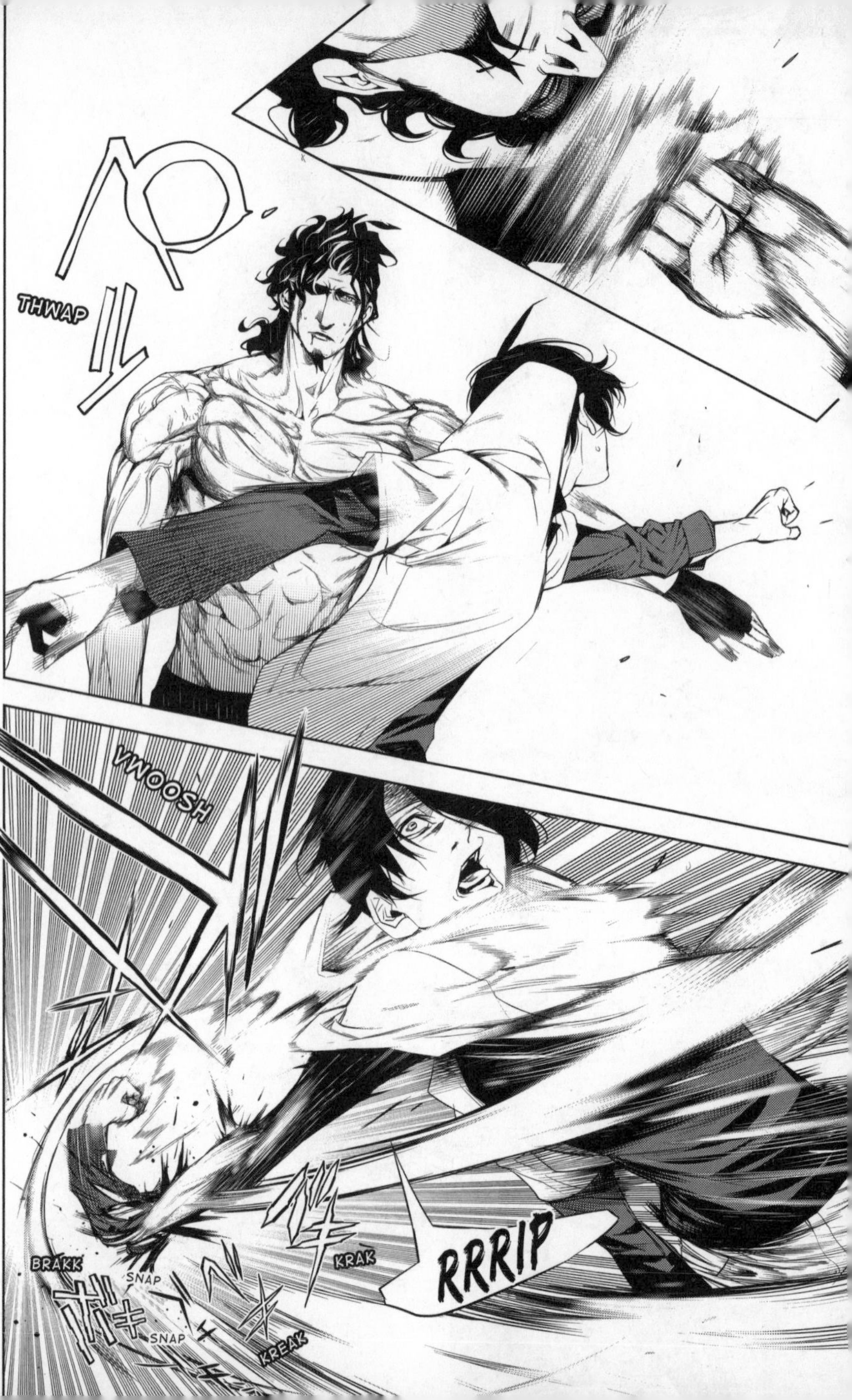
THWAP
VWOOSH
RRRIP
KRAK
BRAKK
SNAP
SNAP
KREAK

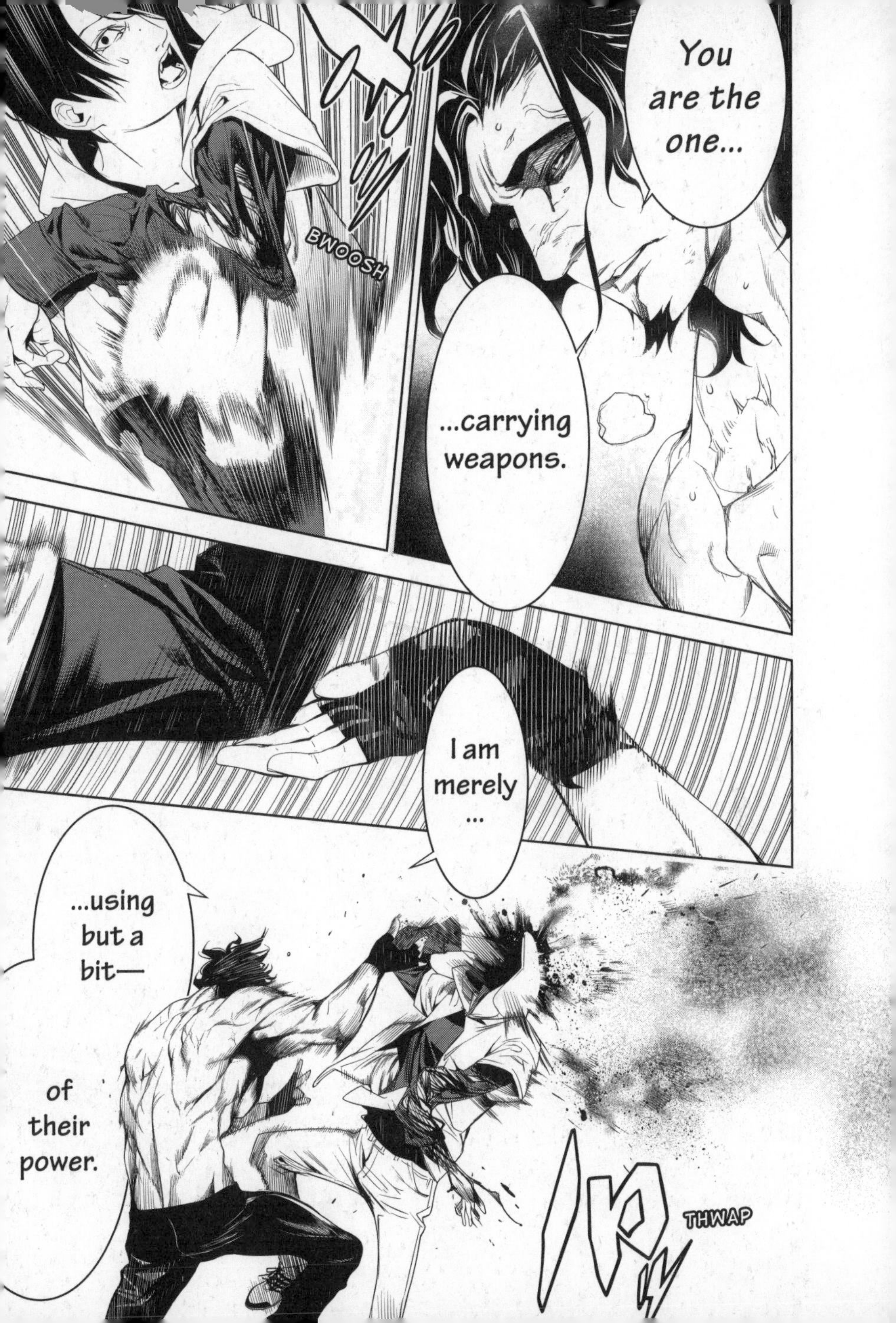
You are the one...
...carrying weapons.
BWOOSH
I am merely ...
...using but a bit—
of their power.
THWAP

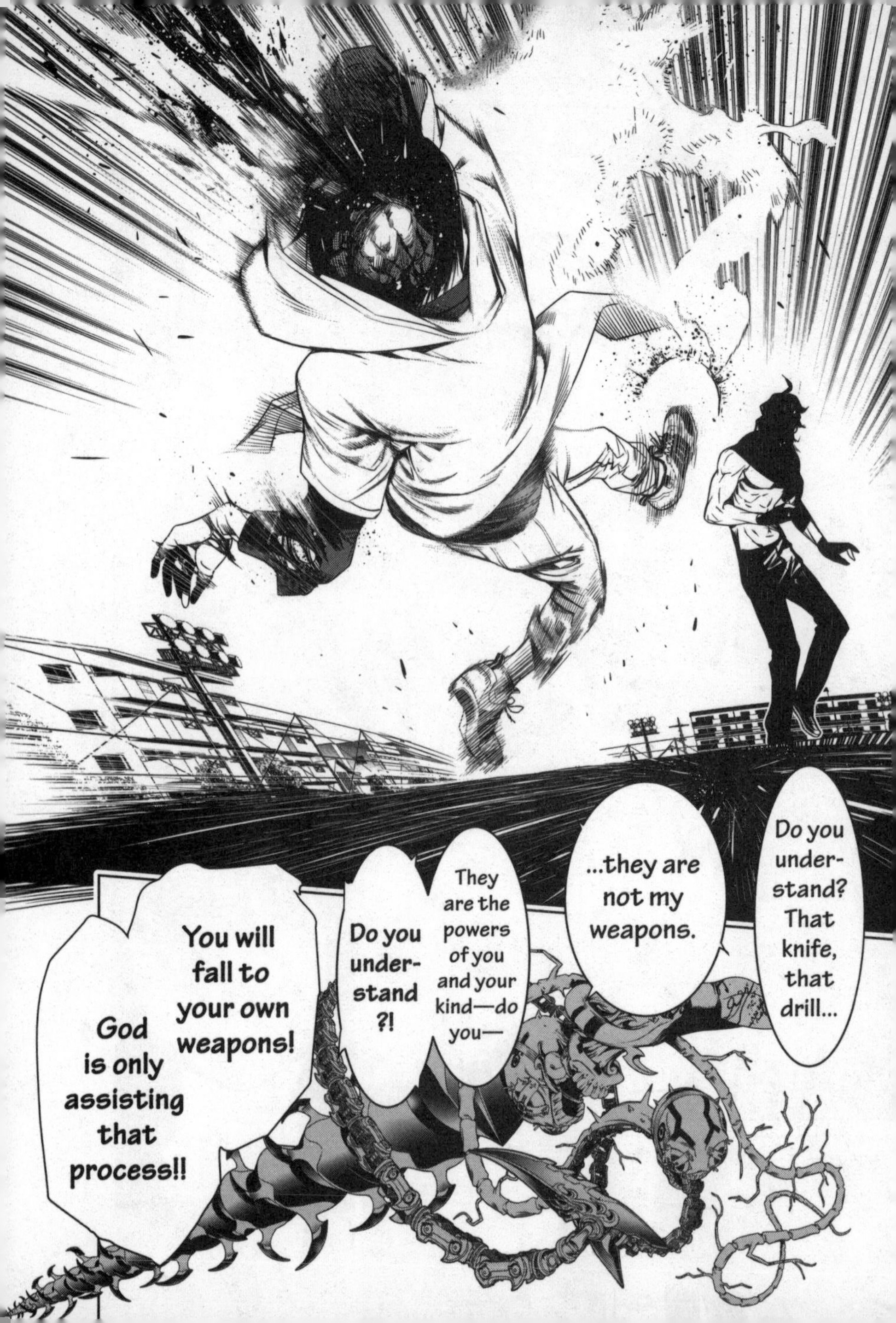
Do you understand? That knife, that drill...
...they are not my weapons.
They are the powers of you and your kind—do you—
Do you understand?!
You will fall to your own weapons!
God is only assisting that process!!

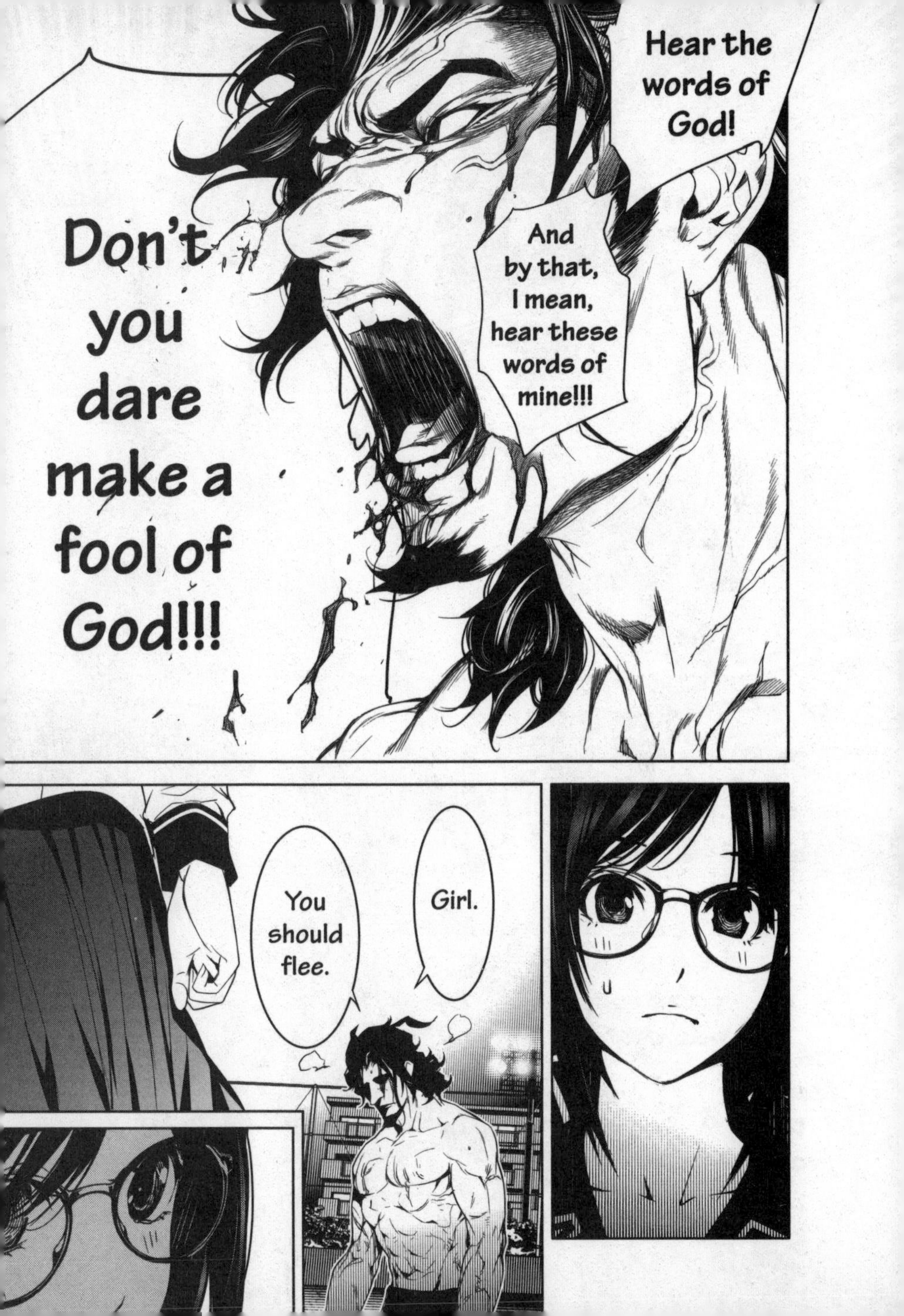
Hear the words of God!
And by that, I mean, hear these words of mine!!!
Don't you dare make a fool of God!!!
Girl.
You should flee.

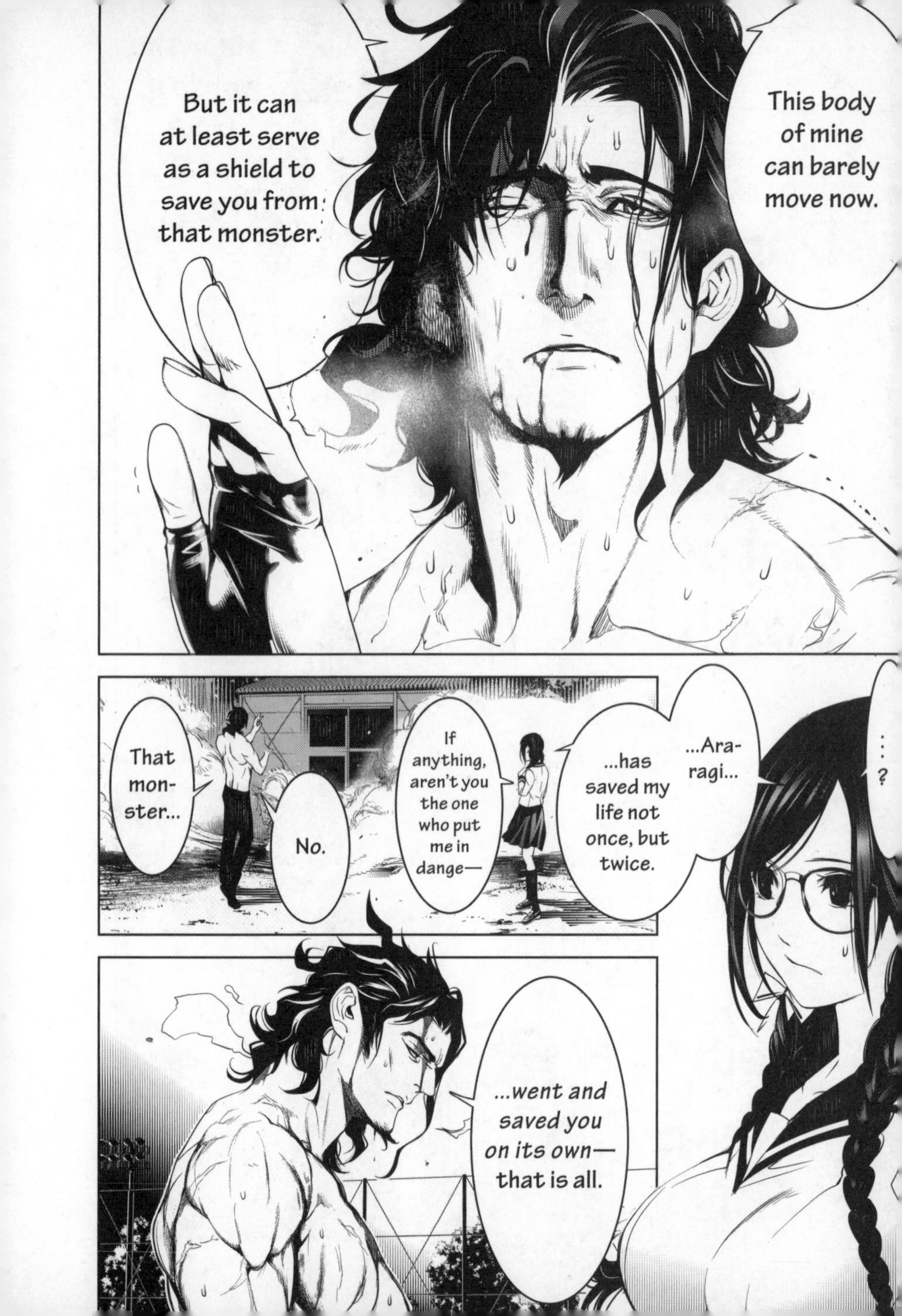
This body of mine can barely move now.
But it can at least serve as a shield to save you from that monster.
...?
...Ara-ragi...
...has saved my life not once, but twice.
If anything, aren't you the one who put me in dange—
No.
That mon-ster...
...went and saved you on its own— that is all.

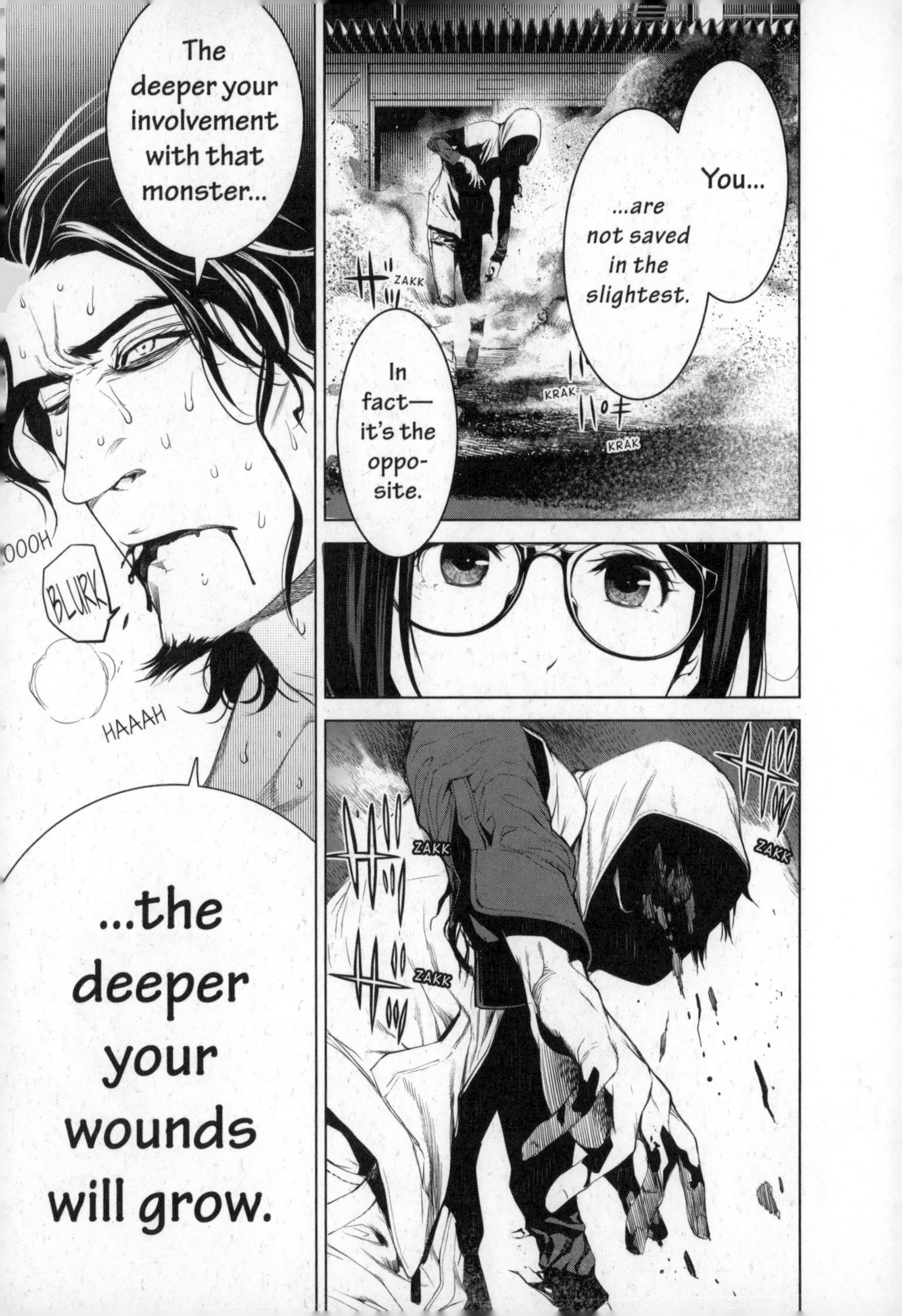
You...
...are not saved in the slightest.
ZAKK
In fact—it's the opposite.
KRAK
KRAK
ZAKK
ZAKK
ZAKK
The deeper your involvement with that monster...
OOOH
BLURK
HAAAH
...the deeper your wounds will grow.

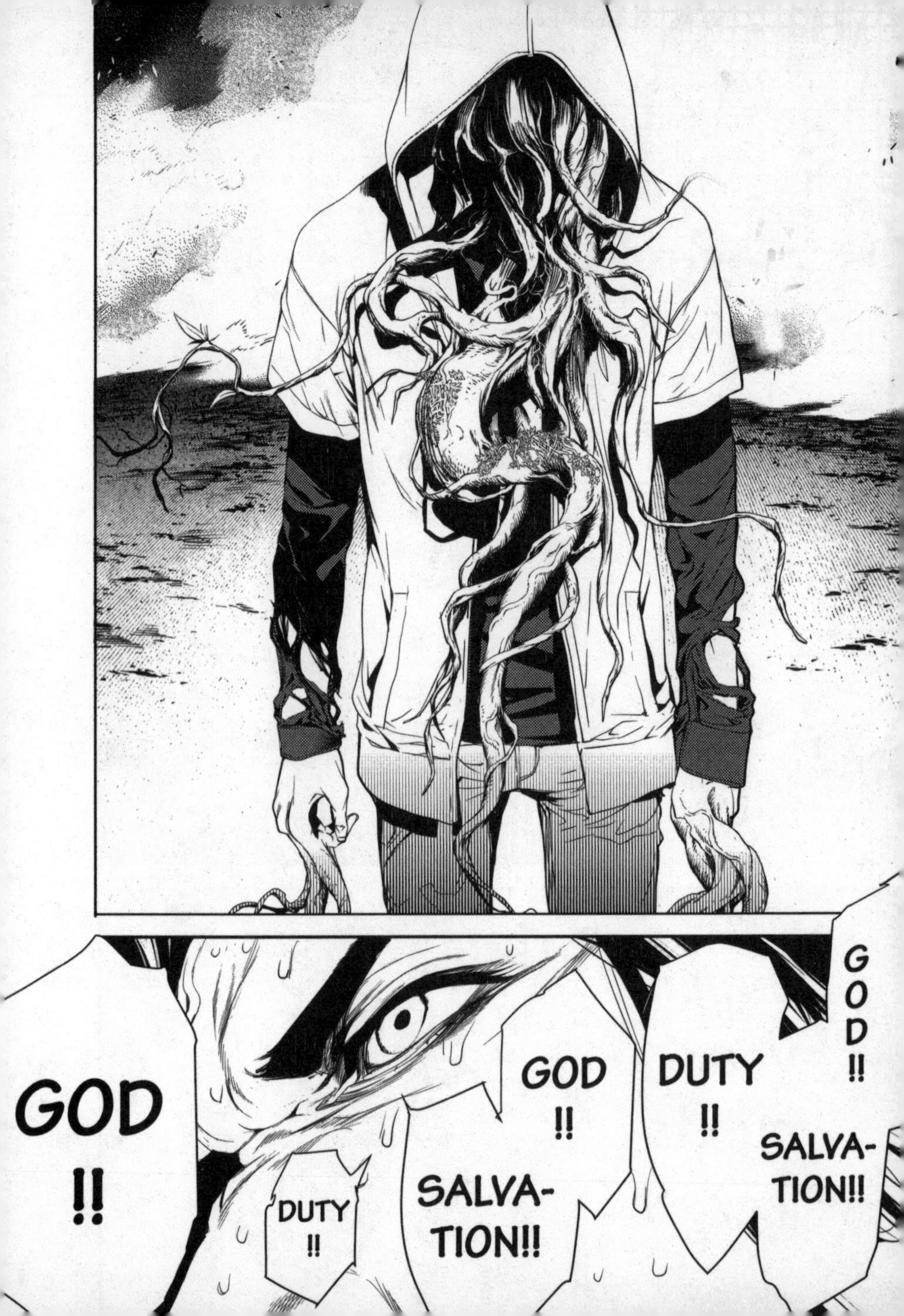
GOD!!
DUTY!!
SALVATION!!
GOD!!
SALVATION!!
DUTY!!
GOD!!

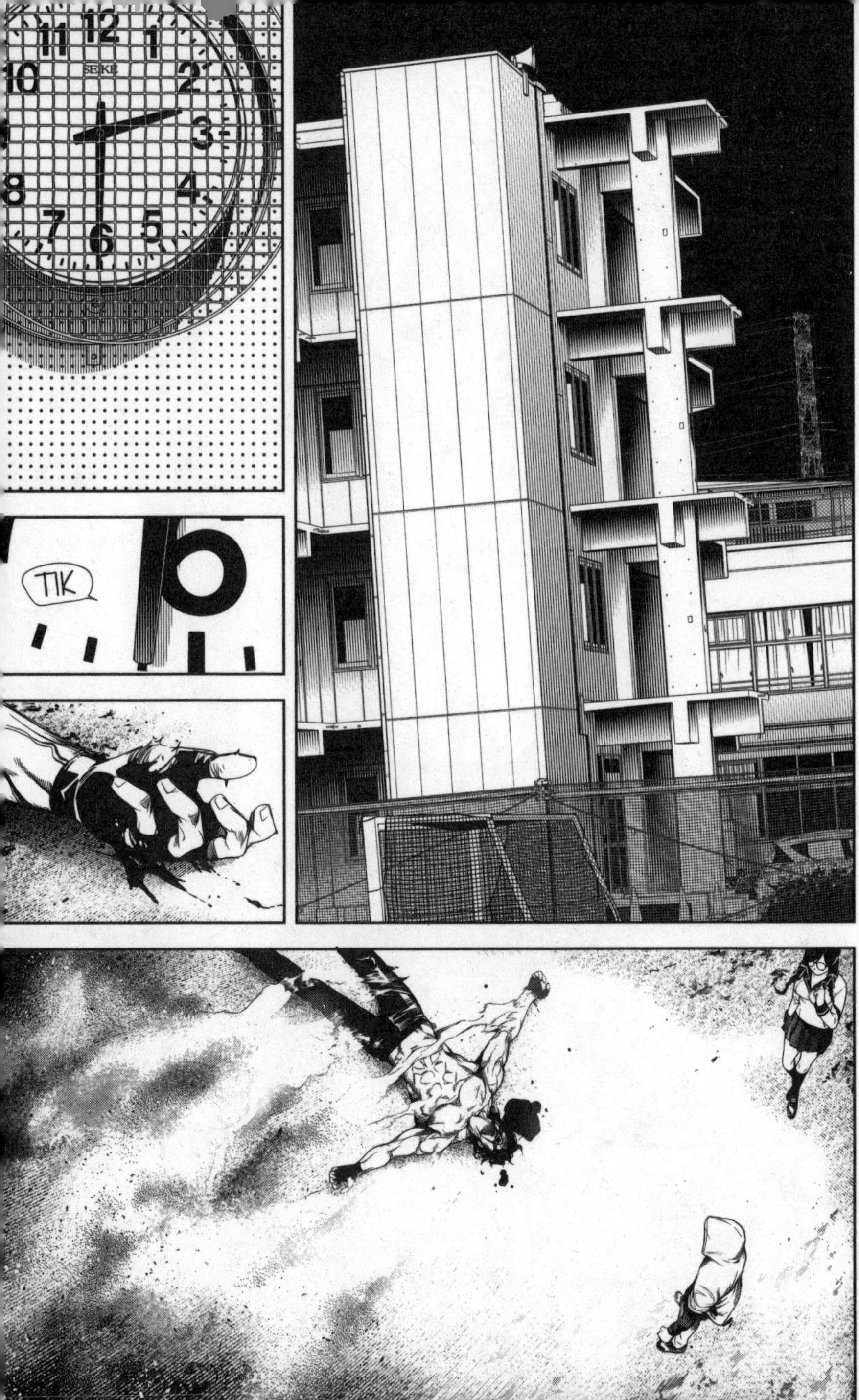
TIK

チュン
CHIRP
チュン
CHIRP
チチチチチチ
CHIRRRP
キイッ
KREAK

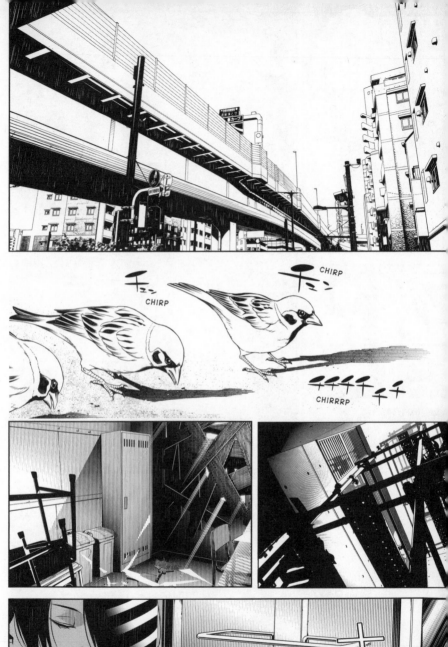

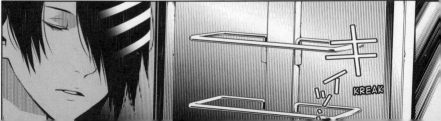

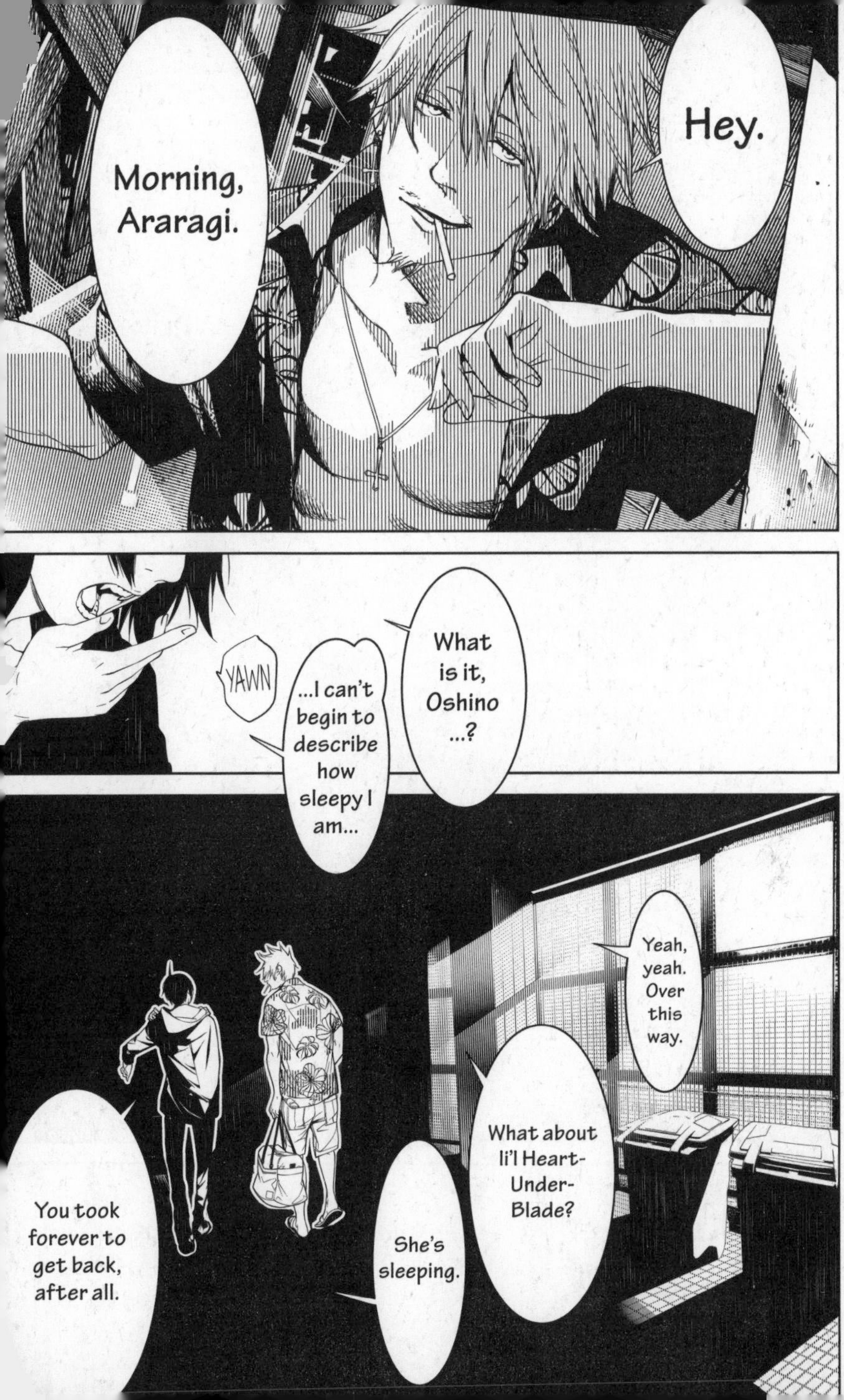
Hey.
Morning, Araragi.
What is it, Oshino ...?
...I can't begin to describe how sleepy I am...
YAWN
Yeah, yeah. Over this way.
What about li'l Heart-Under-Blade?
She's sleeping.
You took forever to get back, after all.

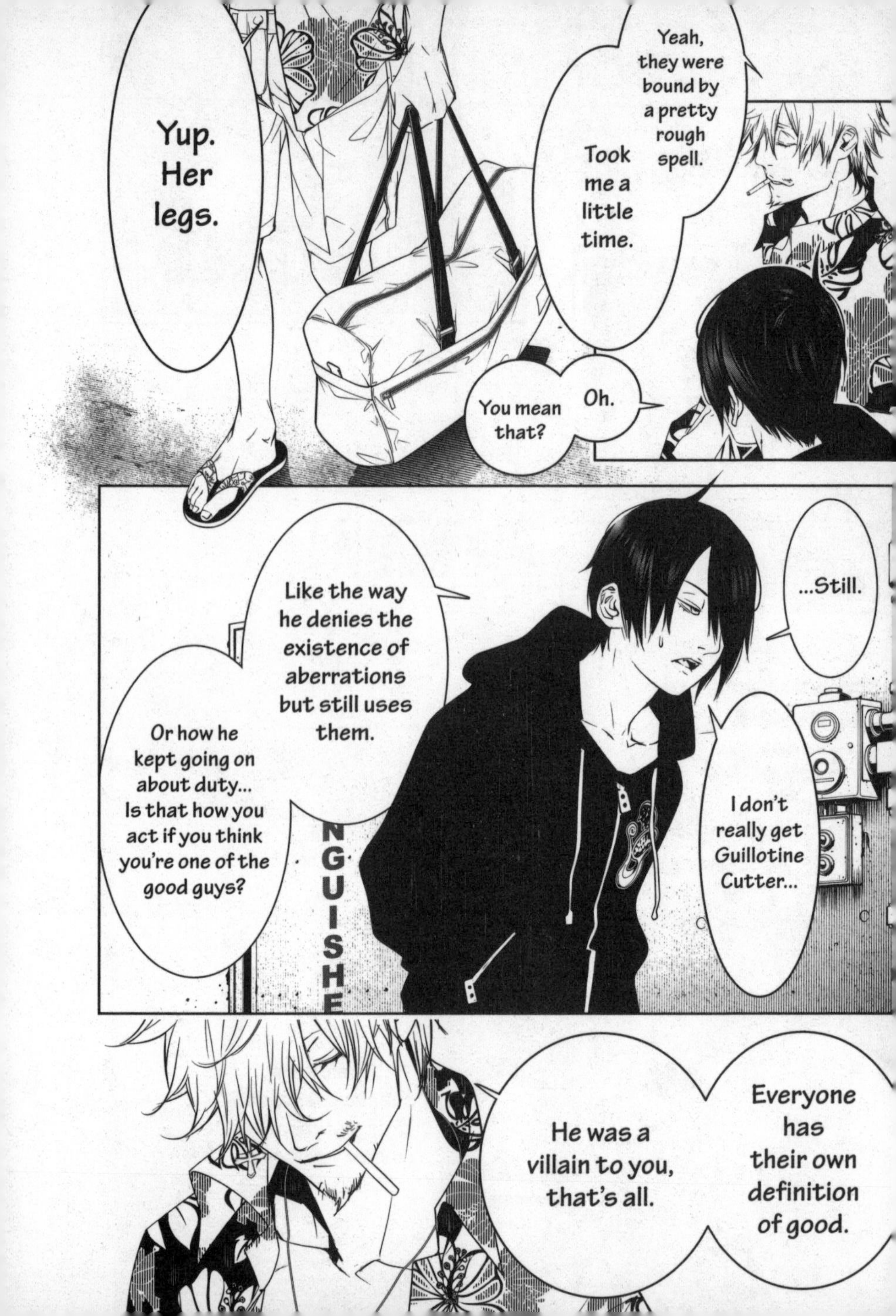
Yeah, they were bound by a pretty rough spell.
Took me a little time.
Oh.
You mean that?
Yup. Her legs.
...Still.
I don't really get Guillotine Cutter...
Like the way he denies the existence of aberrations but still uses them.
Or how he kept going on about duty... Is that how you act if you think you're one of the good guys?
NGUISHE
Everyone has their own definition of good.
He was a villain to you, that's all.

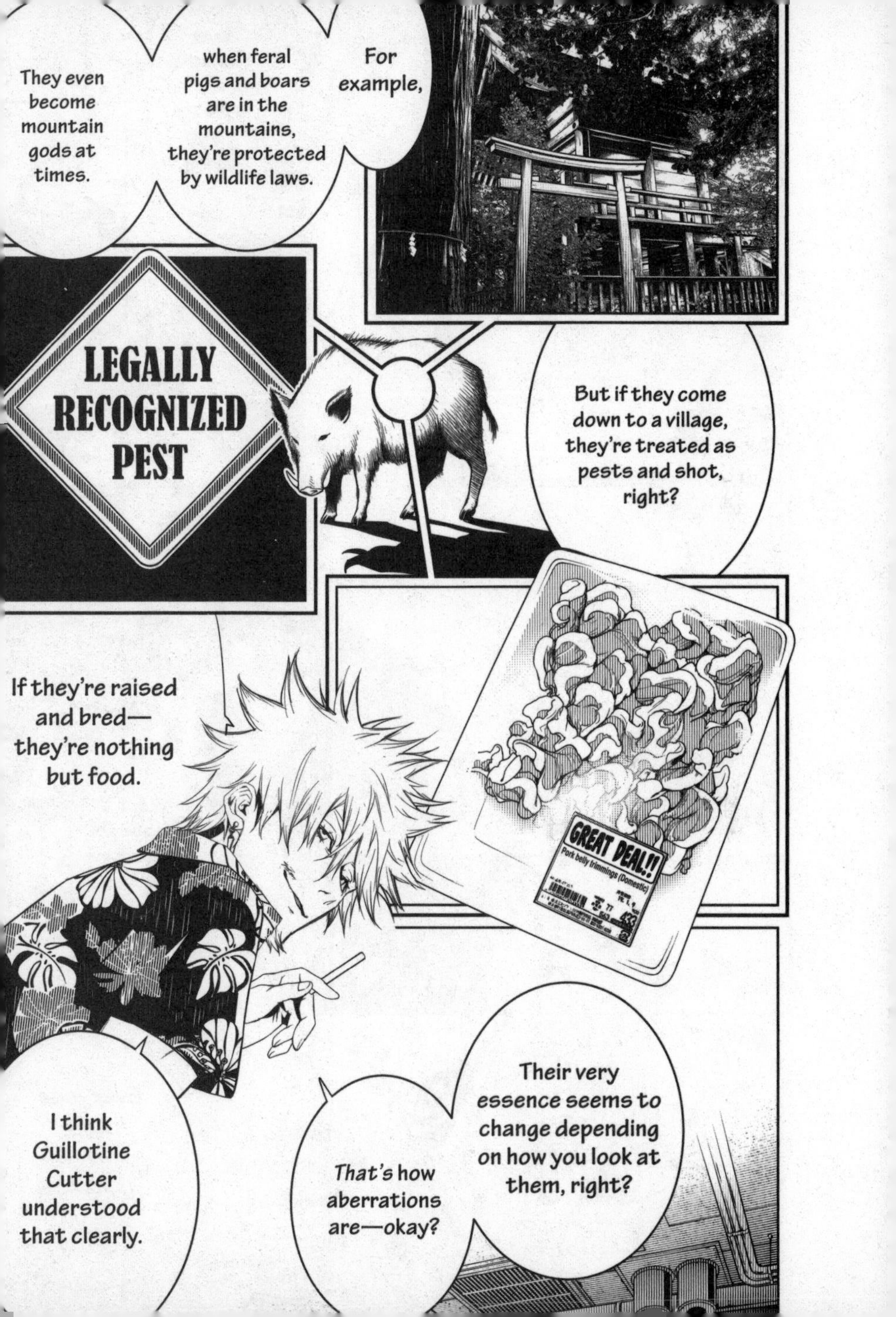
For example,
when feral pigs and boars are in the mountains, they're protected by wildlife laws.
They even become mountain gods at times.
But if they come down to a village, they're treated as pests and shot, right?
LEGALLY RECOGNIZED PEST
GREAT DEAL!!
Pork belly trimmings (Domestic)
If they're raised and bred—they're nothing but food.
Their very essence seems to change depending on how you look at them, right?
That's how aberrations are—okay?
I think Guillotine Cutter understood that clearly.

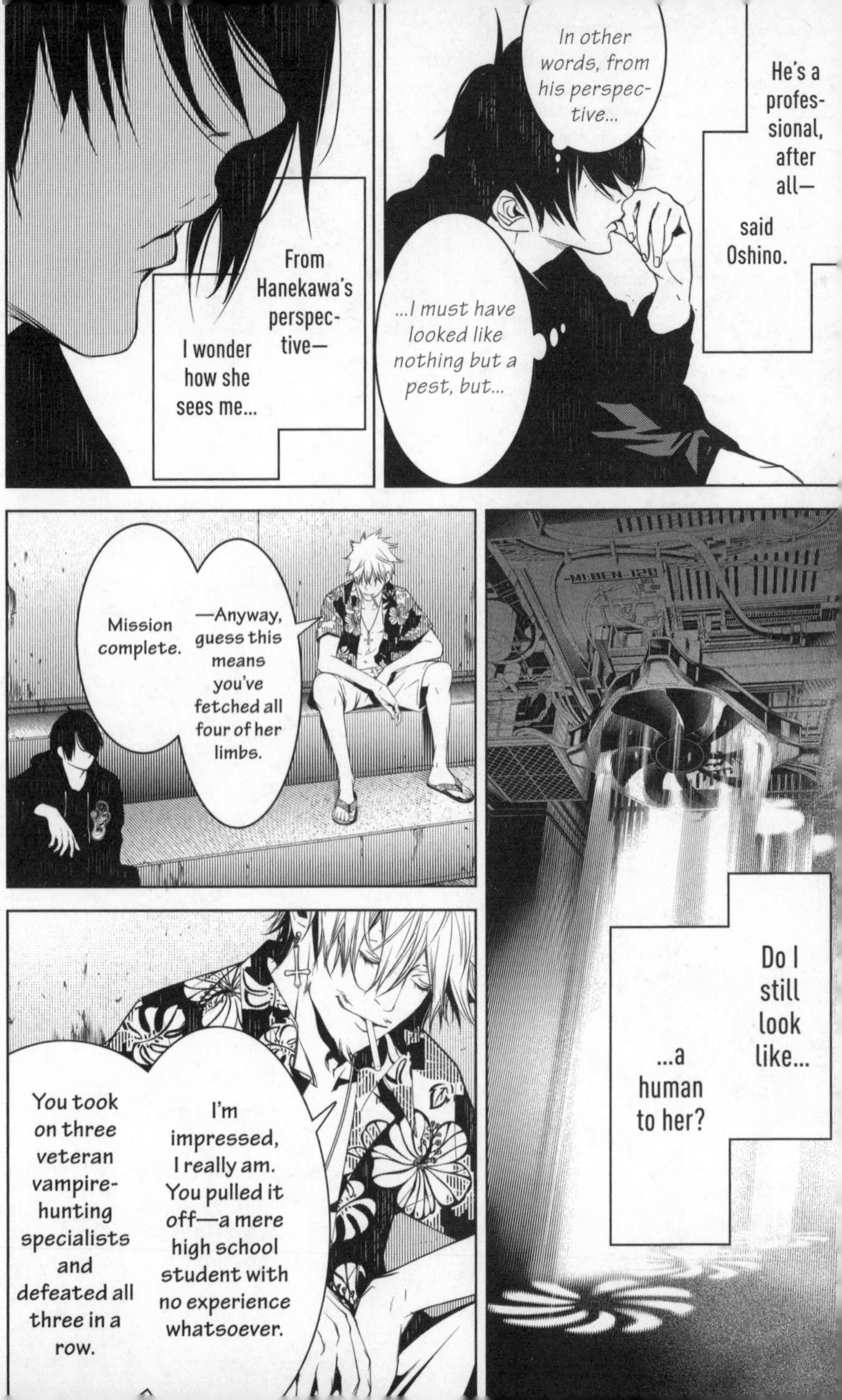
He's a professional, after all—
said Oshino.
In other words, from his perspective...
...I must have looked like nothing but a pest, but...
From Hanekawa's perspective—
I wonder how she sees me...
Do I still look like...
...a human to her?
—Anyway, guess this means you've fetched all four of her limbs.
Mission complete.
I'm impressed, I really am. You pulled it off—a mere high school student with no experience whatsoever.
You took on three veteran vampire-hunting specialists and defeated all three in a row.
-MI:BEN-120

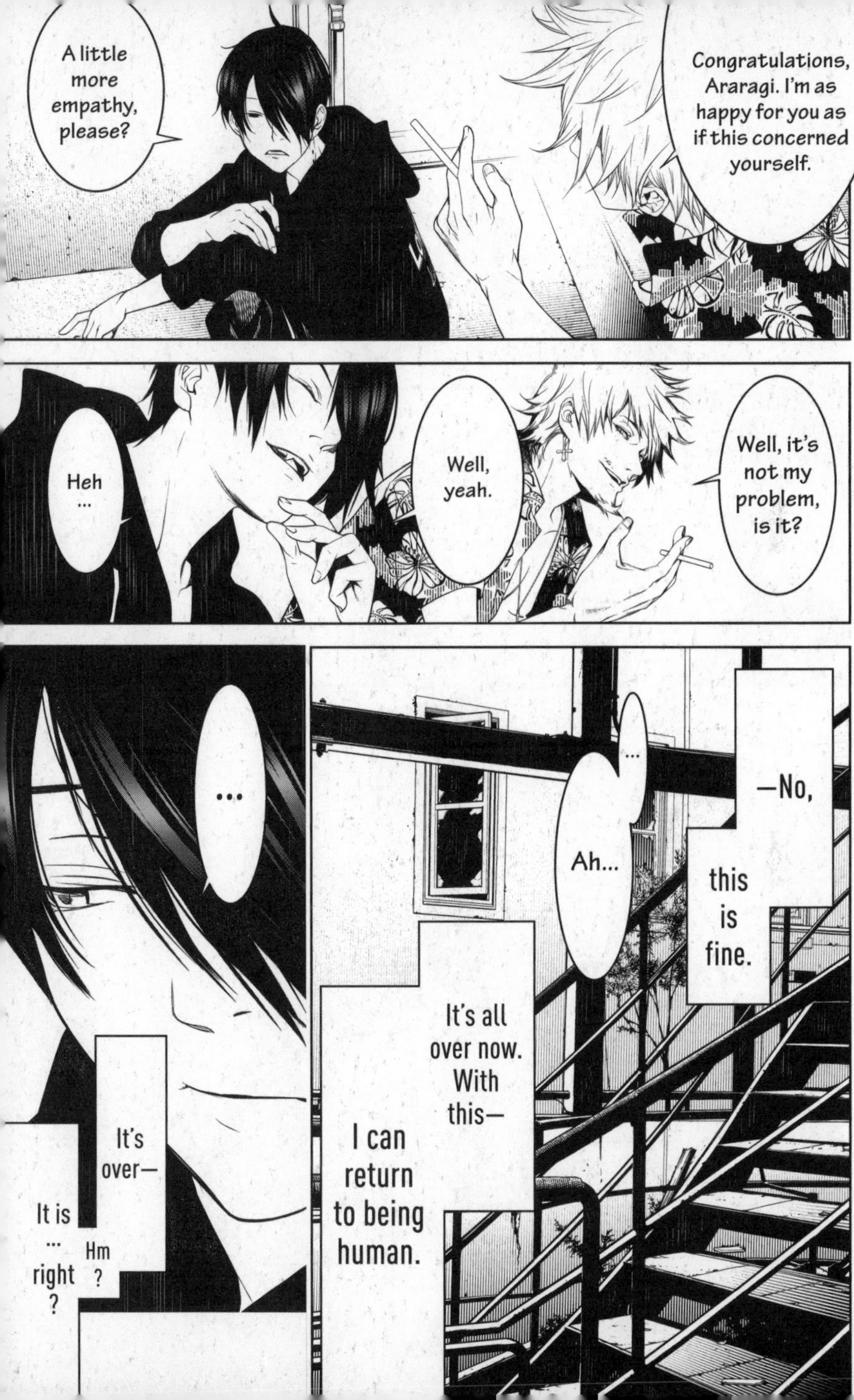
Congratulations, Araragi. I'm as happy for you as if this concerned yourself.
A little more empathy, please?
Well, it's not my problem, is it?
Well, yeah.
Heh ...
—No, this is fine.
...
Ah...
It's all over now. With this—
I can return to being human.
...
It's over—
Hm ?
It is ... right ?

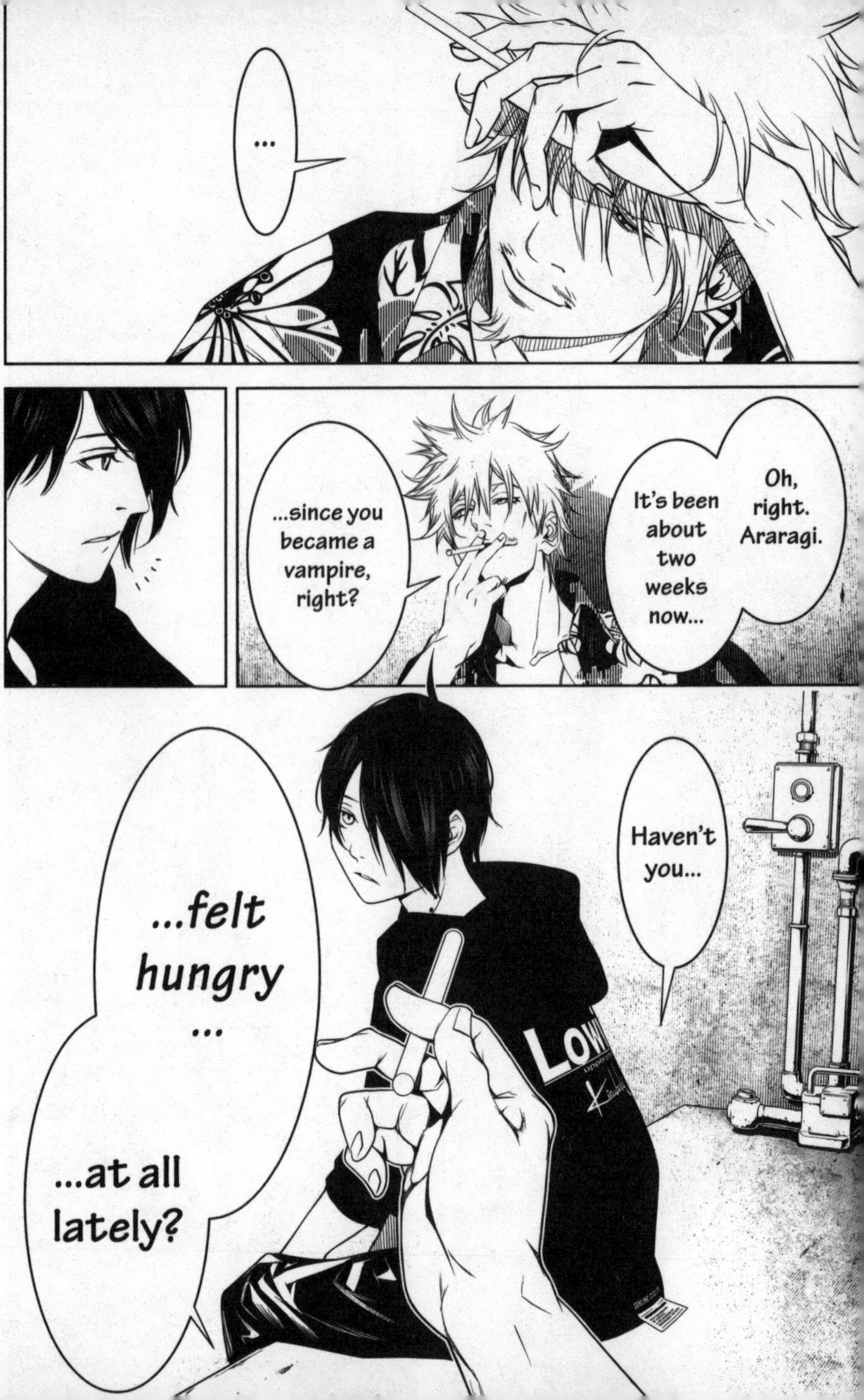
...
Oh, right. Araragi.
It's been about two weeks now...
...since you became a vampire, right?
Haven't you...
...felt hungry...
...at all lately?

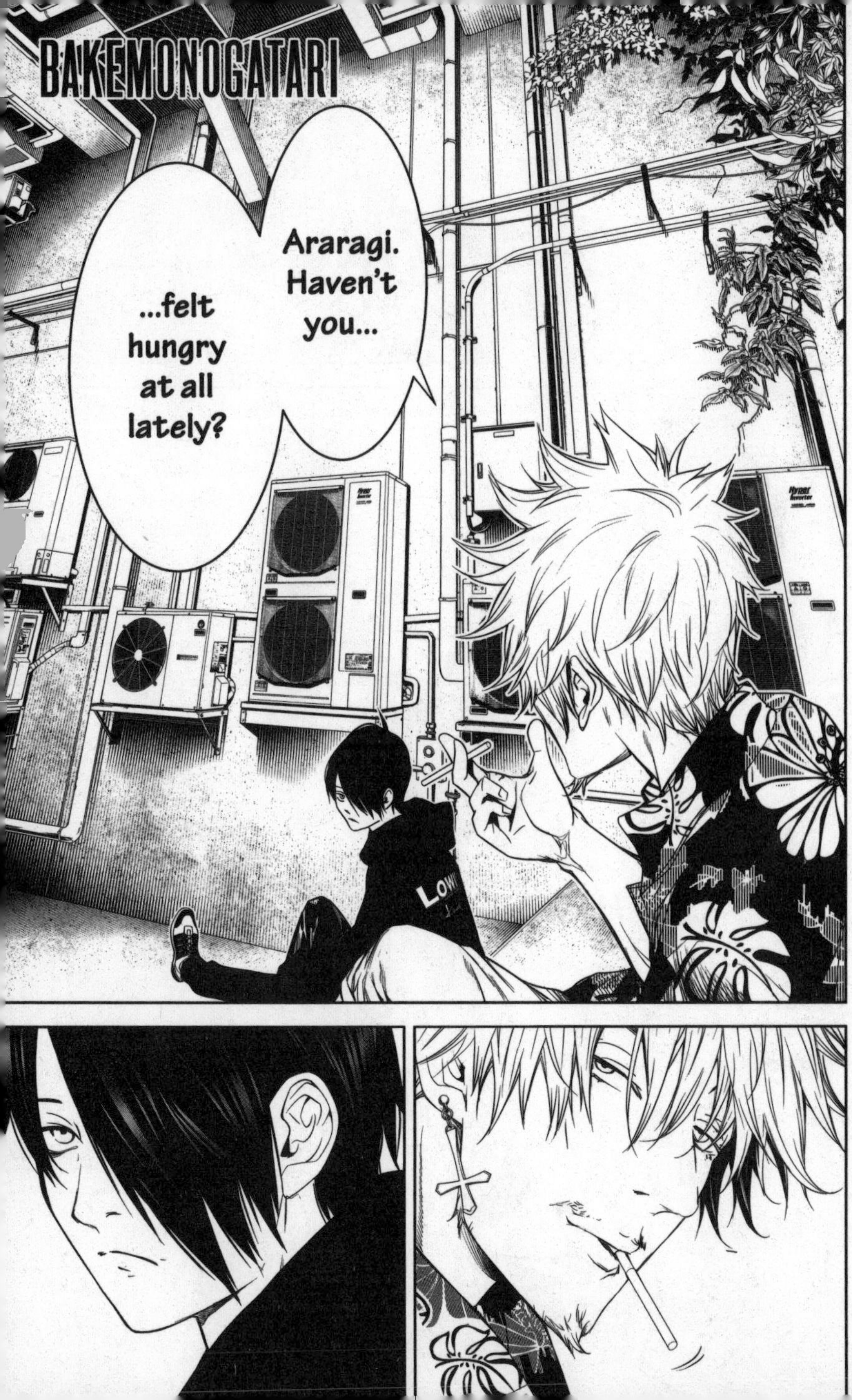
Araragi. Haven't you...
...felt hungry at all lately?

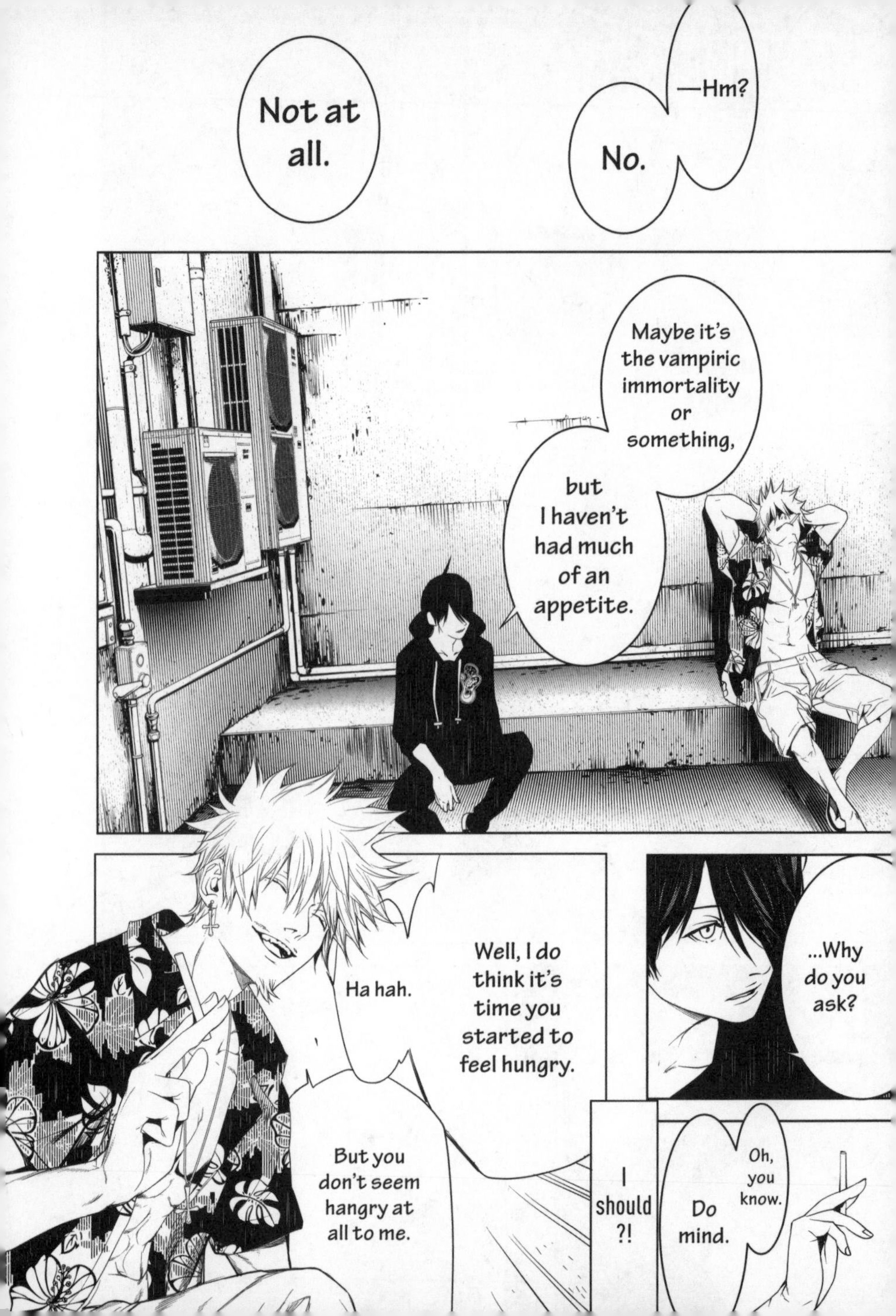
—Hm?
No.
Not at all.
Maybe it's the vampiric immortality or something,
but I haven't had much of an appetite.
...Why do you ask?
Oh, you know.
Do mind.
I should?!
Well, I do think it's time you started to feel hungry.
Ha hah.
But you don't seem hangry at all to me.

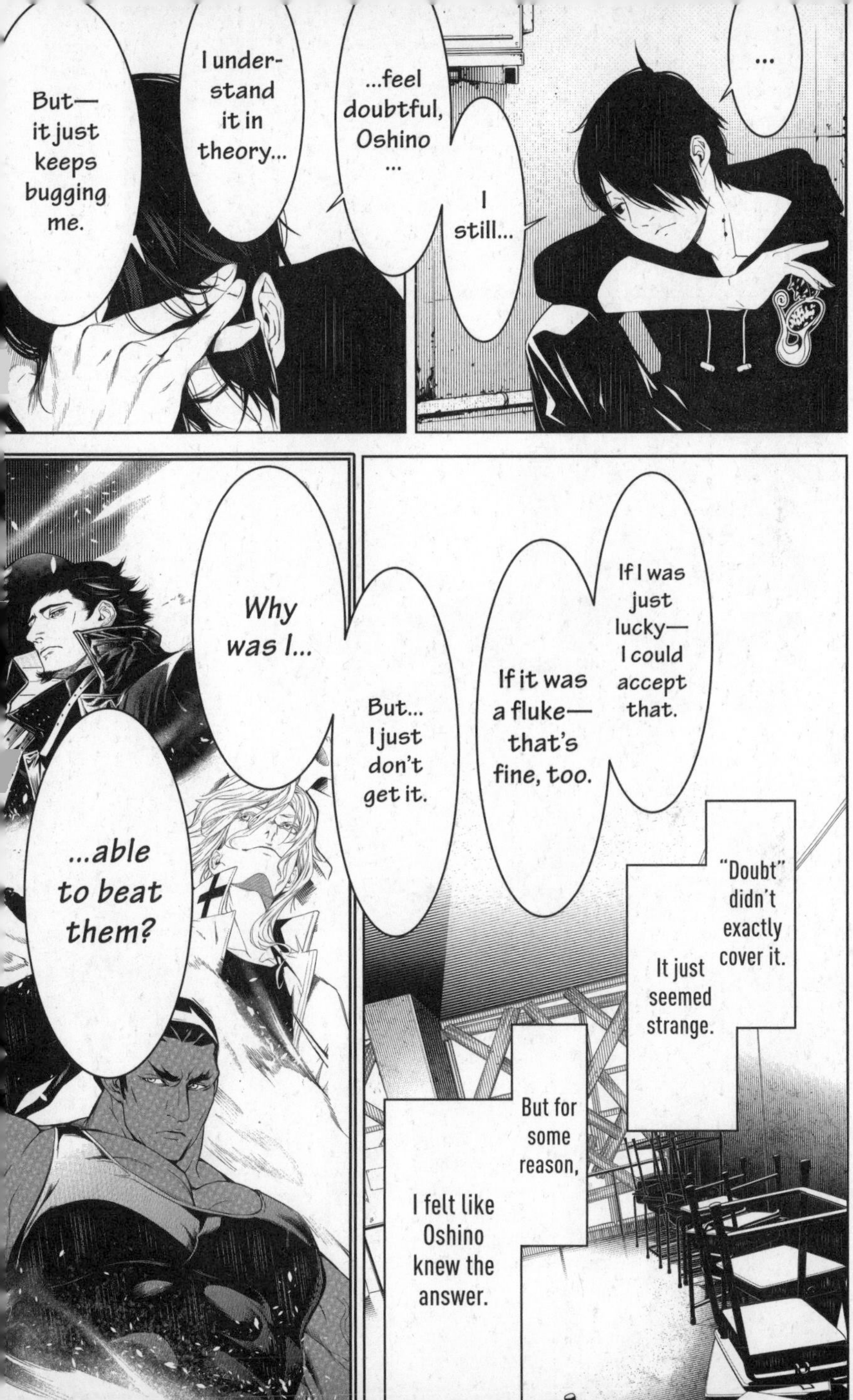
...
I still...
...feel doubtful, Oshino ...
I under-stand it in theory...
But— it just keeps bugging me.
If I was just lucky— I could accept that.
If it was a fluke— that's fine, too.
But... I just don't get it.
"Doubt" didn't exactly cover it.
It just seemed strange.
But for some reason,
I felt like Oshino knew the answer.
Why was I...
...able to beat them?

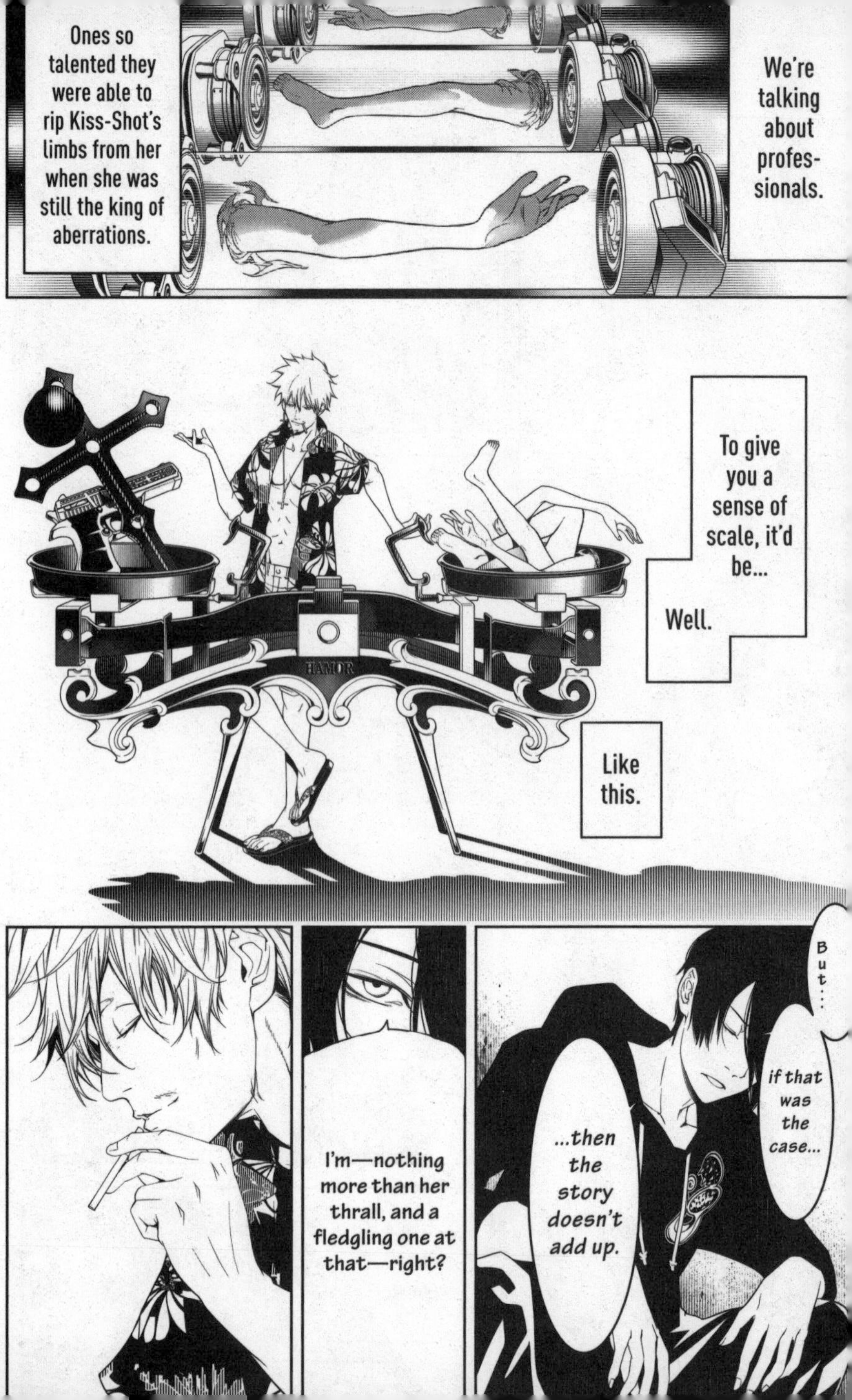
We're talking about profes-sionals.
Ones so talented they were able to rip Kiss-Shot's limbs from her when she was still the king of aberrations.
To give you a sense of scale, it'd be...
Well.
HAMOR
Like this.
But...
if that was the case...
...then the story doesn't add up.
I'm—nothing more than her thrall, and a fledgling one at that—right?

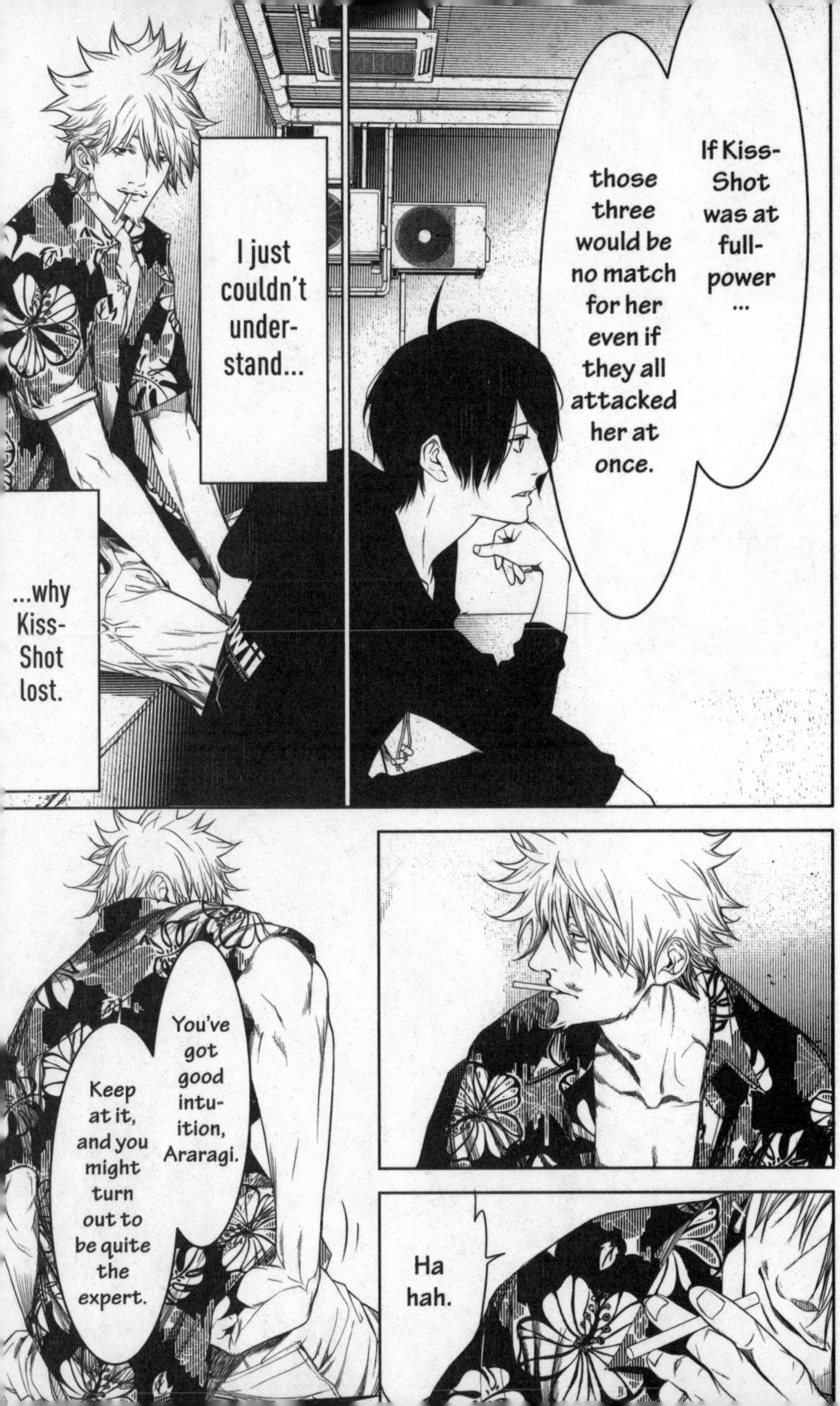
If Kiss-Shot was at full-power...
those three would be no match for her even if they all attacked her at once.
I just couldn't under-stand...
...why Kiss-Shot lost.
Ha hah.
You've got good intu-ition, Araragi.
Keep at it, and you might turn out to be quite the expert.

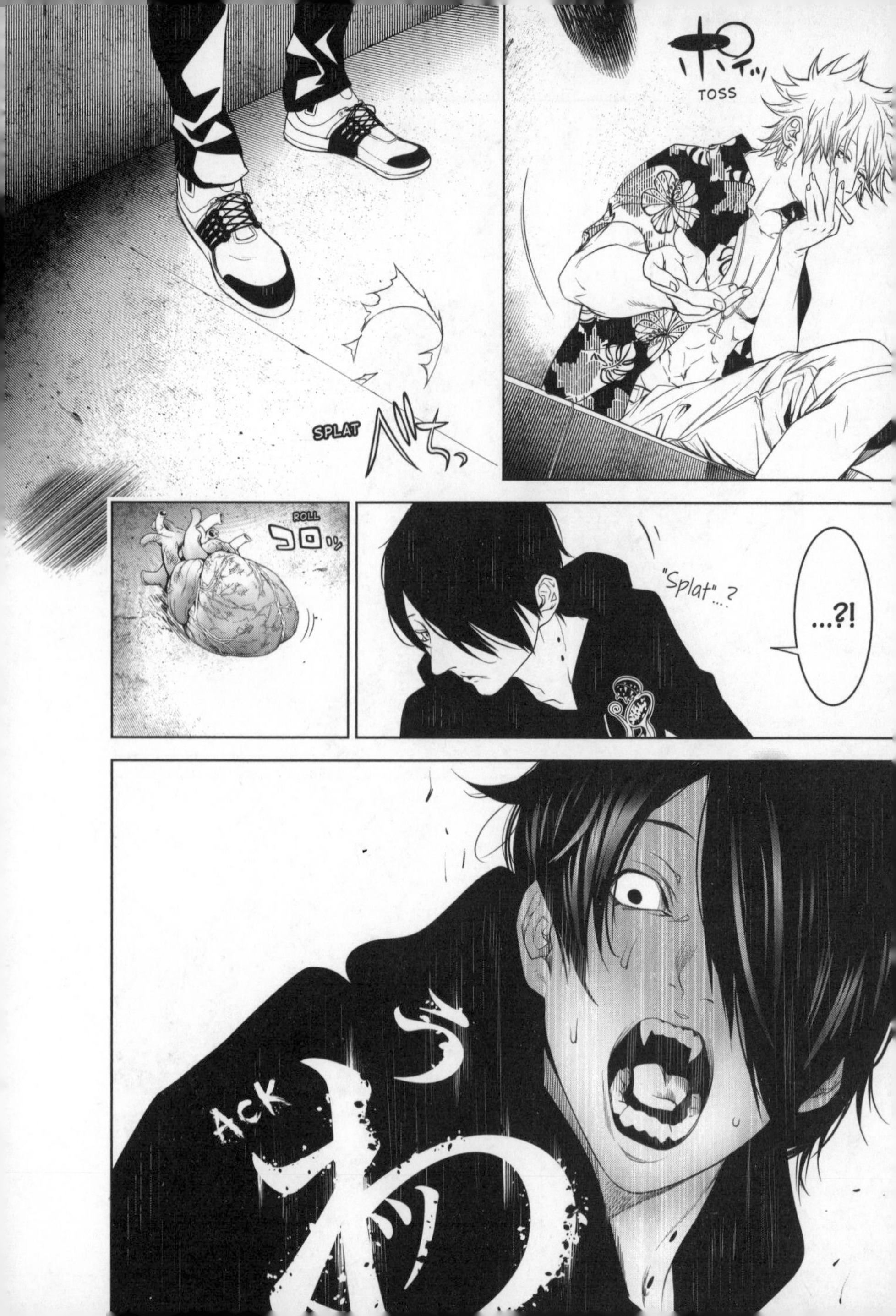
TOSS
SPLAT
...?!
"Splat"...?
ROLL
ACK

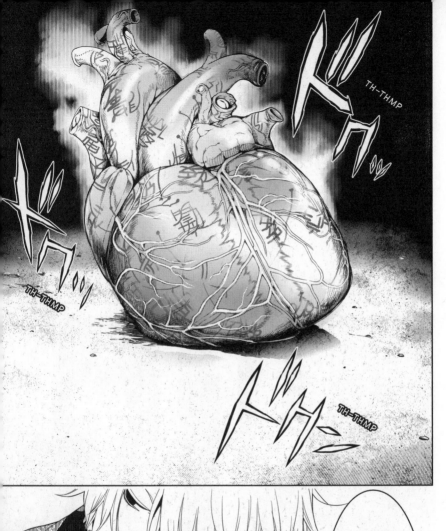

TH-THMP

TH-THMP

TH-THMP

Heart-
Under-
Blade's
...

...
heart.

As you
can see.

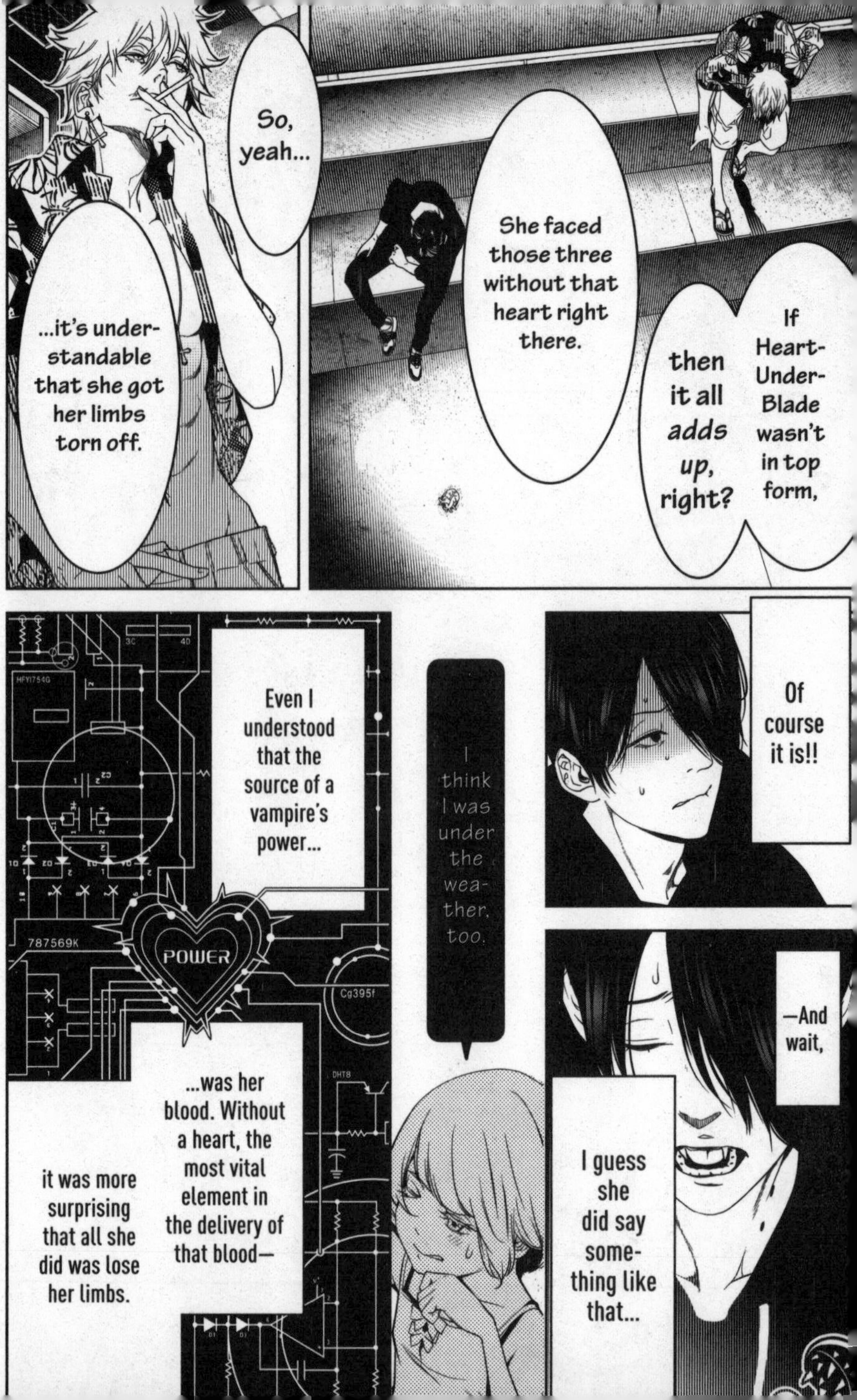

If Heart-Under-Blade wasn't in top form,
then it all adds up, right?
She faced those three without that heart right there.
So, yeah...
...it's understandable that she got her limbs torn off.
Of course it is!!
—And wait,
I guess she did say something like that...
I think I was under the weather, too.
Even I understood that the source of a vampire's power...
POWER
...was her blood. Without a heart, the most vital element in the delivery of that blood—
it was more surprising that all she did was lose her limbs.

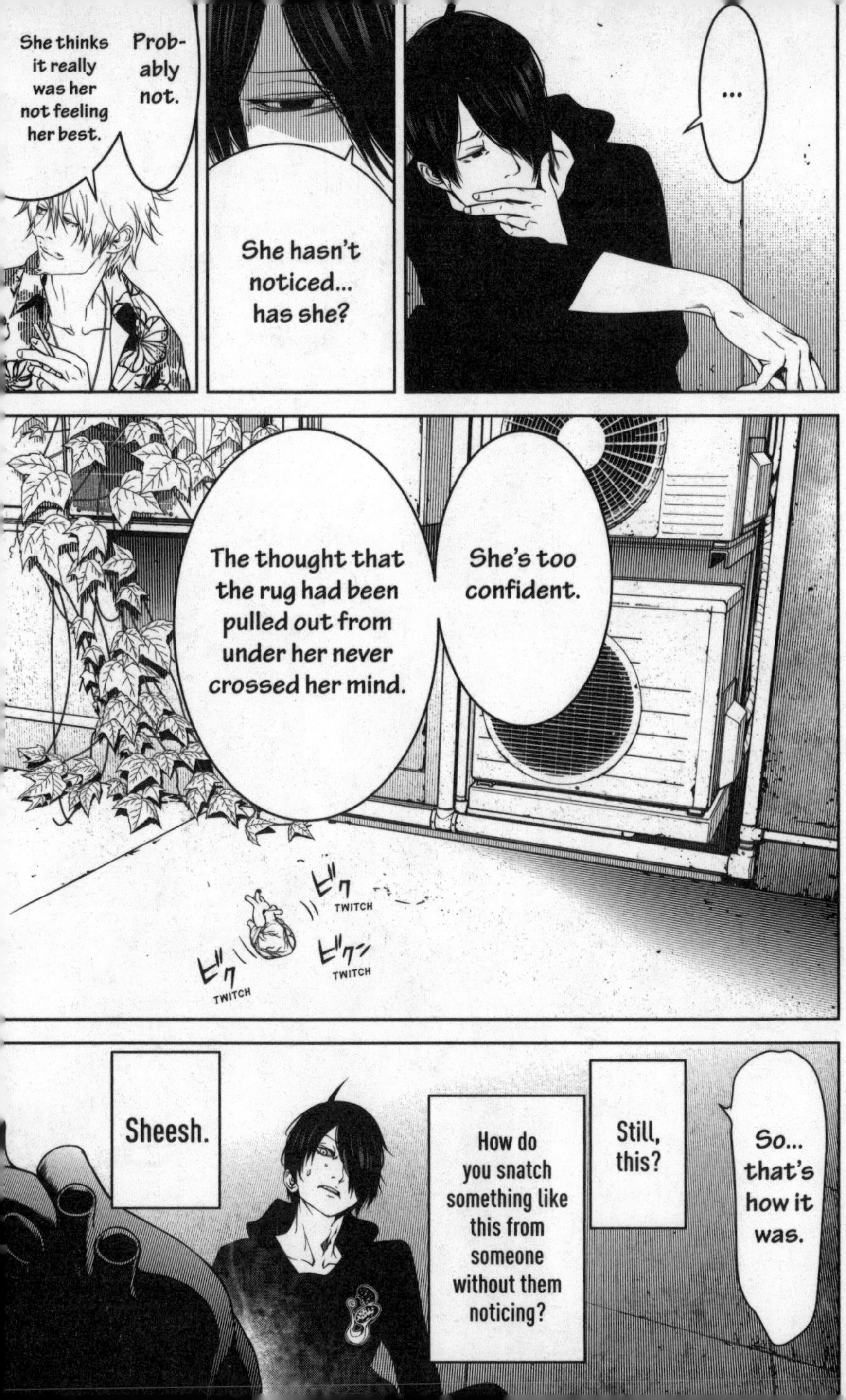
...
She hasn't noticed... has she?
Prob-ably not.
She thinks it really was her not feeling her best.
She's too confident.
The thought that the rug had been pulled out from under her never crossed her mind.
ビク TWITCH
ビクン TWITCH
ビク TWITCH
So... that's how it was.
Still, this?
How do you snatch something like this from someone without them noticing?
Sheesh.

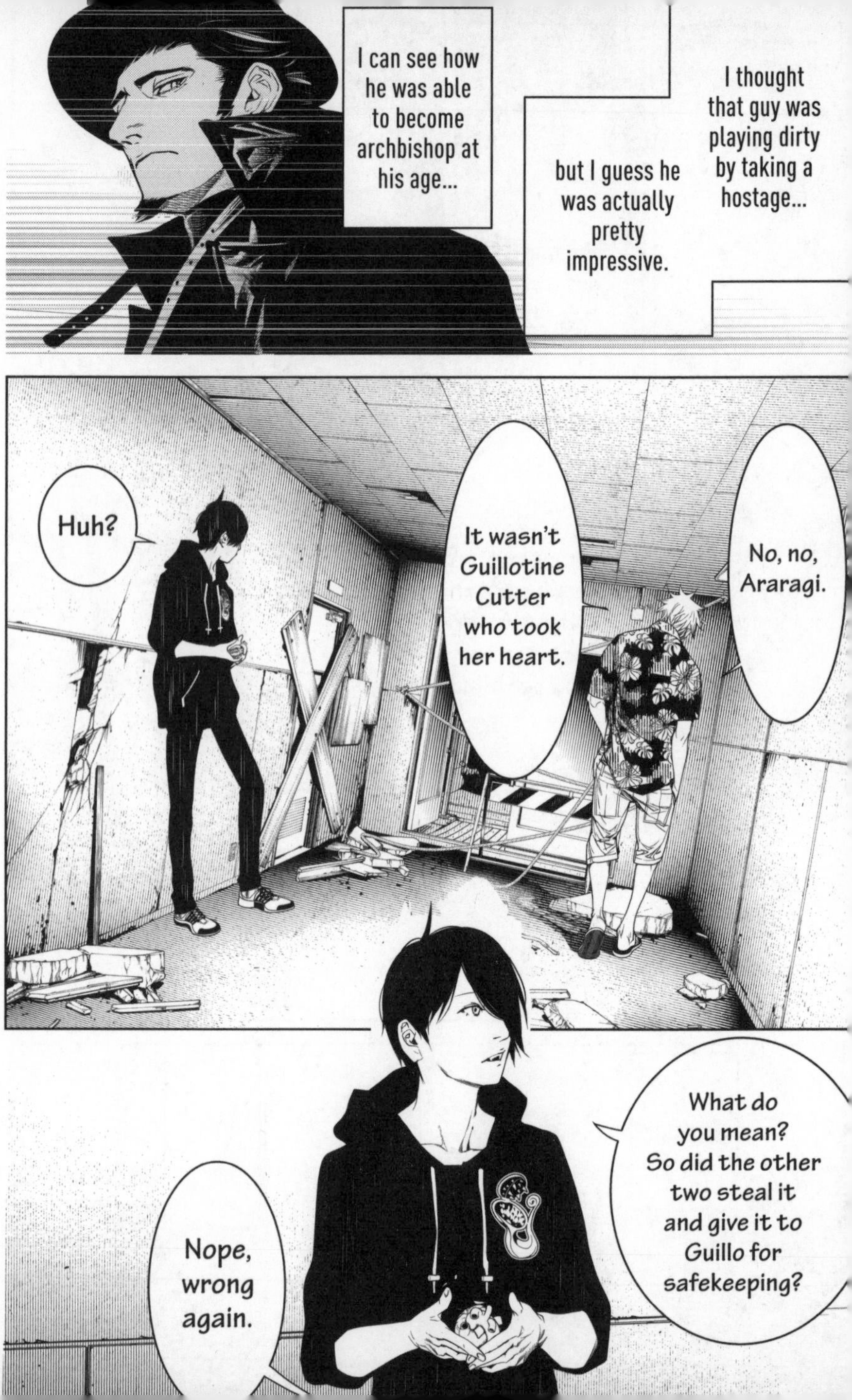
I thought that guy was playing dirty by taking a hostage...
but I guess he was actually pretty impressive.
I can see how he was able to become archbishop at his age...
No, no, Araragi.
It wasn't Guillotine Cutter who took her heart.
Huh?
What do you mean? So did the other two steal it and give it to Guillo for safekeeping?
Nope, wrong again.

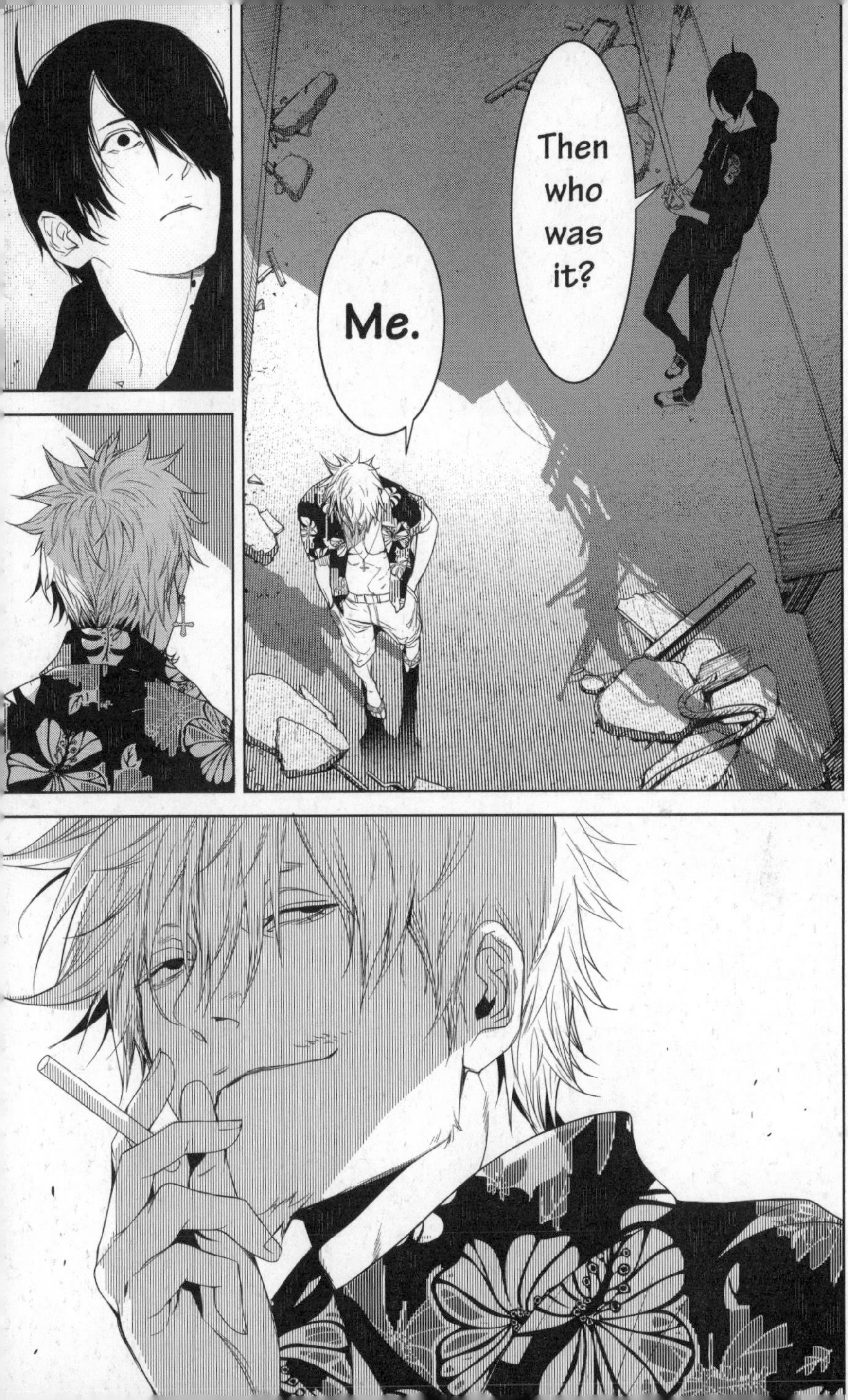
Then who was it?
Me.

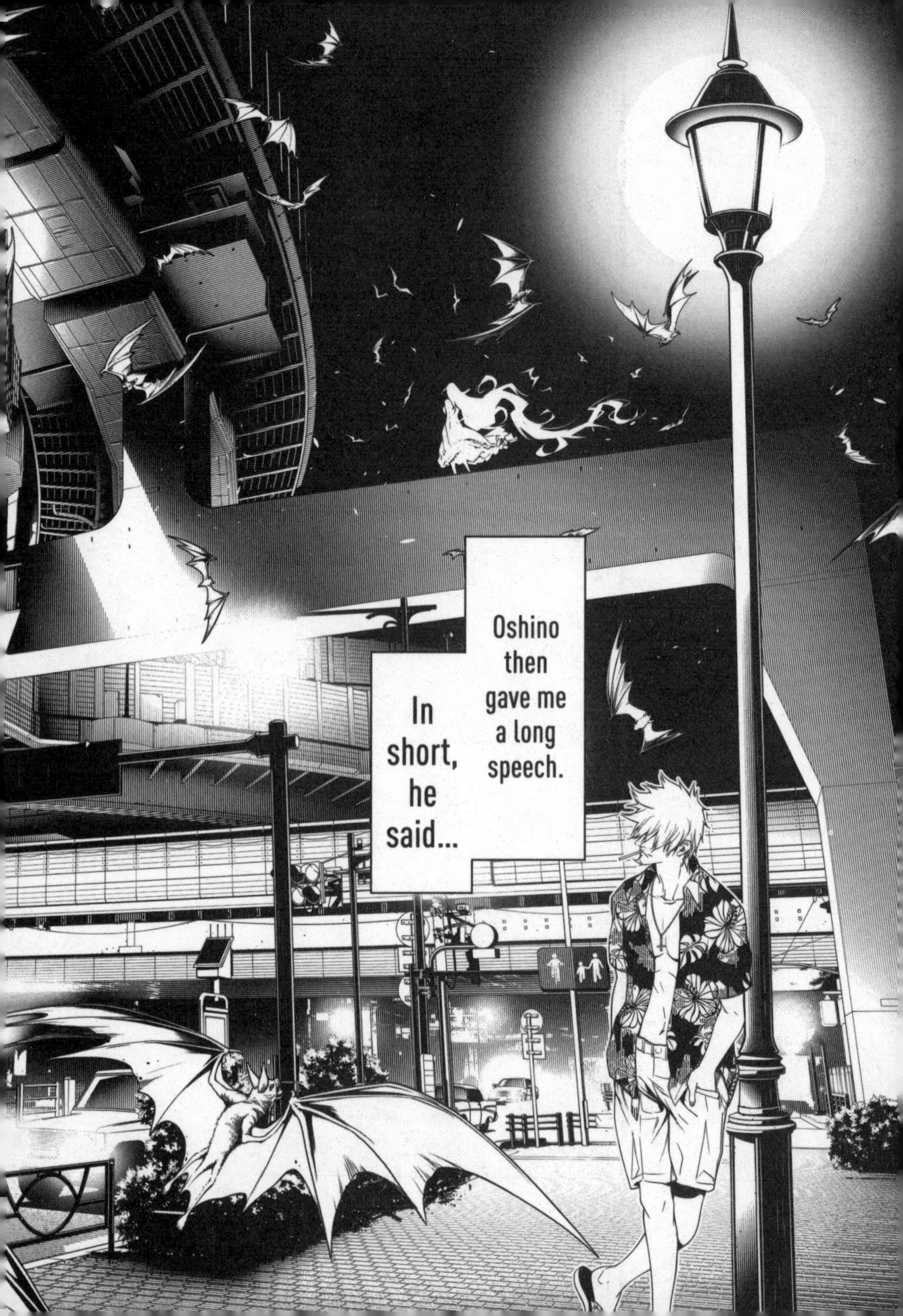
Oshino then gave me a long speech.
In short, he said...

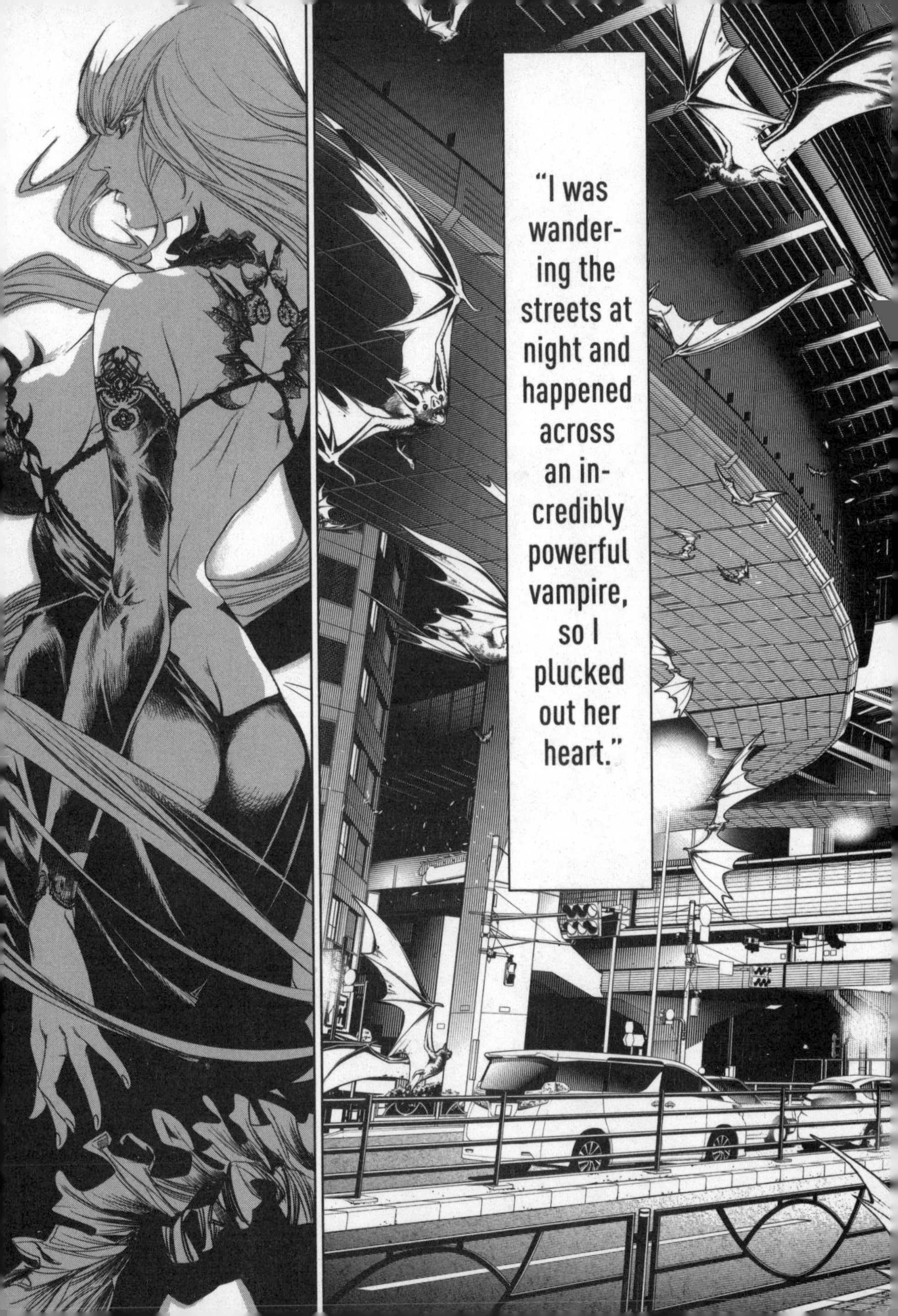
"I was wander-ing the streets at night and happened across an in-credibly powerful vampire, so I plucked out her heart."

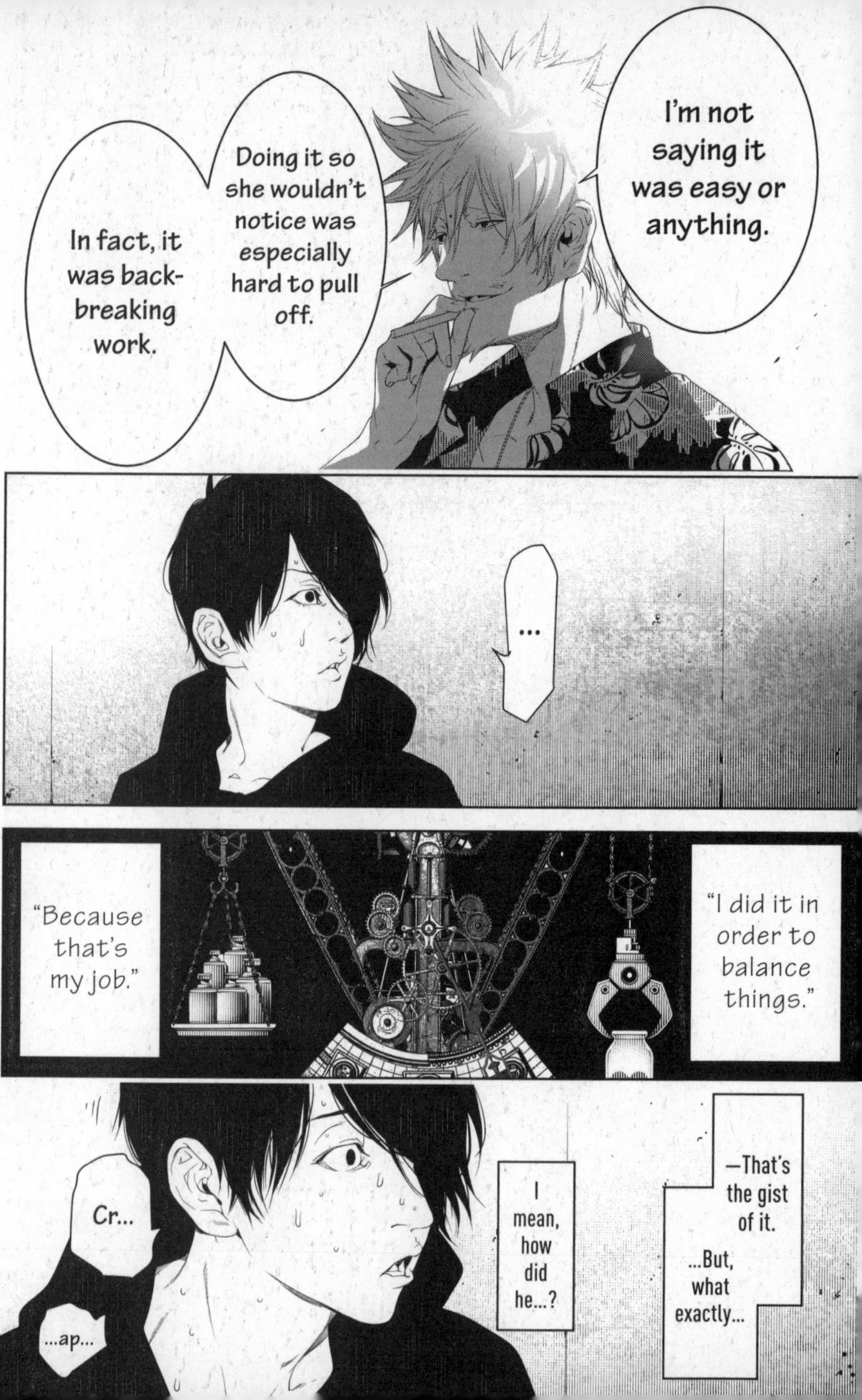
I'm not saying it was easy or anything.
Doing it so she wouldn't notice was especially hard to pull off.
In fact, it was back-breaking work.
...
"I did it in order to balance things."
"Because that's my job."
—That's the gist of it.
...But, what exactly...
I mean, how did he...?
Cr...
...ap...

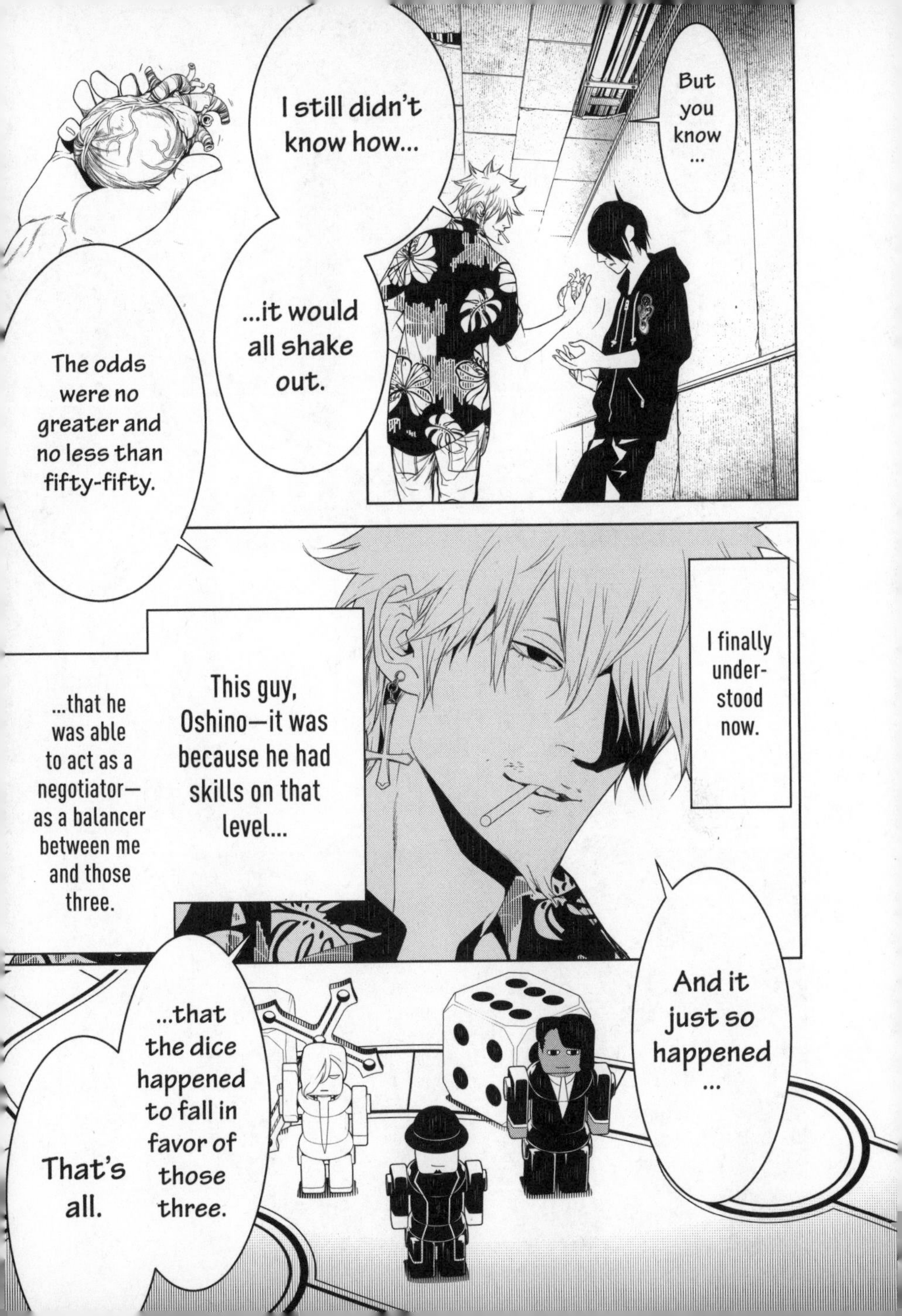
But you know ...
I still didn't know how...
...it would all shake out.
The odds were no greater and no less than fifty-fifty.
I finally under-stood now.
This guy, Oshino—it was because he had skills on that level...
...that he was able to act as a negotiator—as a balancer between me and those three.
And it just so happened ...
...that the dice happened to fall in favor of those three.
That's all.

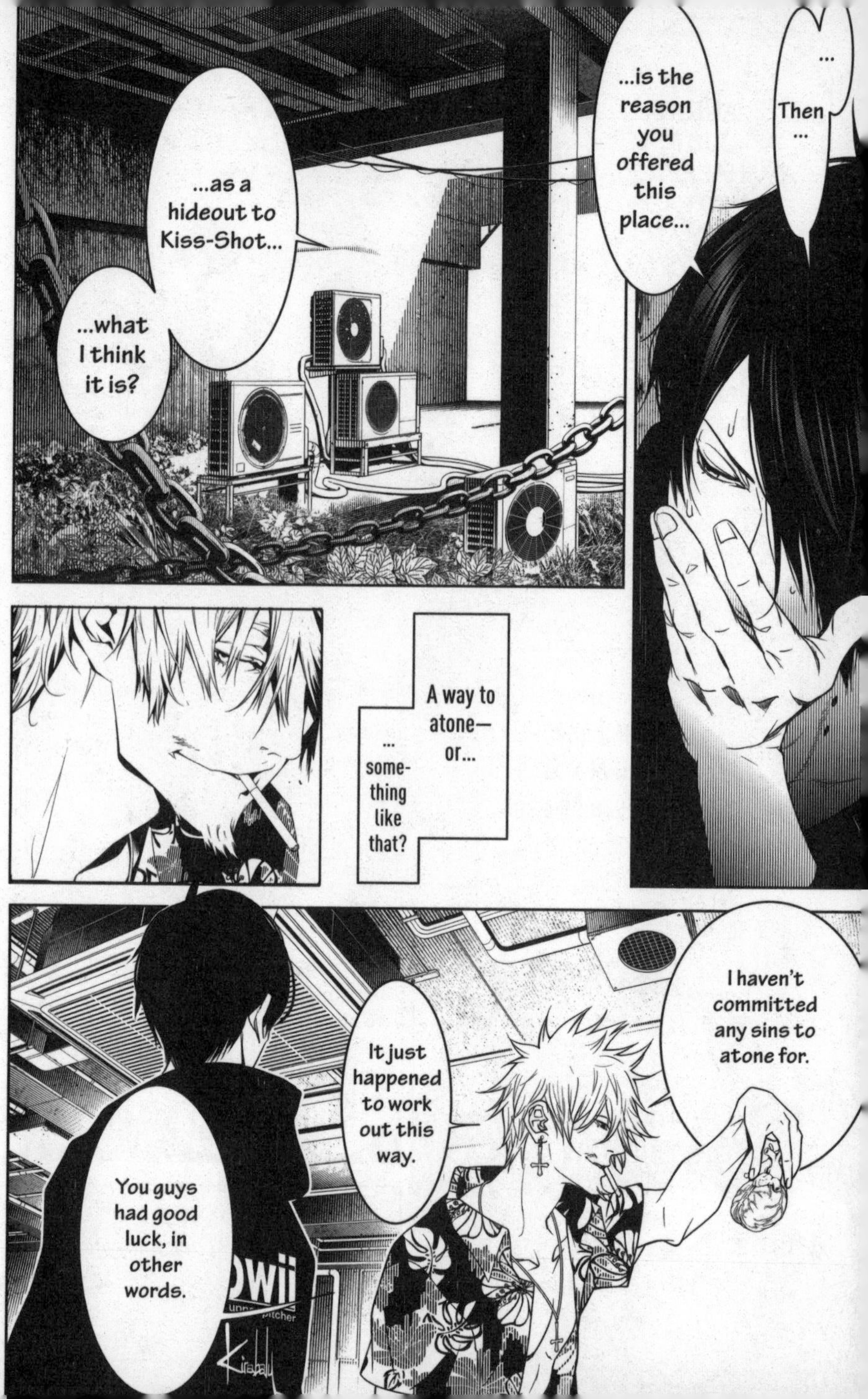
...
Then
...
...is the reason you offered this place...
...as a hideout to Kiss-Shot...
...what I think it is?
A way to atone—or...
...something like that?
I haven't committed any sins to atone for.
It just happened to work out this way.
You guys had good luck, in other words.

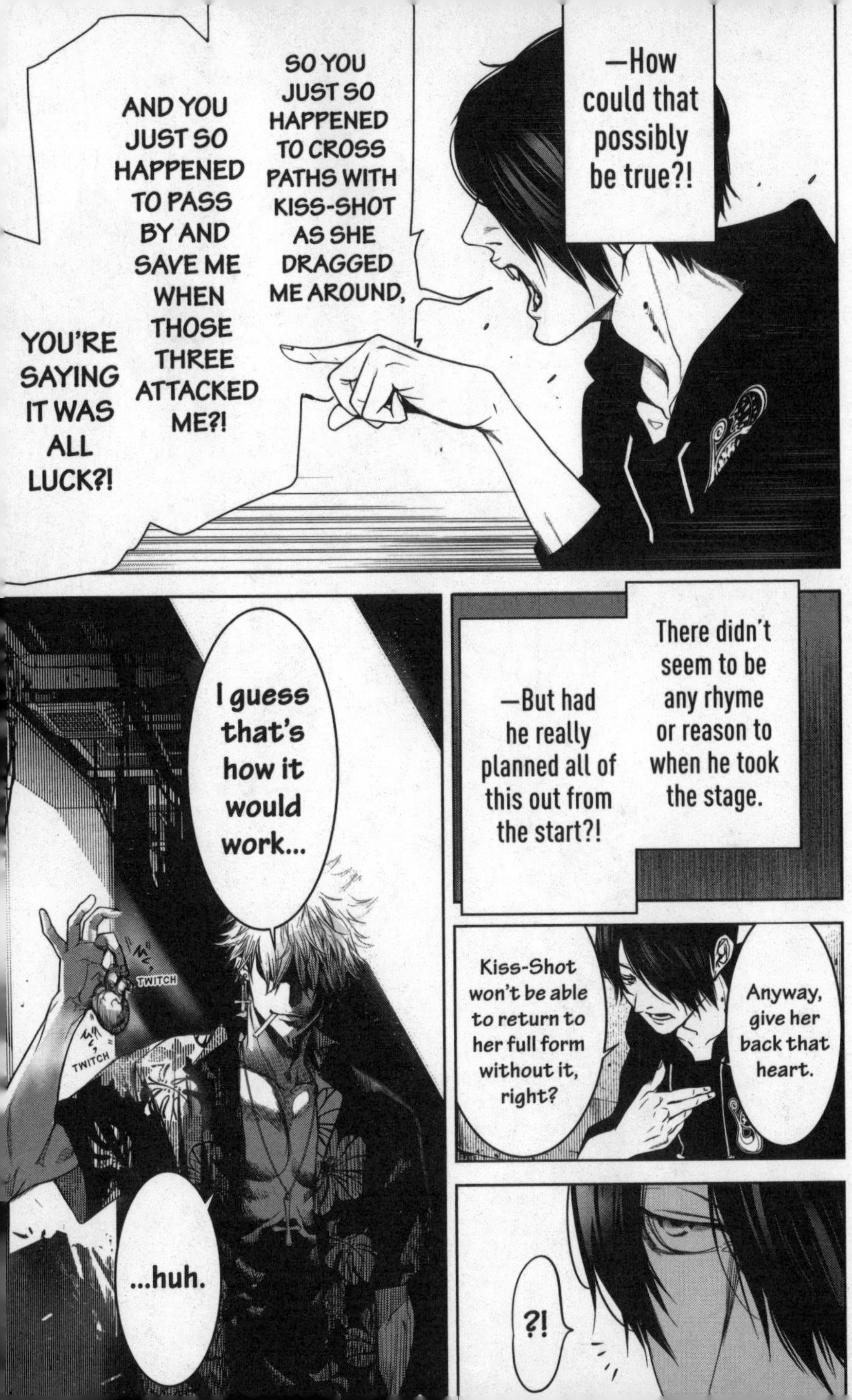
—How could that possibly be true?!
SO YOU JUST SO HAPPENED TO CROSS PATHS WITH KISS-SHOT AS SHE DRAGGED ME AROUND,
AND YOU JUST SO HAPPENED TO PASS BY AND SAVE ME WHEN THOSE THREE ATTACKED ME?!
YOU'RE SAYING IT WAS ALL LUCK?!
There didn't seem to be any rhyme or reason to when he took the stage.
—But had he really planned all of this out from the start?!
Anyway, give her back that heart.
Kiss-Shot won't be able to return to her full form without it, right?
?!
I guess that's how it would work...
TWITCH
TWITCH
...huh.

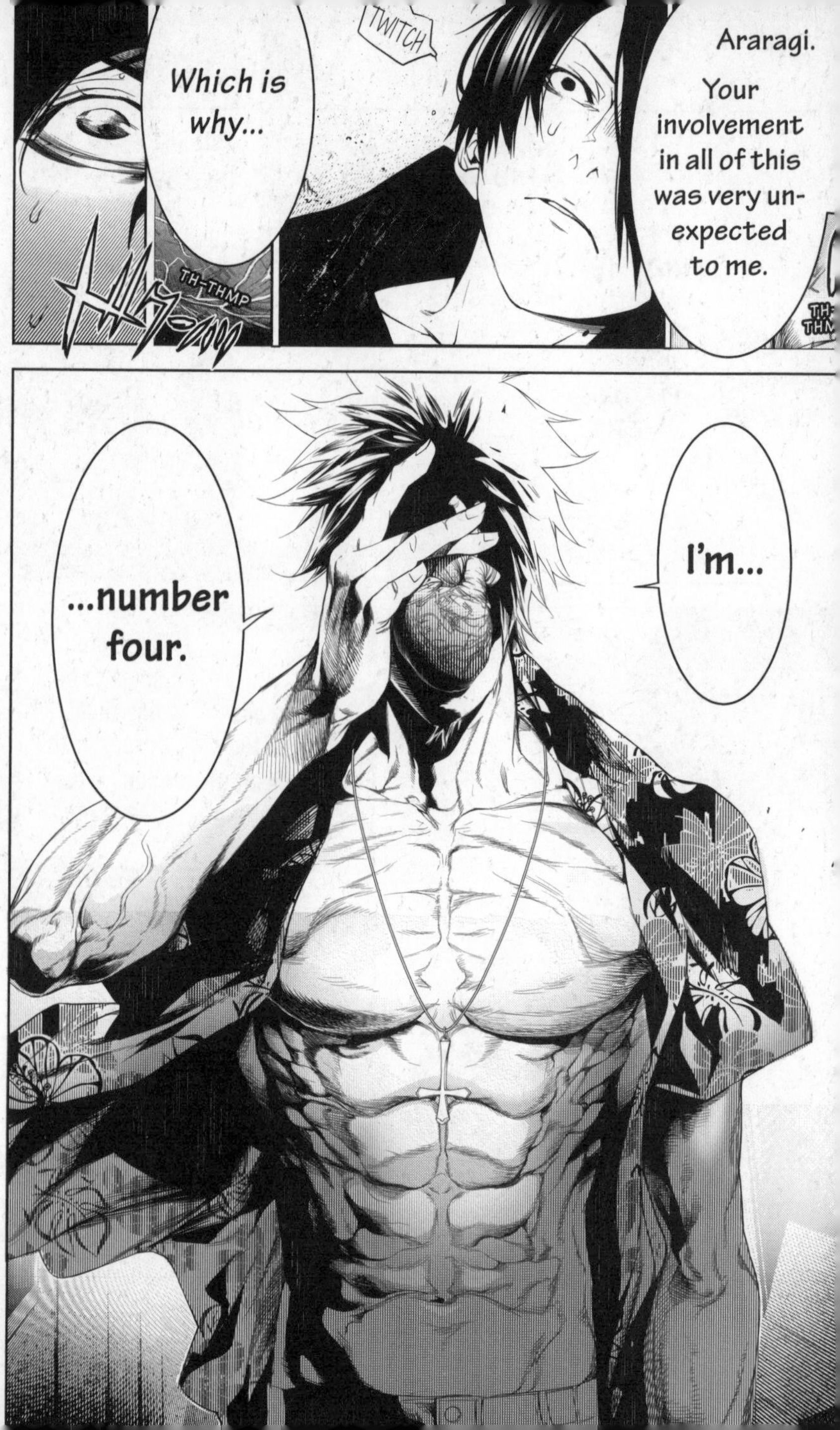
Araragi. Your involvement in all of this was very unexpected to me.
TWITCH
Which is why...
TH-THMP
I'm...
...number four.

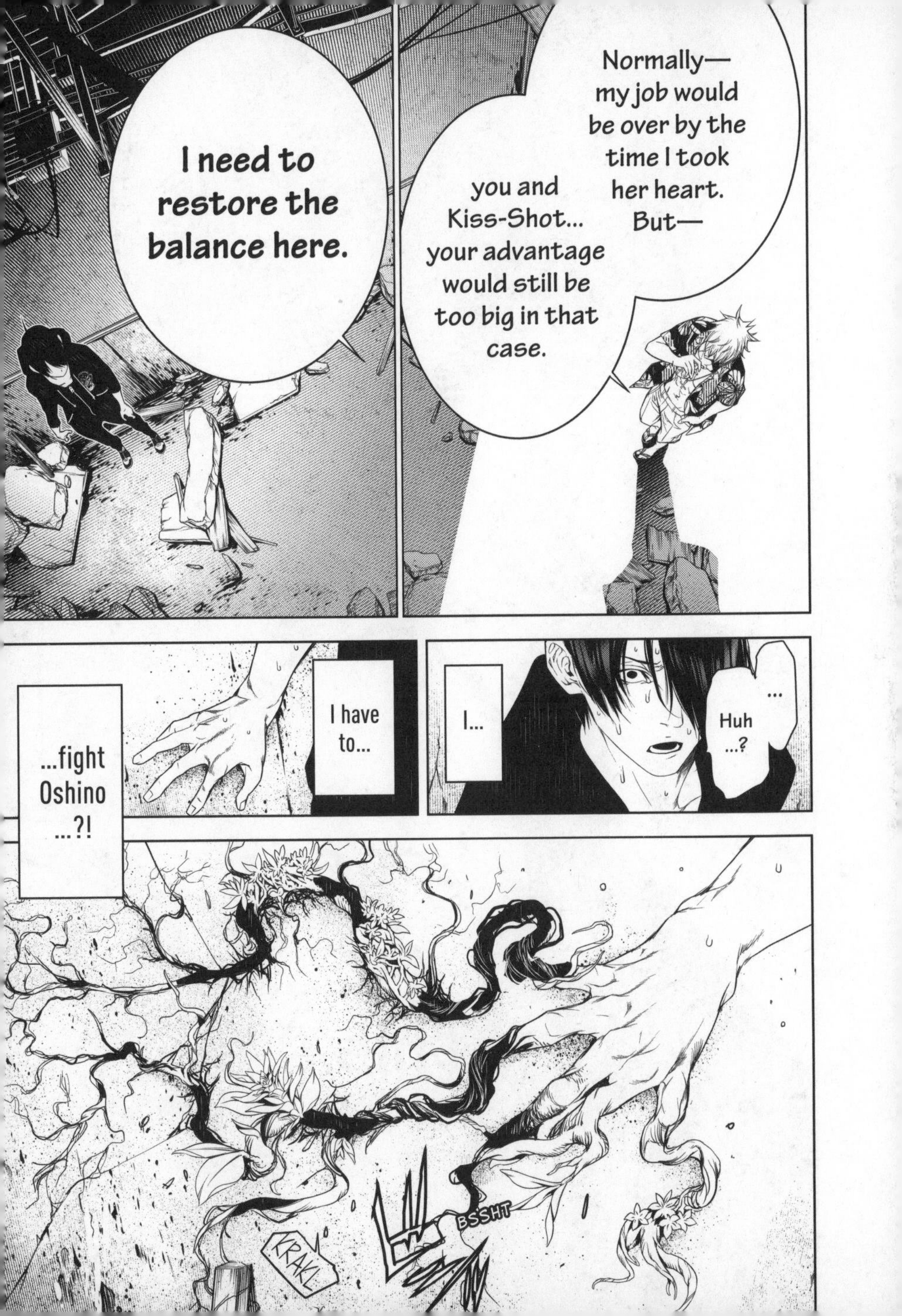

Normally— my job would be over by the time I took her heart. But—
you and Kiss-Shot... your advantage would still be too big in that case.
I need to restore the balance here.
... Huh ...?
I...
I have to...
...fight Oshino ...?!
BSSHT
KRAK!

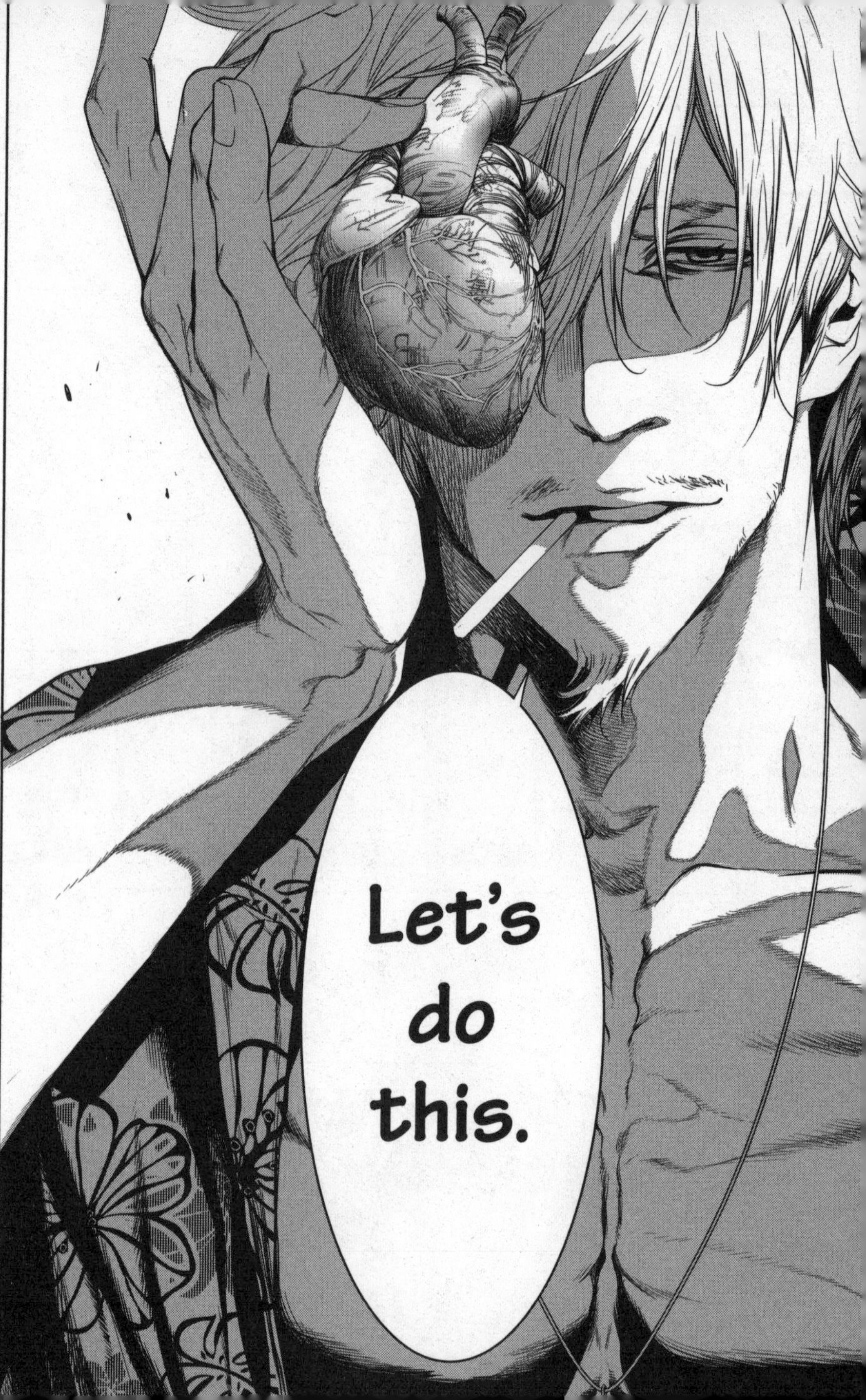
Let's do this.

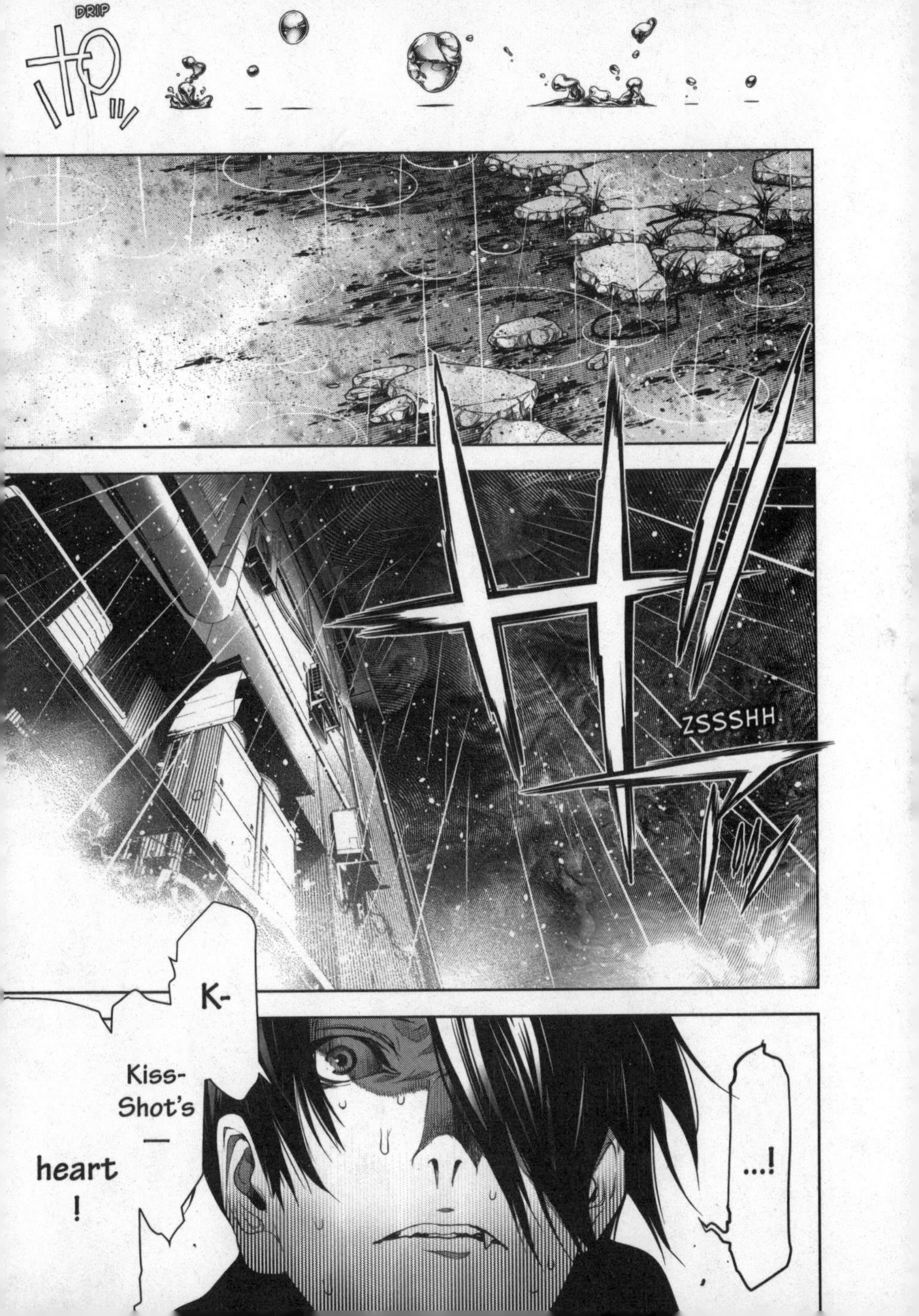
DRIP
ZSSSHH
...!
K-
Kiss-Shot's
—
heart
!

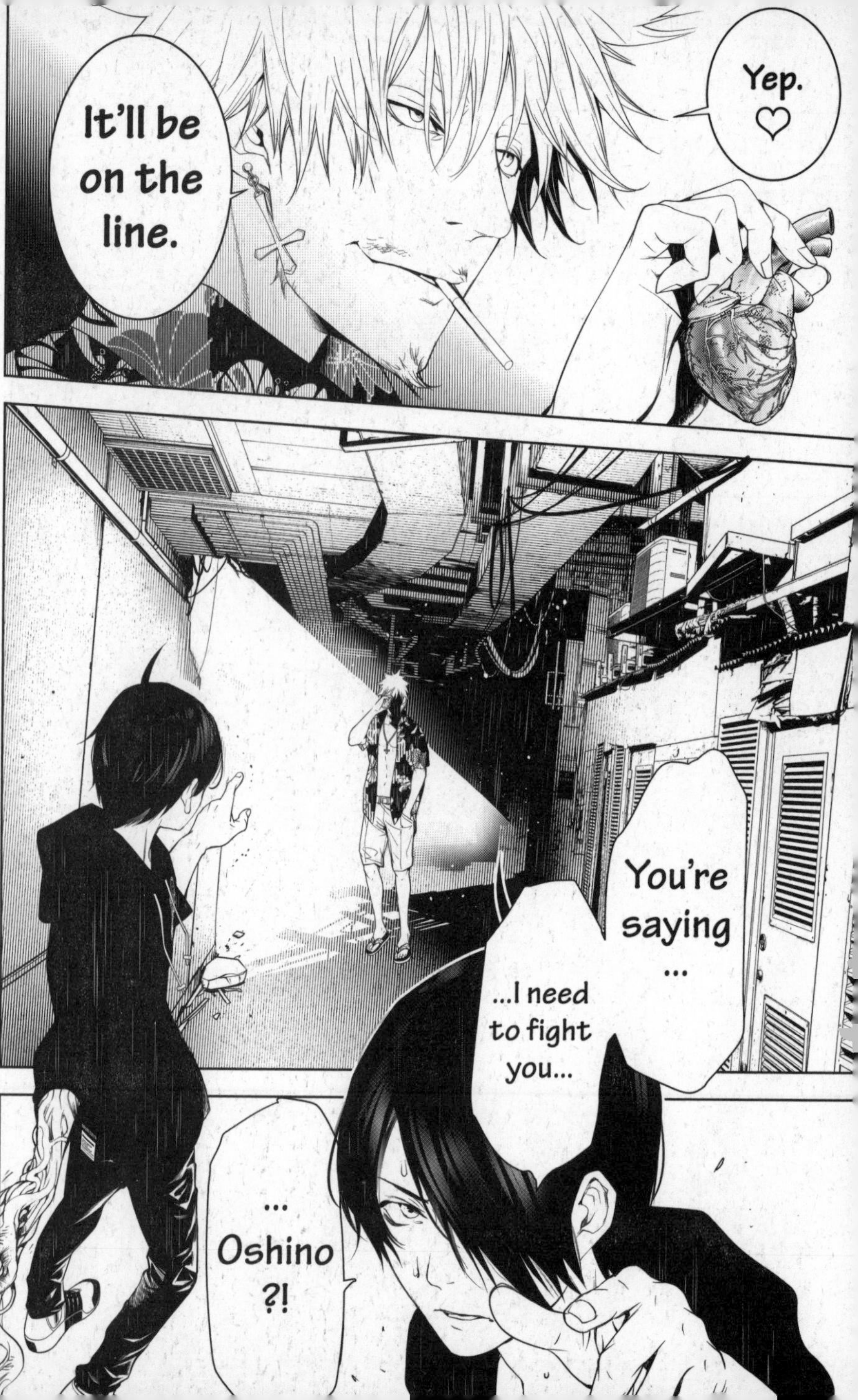
Yep. ♡
It'll be on the line.
You're saying ...
...I need to fight you...
... Oshino ?!

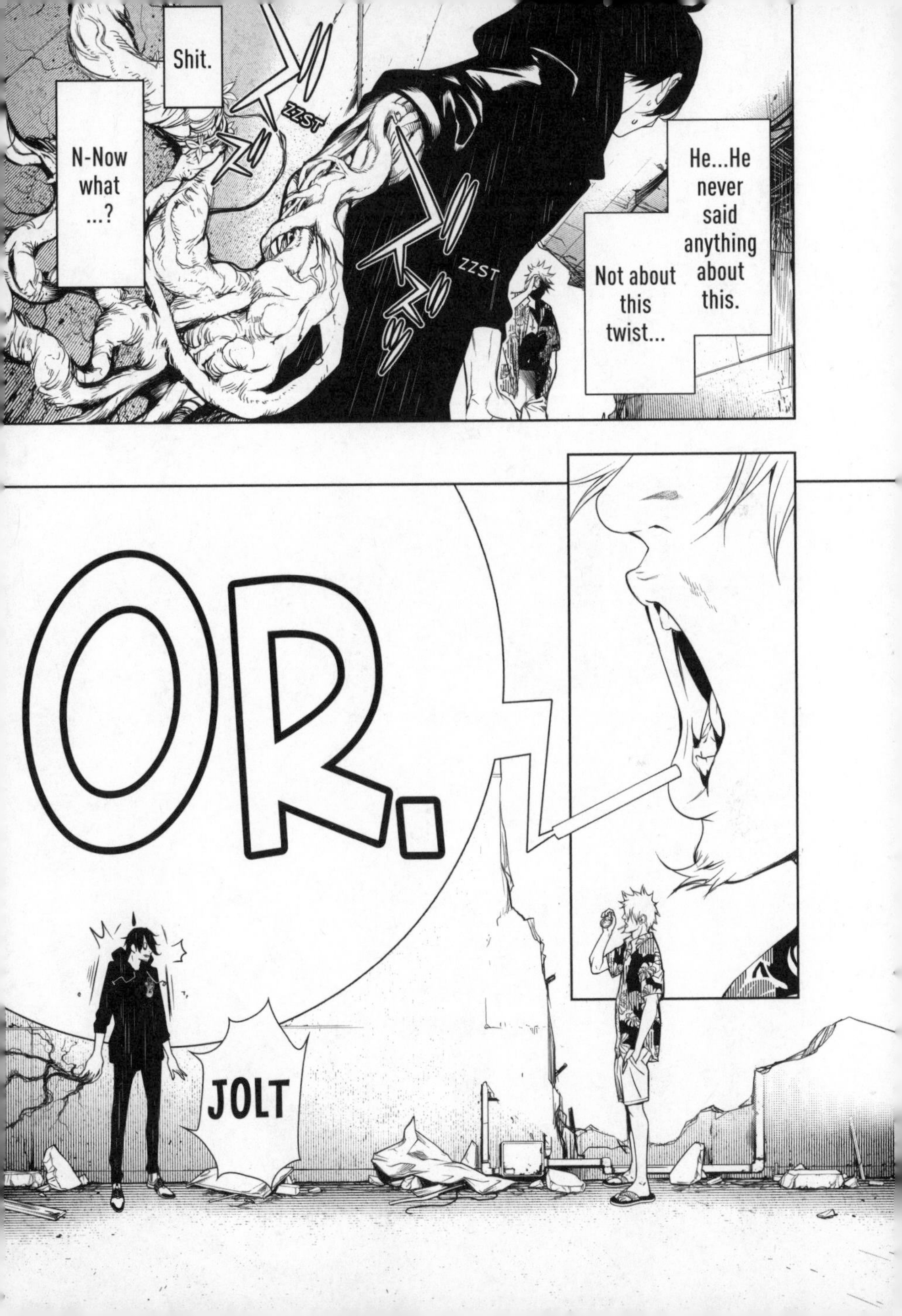
He...He never said anything about this.
Not about this twist...
ZZST
ZZST
Shit.
N-Now what ...?
OR.
JOLT

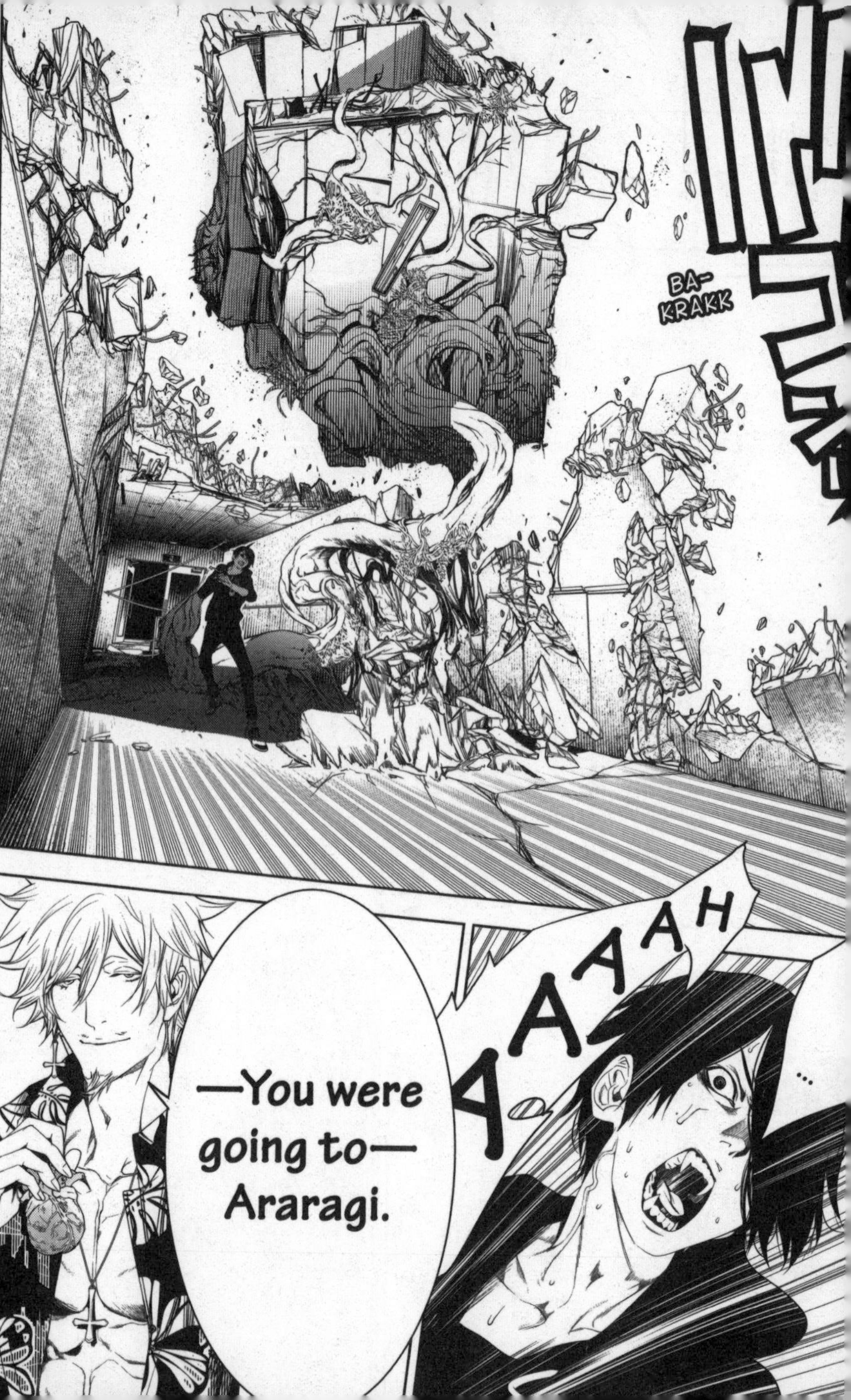
BA-
KRAKK
AAAAAH
...
—You were going to— Araragi.

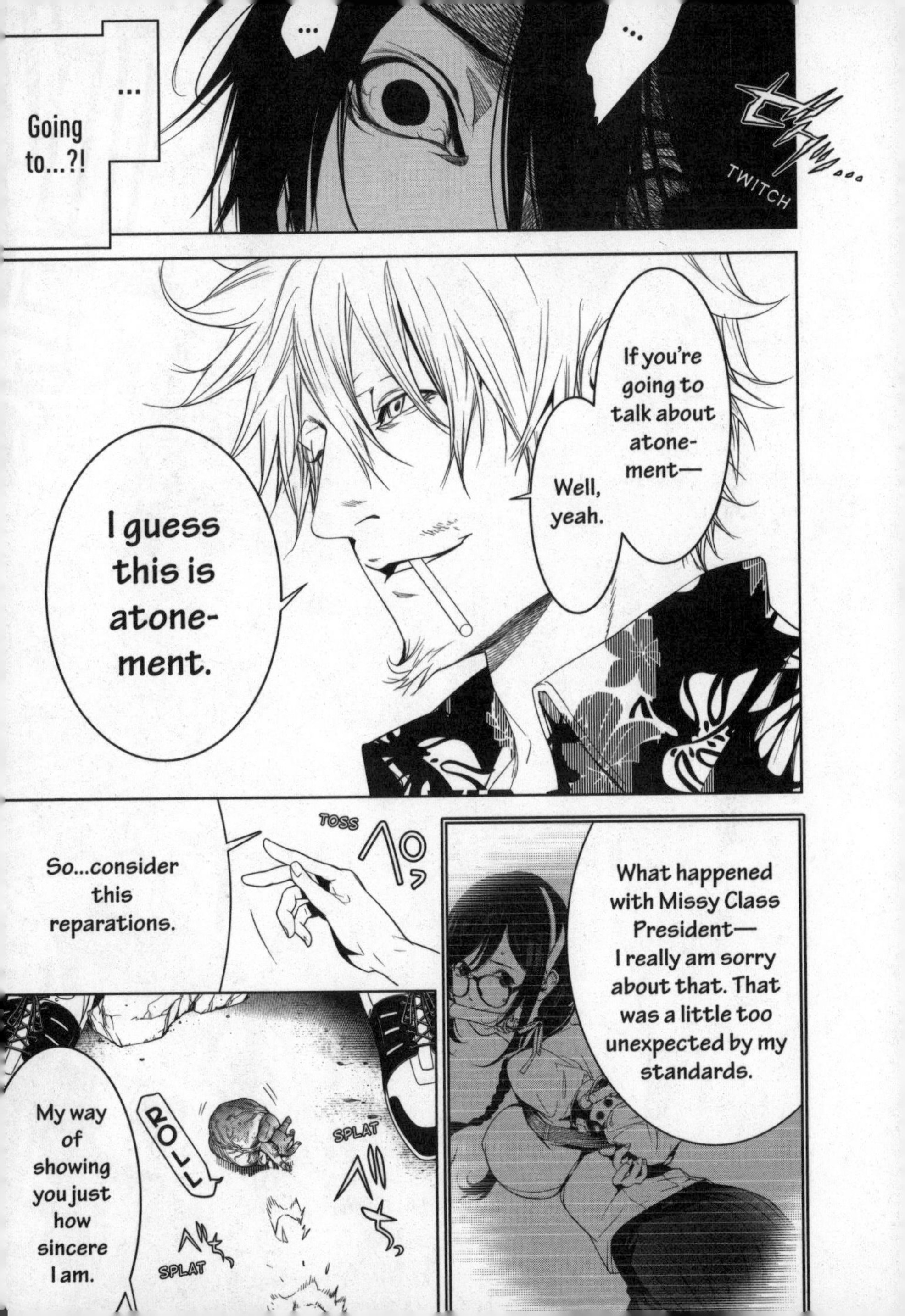
...
...
... Going to...?!
TWITCH
If you're going to talk about atone-ment—
Well, yeah.
I guess this is atone-ment.
What happened with Missy Class President— I really am sorry about that. That was a little too unexpected by my standards.
TOSS
So...consider this reparations.
ROLL
SPLAT
My way of showing you just how sincere I am.
SPLAT

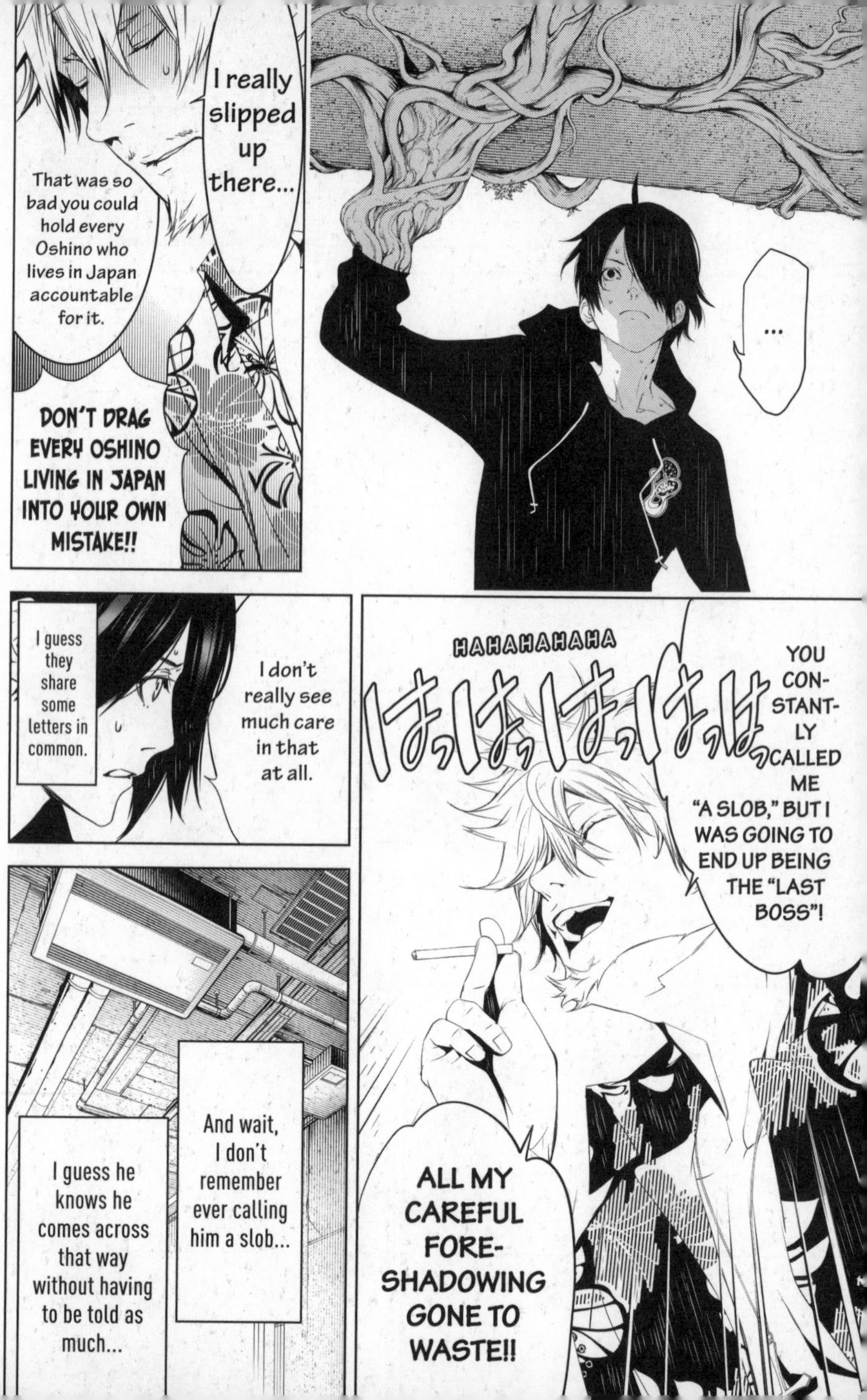
...
I really slipped up there...
That was so bad you could hold every Oshino who lives in Japan accountable for it.
DON'T DRAG EVERY OSHINO LIVING IN JAPAN INTO YOUR OWN MISTAKE!!
はっはっはっはっはっ
HAHAHAHAHA
YOU CONSTANTLY CALLED ME "A SLOB," BUT I WAS GOING TO END UP BEING THE "LAST BOSS"!
ALL MY CAREFUL FORE-SHADOWING GONE TO WASTE!!
I don't really see much care in that at all.
I guess they share some letters in common.
And wait, I don't remember ever calling him a slob...
I guess he knows he comes across that way without having to be told as much...

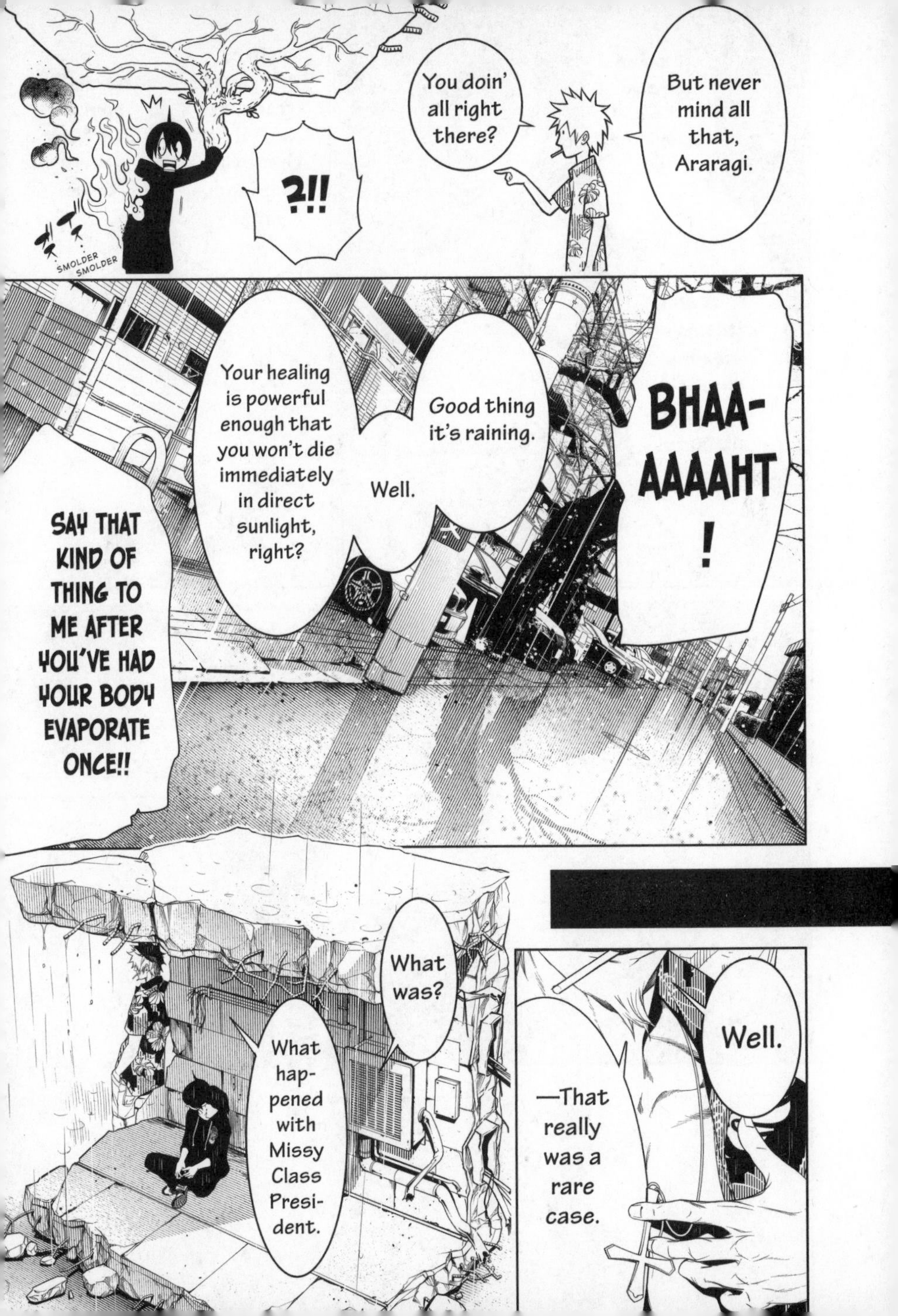
But never mind all that, Araragi.
You doin' all right there?
?!!
SMOLDER SMOLDER
BHAA-AAAAHT!
Good thing it's raining.
Well.
Your healing is powerful enough that you won't die immediately in direct sunlight, right?
SAY THAT KIND OF THING TO ME AFTER YOU'VE HAD YOUR BODY EVAPORATE ONCE!!
Well.
—That really was a rare case.
What was?
What hap-pened with Missy Class Presi-dent.

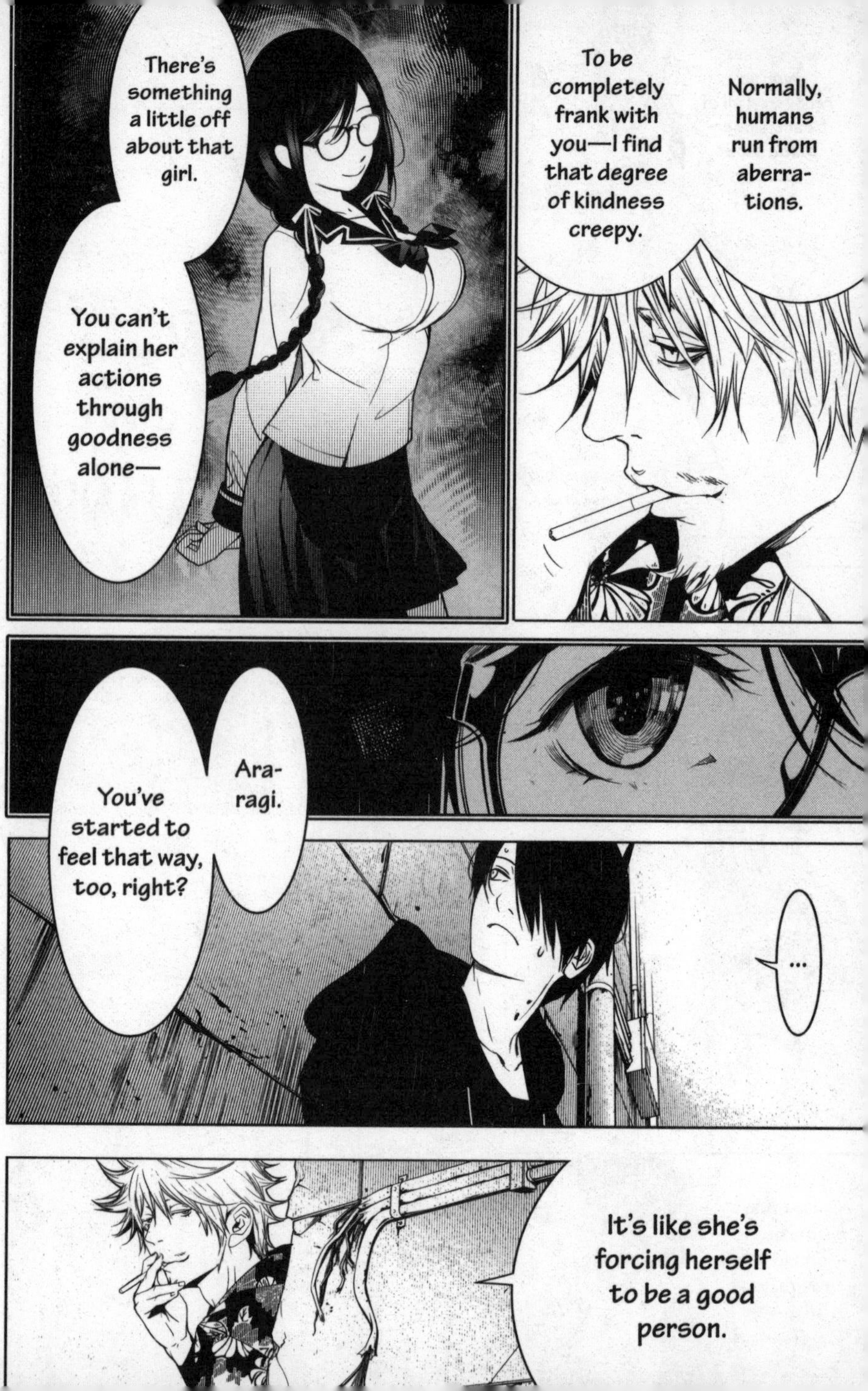
Normally, humans run from aberrations.
To be completely frank with you—I find that degree of kindness creepy.
There's something a little off about that girl.
You can't explain her actions through goodness alone—
Ara-ragi.
You've started to feel that way, too, right?
...
It's like she's forcing herself to be a good person.

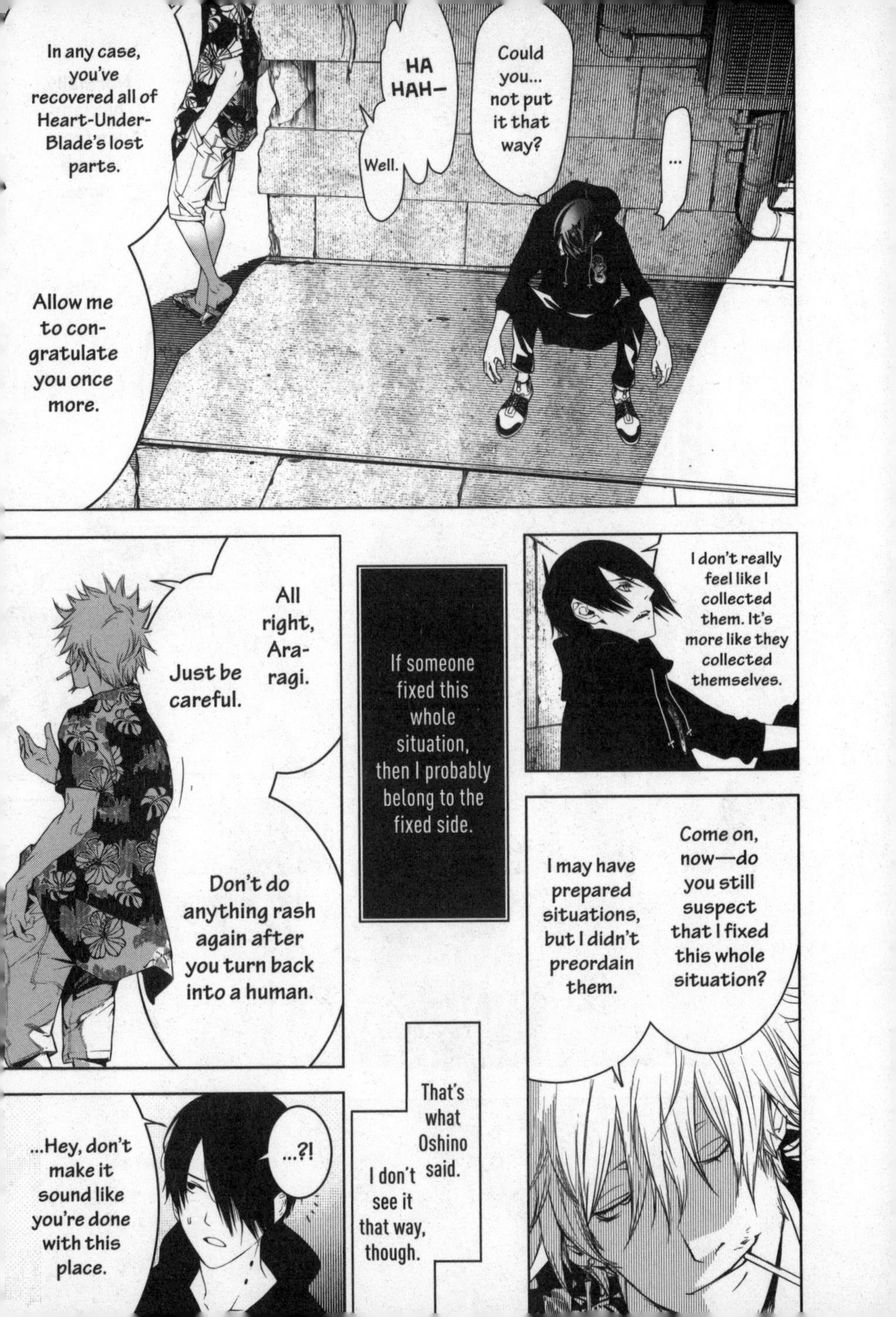
...
Could you... not put it that way?
HA HAH—
Well.
In any case, you've recovered all of Heart-Under-Blade's lost parts.
Allow me to congratulate you once more.
I don't really feel like I collected them. It's more like they collected themselves.
Come on, now—do you still suspect that I fixed this whole situation?
I may have prepared situations, but I didn't preordain them.
If someone fixed this whole situation, then I probably belong to the fixed side.
All right, Araragi.
Just be careful.
Don't do anything rash again after you turn back into a human.
That's what Oshino said.
I don't see it that way, though.
...?!
...Hey, don't make it sound like you're done with this place.

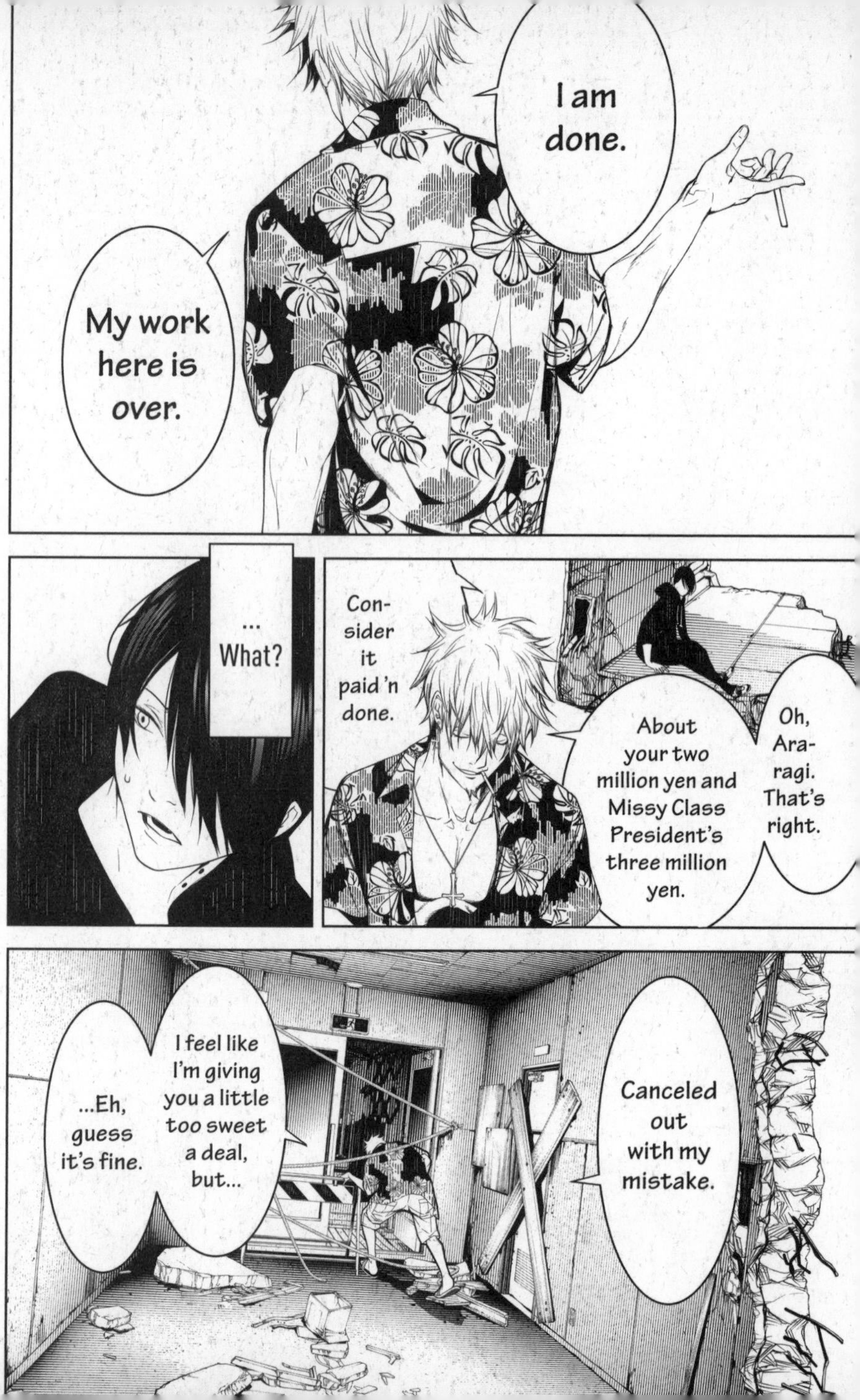
I am done.
My work here is over.
Oh, Araragi. That's right.
About your two million yen and Missy Class President's three million yen.
Consider it paid 'n done.
... What?
Canceled out with my mistake.
I feel like I'm giving you a little too sweet a deal, but...
...Eh, guess it's fine.

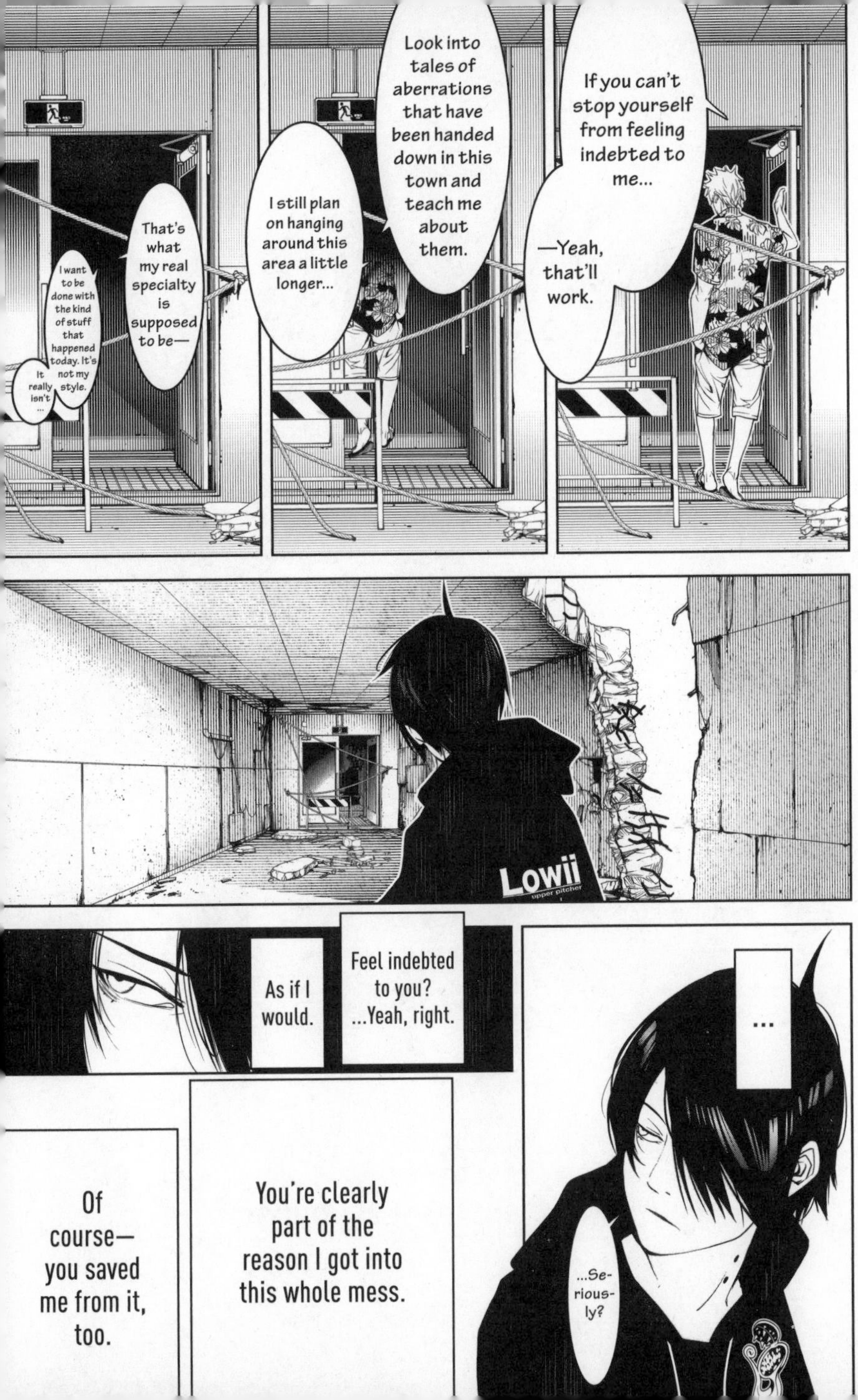
If you can't stop yourself from feeling indebted to me...
—Yeah, that'll work.
Look into tales of aberrations that have been handed down in this town and teach me about them.
I still plan on hanging around this area a little longer...
That's what my real specialty is supposed to be—
I want to be done with the kind of stuff that happened today. It's not my style.
It really isn't ...
Lowii
...
...Se-rious-ly?
Feel indebted to you? ...Yeah, right.
As if I would.
You're clearly part of the reason I got into this whole mess.
Of course— you saved me from it, too.

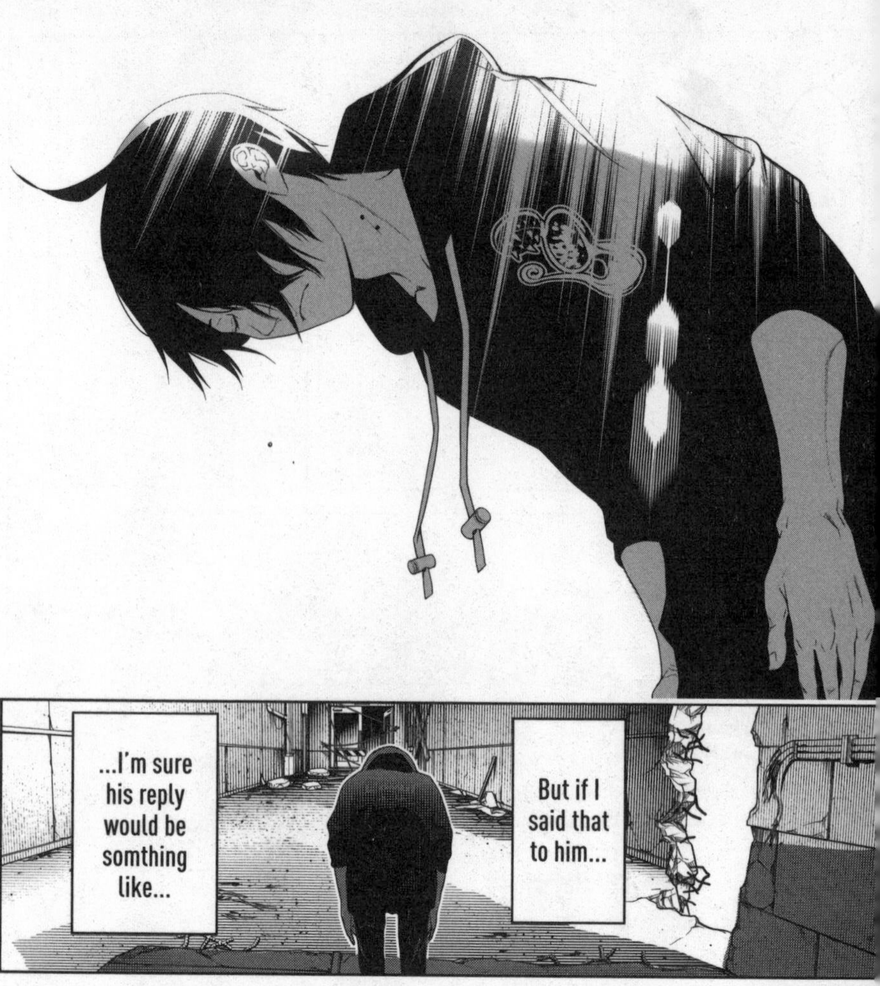
But if I said that to him...
...I'm sure his reply would be somthing like...

"You just went and saved yourself."

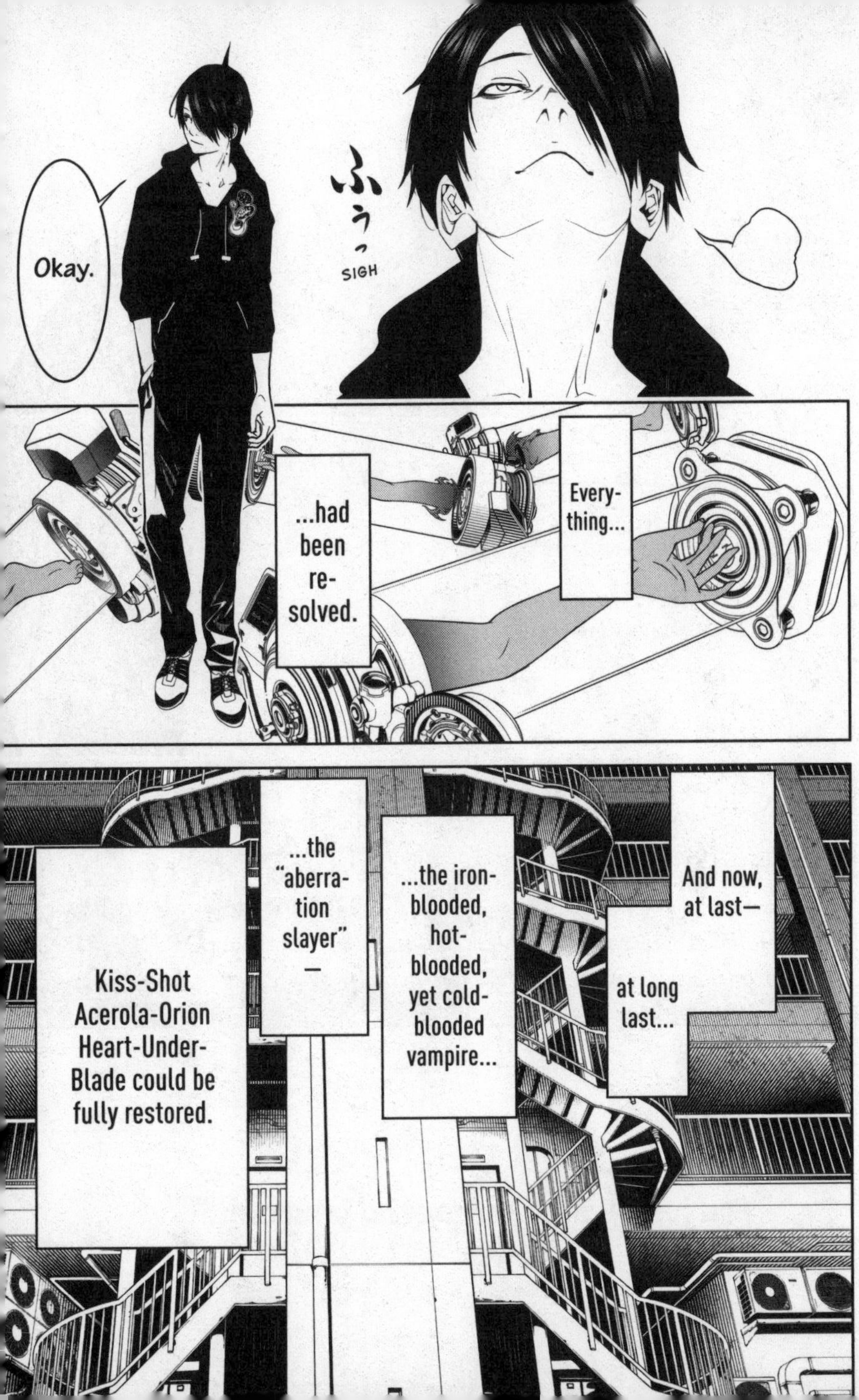

ふぅっ
SIGH
Okay.
Every-thing...
...had been re-solved.
And now, at last—
at long last...
...the iron-blooded, hot-blooded, yet cold-blooded vampire...
...the "aberration slayer" —
Kiss-Shot Acerola-Orion Heart-Under-Blade could be fully restored.

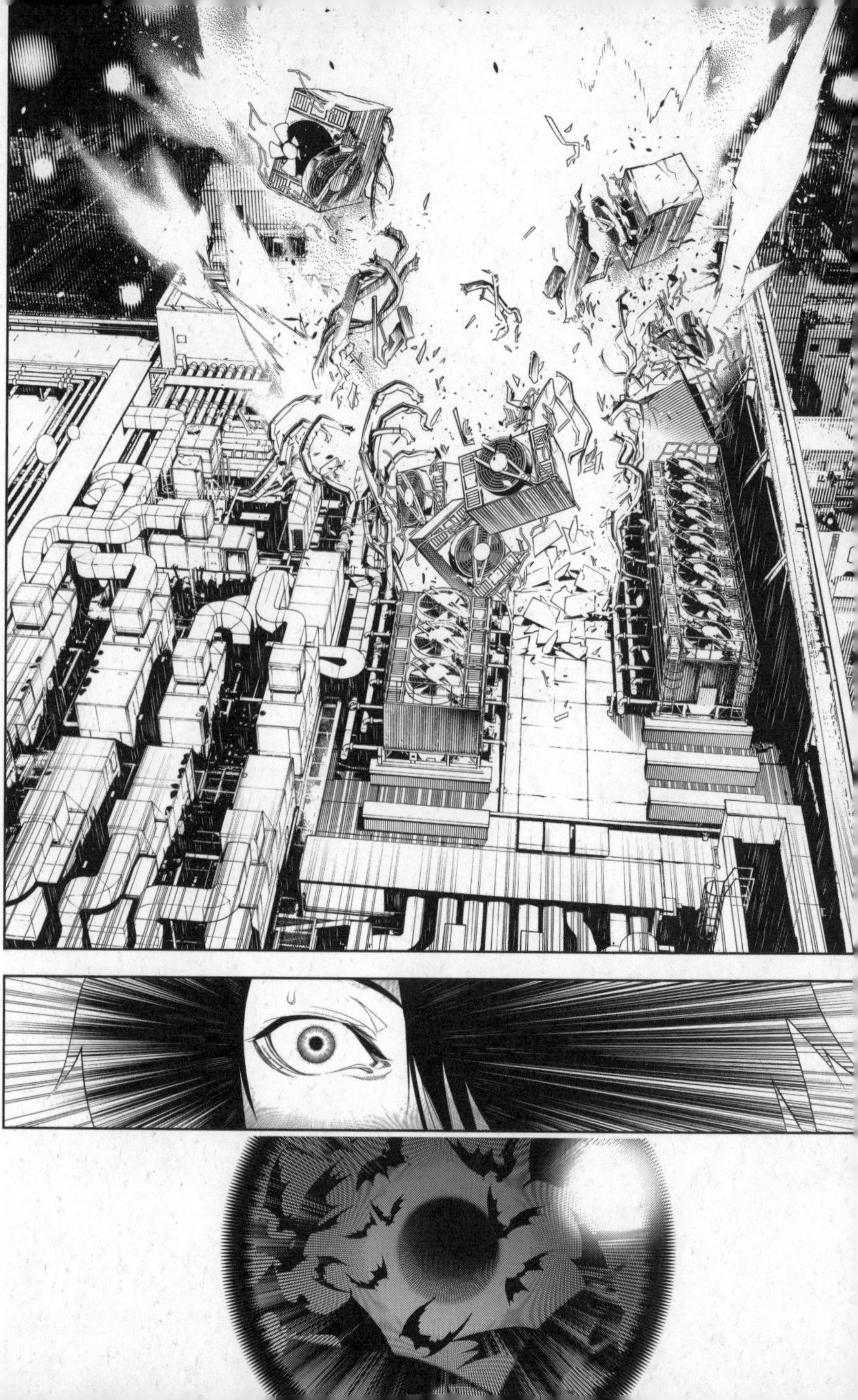

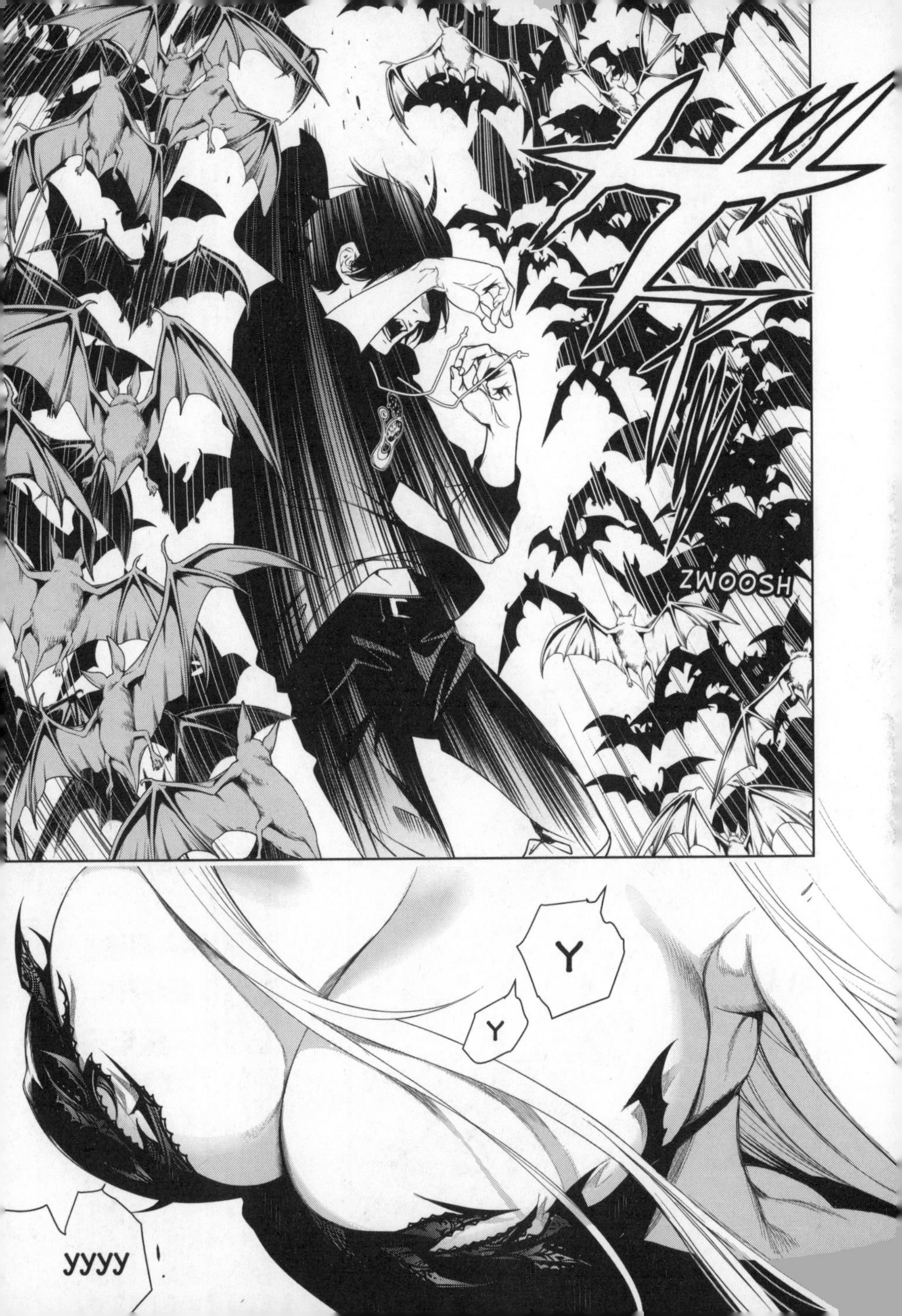
ZWOOSH
Y
Y
YYYY

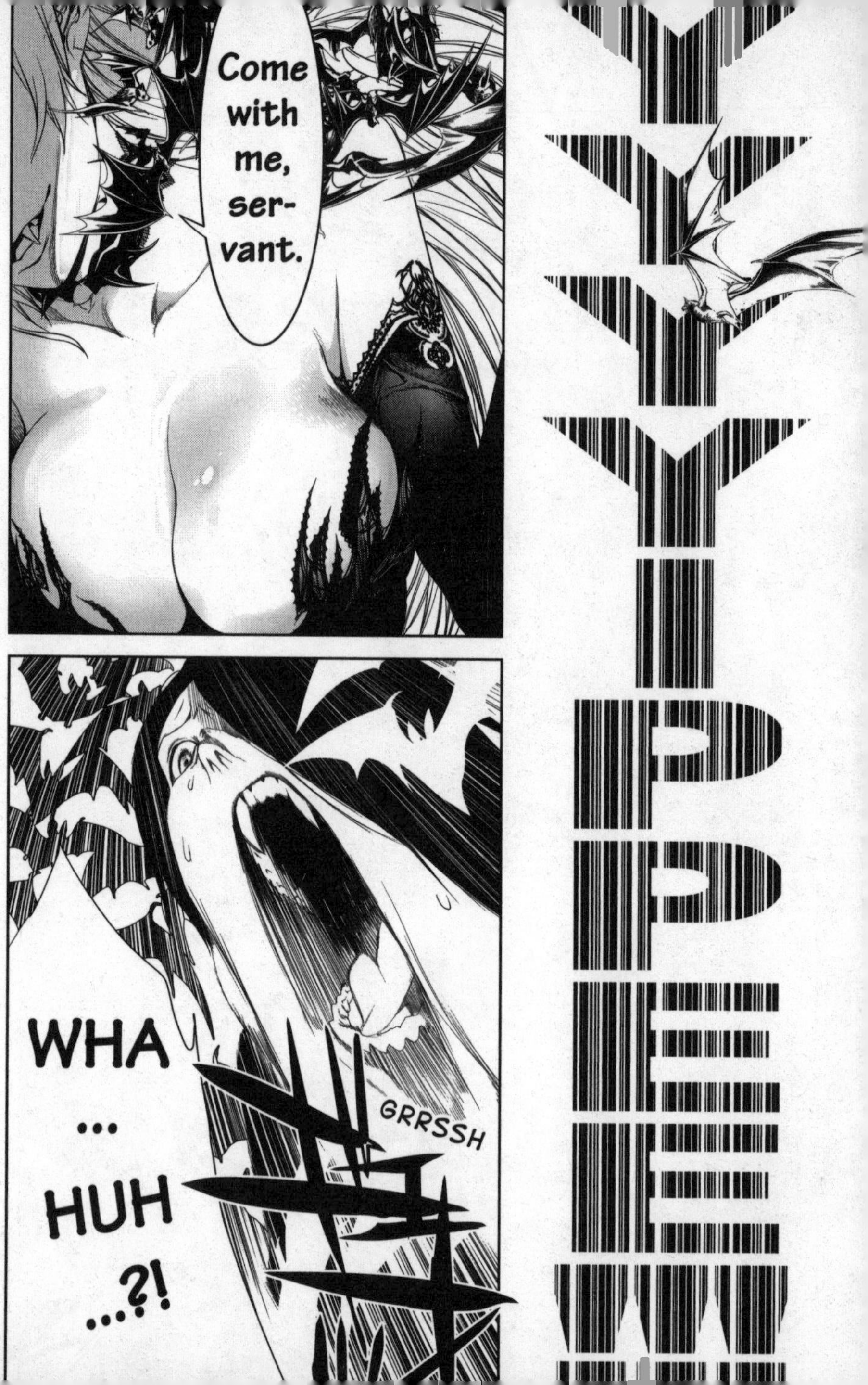
Come with me, ser-vant.
WHA ... HUH ...?!
GRRSSH

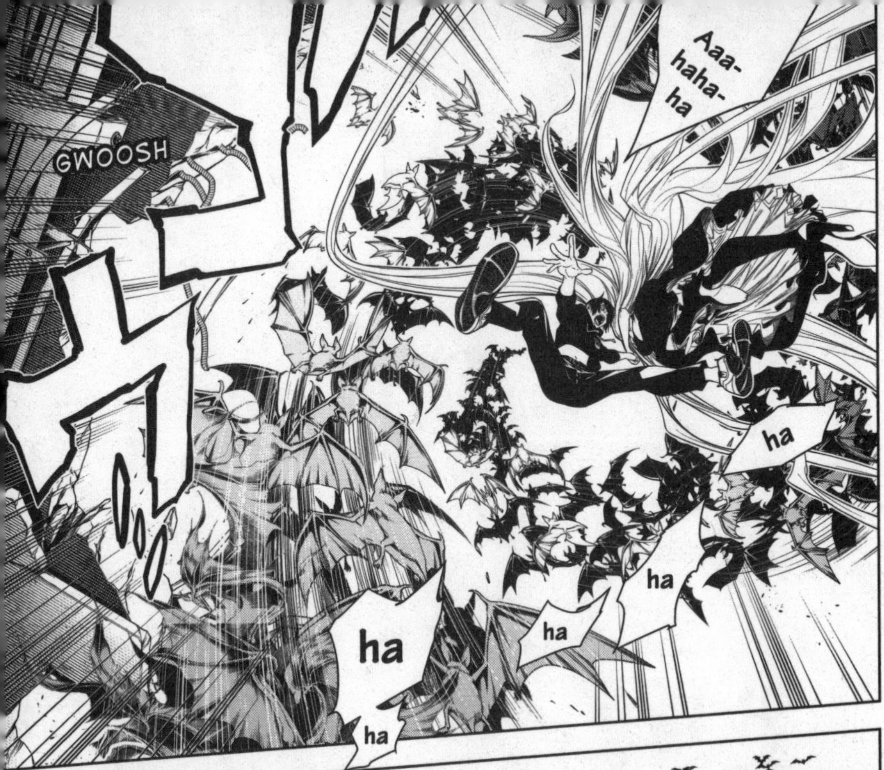
Aaa-
haha-
ha
GWOOSH
ha
ha
ha
ha
ha

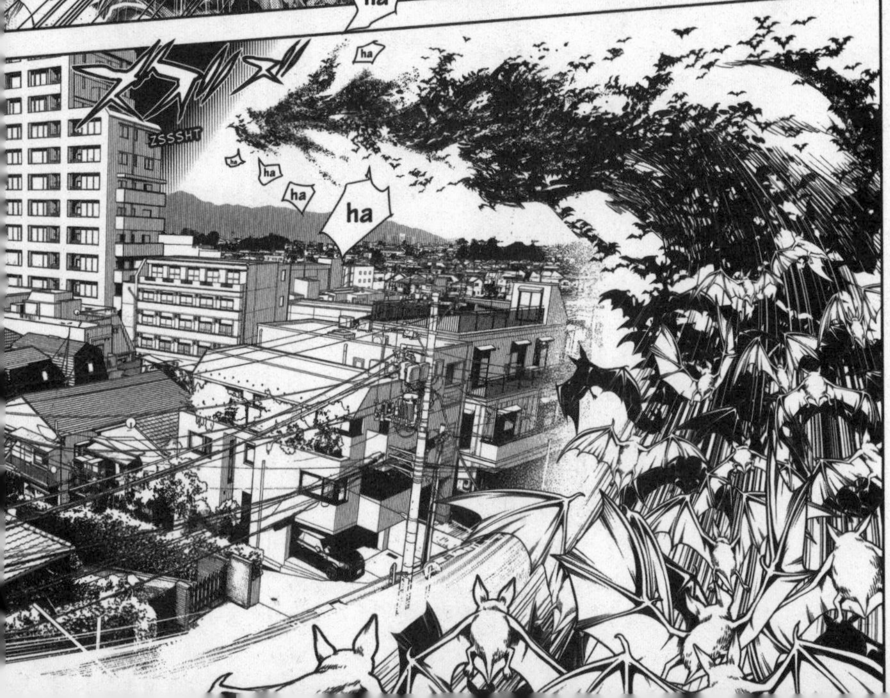
ZSSSHT
ha
ha
ha
ha
ha

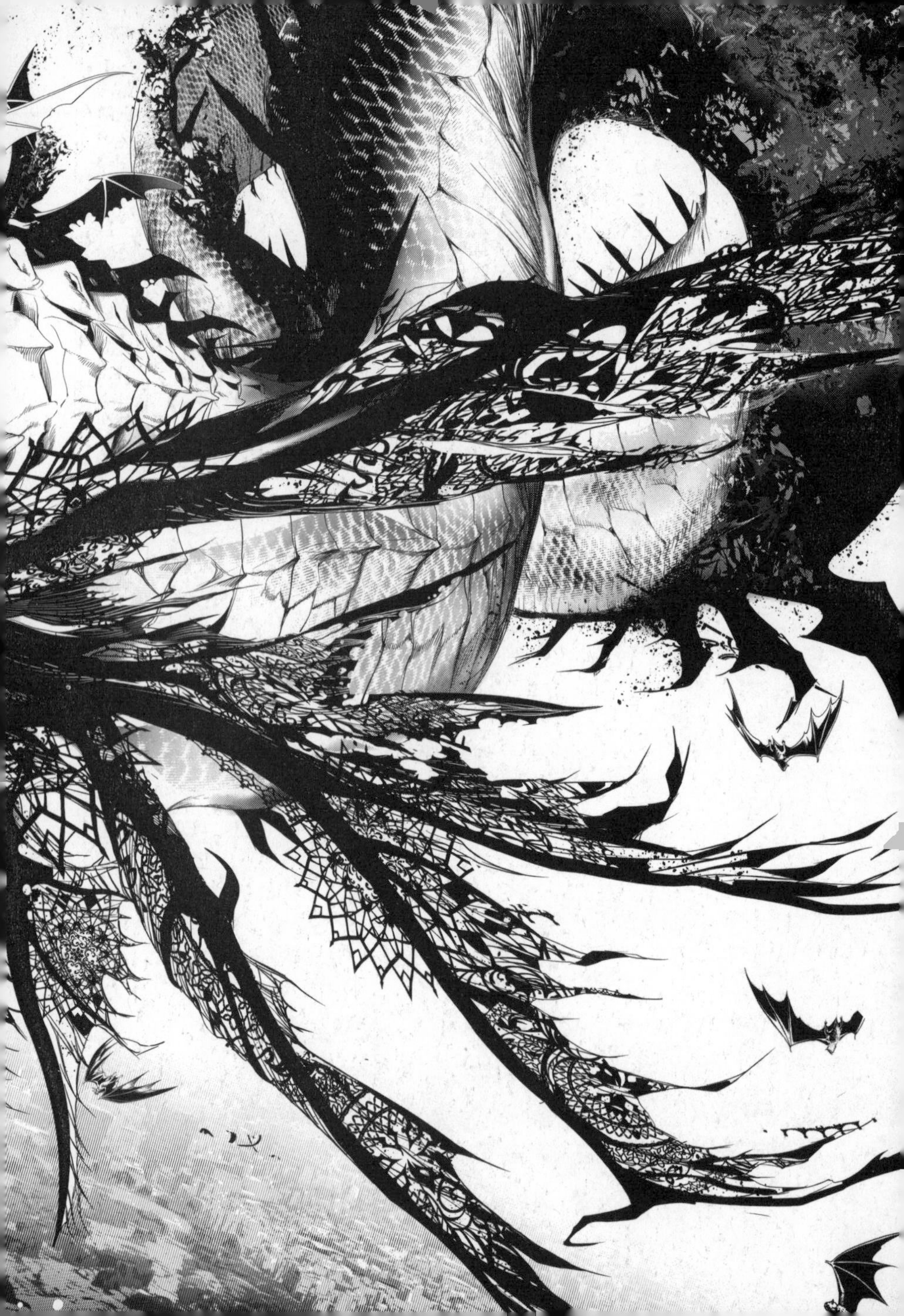